ET   34191

C0-CCO-142

AFRICAN AIMS & ATTITUDES

AFRICAN AIMS & ATTITUDES

SELECTED DOCUMENTS

EDITED BY

MARTIN MINOGUE

Director, Postgraduate Diploma Studies in Development Administration
Department of Administrative Studies for
Overseas Study Fellows, University of Manchester

JUDITH MOLLOY

Assistant Executive Secretary
The World Development Movement

CAMBRIDGE UNIVERSITY PRESS

034191

Published by the Syndics of the Cambridge University Press
Bentley House, 200 Euston Road, London NW1 2DB
American Branch: 32 East 57th Street, New York, N.Y. 10022

Selection & editorial material © Cambridge University Press 1974

Library of Congress Catalogue Card Number: 74-76567

ISBNS
0 521 20426 7
0 521 09851 3

First published 1974

Printed in Great Britain by Alden & Mowbray Ltd
at the Alden Press, Oxford

CONTENTS

034191

PREFACE

The aim of this book is to give the reader some direct acquaintance with the political attitudes and objectives of African leaders and intellectuals, as expressed in their own writings and speeches. We believe that the study of political systems and political activity in Africa is incomplete without reference to the ideas of those who exercise substantial practical or intellectual authority in the African continent. For the purposes of this book, Africa is defined as Africa South of the Sahara; and we include readings from non-Africans who have influenced Africans.

As the Bibliography shows, there is no lack of original material, and we have been compelled to make arbitrary selections, both in terms of the authors to be included and omitted, and of the passages to be selected from their texts. In making these choices, we have tried to reconcile the need to concentrate on material which is not readily available with the need to maintain a representative and coherent selection. Equally, there is an arbitrary air about the groupings of material under particular headings. Political leaders rarely write or think in neatly labelled compartments, and for the convenience of the reader our selections attempt to impose a degree of order and unity on a large output of miscellaneous and overlapping material.

The book is arranged in five parts. Each part has a short introduction linking together the texts which follow. Each text is placed in its particular context, and its source indicated. Together with the detailed biographies which are placed at the end of the book, this introductory material should provide adequate information on the authors and their texts. A discussion of the characteristics and significance of African political ideology is provided in the Introduction.

Spelling and punctuation conventions were retained in their original form in the individual documents, with the exception of the distracting variations on the word Panafricanism; in its ideological meaning it has been spelt 'Panafricanism' and in its geographical meaning as 'panafricanism'.

We owe particular thanks for generous advice and encouragement to Patricia Skinner of the Cambridge University Press. We also wish to thank Anne Griffiths and Chris Knee for help with translations, Thérèse Wong, Marjorie Marchant, and Maureen Stanford for help with typing. Josephine Minogue provided a constant stimulus.

1974   M.M.M.
                                                                J.M.

INTRODUCTION

'We are so poor that we have nothing to earn respect but our principles.' Julius Nyerere
'I am an idea.' Patrice Lumumba

The study of African political ideas raises questions that cannot be answered with any confidence. What is the nature of African political thought? Is there anything so coherent as the term 'political thought' implies? What are the functions of political ideology in the African context? Is there any connection between the ideas expressed by political leaders and their political actions? Do these ideas influence the beliefs and actions of other Africans and in particular, the beliefs and actions of the masses? Do political leaders believe what they say? Do the masses believe what they say?

Confident answers to these questions can only be provided (if ever) by research. For the moment, the student of African politics must confine himself to a speculative discussion of the issues involved in the relationship between political ideas and political actions. Certainly, there can be no complete understanding of African political systems without some insight into the perspectives and motives of the people who play principal roles in those systems. The starting-point for achieving such insight is a consideration of the statements made by political leaders. The intention in presenting this selection of readings from the recorded statements of African political leaders is to enable the student to make this first step, as a necessary preliminary to a more probing analysis of the context and function of African political ideas.

Whether these ideas are true or false, idealistic or pragmatic, is neither here nor there. What matters, in the first place, is that these ideas exist, and are given existence by men who are crucially placed to put the ideas into practice. Their motives in constructing and propagating ideologies are likely to be complex, diverse, and even self-contradicting. The implementation of ideas may be impeded by a variety of obstacles not always amenable to political control. The ideas may be well or badly received by other leading actors in the political drama, and might be viewed with blankness, scepticism, or dismay by the general audience. But

1

they cannot easily be ignored, or avoided; for, in the political systems of developing countries, 'it is the relation to authority that gives ideology its political significance'.[1]

There is a tendency, though, for familiarity with the statements of African political leaders to breed, if not contempt, something akin to boredom. It would be easy enough to dismiss their ideologies as strident, repetitive, rhetorical and unproductive. The political theorist would search in vain for originality; the general reader would more often be mystified than enlightened. Let us, for the sake of argument, accept these strictures. But there remains an irreducible core to these ideologies; and that hard centre is provided by the human condition itself, which is so poignant in the poor regions of the world, and to which these ideologies constantly address themselves. In this context, it is the actions of political leaders which are of immediate concern and interest. But again we are brought up against the fact that these actions find at least a partial explanation in the beliefs and values of the actor; and in trying to uncover those beliefs and values, we must take the formal expressions as one piece of evidence.

The next step is to examine the evidence critically, and I will confine myself here to an identification of what seem to me to be the three most significant areas for discussion. These are the content of African ideology; its political purposes; and the relationship between political ideas and political actions.

'... the philosophy of the African revolution ... is defined by three political components of our liberation movement – namely: Nationalism, Panafricanism, and Socialism.' Kwame Nkrumah

The labels selected by Nkrumah remain the most convenient catch-phrases to summarise the dominant strands in African ideology. They are labels which reflect the pre-eminent day-to-day concerns of African decision-makers, as well as their cultural and intellectual stances. Nationalism was the chosen philosophy of the colonial independence movements. A Western philosophy, it was turned to good effect against embarrassed imperial governments, which had customarily pretended not to notice the blatant contradiction between their own explicitly democratic values and the colonial autocracies for which they were responsible. Leaders like Nkrumah, Azikiwe, Senghor and Sekou Touré lost no opportunity to proclaim this contradiction, and to claim that they represented genuinely nationalist movements rooted in the evident aspirations of the colonial peoples. The clearest evidence that this claim had little foundation in social reality is the post-independence experience of the liberated territories. Ethnic, linguistic, and religious differentiations

2

ensure that these formal political units lack natural cohesion. Political leaders who in the colonial period found in the call for national unity a sharp-edged slogan, in the independence period strive to convert the slogan into reality, or at the least to use the slogan to maintain the national unit they have called into being. Naturally enough, they soon discover the limitations of slogans as an effective political instrument, and increasingly find themselves in the position of exerting their political authority in the direction of imposing a political unity which has only a tentative social basis. The establishment and maintenance of national unity therefore becomes inextricably involved with the establishment and maintenance of the leader's authority. A challenge to national unity is interpreted (and resisted) as a challenge to the political leadership. Likewise political competition is viewed as damaging to that national unity which is seen as the guarantee of genuine independence; *ergo,* political competition is subversive.

It is this progression which underlies the emphasis in African ideology upon the need to restructure political institutions so that they accord with what are believed (or expressed) to be the real needs of the emergent political system. This emphasis invariably centres on the nature of democracy, the irrelevance of institutional models of democracy drawn from Western experience, and the necessity to limit political competitiveness and conflict. Political organisation henceforth is to centre on a single political party which will act to reflect the popular will. The logical extension of this argument is that the state bureaucracy is obliged to act in accordance with the directives of the party; as Sekou Touré puts it, 'the Party constitutes the thought of the people of Guinea at its highest level ... the thought of the Party specifies the principles which ought to direct our behaviour.'[2] The influence of Marxist–Leninist principles of political organisation is evident in this approach: but it is an approach which in more or less radical form is to be found across a wide spectrum of African ideology. And to the charge that this approach is merely a cloak for the pursuit of power, the African leader would reply that, from a cynical viewpoint, the charge applies to all forms of political organisation, and that any political arrangement is valid once it meets the requirements of a given economic and social situation. Since most African countries are in an approximately similar economic and social situation, it is no matter for surprise that common forms of political organisation make their appearance; nor that the question of political institutions and their operation should be a central concern of political ideology. The development of central institutions of State bureaucracy has always been a distinguishing characteristic of the emerging nation-state, and in Africa today the best hope for viable national entities would appear to rest in the creation of effective and authoritative political institutions. In these terms, the self-interest of the political actor and the general interest of the political unit in which he operates could be regarded as indivisible.

Just as all African leaders have to define the arena in which they will operate, so do they have to respond to a common demand from the people brought within these arenas. The demand is for improvements in the social and economic conditions faced by the nation's new citizens. Indeed, political support for anti-colonial leaders was often based in social and economic discontents which the colonial regime could not, or would not, assuage. The political pact between the nationalist leader and his political subjects contained an implied promise that social and economic discontents would be remedied with the overthrow of the offending regime. Again, then, the political self-interest of the leader demanded that he should attempt to honour this pact, quite aside from moral imperatives or social ideals. The attempts to achieve economic and social development vary in tactical and doctrinal scope; but the overall strategy is everywhere the same, and is imposed by the brutal and unyielding facts of economic and social existence in Africa. Nonetheless, tactics and doctrine are of primary political concern; and so a situation obtains where many roads to socialism are declared open, but where all roads lead only to socialism. A common characteristic in African versions of socialism is what has been described as 'reconstructed traditionalism',[3] or the tendency to claim that modern socialist planning is no more than a redefinition of the communaucratic basis of traditional African social organisation. Even Nkrumah, who ultimately rejected the adjective 'African' in favour of 'scientific', insisted that socialism must be informed by traditional African cultural values. Often enough the claim can be regarded as having only a tenuous relation to social reality. Traditional social organisation often did not possess the character attributed to it; the viewpoint is a romantic one. Even where communaucratic qualities did exist, social and economic existence was frequently harsh and unpleasant. Indeed, it is precisely the political dilemma of modern African leaders that such large numbers of traditional groups wish to improve their social and economic position. Nonetheless, the attempt to link modern social and economic planning to traditional and familiar patterns of life is probably essential if the African peasant is to be persuaded into modern ways; in other words, this is the element of African ideology intended to make it adaptive to social reality.

A second, slightly baffling, characteristic of African socialism is the co-existence of significant elements of vagueness and precision. The controlling ideology is only vaguely defined; the precision comes in the concrete planning mechanisms which purport to translate the ideology into practice. The vagueness serves a useful purpose to the politician: it provides symbols around which his supporters may cluster, without the rigidity which might cause embarrassing doctrinal divisions. And if, as so often occurs, concrete plans fail to realise their intentions, the ideology may conveniently be reinterpreted to cover up the failure, or at best, to explain it away. It is this syndrome which, perhaps, explains the recurrence in African socialist ideology of juxtaposed elements of pragmatism and utopianism. But it would be rash to judge the utopianism from a cynical standpoint: there is no reason to doubt the moral earnestness of Kaunda's humanism, or the moral conviction of Nyerere's socialism. One may doubt their ability to achieve what they believe in, or note the inconsistencies which arise in the constant dialectic of theory and reality; but these are separate matters. What is clear, and crucial, is that there is a relationship between theory and practice, between social ideal and social reality which underlines the political significance of socialist ideology.

Nkrumah's third general label, Panafricanism, is one which ideologically is most difficult to pin to political reality; Fanon describes it as 'African unity, that vague formula, yet one to which men and women of Africa were passionately attached'.[4] The nature of the passion can more easily be traced through the causes which Africans take up collectively than through statements by leaders on what constitutes African unity. And it is here, too, that the gap between principle and practice is most evident. Passion there may be; but the collective heart rarely turns the collective head, and Africans have themselves launched stinging attacks on the inadequacy of panafrican institutions. Yet the Organisation for African Unity is, rather like the United Nations, in itself a remarkable translation of ideal into reality; and if it is not a sufficient condition of panafrican unity, it is certainly a necessary one. The chief ideological difficulty with the concept of Panafricanism is that it both contains and conflicts with other strands of African ideology. The concepts of racial identity and continental solidarity were both significant elements in the construction of the ideology of anti-colonial nationalism. It is still a main objective of Panafrican organisation to achieve the national liberation of colonial peoples. Yet the concept of nationalism, and the vigorous efforts by African leaders to build and define their national units, are quite at odds, with the notion of political union across national boundaries; hence the division within the Panafrican movement between supporters of Nkrumah's vision of a continental political union which would erode national distinctions, and opponents of that vision, who would at the very most support only a confederal arrangement. Practical attempts to realise the unionist philosophy, such as the Mali Federation, and the Ghana– Guinea–Mali Union, came quickly to grief, and the emphasis now is on a pragmatic, gradualistic approach, in which regional groupings with a primarily economic character are seen as forerunners of wider unions of a political character.

This wholly realistic position should not be allowed to obscure the significance of the cultural manifestations of the Panafrican idea. The debate over negritude which seemed so significant in the 1950s is no longer an issue wherever politically conscious Africans meet; but it is that debate, and the influence of Senghor's philosophy, which provided a platform for the present outburst of a literature which is regarded as distinctively and uniquely African in its content, its style, and its concerns. Just as the construction of viable nation-states is regarded by African political thinkers as a necessary defence against neo-colonialism, so the construction of an African cultural identity is regarded as a necessary defence against the cultural imperialism imported by Western systems of education and thought. It is impossible to define what the importance is to the political leader of this search for cultural identity, but we must be ready to see it as one more intellectual influence. The most concrete evidence of this influence is to be found in the emphasis on the values of the African past, which are to be rediscovered and reinstated in the existing culture. And it is in the portrayal of African life, and of African modes of behaviour, by existing African writers, that we most readily perceive African reality. To read James Ngugi on psychological and social strains in Kenya, or Chinua Achebe on political and social behaviour in Nigeria, is immensely instructive, and provides for the outsider an invaluable frame of reference in his attempts to understand the social complexity to which African political activity is related. In the long run the African writer may be the most penetrating critical influence in African politics.

'A government does not operate according to theories; practical decisions have to be taken every day of the week.' Tom Mboya

The easiest, and the least useful criticism of African political ideology is that it bears little relation to political practice. It is an easy criticism because it is comfortingly irrefutable; but it is a trite criticism which obscures the real problem to be explored here, that is the nature of the obstacles between theories and their practical implementation. African leaders are themselves well aware of the 'reality gap'. Many of their ideas were expressed in a context in which they were divorced from political responsibility; they were ideas which could only be implemented in the future, when political power came their way. Mamadou Dia acknowledges the situation which then existed: 'we let ourselves be seduced by the mirage of the construct most satisfying to our mind, and taking the ideal for reality, we believed that it would be sufficient to condemn'.[5]

In the independence period, African leaders quickly showed themselves alert to the problem. They were still concerned to construct a new reality, but one which offered hope of realisation. The ideology itself came to include an insistence on the necessary participation of the mass of the people in building the new society. Sekou Touré had already said, in 1959, that 'to take part in the African revolution it is not enough to write a revolutionary song; you must fashion the revolution with the people'.[6] Frantz Fanon was quick to warn political leaders that political activity must be a partnership: 'to educate the masses politically does not mean, cannot mean, making a political speech. What it means is to try, relentlessly and passionately, to teach the masses that everything depends upon them.'[7] The ideologies of Africa reflect this position; they make constant references to the need for self-sacrifice, self-discipline, self-reliance, references which are neatly encapsulated in the blunt statement 'Principles are a good thing, but they are no substitute for hard work.'[8] But then, exhortation is not action; and there is an inherent suggestion in such demands that the masses are in some way themselves to blame for the condition in which they find themselves. As Mboya trenchantly observes, 'it's really no good telling the peasant scratching away at the soil to be self-reliant; he's been self-reliant since he was born'.[9] The fact is, he needs leadership; and resources; and identity. The leader controls, and can provide for all these requirements. Resources are scarce, but government distributes them; identity is nebulous, but ideology can shape it. What shall be the utility of the resources, and what shall be the characteristics of the identity, rests initially with the leaders. But the leader is faced with serious obstacles in both areas. The ideological obstacles are straightforward. Firstly, there is the problem of falsified reality: that is, the ideology constructed to deal with real events may be misplaced if the events have been misinterpreted. African leaders fall into this trap when they attribute to colonialism ills which derive from more fundamental causes. When the ills persist, the leaders then attribute the failure to neo-colonialism and so box the intellectual circle. At this point, the ideology becomes a cover-up for failure instead of a means to productive actions.[10]

Secondly, there is the problem of communication. The spread of an ideology requires more than the mere expression of it. In African countries, even the physical transmission of ideas is a difficult business, since literacy is low, and the radio the only pervasive type of mass medium. Ideas can be passed through the educational system, but this is a long-term process and catches only a limited number of people. Inevitably, the instrument of communication becomes the political party, or political party plus state bureaucracy. The initial step is the indoctrination of the political elite, who then disseminate ideas in a more or less uniform way through political and bureaucratic channels of influence. The acceptability of the ideas will, in this circumstance, be tied closely to the acceptability (and efficiency) of the political and bureaucratic elite which proffers them; and we have evidence to show what a chancy and fragmented process results.[11] The elaboration of ideology into practical proposals is no less difficult. African leaders have attempted to apply rationality here in the form of planning. The hope has been that the implementation of planned social and economic development would lead to self-sustaining economic independence which is the basis of genuine political independence. But this hope has not been realised, and African countries still show the classic signs of economic and social deprivation. The explanation lies partly in adverse environmental factors; and partly in the defects of a world economic system in which primary producing countries are at a permanent disadvantage. These factors are not always amenable to control. But there are internal factors which can be controlled, the most significant being administrative organisation and political communication. The state bureaucracies of Africa suffer from the conventional ailments of the classic bureaucracy, with the additional disadvantage that they lack the resources of technical expertise which the classic bureaucracy is assumed to possess. Moreover, the position of the bureaucracy in the power system has not been clearly defined; the result is a clash of interest between the technical bureaucracy of the state, and the political bureaucracy of the party. This conflict of interest, if unresolved, either prevents the making of decisions, or the implementation of agreed policies, or the evaluation of the results of proposals already implemented; or all these things simultaneously. In this event, not only do plans remain merely paper demonstrations of good intentions, but the ideology ceases to have practical meaning. Only where the bureaucracy and the party have clearly defined and interacting roles (or perhaps where they are fused together in a clear structure of decision-making) can plans be implemented and the first step to real economic growth and social improvement be taken. Where this happens, the ideology will be seen to have some relation to everyday reality. But if it does not happen, the claims of the ideology as a motivating force for action will inevitably be weakened.

In this event, the leader is faced with two alternative approaches. He might grapple with the problem of administrative–political relations in the public administration; and he might redefine the ideology either to explain current failures or to set new objectives. The new objectives might be phrased so as to accord more with social reality, that is they might

8

become less idealistic and more pragmatic. Alternatively, they might present a more deeply etched picture of the future in order to distract attention from unpleasant social reality, while affording an explanation of the persistence of the gulf between present conditions and future expectations. The second type of ideological redefinition will invariably be more radical in its proposals, and this pattern occurs wherever a leadership with an ideological bent enjoys a small economic return on its ideological investments. *The Arusha Declaration* in Tanzania, *The Common Man's Charter* in Uganda, Nkrumah's *Dawn Broadcast* in Ghana, and Sekou Touré's *l'Afrique et la Révolution*, all constitute examples of this pattern; and it seems clear that the point of ideological shift occurs at the moment when the leader realises that the political exhortation which transformed the colonial situation is not by itself sufficient to mobilise the masses for an assault on underdevelopment. Hard thinking about political and administrative organisation is required; at the same time, scapegoats must be found, to provide explanations of the rejection of the earlier ideology. And so, 'what was progressive in 1964 may cease to be so in 1965'.[12]

The shift to the left is not likely to succeed any more than previous ideological positions, unless the fundamental economic and political problems of the state are solved. In some cases the use of the ideology as a substitute for action indicates that the leadership has given up the struggle: the ideology becomes at best a counsel of despair. But where ideology and action are still contemplated in a symbiotic relationship, certain attitudes become apparent. First is the renewal of the call for self-reliance, but with a new and sharp note of self-criticism. Neo-colonialism is still the principal cause of adversity, but the people have their fate in their own hands and if they cannot be persuaded towards a better future, they might have to be compelled. Secondly, the administrative deficiencies of the state are acknowledged, and the remedy proposed here is usually a form of administrative decentralisation, so that the state bureaucracy can be more effectively linked to the grassroots, and better informed about them. Thirdly, the faults of the political leadership are openly proclaimed; the elite has a special role, must obey a special code, and must avoid the privileges and status which open up a social gulf between it and the masses. Austerity is a keynote of both political and economic life. This attack on the privileged position of the political elite is usually linked to a restructuring of the party organisation which brings it more closely within the machinery of the state. Fourthly, political control is exerted more deliberately over those organisations which operate in crucial areas of economic activity and have political affiliations: this normally means the trade unions and the agricultural cooperatives. In short, ideological radicalism precludes a system of autonomous politics. Finally, the controlling status of the ideology is asserted; all political (and economic) activity should have reference to consistent ideological guidelines which will be formulated by the party (or in practice by the leader who is head of state and of party).

The lines are clearly drawn in these circumstances: an established leader (or leadership) enunciates an ideology which is implemented jointly by the party organisation and the public administration. There is no guarantee that the party will function, that the state will be efficient, or that the ideology will be correctly interpreted through these institutions to effect a transformation of the society. There is a vicious circle in operation: the ideology proposes a fundamental economic and social transformation, but cannot be realised because of the existence of economic and political obstacles which are part of the system which the ideology was constructed to transform.

'If we persistently think and cherish good thoughts, good will result; if evil, evil will result.'
Obafemi Awolowo

Fanon has made a searing attack on the set-up where he sees the triumph of a cynical bourgeois elite without real ideals and motivated only by economic self-interest; where the party, rather than a living instrument of communication between the masses and their representatives, becomes a hollow shell inhabited by time-serving placemen; and where the nationalist leader who took his people into independence has become corrupted by power, and uses the weight and authority of the state to manipulate and exploit the people in a manner no colonial system could improve upon. These fiery arrows find numerous targets in contemporary Africa, yet the attack seriously underestimates the difficulty of political stewardship in the third world. A leader may be sincere in his ideals, yet have to be ruthless in his political struggle for survival; he may be tender in his social conscience, but have to be tough-minded in managing his society; he may detest placemen, but otherwise be surrounded by no one. Caught in the web of these contradictions, he may see the enforcement of an ideology as the only instrument which can at once ensure social reconstruction and his own political survival.

This brings us to the question, what influences a leader? What are his motivations? And what are the political purposes or functions of political ideology? Conventional wisdom and sociological analysis unite in ascribing to political leaders motives which have little to do with conscience or morality. Ideology is variously viewed as a weapon in the struggle for power; as a symbol with which to blind the popular gaze; as a veil behind which the politician may conceal his true (and impliedly evil) intents. Such interpretations have a simplistic, even melodramatic air, and rest on assumptions about human behaviour in politics which cannot be proven. It would be at least charitable (and certainly less arrogant) to assume that politicians may have a very complicated and even contradictory set of motivations, not all of them conscious. We could then agree that 'the view that social action is fundamentally an unending struggle for power leads to an unduly Machiavellian view of ideology as a form of higher cunning'.[13] After all, to assume that those who express ideologies mean what they say is not to deny the need for sociological analysis, nor the value of sociological explanation of these ideologies. It is merely to reassert the potential power of individual thought, both on the actions of the individual who originates or elaborates ideas, and upon the thoughts and actions of his wider audience.

Geertz contends that in conditions of social change ideology may 'sustain individuals (or groups) in the face of chronic strain, either by denying it outright or by legitimising it in terms of higher values. . . . Ideology bridges the emotional gap between things as they are and as one would have them be . . . thus ensuring the performance of roles that might otherwise be abandoned in despair or apathy.'[14] He notes, too, that ideology often serves to articulate and identify social strains so that they might the better be remedied; they are, in this light, to be regarded as 'elaborate cries of pain'.[15] It is precisely in the conditions of social and political change which characterise modern African societies that ideologies are expounded and given support. The theory of colonialism permitted no political illusions to its subjects, so that political ideology was unnecessary. But the displacement of the central organising principles of political life left a void to be filled; illusions had to be created if nothing else was to hand. The translation of illusions into reality was possibly less urgent than the creation of a new social identity which would help to avert a breakdown of the social system. This social function of ideology will continue whatever the state of the struggle to turn promise into performance; and this function will even survive administrative incompetence, economic corruption, and social elitism, particularly where the ideology carefully proclaims its hostility to these undesirable and undesired realities. In these terms alone, ideology would serve entirely rational social purposes; when, in addition, it is linked to a reasoned programme of action, it cannot be dismissed as mere myth-making. Certainly there will be a persistent quality of social and political rhetoric, but rhetoric need not be mystifying, nor does a rhetorical element justify condemnation of the general vision. There are political constitutions, like

11

that of India, which have been described as declaratory in function: that is, they declare a vision of the future which, it is generally accepted, will take some time to materialise. So it may be with African political ideologies, which take up the position that the struggle for the future begins in the present.

African political ideas, like other systems of thought, can be all things to all men. To the sociologist, they are 'an organised set of justifications'.[16] To the political leader, they are at once a vision and an instrument. To the political supporter, they are a reason (or an excuse) for existence. To the technocrat, they are a basis for action, a model to measure facts against. To the ordinary African, they may be a means of obtaining resources, a source of social identity, a point of contact with the political system, or just an irritation. So ideology may serve numerous functions in the complex structure of social life, quite apart from the intentions which generate them. The practicality of the ideology may be of concern to the student of political action but is by no means the only touchstone of its usefulness. The originality of the thought constructed by individual leaders may be of compelling interest to the student of ideas, but is rarely the most significant aspect of the vision. African ideas have little originality; but they are original in the sense that established ideas have to be adapted to an original environment and so may take on a distinctive and chameleon-like quality. African ideas are often generalised and vague, and so constitute an imperfect basis for concrete activity; but it is the vagueness which allows the ideology both to be comprehensive and durable, for the ideology cannot be embarrassed by practical failures. As Nyerere puts it: 'one criticises the implementation – not the ideology itself'.[17] The derivativeness and the generality of African political ideas have been designated as their most serious weakness, but in terms of their operation as a functioning part of political systems, these qualities are their strengths. Whatever the intrinsic qualities of the ideas expressed by men holding political power, those ideas are at once significant because of their connection with political power. What a man of power thinks, both publicly and privately, will enable us to understand – even predict – his political actions; and it would be wrong to say that what he thinks publicly is less significant in this context than what he thinks privately, for such a stance disregards the fundamental role of the political actor in social life, which is to provide a public channel for publicised actions which affect the public interest. This clearly defined role incorporates its own constraints upon the private achievement of private aims.

In short, the complexity of social action demands that we should be prepared for a corresponding complexity in the relation of political thought and political action; African leaders may therefore be seen as self-

INTRODUCTION

seeking charlatans, as dignified guardians of their peoples, as flawed visionaries, or as men struggling to control social forces beyond mere manipulation; or as people with several of these elements in their make-up. Whatever the labels we attach to them, and however we decide to interpret them, we cannot avoid the necessity of examining their own statements of belief and intention. Meanwhile, Africa needs as leaders 'men who think as men of action, and men who act as men of thought'.[18]

MARTIN MINOGUE

NOTES FOR INTRODUCTION

1. D. Apter (ed.), *Ideology and Discontent* (New York, 1969), p. 18.
2. Sekou Touré, *La Guinée et l'emancipation Africaine* (Paris, 1959), pp. 234–5.
3. C. Geertz, 'Ideology as a Cultural System' in Apter, *Ideology and Discontent,* p. 65.
4. F. Fanon, *The Wretched of the Earth* (London, 1967), p. 128.
5. Mamadou Dia, *The African Nations and World Solidarity* (New York, 1962), p. 140.
6. Sekou Touré, 'Le Leader politique considéré comme le représentant d'une culture', *Présence Africaine,* Nos. 24–5 (1959).
7. Fanon, *op. cit.,* p. 159.
8. Uganda Peoples Congress, *The Common Man's Charter* (Kampala, 1969).
9. T. J. Mboya, *The Challenge of Nationhood* (London, 1969).
10. These points are explored in greater detail in W. A. E. Skurnik, (ed.), *African Political Thought: Lumumba, Nkrumah, and Touré* (Denver, 1968), pp. 1–12.
11. Particularly for Tanzania, where the most concerted efforts have been made to channel ideology through a political–bureaucratic network. Detailed evidence is provided by J. Molloy, 'Political Communication in Tanzania' (unpublished Ph.D. Thesis, University of Kent, 1970); J. H. Proctor (ed.), *Building Ujamaa Villages in Tanzania;* and *The Cell System of the Tanganyika African National Union* (Dar-es-Salaam, 1971); D. Brokensha, 'Handeni Revisited', *African Affairs,* Vol. 70 (April 1971), pp. 159–68; Clyde R. Ingle, 'Compulsion and Rural Development in Tanzania', *Canadian Journal of African Studies,* Vol. 4 (1970), pp. 77–100.

    For a more general discussion see W. Tordoff, *Government and Politics in Tanzania* (Nairobi, 1967); H. Bienen, *Tanzania: Party Transformation and Economic Development* (Princeton, 1967); and J. R. Nellis, *A Theory of Ideology: The Tanzanian Example* (Nairobi, 1972).
12. Sekou Touré, quoted by R. W. Johnson in 'Sekou Touré and the Guinean revolution', *African Affairs,* Vol. 69 (1969). Johnson illustrates in detail Sekou Touré's 'turn to the left'.
13. Fanon, *op. cit.,* pp. 132–65.
14. Geertz, *op. cit.,* p. 53.
15. Geertz, *ibid.,* pp. 53–65, for a detailed discussion of theoretical categories relating to the social functions of ideology.
16. Nellis, *op. cit.,* p. 41.
17. J. K. Nyerere, *Interview* in *New Internationalist* (May 1973).
18. K. Nkrumah, *Consciencism* (London, 1964), p. 25.

Part I
Colonialism and
Decolonisation

There are many strands in anti-colonial movements and beliefs, reflecting in part the variety of colonial systems and practices. The extracts in this part serve to illustrate the varied responses to colonialism, while demonstrating a common feature: emergent nationalism.

Nationalist sentiments were expressed, if mildly, almost as soon as colonialism was implanted in Africa. People like Africanus Horton, while welcoming the 'civilising' paternalism of the British in the 1870s, foresaw a time when West African nations would be self-governing. By the 1920s, his compatriot, Casely Hayford, had rejected paternalism and championed self-determination for West Africa, although he felt that it should still hold allegiance to the British Crown and Empire. But it was not until after the Second World War, when British and French colonies in South-East Asia had become independent, that nationalism in Africa gained impetus. Then, most of the men who were, eventually, to lead their countries to independence, formed strong nationalist organisations with the aim of ending political domination by the colonial powers. The variety in their methods is demonstrated by the difference between Danquah's insistence on using only constitutional means, no matter how long the attainment of independence took, and Nkrumah's use of non-violent but unconstitutional methods of pressurising the colonial regime for immediate self-government. With surprising ease, leaders like Nkrumah of Ghana and Azikiwe of Nigeria got what they asked for. But the West Africans did not have to contend with large white settler populations, determined to defend their economic interests, who would not recognise nationalist aspirations. Such was the case in parts of East and Central Africa, where nationalist movements eventually turned to violence, or the threat of violence, as the only way of making their voices heard.

For the post-war nationalists, political independence was regarded as the *sine qua non* of economic independence. But political independence was only the beginning of the struggle by African countries to emancipate themselves economically and culturally from their colonial masters. Their nationalist organisations, formed to attain independence, had to be transformed to build new nations. They had to choose between capitalism and socialism; they had to try and meet the demands of the masses; and they had to work out their foreign policies. More fundamentally, as Touré points out, echoing Césaire, they had to try and alter the attitudes of people who had been imbued with the values of colonialism. But, Fanon argues, this is no easy task; not only is decolonisation a 'programme of complete disorder', but the leaders themselves are still oriented to colonialist values, and there arises a gulf between them and the masses which ultimately may only be bridged through violence.

1: Africanus Horton

From J. A. B. Horton, *Letters on the Political Condition of the Gold Coast,* 2nd edn (Frank Cass, 1970).

These letters were written by Horton between 1868 and 1870, just after the British had taken over the Gold Coast from the Dutch. They were addressed to Edward Cardwell, British Secretary of State for War and to Earl Granville, Secretary of State for the Colonies. This extract is from a letter to Earl Granville, dated 2 May 1870, and advocates a Confederation of the Fanti, one of the earliest schemes for local self-government by Africans.

On this Coast the English element is unquestionably the best civilizing agency. Their liberality in matters of Christianity, their sound and healthy judgment in colonization, their profound legislative ability, exhibited frequently in adopting proper means to suit the wishes and desires of the colonists, and their commercial policy, all greatly tend to foster the growth of civilization in a young colony.

I verily believe, my Lord, that in the government of a semi-barbarous race, where the aim is to bring up the governed rapidly to advancement in industrial pursuits, education, and general social condition, *a little despotism is absolutely necessary*. But it must be understood that this despotism must not be used for the exertion of uncalled-for arbitrary power, which an intelligent race might think, simply from its superior intelligence, it ought to exact over the other as being less informed. But it should be more on principles of equity, having this object in view – the *material advancement of the people*. It will, however, be a most deplorable thing for any Government if this little despotism is exercised for revenge, or for the purpose of satisfying private pique.

. . . . . .

15

The political constitution of the interior tribes on the Gold Coast is of a very primitive order, and their social organization resembles most closely the feudal system of Europe in the middle ages ...

Before the English became influential on the Gold Coast, this feudal system was carried on to a very high degree. The feudal kingdoms were conglomerations of many heterogeneous states, who acknowledged a king as their feudal lord, and he, on his part, was to a considerable extent a vassal of the powerful King of Ashantee. But since the English Government has had a complete hold on the sea-coast towns, and made the feudal lords or kings independent of the Ashantee potentate, as well as since it has exercised considerable influence over the institutions of each feudal kingdom, a universal spirit of disaffection and sedition reigns in the interior; the influence of each regal Government has declined in a very considerable degree; each feudal-baron or chief, according to his strength, power, and audacity, finding that he is not dependent on the king or feudal lord, but the kings on him, according to the number of vassals under his command, pays but very little attention to his orders, in many cases, in fact, defying him openly. In many places the king is deprived of all regal power, and his retinue or *comitatus* is of the poorest order, and even the external honour of royalty is but meagrely accorded him. Internal convulsions without much violence are not unfrequent; and now a state of agitation exists in the interior; the feudal system is tottering to its foundation; a more enlightened Government is earnestly demanded by even the nominal feudal lords or kings and the wealthy caboceers (barons) and people. But the people are most woefully deficient in the two essential elements of real liberty and the means of having a settled order of things – viz., *education* and *industry*.

If the Government of the interior tribes is to be continued in the very unsatisfactory and undefined manner in which it has been carried on for the last century by the Government on the coast, it will take more than three hundred years to bring it to that state of political civilization which will fit them for independence after fully shaking off the yoke of their feudal lords. And I hazard the opinion, my Lord, that if the regeneration and civilization of the fine race of interior tribes is to be left to the present system of Coast Government, it will certainly take another hundred years to infuse only the germ of civilization amongst them and to enlighten them in the true principles of a civilized Government ...

I do not believe, my Lord, that any European Government can effect this improved state of things in the interior without an enormous outlay, and we natives of the Coast believe your Lordship personally, and the Government of Her Majesty the Queen ... hail with delight any loyal, legitimate, and approved means employed by the natives of the Coast to further any political improvement amongst their countrymen, so as not only to relieve the Imperial exchequer from its heavy outlay, but also to lessen the awful responsibility of the Home Government on matters relating to so distant and unhealthy a colony. That means, in the interior of the Gold Coast, is the formation of a Confederation of all their kings, recognizing one person of influence as their superior, and organizing a constitutional Government, loyal to the British sea-coast Government.

The Fantee Confederation ... sprung into existence soon after the exchange of territory between the English and Dutch Governments, and its main object is to advance the interests of the whole of the Fantee nation, and to combine for offence and defence in time of war ... It is, therefore, the anxious wish of every civilized native of the Gold Coast, who has the interest of his country at heart, that in this agitated political state of the interior, a great desideratum to their country would be to get a *Codex Constitutionum* from the British Government on the sea-coast, defining their powers, giving them extensive latitude to improve the interior, without their President ... being subjected to constant humiliation by being ordered up to Cape Coast.

2: Casely Hayford

From Magnus J. Sampson (ed.), *West African Leadership* (Frank Cass, 1969).
J. E. Casely Hayford was in a strong position to press his ideas on African political progress, both within nationalist organisations, and as an unofficial member of the Legislative Council. These extracts are from a presidential address to the National Congress of British West Africa (January 1923); from a speech to the Legislative Council (March 1923); and from a speech to the Cape Coast Literary and Social Club (date unknown).

We are living in a new age and a new order of which we, who participate in them, are hardly aware. One important element of this new order is the growing consciousness of our race the world over, of which practical statesmanship must take cognisance. Among world problems to-day is the appeal which goes from the heart of the African to be accorded certain rights which are common to humanity; and it is important to address ourselves to the facts and to find a solution to the problems which confront us.

One result of this race consciousness is its growing articulateness. What enlightened African opinion is at present upon most matters affecting

African interests may easily be gleaned by anyone who takes the trouble to find out. We claim that we have the right to our opinion and to the expression of it. We say that we have passed the childhood stage, and that, much as we appreciate the concern of our guardians, the time has come for us to take an intelligent, active part in the guiding of our own national destiny; and that is the primary fact that has called into being the National Congress of British West Africa.

Now, speaking broadly, there are certain fundamental considerations that are common to the whole race. We claim, in common with the rest of mankind, that taxation without representation is a bad thing, and we are pledged, as all free peoples have had to do, that in our several communities the African shall have that common weapon for the protection and safe-guarding of his rights and interests, namely, the franchise. It is desirable, we hold, that by our vote we shall determine by what laws we shall be governed and how the revenues which we help to put together shall be utilised.

Equally do we hold with others that there should be free scope for the members of the community, irrespective of creed or colour, to hold any office under the crown or flag to which a person's merits entitle him or her. We hardly think that in these enlightened days there are any to be found who can seriously quarrel with that proposition, indeed the time is past when the African can be expected to continue the burden-bearer of the world.

. . . . . .

But it is our duty, as a Congress, to define our attitude as to the methods that should be pursued in attaining the liberties that we seek . . . the policy of the National Congress "is to maintain strictly and inviolate the connection of the British West African Dependencies with the British Empire, and to maintain unreservedly all and every right of free citizenship of the Empire and the fundamental principle that taxation goes with effective representation." That implies that we are resolved to honour the choice of our forbears in selecting the Union Jack as the flag under which we shall work out our national destiny; and I may say, as one of the leaders of the people, that notwithstanding any local differences that may exist with local Administrations, the heart of British West Africa to-day beats true in loyalty and devotion to the throne and the person of His Majesty the King-Emperor. It further implies that in seeking our rights we shall do so firmly and yet constitutionally.

Now, remember that this is not only a matter of sentiment. It is one of wisdom and practical common sense. We understand the British Constitution. We have no first-hand acquaintance with other constitutions. From Magna Carta to the Bill of Rights we know the path that has been trod to win British liberty; and we prefer to believe that, although in some cases local Administrations are slow to yield, in the end we shall gain our rights by constitutional persistence and insistence; and, at all events, we shall give the British Government the opportunity of proving that we have not trusted in vain.

I have said in this Council on more than two occasions that the interests of the European community and the African community of this country are identical; and every year I am more and more impressed by the same fact. It is true that the different European pioneers by their enterprise and by the capital sunk in this country have so far identified themselves with the progress of this country and its advancement; and we who are sons of the soil so very well recognise the fact that it is correct to say that our interests are identical. That fact leads, as I have said, to the formation of a strong public opinion, and that public opinion year by year becomes more articulate and more pronounced. At the same time it is true that there is no Party Government in the Gold Coast, nor can there be one. I, personally, deprecate anything in the form of Party Government; in other words, opposition for the sake of opposition. I am asking respectfully, therefore, that any criticism we pass in this House, either in the past, or in the present, or in the future, may be taken as coming from us after careful thought and consideration with a view to securing the successful administration of this country in the interests of all classes – European and African – and it is in that spirit that I desire today to say a few words. In other words, I believe that the co-operation of all classes is absolutely necessary – the Government must co-operate with the public and the public with the Government in order to make a successful administration possible.

The black man has served civilisation in a wonderful way, in a way that men hardly dreamt of, scarcely yet realise. The moral support of Ethiopia has been worth more than gold and lead and blood to the Allied cause. The enemy has stood condemned before the public conscience of the black man, and that is the severest censure that could be recorded against German remissness and wrong to mankind. Henceforth the sons of Ethiopia shall count, must count in the counsels of man. Henceforth any man worth the name of man, whatever his pretensions, whatever his clime, whatever his nationality, must hail him brother and fellow-co-worker in the uplift of man.
. . . . . .
  If you want to be saved in these days of stress, when you cannot keep away from the coming hurricane, you must have articulation, which

depends upon enfranchisement, which, to be effective, depends upon education. And your patriotism will dictate to you the necessity of bearing your own burdens in this respect. Allow me, therefore, to commend to you the idea of a national educational scheme, which aims at the provision of the most liberal standards of culture and training in the arts, the sciences, and industries at a national common ground or centre, call it a University or by what name soever you please. We have spoken of a new era, the people's era, the era of democracy. Like as the Christ in the fullness of time came and revolutionised the world of ideas by the introduction of the Golden Rule, even so now must patriotism be given a new twist in the concepts of man to take in the cause of the weak being taken up by the strong in the remaining chapters of man's history. But such is human imperfection that before the strong can hear the weak, the weak must appeal in no uncertain voice. Indeed, the strong cannot be blamed, if they regard not where there is no outcry, for the simple reason that the world is passing through a storm, and it is difficult to hear sounds of distress, even though one strains one's ears. Hence the necessity, the urgent necessity, for the uplifted voice of him, who is likely to drown. That being so, I venture to commend to you also the coming together of entire West Africa as one man to think together, and to act together in matters of common need on a common constitutional platform. If you meet with the weak-kneed and the prophet of evil in this grand enterprise, pray pass him by on the other side, and say this is not the day of petty considerations; this is Ethiopia's day, and Ethiopia must march on to triumph.

Once more I bring West Africa a message of hope, a message of triumph. The last message that I had the privilege and the honour of delivering has, under God, borne fruit. Today entire West Africa has clasped hands over a common need, a common constitutional demand. She is asking for an effective voice in her affairs. She is asking for self-determination, and we believe she will not ask in vain. It will be uphill we know. There will be slackers; there will be obstructionists; there will be traducers. But the Eternal Power, whose fiat set our sphere going, will sustain us until our little world attains unto that degree of free and democratic life, which will enable us to develop according to the genius of our race within a free United British Empire.

3: Kwame Nkrumah

(a) Extracts from *Towards Colonial Freedom: Africa in the against world imperialism* (Heinemann Educational Books, 1962; Panaf, 1973). Copyright and all rights reserved, Panaf Books Ltd.

Since this book was written in 1945, while Nkrumah was still a student in London, it should be seen in that context and not in the context of 1962 when it was first published.

(b) Extracts from K. Nkrumah, *I Speak of Freedom* (Heinemann, Educational Books, 1961; Panaf, 1973). Copyright and all rights reserved, Panaf Books Ltd.
These extracts are from speeches made in the period 1953 to 1958, as the Gold Coast moved to independence under Nkrumah's political leadership. The context of each speech is indicated after the extract.

(a) The aim of all colonial governments in Africa and elsewhere has been the struggle for raw materials; and not only this, but the colonies have become the dumping ground, and colonial peoples the false recipients, of manufactured goods of the industrialists and capitalists of Great Britain, France, Belgium and other colonial powers who turn to the dependent territories which feed their industrial plants. This is colonialism in a nutshell.

The basis of colonial territorial dependence is economic, but the basis of the solution of the problem is political. Hence political independence is an indispensable step towards securing economic emancipation. This point of view irrevocably calls for an alliance of all colonial territories and dependencies. All provincial and tribal differences should be broken down completely. By operating on tribal differences and colonial provincialism, the colonial powers' age-long policy of 'divide and rule' has been enhanced, while the colonial national independence movement has been obstructed and bamboozled.

In an attempt to reconcile the inherent contradictions within her capitalistic economy, [Britain] has two courses only left to keep her home population from starvation; either her population must be dispersed in the colonial territories, or she must guarantee subsistence to them by exploitation of the colonies.

. . . . . .

The colonies are thus a source of raw materials and cheap labour, and a 'dumping ground' for spurious surplus goods to be sold at exorbitant prices. Therefore these colonies become avenues for capital investments, not for the benefit and development of the colonial peoples, but for the benefit of the investors, whose agents are the governments concerned. That is why it is incoherent nonsense to say that Britain or any other colonial power has the 'good intention' of developing her colonies for self-government and independence.

In general, imperialism is the policy which aims at creating, organizing

034191

and maintaining an empire. In other words, it is a state, vast in size, composed of various distinct national units, and subject to a single, centralized power or authority. This is the conception of empire: divers peoples brought together by force under a common power.

The purpose of founding colonies was mainly to secure raw materials. To safeguard the measures for securing such raw materials the following policies were indirectly put into action: (i) to make the colonies non-manufacturing dependencies; (ii) to prevent the colonial subjects from acquiring the knowledge of modern means and techniques for developing their own industries; (iii) to make colonial 'subjects' simple producers of raw materials through cheap labour; (iv) to prohibit the colonies from trading with other nations except through the 'mother country'.

The most searching and penetrating analysis of economic imperialism has been given by Marx and Lenin . . .

The Marxist–Leninist position may be stated thus: In the capitalist system of production labour is treated as a commodity to be bought and sold in the market like any other commodity. As such, it figures in the capitalist-producer's calculations merely as one production cost among others. But since the system is a competitive system, the capitalist-producer is compelled to keep wages down in order to keep the margin of profit high . . . This means that under the capitalist system of production a point is soon reached where wages appear a necessary evil even to the capitalist-producer, who now realizes that the incomes distributed as wages form the body of the market for what he wants to sell . . .

The capitalist-producer, in seeking profit by limiting his wage bill, impedes his own effort to find buyers for the increasing volume of his production.

. . . . . .

To find a way out of this contradiction the capitalist-producer turns his profit-seeking eyes to the colonies and dependent territories. He does so first by killing the arts and crafts in these areas through the competition of his cheaper machine-made goods (exports) and, secondly, by thrusting capital loans upon them for the construction of railways, harbours and other means of transportation and communication in so far as these constructions cater to his profits and safeguard his capital . . .

The question may be raised to the effect that the colonial powers utilize part of these profits for public works, health projects and 'loans'. The fact generally forgotten is that such 'loans' come from taxing the colonial 'subjects', and the profit gotten from their produce and mineral resources, and the greater part of these very loans is used in paying European officials in the colonies.

. . . . . .

The mandate system is ... a cowardly compromise between the principle of self-determination for dependent territories and imperialism. It becomes nothing but a useful tool in the hands of the powers to whom the territories are mandated in order to carry out their intentions and to perpetuate the economic exploitation of these territories by a combination of colonial powers ...

The doctrine of 'trusteeship' is supposed to be more humanitarian in its significance and approach than exploitation. It is the fundamental factor underlying the system of 'dual mandate', exponents of which think that exploitation involves a sacred duty towards the exploited peoples. The colonial subjects must be exploited and 'civilised', but, in doing so, their 'rights' must be 'respected' and 'protected'.

. . . . . .

The duty of any worthwhile colonial movement for national liberation ... must be the organization of labour and of youth; and the abolition of political illiteracy. This should be accomplished through mass political education which keeps in constant contact with the masses of colonial peoples. This type of education should do away with that kind of intelligentsia who have become the very architects of colonial enslavement.

Then, the organizations must prepare the agents of progress, must find the ablest among its youth and train their special interests (technological, scientific and political) ... The organization must root itself and secure its basis and strength in the labour movement, the farmers (the workers and peasantry) and the youth. This national liberation movement must struggle for its own principles and to win its aims.

It must have its own press. It cannot live separately from, nor deviate from the aims and aspirations of the masses, the organized force of labour, the organized farmers, and the responsible and cogent organization of youth ...

The peoples of the colonies know precisely what they want. They wish to be free and independent, to be able to feel themselves ... equal with all other peoples, and to work out their own destiny without outside interference, and to be unrestricted to attain an advancement that will put them on a par with other technically advanced nations of the world. Outside interference does not help to develop their country. It impedes and stifles and crushes not only economic progress, but the spirit and indigenous enterprise of the peoples themselves.

(b) It had become evident that unless we organised our potential strength more vigorously, the granting of Independence might be delayed indefinitely ...

It was therefore necessary to adopt a definite programme of political action. I explained what I meant by Positive Action. It was, I said, the application of constitutional and legitimate means to cripple the imperialist forces in the country. The weapons would be strikes, boycotts and non-co-operation, based upon the principle of non-violence.

It is our ambition to improve the standard of living of the people of Ghana, by making great achievements such as the gigantic agricultural scheme, leading to the abolition of unemployment and idleness; the introduction of progressive socialist schemes like housing, sanatoria, the establishment of workers' compulsory education for children of all classes, maternity and child welfare clinics, and other intricate and progressive social economic schemes that will surely transform Ghana into a modern country.

Our support has come from the masses, and in the masses we place our greatest belief and faith. And we shall not be let down . . . we have no place for shirkers, we have place for workers, thinkers and doers . . . And so before long this country of ours will be the land of self-help, efficiency and enterprise. (Address to public rally, Accra 1953)
. . . . . .

Democracy, as against imperialism, despotism and autocracy in the Gold Coast, must have its roots in rural reconstruction. It is in the rural areas that the forces of feudalism are entrenched. There can be no social advancement or complete overthrow of imperialism as long as the vestiges of feudalism still remain in this country. An effective system of democratic regional, district and local councils must therefore be established in order to make the wishes of the common man decisive in the consideration of rural problems and programmes. Homes for the people, education for the masses, rural communications, health and sanitary needs, water supplies, facilities for education with special emphasis on the acquisition of modern skills, housing and social amenities will be in importance second only to that of the development of rural industries. Our development plan must be essentially a plan for rural reconstruction. (Address to CPP Annual Delegates Conference 1955)

Now let me come to the general principles which, I hope, will govern the country's future constitution. First and foremost, the Government consider that the constitution should be based on the principle that all citizens of Ghana are equal and are all entitled to the same rights.
. . . . . .

I come now to what I believe to be the second great principle which is essential in any constitution of a democratic country. This principle can be expressed by saying that the people of the country must be sovereign. The Convention People's Party has not fought for self-government in order to have a sham form of independence. We are determined not only to see that this country is independent of any foreign country, but also that power passes into the hands of the people and is effectively exercised by them.

The way in which a sovereign people exercise their power is through organs of government which are freely elected by them.

......

If there is any one matter above all else which I would describe as the first essential of democracy, it is the existence of machinery to provide for impartial supervision of elections ... The Government attach the greatest importance to the compilation of accurate registers and to the setting up of impartial bodies to see to it that elections are carried out in a fair and non-partisan spirit ...

Allied to minority rights and of equal importance are the rights of individuals. The Government believe that the individual citizen of Ghana ought to be guaranteed by law freedom from arbitrary arrest. The Government believe that the individual's home should be inviolate and not subject to arbitrary search, and that his property should not be arbitrarily confiscated and that he should have the right of free speech. The Government believe that any individual should be entitled to join any trade union, political party or other association of his choice. The Government consider that freedom to practise whatever religion a citizen follows should be guaranteed by law; the Government think that it is an essential part of democracy that there should be a free press and that provision should be made by law that any state broadcasting system is as free to put the Opposition's point of view as that of the Government. Above all, the Government believe that the courts of law should be absolutely independent of the Executive and should be a bulwark for the defence of the rights of the individual.

... it is the Government's intention to include these fundamental rights in the constitution once Independence has been granted. (Speaking on the motion for Approval of the Government's Revised Constitutional Proposals, National Assembly, 12 November 1956)

The Gold Coast Government believes that the trade union movement is of the utmost importance in the development of Africa as a whole and I can assure you that my Government will give all the support which it can to the establishment and maintenance of independent and free trade unions in the new state of Ghana. (Inauguration ceremony of the All African Regional Conference of ICFTU, 1957)

Many of the advocates of colonialism claimed in the past − as some of them do now − they were racially superior and had a special mission to colonise and rule other people. This we reject. We repudiate and condemn all forms of racialism, for racialism not only injures those against whom it is used but warps and perverts the very people who preach and protect it; and when it becomes a guiding principle in the life of any nation, as it has become in some other parts of Africa, then the nation digs its own grave. It is inconceivable that a racial minority will be able for ever to maintain its totalitarian domination over an awakened majority.

We, the independent states of Africa, seek to eliminate racialism by our own example of a tolerant, multi-racial community reflecting the freely expressed will of the people based upon universal adult suffrage.

4: J. B. Danquah

(a) Extracts from *Dr. J. B. Danquah's Letters 1949–1951: Journey to Independence and After,* compiled by H. K. Akyeampong (Waterville Publishing House, 1971).
These extracts illustrate Danquah's hostility to Nkrumah's Convention People's Party, formed in opposition to his own United Gold Coast Convention; and to Nkrumah's more radical policy of 'Positive Action', involving strikes, boycotts, and other forms of non-cooperation.

(b) Extract from J. B. Danquah, *Historic Speeches and Writings on Ghana,* compiled by H. K. Akyeampong (George Boakie, Accra, no date).
This extract is from a Christmas message to the nation, 20 December 1959, by which time he was a leading critic of the ruling Convention People's Party. None of the Ghanaian newspapers would publish this message.

(a) The truth is that by establishing the [United Gold Coast] Convention we have succeded to make the masses fall in with our aspirations of self-government. We have pledged ourselves to secure this for the country within the shortest possible time, constitutionally. But certain of the masses who accept the C.P.P. doctrine believe that they can take self-government 'now', by positive action. It does not occur to them that 'now', as a portion of time, may be longer than the 'shortest' possible time e.g. two seconds.

I do not believe in the soundness or reasonableness of the C.P.P. doctrine that by positive action of the type usually paraded in their newspapers and on their platforms it will be possible for the Gold Coast to win the sympathy of international opinion, by which I mean, in particular, the U.N.O. and the U.S.A., so as to compel the British to yield to our demands.

However, I am constantly keeping my eyes open on the party situation, and I will not fail to take advantage of any opportunity for members of the C.P.P. to be won over completely. The recognition of the U.G.C.C. policy as the soundest, most constitutional and most reasonable for the people of this country, both young and old, to follow is not doubted in any intelligent circle, and anything hotter than what is lawful is beyond my acceptance.

I must add that I do not accept the C.P.P. doctrine that the masses are to lead the leaders, or that the leaders are to follow the masses. That policy is suicidal, and it is not in good taste for me to advise the Gold Coast people to commit political suicide. (Extract from letter to J. K. Dadson, 15 September 1949)

My Dear Kwame Nkrumah,

I write to you as a Gold Coast citizen, loving this country as much as any one. The report to hand is that you have given a fortnight's notice as from December 15 to commence operations for positive action on the expiration of the period, unless the Governor by that time should have summoned a national constituent assembly or should have granted us 'dominion status on the so-called model of the Westminster Statute'.
......

As you well know, in 1947 Mr. George Alfred Grant took positive action when he gave birth to his conception of a United Gold Coast becoming militant in the struggle for this country's liberation by forming a Convention of the Chiefs and people for the purpose.
......

Indeed, Kwame, you know that by pursuing Mr. Grant's mode of positive action we captured the political initiative from Government and brought about the Coussey Committee. The country, on the crest of a wave of success, was surging forward in the silent and confident strength of a united nation when, like a bolt from the blue, that united front was shattered and battered and smashed into smithereens by a new brand of positive action. That new brand of positive action, at an evil hour, created a bastard kind of Convention, a partisan Convention, the Convention People's Party, inconsistent with its putative parent, Grant's United Convention.

Indeed, Kwame, you know that from that evil hour, from that grossest of all our national mistakes, the ground started to shift from beneath us; Government regained its lost initiative, and breathed free again 'with excess of joy' that 'Divide et impera' had triumphed even against the

27

invincible Convention!

The entire country has since this event experienced a harassing, bewildering and an anguishing despair, apprehensive that the . . . policy to achieve self-government in the shortest time possible upon the crest of a united front, had been illusory.

In the midst of that perplexity and embarrassment, . . . thousands of our people were made to believe that you had discovered for them a new heaven in the slogan 'S.G. Now!'

. . . . . .

We are told that the implements of your positive action are boycotts, strikes and demonstrations, the same which you defined before the Ga State Council on the 20th October as 'positive action with absolute non-violence'.

I confess I did not understand it then and I do not understand it now. Human nature being what it is; the fortified Government of Imperialism on our soil being what it is; and our unarmed or, if possible, wretchedly armed people being so completely at the mercy of the armed strength of the imperial power, how can anyone in his senses guarantee that what happened on the day of your trial for contempt of court may not happen again in a worse, heightened and more widespread form on December 30 and thereafter? Who can guarantee that the blood of old and young will not be shed, that heads will not be broken, that liberties may not be restrained behind bars, and that brilliant and promising careers of young men who in the future to come could have achieved greater things for us might not be cut short?

We all agree in this: that if, for the sake of this Ghana death or prison bars or broken heads should come, we welcome them as part of the game. But only those without charity fail to agree in this: that the destructive brand of positive action will not advance us ahead of the great Foe, nor wrest initiative from him. It may, on the contrary, strengthen his hold, or even worse, retard our own advance and even destroy some of our present gains.

Can anyone guarantee that after a day, or a year and a day, of destructive positive action, this British Imperialist will come forward with outstretched arms and say: 'Hello, Ghanaians: Here's your S.G., take it!'

I counsel you . . . be not rash to waste your strength upon an impracticable ideal. Instead, resort to creative positive action, and abandon the destructive kind.

. . . . . .

Like yourself I would gladly have self-government this second this minute, even this moment . . . But it is said that hasty climbers have sudden falls, and believe me, my dear Kwame, there is wisdom in it.

(Extract from a letter to Kwame Nkrumah, December 1949)

(b) In the past twelve months, our country has witnessed a great display of the power of the State as against the individual. Laws have been passed or put into execution, which have made it possible for the individual to be deprived of his liberty and imprisoned for five years without trial.

Laws have been passed which have put the verdict of the Courts to nothingness and have elevated the power of the State above the right of the individual, even to the extent of depriving the individual of his property, even of his or her money.

By a resolution adopted by the executive of a farmers' organisation, the poorest entity among us, the Ghana cocoa farmer, whose average income is about £85 a year, has been exploited for one-sixth of his fixed cocoa price of 72 shillings a load, to help the Development Fund. This exploitation has been deliberately accepted by the Government to enrich the State by £25 million, to the loss of the individuals.

Again, in the past twelve months, laws have been passed or put into execution, which have deprived the worker of his freedom to join any trade union of his choice, or his own organisation, and have compelled him to belong to one or other of a few organisations approved by law.

. . . . . .

... we are veering away from the liberalism of Christianity to the absolutism of Communism, and we are acquiring the habit of thinking that while the State matters, the individual does not count. We happen to know of course, that without individuals there can be no State, but without a State individuals can be.

5: Nnamdi Azikiwe

Extracts from N. Azikiwe, *Renascent Africa* (Frank Cass, 1968).
This book was first published in 1937 while Azikiwe was editor of the *African Morning Post* in Accra. In the same year, Azikiwe returned to Nigeria to found the newspapers which were an important instrument in his campaign against British colonialism in Nigeria.

The Renascent African exists in a transitional stage between the Old and the New Africans. He refuses to view his future passively. He is articulate. He is destined to usher forth the New Africa. To avoid ambiguity, it is necessary to explain what is meant by the New Africa.

. . . . . .

The term is used in a psycho-social sense. It is the renascence of Africans and the reformation of African society.

. . . . . .

The philosophy of the New Africa hinges itself on five bases. These are indispensable to its realization.

1. *Spiritual Balance* must be cultivated by Renascent Africans. This means respect for the views of others ... It means that the feelings of others must be taken into consideration, and that no ulterior motives should influence one's criticisms of others.

2. *Social Regeneration* must be experienced in African society. African conventions cannot be said to be consistent with what is ethical, just, and equitable. African society must be democratic. The ills of the present social order hinge on the continuation of the forces of man's inhumanity to man. Let the Renascent African take upon himself the burden of looking at his fellow African as a man, nothing more, nothing less. Tribal appellations cause tribal idiosyncrasies; these lead ultimately to vanity and superciliousness and disharmony.

. . . . . .

3. *Economic Determinism* must be the basis of African economic thought ...

The Renascent African cannot create a new social order without an economic foundation. No longer must wealth be concentrated in the hands of the few. No longer must the profit motive guide and control the aims in life of the African. No longer must the wage-earners be told of a dignity that does not seem to exist in labour.

Let the Renascent African make to-morrow secure for posterity, and a milestone is reached toward African economic interdependence with the rest of the world.

4. *Mental Emancipation* is necessary in order to crystallize the New Africa. This includes education of the sort which should teach African youth to have faith in his ability; to believe that he is the equal of the people of other races of mankind – mentally and physically.

. . . . . .

5. *National Risorgimento* is inevitable. When the Renascent African has cultivated spiritual balance, regenerated his society, planned his society economically, and has experienced mental emancipation, his political status cannot be in doubt.

. . . . . .

... to understand the significance of imperialism, it must be analyzed from the following standpoints: causes, ethics, problems, and results.

Now, what are the causes of imperialism? They may be social, economic, political, military, religious.

30

Socially speaking, I may refer to Darwin, Malthus, Spencer, Wallace, and other biologists, for giving me an idea as to the nature of the struggle for existence and the survival of the fittest. In this respect the law of natural selection plays no less an important part.

In other words, the instinct of pugnacity (to dominate) is innate in man . . . It fortifies his pride with a desire to conquer . . .

Economically speaking, I may refer to Karl Marx, Friedrich Engels, and other economists for establishing the economic interpretation of history, through which one learns that the quest for food, shelter and clothing is the dominating factor in human society.

In other words, since the Industrial Revolution has made society to manufacture goods and commodities by machine, and since mass production is the rule and not the exception, raw materials are essential to a stabilization of home industries. And since colonies produce raw materials, they are necessary to the economic life of the industrial countries.

Politically speaking, I am grateful to Jules Ferry (France), Friedrich Fabri, Dr Paul Rohrbach (Germany), Rudyard Kipling, Lord Lugard (Great Britain), and other advocates of colonial possessions who believe that in the imposition of the will of the superior on the will of the inferior, there must be a political symbiosis which will enable the inferior to graduate from tutelage.

In other words, the strong are destined to rule the weak . . .

From a military point of view, if the fittest must survive the struggle, and if economics motivate human life more predominantly than any other factors, and if the prestige of *map-itis* must be maintained, colonies are essential in order to co-ordinate the military organizations of the empire.

In other words, coaling stations are essential for the mercantile fleet of the imperialist countries; naval bases and fortifications are also of prime importance; not to mention the paramount need for using the colonial possessions as a reservoir of troops . . .

From a religious point of view, it is essential that the strong must weaken the weak, not only physically but psycho-physically . . .

. . . . . .

The religious man must, and did, teach the Native not to lay up treasures on earth; this enabled the commercial man to grab the earthly treasures; and this facilitated the role of the Government to regulate how these earthly treasures are to be exported for the use of the world's industries.

. . . . . .

There are two main doctrines in the philosophical analysis of imperialism from an ethical point of view: (a) the Doctrine of Exploitation; and (b) the

31

Doctrine of Trusteeship.

. . . . . .

[The philosophy of the Doctrine of Exploitation] is identical with that of Thucydides: 'Gods and men alike always maintain dominion wherever they are stronger' . . .

In other words, 'To the victor belong the spoils'. And if man needs the pathway of the deer for the construction of a highway or for any purpose whatsoever, the deer must surrender its path. *Therefore, the ethics underlying the Doctrine of Exploitation is a glorification of force as a means to an end.*

. . . . . .

[The] doctrine [of Trusteeship] is more or less humanitarian in its approach. Its basis is a dual mandate. That is, a belief that exploitation involves a duty.

In other words, this doctrine is not opposed to exploitation, necessarily, but it suggests that exploitation should be a complement of responsibility. It says: Exploit the weaker races, develop their mineral resources, civilize backward peoples, but in so doing respect their rights and protect them.

. . . . . .

Many problems have been raised by the practicalization of the ethics of imperialism. They are racial, social, educational, economic, political.

Racially speaking, the contact of two races which belong to an imperialist country and an exploited country, respectively, leads to an arrogation of superiority and inferiority, respectively.

. . . . . .

Socially speaking, the policy which arrogates innate superiority to the race of the imperialist State reinforces its social ideology by enabling such 'superior' race to pass unfair measures directed against the Native races, to impress upon the latter their status of inferiority.

. . . . . .

Educationally speaking, the education of the backward races has been regarded as a 'problem'. In the attempt to solve this 'problem', efforts have been made to reduce education to the lowest minimum, possibly *the four R's* – Reading, 'Riting, 'Rithmetic, and Religion.

The restriction of the education of the natives is based on fear, because the imperialist believes that the more educated the backward races become, the more will they demand for an increased share and participation in the governance of their countries, which is natural. This, the imperialist States are not prepared to grant, at least at the present time.

. . . . . .

Economically speaking, the problems of imperialism are based on the following: production, distribution, consumption, and exchange. The production of raw materials is necessary to the manufacturing industries of the home country. There must be a large source of labour supply which consequently brings problems of wages, conditions of work, industrial accidents, forced labour, etc., to the fore.

In addition to this, goods and other commodities must be distributed to the colonies, at prices which must pay appreciable dividends to the investors of the mother country, and the raw materials must be bought from Natives at the prices dictated by the imperialist firms according to their rate of exchange.

Native lands have also been confiscated on the ground of the right of eminent domain; and among some Powers, these unfairly acquired lands have been leased and subleased to plantation owners where native labourers have suffered all sorts of inhumanity . . .

Politically speaking, the question arises whether the period of tutelage is definite or indefinite? If it is the former, who is entitled to decide when a ward is ready to assume the task of autonomy – the imperialist State or the exploited Native? If it is the latter, is it consistent with the policy of trusteeship, and must it be accepted as revealed law, handed down from Mount Sinai, without the Natives making just demands, in accordance with the verdict of history?

. . . . . .

Unless the Natives are allowed to participate in the governance of their own lands, on a sound basis of democracy, that is, the application of the doctrine of natural, civil, political, social, and economic rights and equalities, in the administration of their country, by a system which will not only educate them to make use of the ballot, but will also educate them to make it possible for them to *participate* in the higher political offices which are now restricted to Caucasoid foreigners, the future is not assuring.

Writing on such a subject as imperialism, it is not academic to define it at the outset, in view of its nature. However, since the causes, ethics and problems of imperialism have been considered, it is safe to attempt a definition.

Imperialism may be defined as the imposition of the will of one political organization, which is backed by superior armaments, upon the will of another political organization or organizations, whose physical force is incapable of resisting the will of the State which is bent on a civilizing mission. This is a general definition, and some of the factors hitherto discussed come under its various ramifications.

. . . . . .

Historically speaking, imperialism is inevitable, . . . for self-preservation is the first law of nature. Since imperialism is a *sine qua non* in the evolution of organisms, the main problem of Africans is to adjust themselves to it, for what cannot be helped cannot be helped, especially if it be an obeisance to the law of nature.

What is needed to-day to strengthen the constructive phases of imperialism is the unequivocal acceptance of the postulate of the equality of the races. Inability to organize a stable civilization does not necessarily imply inherent racial inferiority or lack of political capacity.

It is desirable, from the standpoint of universal order, for the stronger races to rule the weaker races (*it is inevitable and cannot be helped; and since this is the predicament of the weaker races, they must cultivate tolerant skepticism to accept their fate, if even it may be temporary*) provided that the rulers will act merely as guides and guardians, on the dual mandate principle — exploitation for development, trusteeship and tutelage — and provided that the ruling Power is willing to surrender its suzerainty if and when the ward is convinced that he is fledged for political independence.

......

Mutual aid is an important factor in the evolution of human society. Without co-operation, society will deteriorate. Each individual will be left to himself, and the strong will prey upon the weak.

Among subject races, it is very essential that this fundamental principle of societal life should be taken into consideration, else the future cannot be assuring.

......

If it is conceded that the African is *communalistic* in his societal relationship, then there can be no doubt that the ethos of individualism is an outside force which the African has had to contend with as a result of the impact of other culture-complexes. That being the case, it means that in the cultural assimilation thus occasioned, the African seems to be gradually effacing his original societal philosophy, in favour of an alien idea.

......

I am not saying that African society is not *individualistic* in certain respects, yet I am not saying that African society has been *communistic* or *collectivistic*. What I am suggesting is that pristine African society was *communalistic,* in that the welfare of the group was paramount to the welfare of the individual.

......

In the present stage of the evolution of West Africa, it is essential that mutual aid should be practicalized, else Africans shall devolutionize into something which is not only alien to their societal structure but also inimical to the progress of any people.

34

If Africans must evolve better forms of political institutions, certain realities must be faced, and unless they are prepared to bear one another's burden, their aspirations will never materialize.

The struggle for political emancipation has just begun. In different sections of West Africa, the right of self-determination is being doctrinated and evangelized.

. . . . . .

If he who strikes the first blow [for political autonomy] does so sincerely for the benefit of the many, then the many must rally round him, especially in time of distress. This is a practical way of demonstrating mutual aid as a factor of political evolution.

. . . . . .

Are Africans not the authors of their doom? Africans must realize that he who pays the piper calls the tune. They should appreciate what this expression denotes and connotes. If Africans are not mentally matured enough to realize that only through African philanthropy can this continent be saved from its impending doom, then they are lost.

6: Kenneth Kaunda

Extracts from K. Kaunda, *Zambia Shall Be Free* (Heinemann Educational Books, 1962). Reprinted by permission of Praeger Publishers, Inc.

These extracts illustrate Kaunda's consistent campaign for rapid African political advance which he first mounted through the Northern Rhodesia African National Congress, then from 1960 through his own United National Independence Party.

Your membership of the African National Congress, entered now, will help make possible
   the fight for the franchise;
   the fight against colour discrimination in public places like post offices, hotels, rest rooms, eating places, theatres, parks, playgrounds and many others;
   the fight to get Africans safeguarded against the prevailing police brutality and unlawful arrests;
   the fight for getting higher posts for Africans in the Protectorate's and Federal Civil Services, and in military and police forces according to merit and not according to their colour;
   the fight for better treatment of our Chiefs in the way of allowances ... and to stop all intimidation and ill-treatment of Chiefs and their Native Authority servants by Government officials;

the fight for more and better educational and health facilities and to fight for free economic progress of Africans both in urban and rural areas;

the fight against the establishment of a common native policy for the Federation;

the fight against the final stage of this dreadful monster Federation which is intended to be a Central African Dominion, in other words the fight for remaining a Protectorate under the direct control of the Colonial Office until we are ready to participate fully in the running of our Protectorate's affairs;

in short, all the above mean the fight for self-guards and not safeguards by someone else! (Extract from a circular sent out by Kaunda, as Secretary-General of the ANC, 1955.)

The primary objective of Congress is to improve the lot of the up-to-now badly exploited African, either by negotiation, or by action, where negotiation fails. In this way, the gap between the privileged and the underdog is being narrowed; and the narrower the gap, the greater chance there is of the different races living together in peace and harmony.

......

Northern Rhodesia is a country of deep-rooted contrasts, deep-rooted because everything has been planned on *apartheid* lines, everything has been running, is running and within the foreseeable future will continue to run, on those lines. In this lies the root of all the present trouble. This 'apartheid' of political, economic and social planning is admittedly more pronounced here because it takes racial lines and so must be faced as such.

The white man lords it over us in all walks of life not because he happens to be white but because he is better organized than we are; that is his secret. Our task is now to mobilize all the forces that we can for *self-government now*. This is no small task at all. It means choosing your friends well here and abroad, it calls for sincerity of purpose, determination and courage, self-discipline ... Nothing can be achieved anywhere and in any field without good organization. For those who have succeeded in life good and effective organization were their watchwords. We are capable of organizing effectively here if only we can seriously put our heads together.

To organize for anything effectively, you must have clear in your own mind what you want, and how you mean to get it. We of U.N.I.P. know what we want, self-government now, and we also know how to get it, through non-violent means plus positive action.

When we organize our people, it is important to note that we are building an organization that should not only get us self-government and, ultimately, independence, but an organization sufficiently strong to run our government. Putting it briefly, we are organizing to bring into being here a government of the people, by the people and indeed for the people. We criticise and condemn the present set-up as undemocratic, unethical and entirely unchristian and, therefore, unworthy of self-respecting people. It is a government of the privileged few, by the privileged few and for the privileged few. It is these few that the Welensky governments in Central Africa are arming. He is creating all-white battalions, in spite of the existing regiments which are mixed racially. All this should not surprise us, although we condemn it unreservedly, because it is part of the privileged few's organization in order to perpetuate here their rule of oppression and suppression. (Extracts from speech to delegates at a UNIP working committee, August 1960)

At meetings up and down the country I repeatedly stressed the need for a well-lubricated party political machine. Every single member of the party must be kept in constant and close touch with party headquarters. The party must become the trusted mouthpiece of all the people, so that each and every one would be ready to suffer, if necessary, together, in the cause of freedom. This kind of solidarity was even more necessary after independence had been achieved.

No organization of any type, industrial, social or political, can survive without discipline. It brings self-control, and is of the utmost importance in a political party. Both leaders and ordinary members must submit to it, but the leaders particularly, must set a good example. They are closely watched by their followers and much depends on how they conduct themselves. In a campaign employing methods of non-violence, discipline is even more vital, especially when the tide of nationalism is rising all the time.

7: Oginga Odinga

Extracts from O. Odinga, *Not Yet Uhuru* (Heinemann Educational Books, 1967). Reprinted by permission of Farrar, Straus & Giroux, Inc.
This book was published while Odinga was Vice-President of Kenya.

The mission schools supplied the servants of the [colonial] administration. The products of the schools rose to be clerks, census and tax counters, interpreters, and chiefs. The teaching in the classrooms stressed memory rather than reasoning, repetition by rote instead of thinking and originality, for these were the ideal moulds for docile civil servants. The purpose of education was not to train for independence, but for subservience.

It was also to teach the African that his ways were alien to civilized living. Christianity could not be accepted without the rejection of African customs and religion. White and African religions were not only different, but Christianity had to be recognized as unquestionably superior. The new religion had to be the *only* way of life. In turning his back on old ways to embrace the new, the African was made ashamed of the traditions of his own society.

In this way docile African hangers-on, who deferred without murmur to the moral superiority of all things White and Christian, were enlisted to serve the White government; and an educated leadership group emerged that was separated by a great gulf from the mass of the people ... The price for education had been Christianity; now the price for approval and acceptance was deferring not to the African will, but to the purpose of the Whites. Here were sown early the seeds of estrangement of the educated leadership from the people which has bedevilled Kenya's political life for so long. A man could be a leader by virtue of his education, but his very education estranged him from his people and fostered in him the illusion that he need not be answerable to them. Only this can explain the ease with which leaders of later generations of political activity switched policy and party, allegiance and principle without any consultation of their followers and voters.

African society had a very distinct image of leadership. Leadership was generally associated with maturity, experience, steadfastness, and wisdom, and a thorough absorption of the teachings of the elders passed on by them or sung by our traditional musicians. The new education took leadership from the elders and bestowed it on the youth, but a youth which was steeped in the colonial philosophy and that rejected not only the traditional way of life, but also respect for the will of the people.

. . . . . .

I was convinced that to start the battle against White domination we had to assert our economic independence. We had to show what we could do by our own effort. We had had it drummed into us that the Whites had the brains to give the orders and it was for Africans to carry them out. We had to show we were capable of enterprise and development in fields beyond our shambas. It was no good bridling at accusations of our inferiority. We had to prove our mettle to the government, to the Whites. We Luo had also to assert ourselves among the other peoples of Kenya. I

38

was haunted by the view which other Africans had of the Luo people . . . that the Luo were extravagant, self-centred, and exhibitionist; that they used their money for show and not to save to improve themselves. The Luo needed to build a sense of unity, common purpose, and achievement.

I was growing increasingly sceptical of the advice we heard from the government that we had to seek economic advance before political power could be given to us: wherever we turned government-made obstacles seemed to loom in the way of our economic advance.

I was being forced to the conclusion that the admonitions to us to seek economic power before political rights were not genuine advice from the colonial government; these were devices by the authorities to mislead us, and gain time for the administration. I was becoming more and more convinced that political power had to be struggled for and achieved as a stepping-stone to any advance at all.

. . . . . .

A ten-year development plan for African agriculture was launched in 1946. In 1948 the Governor, Sir Philip Mitchell, wrote a paper on 'The Agrarian Problem in Kenya'. He put his finger on the issue: African unrest was not just a political and a security question, but an economic one. Mitchell asked for a commission of investigation into the economic conditions of the three East African territories. His pressure resulted in the appointment of the East African Royal Commission of 1953–55, which announced, when it reported, that something in the nature of an agrarian revolution was essential . . .

It was an economic solution that was needed but it was already too late and priorities were wrong. In the drive for increased production the interests of the people of Kenya were subordinate to Britain's needs, and so the schemes were not devised to change the basic dependency of Africans in the settler economy, and they did not thus go far enough to meet African needs and demands.

. . . Government policy was not to extend African land holdings, but to devise new systems of land usage and control to make more productive the land on which Africans were already overcrowded. A system of individual land tenure was to be imposed. Land consolidation would be the first step towards the registration of individual ownership.

The Governor had gone on record that the most urgent problem was not the question of the alienated land but 'the need to discover and apply systems of land usage'. It was obvious that the purpose of intensifying land use in the African reserves was to block African demands for the return of their stolen lands. There was another motive behind the new land policy. The Royal Commission stated that it aimed at achieving 'economic mobility designed to ensure that the land finds its way into the hands of those best able to use it in the interests of the community as a whole'. In other words, a stable middle class would be created to serve as a buffer between the government and the mass of the people, and to absorb political resistance among the people as mission education and plums of minor office had done in a previous generation.

The government put its new policies into effect as it had always done in the past, by imposing them on the people without consultation. If the people would not cooperate, out of deep distrust of all government policy, then the government would order the chiefs and the headmen to push its policies through by force. This added fuel to an already fiercely burning fire. Resistance to government soil conservation measures and land consolidation gave the mass backing to the political movement that had searched for peaceful solutions and, when it found none, was forced by the pressure of events to embark on altogether new forms of struggle.

......

Kenya nationalism turned violent because for thirty years it was treated as seditious and denied all legitimate outlet. KAU [Kenya African Union] spokesmen were dismissed as agitators instead of being recognized as the vocal cord of a whole people.

The irony was that the preparations for an uprising were not only not initiated by KAU, but were deliberately kept away from it, and yet when the government cracked down, it was KAU that was made the scapegoat and Kenyatta the evil genius. To explain the revolt as the organized plot of KAU was to totally distort the facts and misunderstand the nature of the struggle in Kenya. The date and place of birth of the revolt cannot be clearly pointed out; there were many beginnings and many origins. There was seething revolt among the people, on numerous levels, some national, some tribal, some clan, some of a sophisticated political nature, some expressive of the simplest form of anti-White hostility. There was a labyrinth of clandestine committees and organizations of one kind or another.

......

The government's handling of the Emergency forced a state of civil war on the Kikuyu people. In the beginning the government had virtually no support among the people; from Chiefs, wealthy landholders, tribal police, shop-keepers, government employees, people who ate crumbs from the settler table, perhaps, but from no significant cross-section of the people. The government realized it could never defeat the people until it divided them. The Home Guard movement was begun to turn men into collaborators, to turn father against son, and to enlist brother to betray brother. Men who did not volunteer for the Home Guard were immediately suspect to the security forces ...

40

The two sides of the Emergency persisted into later years; freedom-fighters were unemployed and landless; and the loyalists had entrenched themselves and had become the dependable middle group that government had aimed to create. Those who had sacrificed most in the struggle had lost out to the people who had played safe. Political divisions had been given concrete economic shape, and so would persist into the post-Emergency period. This, as much as the toll of dead, injured, and detained, was the harvest that government policy reaped: the creation of a group that had vested interests to defend would, it was hoped, block the struggle rising again in open revolt and would capture not only the military but the political victory of the years to come.

Throughout the Emergency years the nightmare of the government was that the revolt would spread to the other tribes. Immediate steps were taken to seal off the Kikuyu reserves and to subject the rest of the country to a continuous barrage of propaganda to inflame anti-Kikuyu feeling. Government and settler tactics seemed designed at little less than the extinction of the Kikuyu (for the accusation 'Mau Mau' was interchangeable with 'Kikuyu') and to win over the Luo, the second largest tribe in Kenya, as an army of loyalists. My primary objective was to block this government offensive to enrol the Luo as pro-government belligerents, and thus fatally to divide the African people of our country.

. . . . . .

We had gone into the Legislative Council with a clear set of aims. These were to make the council a platform from which settlers and the governments of Kenya and Britain could hear African opinion. We were pledged to campaign for more African representation, to use this, in turn, to remove the political, economic, and social restrictions on our people. National political organizations were prohibited; above all we would use the Legislative Council as a national forum to build national unity.

. . . . . .

Our rejection of the special seats and African Ministries was in anticipation of the search by government and settlers for Africans who would try to deflect our people from our struggle. Plums of office might tempt men to accept the continuance of White domination if there was a comfortable seat somewhere in government for themselves.

KANU, the party, it seemed to me, was the key to our advance. If the party could be associated with policy-making at all levels, including the Cabinet level, the whole national effort could be galvanized for advance. No popular policy would be possible without a strong and vigorous party. Where there was no united and powerful national movement neo-colonialism moved in and thrived.

. . . We regarded the *uhuru* period [*uhuru* = freedom, independence] as a culmination of the struggle for independence, when national mobilization was needed for a set of political and economic *uhuru* aims—expressed as African socialism—to which all forces and economic groups in the country would subjugate their efforts. But a one-party government could be democratic only if the mass of the people were associated with policy-making at all levels, if the people were drawn into the running of the party, if national issues were discussed in the branches, at public meetings, at conferences, in our newspapers, among the women and the youth; if careful thought was given to the role of the party in relation to the administration so that civil servants trained in pre-colonial attitudes could not, in the day-to-day running of the country, undo the best plans made by the political leadership. The existence of one party, an umbrella party, meant that all policy decisions and differences had to be hammered out within the party. There could be fierce controversy, but once majority decisions were taken through democratic process they had to be accepted.

8: Patrice Lumumba

Extracts from P. Lumumba, *Congo, My Country* (Pall Mall, 1962).
This book, written between 1956 and 1957, before Lumumba had become a leading figure in Congolese politics, reflects the liberal attitudes he held at that time when he still felt confident that the Belgians should and would develop the Congo in the interests of both the Belgians and the Congolese. The book was published posthumously.

... Contrasting the Congo of yesterday and today, we can freely admit that Belgium has not failed in its mission and that, apart from a few mistakes which are inherent in any human activity, much that is fine and great has been achieved and is still being achieved.

We would urge those who are only willing to see the bad side of colonisation to weigh up the good and the bad to see which is the greater.

To whom do we owe our liberation from that odious trade practised by the bloodthirsty Arabs and their allies, those inhuman brigands who ravished the country?

......

Belgium, moved by a very sincere and humanitarian idealism, came to our help and, with the assistance of doughty native fighters, was able to rout the enemy, to eradicate disease, to teach us and to eliminate certain barbarous practices from our customs, thus restoring our human dignity and turning us into free, happy, vigorous, civilised men.

. . . . . .

The Congolese élite . . . only wish to be 'Belgians' and to be entitled to the same well-being and the same rights, given equal merits, of course. This desire is praiseworthy and in accordance with human justice.

. . . . . .

To introduce the ferment of political life prematurely among the ignorant and irresponsible masses in response to a craving for modernisation would be to introduce the ferments of discord and dissension; it would not be a victory for the democratic idea nor would it lead to such a victory; it would open the way for a return to the old tribal concepts with each person wishing to be head of the new tribe; this would give rise to petty quarrels which would be detrimental to harmonious social relationships. It has proved necessary to give the people peace and happiness instead of disorder and wrangling, disguised as democracy.

. . . . . .

The Congo cannot, of course, escape the laws of nature; it will follow the same course of development as Belgium, and finally its inhabitants will have to enjoy political rights. I believe that it would be possible, in the relatively near future, to grant political rights to the Congolese élite and to the Belgians of the Congo in accordance with certain criteria to be laid down by the Government. In my view, there would be no question of granting these rights to people who were unfit to use them, to dull-witted illiterates; that would be to put dangerous weapons in the hands of children.

. . . . . .

The *status quo* could be maintained for the uneducated masses who would continue to be governed and guided – as in all countries – by the responsible élite: the white and African élite.

The work of colonisation undertaken in a country cannot be crowned with success or achieve its ends without the whole-hearted collaboration of the élite of the country, the leaders of the mass of the population.

The native élite, whose loyalty and level of civilisation have been officially recognised by a decision of the High Court, should be regarded as genuine allies, valuable collaborators of the Belgians, with whom they should form a united and dynamic team to continue the work of civilisation and to defend their common interests. They must be closely associated with the achievements of the Belgo-Congolese community and act as intermediaries between their people and the colonisers, by taking an adequate share in the conduct of public affairs and the direction of national policy.

. . . . . .

43

I am in favour of retaining good customs, as I have a distaste for any policy which would involve making Africans poor imitations of the Whites. We are proud to *remain* what we are, but we are also civilised Africans, imbued with respect for our personalities, our traditional institutions, and our moral standards – in so far (of course) as they are consistent with the principles of human civilisation towards which the Congo is irresistibly advancing.

......

The task for Africa in this modern age must be the task *of humanising and harmonising opposing interests and relations* between Europeans and Africans.

What rather disturbs us about large-scale settlement is the later and possibly distant *consequences* which this settlement *might* involve: *Occupation of all the good land by Europeans – impossibility for Congolese to secure land in the vicinity of the large towns or urban centres – compulsion on future African settlers (agricultural and industrial) to establish themselves in very distant parts of the country, since the approaches to large and industrialised centres will all be occupied by European settlers – Difficulties for the small African tenant-farmer in developing his land by the side of the powerful European tenant-farmer – Occupation of all important posts by Europeans – Priority of employment for Europeans, which would probably cause unemployment amongst some of the African élite or reduce them to minor functions, as is the case at present . . .*

......

Provided that European settlement does not threaten to destroy African settlement; provided that the black settlers place themselves under the sponsorship of the white settlers and the latter support them and help them to develop; provided that the European settlers and the black settlers live in harmony and form a unified, single group; provided that the European population fraternises with the Congolese population; provided that we can have firm and sincere guarantees; then we shall meet at the gateway to the Congo to shout a loud WELCOME to this large-scale influx of people, and wish them a happy stay amongst us.

......

The inadequate education of African women has considerably retarded the cultural development of the Congo. We cannot lay claim to any kind of civilisation as long as our wives remain in this state of stagnation.

When you civilise a man, you only civilise an individual; but when you civilise a woman you civilise a whole people.

......

What in effect would happen if the Whites left the Congo today? It

44

would spell complete ruin. And what would happen if the Africans withdrew completely from the Europeans, abandoned them and returned to till their own fields? The Europeans would be able to do nothing with their capital and machines; they would go bankrupt and would have to pack up their bags and go home.

This interdependence should suffice to bring together White and Black, not merely for their immediate material advantages but in a spirit of genuine human solidarity.

The bond of common interest would be frail indeed if it were not strengthened by the bond of sentiment and mutual affection.

The interpenetration of races and the fusion of interests form the only foundations for a firm and lasting Euro-African society.

......

Let us not stand aloof from our brothers because they are less educated, less cultured, less fortunate than ourselves; this would create an unfortunate gulf between us. We want to bridge the gulf which separates us from the Whites but we must not create another one behind us. Who will work for them if we abandon them? May they not one day turn against us? Our concern must be not to satisfy personal ambitions but to achieve the harmonious development of all Africans. We must give up any activities which may cause cleavages within our society.

......

Some Europeans of the less desirable kind exploit the credulity of the still largely uneducated Africans by urging them to claim immediate independence; they go so far as to suggest that autonomy will never be obtained without the spilling of blood, that all the Western countries had to fight in order to obtain their independence and that the Congolese must do the same if they wish to free themselves from the Belgians. This is indeed a sad state of mind!

We must reject these ideas, from whatever source they may come. The Congo will obtain its independence with dignity and not with barbarism. Civilisation and war are incompatible.

......

The first stage of the colonisation has been completed: the stage of the conclusion of treaties, construction of roads, liberation of the people, etc. After these three-quarters of a century of hard work, of groping steps which have now led to success, the people of the colony put forward a confident and dignified plan to leave this stage, which has been out-dated by the course of development, and to enter stage two.

......

What is this *second stage?* It is the stage of *integration* (not of assimilation which involves the absorption of one people by another) of

45

the *democratisation of the country* and of the *Africanisation of the leader-ship.*

. . . . . .

In their co-existence with the Whites, the Africans are greatly worried, not by the fact of living alongside them, but by the idea that they may never be able to attain complete emancipation and liberty whilst under European domination.

Hence the African's dream of independence does not arise from hatred for the Whites or a desire to drive them out of Africa, but simply from the wish to be not merely a free man but also a citizen in the service of his country and not perpetually in the service of the European. He believes, moreover, that, even if he is able to obtain complete emancipation under white domination, it will only come after centuries, because the European will hamper that emancipation by all sorts of tricks and political schemes, and that the Blacks will therefore be kept in a state of inferiority as long as possible. Finally, he believes that once the country becomes independent, the emancipation of the inhabitants will be much more rapid than it would have been under the system of tutelage and colonialism.

9: Mamadou Dia

From Mamadou Dia, *The African Nations and World Solidarity* (Praeger, 1961). Reprinted by permission of Thames and Hudson Ltd.
This book was published while Dia was Prime Minister of Senegal.

Willingly or unwillingly, colonization carries the germ of liberation, by virtue of the transformations that it involves, the changes it introduces in ideas, institutions, and mores, and the basic services it implants, indispensable for the activity of the colonial society, which is itself obliged to evolve from the traditional to the transitional stage.

Let us not expect colonization to be more than it could possibly become, namely, an ethic. Let us agree to judge it by its results and we shall have to admit that, along with its ravages, colonization – any colonization – makes some favourable contributions . . . African nations, like all nations torn by dissension, anarchy, and neglect of the collective welfare, have become easy prey. Colonization has provided the shock that awakened them and inspired a new spirit. It is not paradoxical to contend that colonization engendered nationalism, not only that of clans and tribes, but also doctrinal, unifying nationalism, which transforms the struggle of colonized nations into a struggle on a world-wide scale.

. . . . . .

We must remember that while no nation is valid without morality, it certainly cannot be valid without economic and technical efficiency in this cruel world. The nationalism of colonial and former colonial territories, if it is to attain the desired result, owes it to itself to be an active, constructive nationalism, determined to transform a state of revolt into an effective revolution. In this light, the concept of "African nations" finds theoretical and practical justification, even in the absence of an impressive past (and we know that this is not the case), even in the absence of perfectly organized institutions. What matters primarily is the consciousness of being, the will to be born, to participate in world growth, and to require justice of other nations. Such is the meaning of the revolution that is being waged before our eyes and that henceforth will take the initiative away from the West.

Nationalism in this sense is something quite different from a theory founded on racial or religious ideology. Nationalism with a racial or religious basis is an irrational construction depending not so much on a national conscience as on the collective folly of the crowd, on the destructive force of exasperated instincts. It is a blind, closed nationalism, inaccessible to the concept of nation-solidarity, and not conducive to a universal humanism.

. . . . . .

Nothing is less certain than that the solution of the future, the equilibrium of the world, lies in the realization of economic, social, and cultural equality. The works on paleontology produced by a mind as original as that of Teilhard de Chardin suggest, on the contrary, that the evolution of humanity seems to be headed less toward equality than toward complementarity. One has only to consider the development of the different rival economies and the relative condition of the techniques at their disposal to become convinced that the solution of the conflict between the *Tiers-Monde* [Third World] and the rich world lies neither in a levelling process nor in open or secret competition based on hatred, but rather in frank and loyal co-operation, assuring mutual harmonious development.

The influence of Marxist theories on the affirmation of nationalism in the dominated countries, though far from negligible, must not be exaggerated. There is even cause to anticipate, once the young nations have acquired political independence from their former Metropoles, a new period of struggle between nationalism and foreign ideology, and more specifically, between emergent national economies and evolved economies of the capitalist or socialist types.

... Doubtless, if they are to have any real national existence, African nations will not accept second-class nationhood. They will, instead, throw

47

off the tutelage of all competing dialectics, of every paternalism old or new, to affirm their own vocation, which basically is that of realizing a new world, a new humanity, by realizing themselves according to a new pattern. Some will probably describe this as proud pretence or extremism. We are convinced that it is on this condition that African nations will justify their birth.

For what would be the use of creating new nations, only to remain enslaved to one or another established ideology; to renounce, upon liberation, the right to liberty; or, instead of being an instrument for building an interdependent civilization, we accept a cowardly, servile role? ... Like every movement against the established order, the process of forming twentieth-century nations, and therefore African nations, upsets our usual system of reasoning, challenges rules generally admitted by all, including those of Marxism–Leninism. Unless there is an ideological revision on the national question, the present alliances against capitalist imperialism will give way, in time, to merciless struggles between young nations and Communist imperialism.

10: Aimé Césaire

Extracts from A. Césaire, *Discourse on Colonialism* (Monthly Review Press, 1972).
Originally published as 'Discours sur la colonialisme' by Présence Africaine in 1950, this attack on the concept of colonialism became a classic text for the French-speaking African intelligentsia.

The fact is that the so-called European civilization – 'Western' civilization – as it has been shaped by two centuries of bourgeois rule, is incapable of solving the two major problems to which its existence has given rise: the problem of the proletariat and the colonial problem; that Europe is unable to justify itself either before the bar of 'reason' or before the bar of 'conscience'; and that, increasingly, it takes refuge in a hypocrisy which is all the more odious because it is less and less likely to deceive.

. . . . . .

... what, fundamentally, is colonization? To agree on what it is not: neither evangelization, nor a philanthropic enterprise, nor a desire to push back the frontiers of ignorance, disease, and tyranny, nor a project undertaken for the greater glory of God, nor an attempt to extend the rule of law. To admit once for all ... that the decisive actors here are the adventurer and the pirate, the wholesale grocer and the ship owner, the gold digger and the merchant, appetite and force, and behind them, the baleful projected shadow of a form of civilization which, at a certain point in its history, finds itself obliged, for internal reasons, to extend to a world scale the competition of its antagonistic economies.

... the chief culprit in this domain is Christian pedantry, which laid down the dishonest equations *Christianity = civilisation, paganism = savagery*, from which there could not but ensue abominable colonialist and racist consequences, whose victims were to be the Indians, the yellow peoples, and the Negroes.

That being settled, I admit that it is a good thing to place different civilizations in contact with each other; that it is an excellent thing to blend different worlds; that whatever its own particular genius may be, a civilization that withdraws into itself atrophies; that for civilizations, exchange is oxygen; that the great good fortune of Europe is to have been a crossroads, and that because it was the *locus* of all ideas, the receptacle of all philosophies, the meeting place of all sentiments, it was the best centre for the redistribution of energy.

But then I ask the following question: has colonization really *placed civilizations in contact?* Or, if you prefer, of all the ways of *establishing contact,* was it the best?

I answer *no.*

And I say that between *colonization* and *civilization* there is an infinite distance; that out of all the colonial expeditions that have been undertaken, out of all the colonial statutes that have been drawn up, out of all the memoranda that have been despatched by all the ministries, there could not come a single human value.

......

... it would be worth while to study clinically, in detail the steps taken by Hitler and Hitlerism and to reveal to the very distinguished, very humanistic, very Christian bourgeois of the twentieth century that without his being aware of it, he has a Hitler inside him, that Hitler *inhabits* him, that Hitler is his *demon,* that if he rails against him he is being inconsistent and that, at bottom, what he cannot forgive Hitler for is not *crime* in itself, *the crime against man,* it is not *the humiliation of man as such,* it is the crime against the white man, the humiliation of the white man, and the fact that he applied to Europe colonialist procedures which until then had been reserved exclusively for the Arabs of Algeria, the coolies of India, and the blacks of Africa.

......

But let us speak about the colonized.

I see clearly what colonization has destroyed: the wonderful Indian

49

civilizations – and neither Deterding nor Royal Dutch nor Standard Oil will ever console me for the Aztecs and the Incas.

I see clearly the civilizations, condemned to perish at a future date, into which it has introduced a principle of ruin ... I see less clearly the contributions it has made.

Security? Culture? The rule of law? In the meantime, I look around and wherever there are colonizers and colonized face to face, I see force, brutality, cruelty, sadism, conflict, and, in a parody of education, the hasty manufacture of a few thousand subordinate functionaries, 'boys', artisans, office clerks, and interpreters necessary for the smooth operation of business.

I spoke of contact.

Between the colonizer and colonized there is room only for forced labour, intimidation, pressure, the police, taxation, theft, rape, compulsory crops, contempt, mistrust, arrogance, self-complacency, swinishness, brainless elites, degraded masses.

No human contact, but relations of domination and submission which turn the colonizing man into a classroom monitor, an army sergeant, a prison guard, a slave driver, and the indigenous man into an instrument of production.

......

I hear the storm. They talk to me about progress, about 'achievements', diseases cured, improved standards of living.

I am talking about societies drained of their essence, cultures trampled underfoot, institutions undermined, lands confiscated, religions smashed, magnificent artistic creations destroyed, extraordinary *possibilities* wiped out.

They throw facts at my head, statistics, mileages of roads, canals, and railroad tracks ...

I am talking about those who, as I write this, are digging the harbour of Abidjan by hand. I am talking about millions of men torn from their gods, their land, their habits, their life – from life, from the dance, from wisdom.

I am talking about millions of men in whom fear has been cunningly instilled, who have been taught to have an inferiority complex, to tremble, kneel, despair, and behave like flunkeys.

They dazzle me with the tonnage of cotton or cocoa that has been exported, the acreage that has been planted with olive trees or grapevines.

I am talking about natural *economies* that have been disrupted ..., about food crops destroyed, malnutrition permanently introduced, agricultural development oriented solely toward the benefit of the metropolitan countries, about the looting of products, the looting of raw materials.

They pride themselves on abuses eliminated.

I too talk about abuses, but what I say is that on the old ones – very real – they have superimposed others – very detestable. They talk to me about local tyrants brought to reason; but I note that in general the old tyrants get on very well with the new ones, and that there has been established between them, to the detriment of the people, a circuit of mutual services and complicity.

They talk to me about civilization, I talk about proletarianization and mystification.

For my part, I make a systematic defence of the non-European civilizations.

Every day that passes, every denial of justice, every beating by the police, every demand of the workers that is drowned in blood, every scandal that is hushed up, every punitive expedition, every police van, every gendarme and every militiaman, brings home to us the value of our old societies.

They were communal societies, never societies of the many for the few.

They were societies that were not only ante-capitalist, as has been said, but also *anti-capitalist*.

They were democratic societies, always.

They were cooperative societies, fraternal societies.

. . . . . .

. . . the great historical tragedy of Africa has been not so much that it was too late in making contact with the rest of the world, as the manner in which that contact was brought about; that Europe began to 'propagate' at a time when it had fallen into the hands of the most unscrupulous financiers and captains of industry; that it was our misfortune to encounter that particular Europe on our path, and that Europe is responsible before the human community for the highest heap of corpses in history.

. . . . . .

. . . I maintain that colonialist Europe is dishonest in trying to justify its colonizing activity *a posteriori* by the obvious material progress that has been achieved in certain fields under the colonial regime – since *sudden change* is always possible, in history as elsewhere; since no one knows at what stage of material development these same countries would have been if Europe had not intervened; since the technical outfitting of Africa and Asia, their administrative reorganization, in a word, their 'Europeanization', was (as is proved by the example of Japan) in no way tied to the European *occupation*; since the Europeanization of the non-European continents could have been accomplished otherwise than under the heel of Europe; since this movement of Europeanization *was in progress*; since it was even slowed down; since in any case it was

51

distorted by the European takeover.

The proof is that at present it is the indigenous peoples of Africa and Asia who are demanding schools, and colonialist Europe which refuse them; that it is the African who is asking for ports and roads, and colonialist Europe which is niggardly on this score; that it is the colonized man who wants to move forward, and the colonizer who holds things back.

For us, the problem is not to make a utopian and sterile attempt to repeat the past, but to go beyond. It is not a dead society that we want to revive. We leave that to those who go in for exoticism. Nor is it the present colonial society that we wish to prolong, the most putrid carrion that ever rotted under the sun. It is a new society that we must create, with the help of all our brother slaves, a society rich with all the productive power of modern times, warm with all the fraternity of olden days.

. . . . . .

. . . unless, in Africa, . . . Western Europe undertakes on its own initiative a policy of *nationalities,* a new policy founded on respect for peoples and cultures – nay, more – unless Europe galvanizes the dying cultures or raises up new ones, unless it becomes the awakener of countries and civilizations, . . . Europe will have deprived itself of its last chance and, with its own hands, drawn up over itself the pall of mortal darkness.

Which comes down to saying that the salvation of Europe is not a matter of a revolution in methods. It is a matter of the Revolution – the one which, until such time as there is a classless society, will substitute for the narrow tyranny of a dehumanized bourgeoisie the preponderance of the only class that still has a universal mission, because it suffers in its flesh from all the wrongs of history, from all the universal wrongs: the proletariat.

11: Sekou Touré

Extract from Sekou Touré, *L'Expérience Guinéenne et l'Unité Africaine* (Présence Africaine, 1959).
In this typical attack on the pervasive nature of the colonial system, one of the most articulate of French-speaking African political leaders stressed the need for 'individual decolonisation'.

Decolonisation can only be achieved by the destruction of colonial institutions. Colonialism as a system weighed heavily upon the economic, social, political and cultural life of the country. In the first place, therefore, we must destroy the colonial structures and replace them with structures which corresponded as closely as possible to our own needs and our own evolutionary course.

......

... but social and economic revolution requires a moral revolution and there can be no profound transformation without the total support and full comprehension of the people. What is needed is that each person should convert himself, on his own initiative; without individual decolonisation there can be no hope of liquidating the evils of colonialism. We have henceforth to combat colonialism in its most insidious form and it is chiefly our own behaviour that we have to change.

Whether we like it or not, whether we take any notice of it or not, each one of us is marked by the colonialism to which we have been subjected ... the greater our contact with colonialism, the more have we been affected, the more deeply are the roots of colonialism embedded in us. So is perpetuated a system which we have deliberately rejected in choosing independence and full sovereignty.

The civil servant or the worker of the Guinean Republic who thinks more of his salary than of his active contribution to the country ... is putting colonialism before Africa; while the Africa of which we dream will be constructed neither by speeches nor by theories, but by constant sacrifice and ceaseless devotions; the efforts of the cultivator, ... of the nurse and the doctor ... above all the efforts of those who work with the constant intention that their task should provide a real support to the Guinean nation, and by reflection, to the whole of Africa, and destroy not only the institutions of colonialism, but its spirit.

......

To love the country, is to love the man who lives in it, and who must come before all else.

To love the man, is to keep him healthy, to teach him enlightenment, to educate him into sociable ways, to keep him human.

The African elite in particular, has the opportunity to achieve great things because the pursuit of justice, liberty, and democracy is the most elevated ideal of humanity. In this respect, the African leaders will be recognised not by their diplomas, not by their theoretical or practical knowledge, not by their status, but, significantly, by the degree of devotion with which they serve African evolution ... such leaders are to be found amongst ... workers, bureaucrats, the young, the old, the women, amongst both the literate and the illiterate, the rich or the poor.

The struggle on behalf of the African fatherland rests not in the adoption of a specific programme, but rather in the voluntary acceptance of a continuous activity which will eventually result in the transformation of the existing hard realities of Africa; the struggle for the future begins in the present.

12: Frantz Fanon

Extract from F. Fanon, *The Wretched of the Earth,* translated by Constance Farrington (Penguin, 1967).
Originally published as 'Les Damnés de la Terre' by F. Maspero (Présence Africaine, 1963), this book was written during the Algerian war. This extract illustrates Fanon's views on the nature and uses of violence in the colonial context.

National Liberation, national renaissance, the restoration of nationhood to the people, commonwealth: whatever may be the headings used or the new formulas introduced, decolonization is always a violent phenomenon. At whatever level we study it – relationships between individuals, new names for sports clubs, the human admixture at cocktail parties, in the police, on the directing boards of national or private banks – decolonization is quite simply the replacing of a certain 'species' of men by another 'species' of men. Without any period of transition, there is a total, complete and absolute substitution. It is true that we could equally well stress the rise of a new nation, the setting up of a new state, its diplomatic relations, and its economic and political trends. But we have precisely chosen to speak of that kind of *tabula rasa* which characterizes at the outset all decolonization. Its unusual importance is that it constitutes, from the very first day, the minimum demands of the colonized. To tell the truth, the proof of success lies in a whole social structure being changed from the bottom up. The extraordinary importance of this change is that it is willed, called for, demanded. The need for this change exists in its crude state, impetuous and compelling, in the consciousness and in the lives of the men and women who are colonized. But the possibility of this change is equally experienced in the form of a terrifying future in the consciousness of another 'species' of men and women: the colonizers.

Decolonization, which sets out to change the order of the world, is, obviously, a programme of complete disorder. But it cannot come as a result of magical practices, nor of a natural shock, nor of a friendly understanding. Decolonization, as we know, is a historical process: that is to say that it cannot be understood, it cannot become intelligible nor clear to itself except in the exact measure that we can discern the movements which give it historical form and content. Decolonization is the meeting of two forces, opposed to each other by their very nature, which in fact owe their originality to that sort of substantification which results from and is nourished by the situation in the colonies. Their first encounter was marked by violence and their existence together − that is to say the exploitation of the native by the settler − was carried on by dint of a great array of bayonets and cannon. The settler and the native are old acquaintances. In fact, the settler is right when he speaks of knowing 'them' well. For it is the settler who has brought the native into existence and who perpetuates his existence. The settler owes the fact of his very existence, that is to say his property, to the colonial system.

Decolonization never takes place unnoticed, for it influences individuals and modifies them fundamentally. It transforms spectators crushed with their inessentiality into privileged actors, with the grandiose glare of history's floodlights upon them. It brings a natural rhythm into existence, introduced by new men, and with it a new language and a new humanity. Decolonization is the veritable creation of new men. But this creation owes nothing of its legitimacy to any supernatural power; the 'thing' which has been colonized becomes man during the same process by which it frees itself.

In decolonization, there is therefore the need of a complete calling in question of the colonial situation. If we wish to describe it precisely, we might find it in the well-known words: 'The last shall be first and the first last'. Decolonization is the putting into practice of this sentence. That is why, if we try to describe it, all decolonization is successful.

The naked truth of decolonization evokes for us the searing bullets and bloodstained knives which emanate from it. For if the last shall be first, this will only come to pass after a murderous and decisive struggle between the two protagonists. That affirmed intention to place the last at the head of things, and to make them climb at a pace (too quickly, some say) the well-known steps which characterize an organized society, can only triumph if we use all means to turn the scale, including, of course, that of violence . . .

Thus the native discovers that his life, his breath, his beating heart are the same as those of the settler. He finds out that the settler's skin is not of any more value than a native's skin; and it must be said that this discovery shakes the world in a very necessary manner. All the new, revolutionary assurance of the native stems from it. For if, in fact, my life is worth as much as the settlers, his glance no longers shrivels me up nor freezes me, and his voice no longer turns me into stone. I am no longer on tenterhooks in his presence; in fact, I don't give a damn for him. Not only does his presence no longer trouble me, but I am already preparing such efficient ambushes for him that soon there will be no way out but that of flight.

......

What are the forces which in the colonial period open up new outlets and engender new aims for the violence of colonized peoples? In the first place there are the political parties and the intellectual or commercial elites. Now, the characteristic feature of certain political structures is that they proclaim abstract principles but refrain from issuing definite commands. The entire action of these nationalist political parties during the colonial period is action of the electoral type: a string of philosophico-political dissertations on the themes of the rights of peoples to self-determination, the rights of man to freedom from hunger and human dignity, and the unceasing affirmation of the principle: 'One man, one vote.' The national political parties never lay stress upon the necessity of a trial of armed strength, for the good reason that their objective is not the radical overthrowing of the system. Pacifists and legalists, they are in fact partisans of order, the new order – but to the colonialist bourgeoisie they put bluntly enough the demand which to them is the main one: 'Give us more power'. On the specific question of violence, the elite are ambiguous. They are violent in their words and reformists in their attitudes. When the nationalist political leaders say something, they make quite clear that they do not really think it.

This characteristic on the part of the nationalist political parties should be interpreted in the light both of the make-up of their leaders and the nature of their followings. The rank-and-file of a nationalist party is urban. The workers, primary school teachers, artisans and small shopkeepers who have begun to profit – at a discount, to be sure – from the colonial set-up, have special interests at heart. What this sort of following demands is the betterment of their particular lot: increased salaries, for example. The dialogue between these political parties and colonialism is never broken off. Improvements are discussed, such as full electoral representation, the liberty of the Press, and liberty of association. Reforms are debated. Thus it need not astonish anyone to notice that a large number of natives are militant members of the branches of political parties which stem from the mother country. These natives fight under an abstract watchword: 'Government by the workers', and they forget that in their country it should be nationalist watchwords which are first in the field. The native intellectual has clothed his aggressiveness in his barely veiled desire to assimilate himself to the colonial world. He has used his aggressiveness to serve his own individual interests . . .

The peasantry is systematically disregarded for the most part by the propaganda put out by the nationalist parties. And it is clear that in the

56

colonial countries the peasants alone are revolutionary, for they have nothing to lose and everything to gain. The starving peasant, outside the class system, is the first among the exploited to discover that only violence pays. For him there is no compromise, no possible coming to terms; colonization and decolonization are simply a question of relative strength. The exploited man sees that his liberation implies the use of all means, and that of force first and foremost . . .

What is the real nature of this violence? We have seen that it is the intuition of the colonized masses that their liberation must, and can only, be achieved by force. By what spiritual aberration do these men, without technique, starving and enfeebled, confronted with the military and economic might of the occupation, come to believe that violence alone will free them? How can they hope to triumph?

It is because violence (and this is the disgraceful thing) may constitute, in so far as it forms part of its system, the slogan of a political party. The leaders may call on the people to enter upon an armed struggle. This problematical question has to be thought over. When militarist Germany decides to settle its frontier disputes by force, we are not in the least surprised; but when the people of Angola, for example, decide to take up arms, when the Algerian people reject all means which are not violent, these are proofs that something has happened or is happening at this very moment. The colonized races, those slaves of modern times, are impatient. They know that this apparent folly alone can put them out of reach of colonial oppression. A new type of relations is established in the world. The under-developed peoples try to break their chains, and the extraordinary thing is that they succeed. It could be argued that in these days of sputniks it is ridiculous to die of hunger; but for the colonized masses the argument is more down-to-earth. The truth is that there is no colonial power today which is capable of adopting the only form of contest which has a chance of succeeding, namely, the prolonged establishment of large forces of occupation.

As far as their internal situation is concerned, the colonialist countries find themselves faced with contradictions in the form of working-class demands which necessitate the use of their police forces. As well, in the present international situation, these countries need their troops to protect their regimes. Finally there is the well-known myth of liberating movements directed from Moscow. In the régime's panic-stricken reasoning, this signifies 'IF that goes on, there is a risk that the communists will turn the troubles to account and infiltrate into these parts'.

In the native's eagerness, the fact that he openly brandishes the threat of violence proves that he is conscious of the unusual character of the contemporary situation and that he means to profit by it. But, still on the level of immediate experience, the native, who has seen the modern world penetrate into the furthermost corners of the bush, is most acutely aware of all the things he does not possess. The masses by a sort of (if we may say so) childlike process of reasoning convince themselves that they have been robbed of all these things. That is why in certain under-developed countries the masses forge ahead very quickly, and realize two or three years after independence that they have been frustrated, that "it wasn't worth while" fighting, and that nothing could really change. In 1789, after the bourgeois revolution, the smallest French peasants benefited substantially from the upheaval. But it is a commonplace to observe and to say that in the majority of cases, for ninety-five per cent of the population of under-developed countries, independence brings no immediate change. The enlightened observer takes note of the existence of a kind of masked discontent, like the smoking ashes of a burnt-down house after the fire has been put out, which still threaten to burst into flames again.

So they say that the natives want to go too quickly. Now, let us never forget that only a very short time ago they complained of their slowness, their laziness and their fatalism. Already we see that violence used in specific ways at the moment of the struggle for freedom does not magically disappear after the ceremony of trooping the national colours. It has all the less reason for disappearing since the reconstruction of the nation continues within the framework of cut-throat competition between capitalism and socialism . . .

But it so happens that for the colonized people this violence, because it constitutes their only work, invests their characters with positive and creative qualities. The practice of violence binds them together as a whole, since each individual forms a violent link in the great chain, a part of the great organism of violence which has surged upwards in reaction to the settler's violence in the beginning. The groups recognize each other and the future nation is already indivisible. The armed struggle mobilizes the people; that is to say, it throws them in one way and in one direction.

The mobilization of the masses, when it arises out of the war of liberation, introduces into each man's consciousness the ideas of a common cause, of a national destiny and of a collective history. In the same way the second phase, that of the building-up of the nation, is helped on by the existence of this cement which has been mixed with blood and anger. Thus we come to a fuller appreciation of the originality of the words used in these under-developed countries. During the colonial period the people are called upon to fight against oppression; after national liberation, they are called upon to fight against poverty, illiteracy and under-development. The struggle, they say, goes on. The people realize that life is an unending contest . . .

. . . . . .

At the level of individuals, violence is a cleansing force. It frees the native from his inferiority complex and from his despair and inaction; it makes him fearless and restores his self-respect. Even if the armed struggle has been symbolic and the nation is demobilized through a rapid movement of decolonization, the people have the time to see that the liberation has been the business of each and all and that the leader has no special merit. From thence comes that type of aggressive reticence with regard to the machinery of protocol which young governments quickly show. When the people have taken violent part in the national liberation they will allow no one to set themselves up as 'liberators'. They show themselves to be jealous of the results of their action and take good care not to place their future, their destiny or the fate of their country in the hands of a living god. Yesterday they were completely irresponsible; today they mean to understand everything and make all decisions. Illuminated by violence, the consciousness of the people rebels against any pacification. From now on the demagogues, the opportunists and the magicians have a difficult task. The action which has thrown them into a hand-to-hand struggle confers upon the masses a voracious taste for the concrete. The attempt at mystification becomes, in the long run, practically impossible . . .

What is the reaction of the nationalist parties to this eruption of the peasant masses into the national struggle? We have seen that the majority of nationalist parties have not written into their propaganda the necessity for armed intervention. They do not oppose the continuing of the rebellion, but they content themselves with leaving it to the spontaneous action of the country people. As a whole they treat this new element as a sort of manna fallen from heaven, and pray to goodness that it'll go on falling. They make the most of the manna, but do not attempt to organize the rebellion. They don't send leaders into the countryside to educate the people politically, or to increase their awareness or put the struggle on to a higher level. All they do is to hope that, carried onwards by its own momentum, the action of the people will not come to a standstill. There is no contamination of the rural movement by the urban movement; each develops according to its own dialectic . . .

The different strata of the nation never have it out with each other to any advantage; there is no settling of accounts between them. Thus, when independence is achieved, after the repression practised on the country people, after the *entente* between colonialism and the national parties, it is no wonder that you find this incomprehension to an even greater degree. The country dwellers are slow to take up the structural reforms proposed by the government; and equally slow in following their social reforms, even though they may be very progressive if viewed objectively, precisely because the people now at the head of affairs did not explain to the people as a whole during the colonial period what were the aims of the party, the national trends, or the problems of international politics . . .

The temptation therefore will be to break up this body by centralizing the administration and surrounding the people by a firm administrative framework. This is one of the reasons why you often hear it said that in under-developed countries a small dose of dictatorship is needed. The men at the head of things distrust the people of the countryside; moreover this distrust takes on serious proportions . . . For all practical purposes, the interior ranks with the unknown. Paradoxically, the national government in its dealings with the country people as a whole is reminiscent of certain features of the former colonial power. 'We don't quite know how the mass of these people will react' is the cry; and the young ruling class does not hesitate to assert that 'they need the thick end of the stick if this country is to get out of the Middle Ages'. But as we have seen, the off-hand way in which the political parties treated the rural population during the colonial phase could only prejudice national unity at the very moment when the young nation needs to get off to a good start.

. . . . . .

The many peasant risings which have their roots in the country districts bear witness wherever they occur to the ubiquitous and usually solidly massed presence of the new nation. Each native who takes up arms is a part of the nation which from henceforward will spring to life. Such peasant revolts endanger the colonial regime; they mobilize its troops, making them spread out, and threaten at every turn to crush them. They hold one doctrine only: to act in such a way that the nation may exist. There is no programme; there are no speeches or resolutions, and no political trends. The problem is clear: the foreigners must go: so let us form a common front against the oppressor and let us strengthen our hands by armed combat.

So long as the uncertainty of colonialism continues, the national cause goes on progressing, and becomes the cause of each and all. The plans for liberation are sketched out; already they include the whole country. During this period spontaneity is king, and initiative is localized. On every hill a government in miniature is formed and takes over power. Everywhere — in the valleys and in the forests, in the jungle and in the villages — we find a national authority. Each man or woman brings the nation to life by his or her action, and is pledged to ensure its triumph in their locality. We are dealing with a strategy of immediacy which is both radical and totalitarian: the aim and the programme of each locally constituted group is local liberation. If the nation is everywhere, then she is here. One step further, and only here is she to be found. Tactics are mistaken for strategy. The art of politics is simply transformed into the art of war; the political militant is the rebel. To fight the war and take part in politics: the two things become one and the same . . .

The native must realize that colonialism never gives anything away for nothing. Whatever the native may gain through political or armed struggle is not the result of the kindliness or good will of the settler; it simply shows that he cannot put off granting concessions any longer. Moreover, the native ought to realize that it is not colonialism that grants such concessions, but he himself that extorts them. When the British government decides to bestow a few more seats in the National Assembly of Kenya upon the African population, it needs plenty of effrontery or else a complete ignorance of facts to maintain that the British government has made a concession. Is it not obvious that it is the Kenyan people who have made the concession? The colonized peoples, the peoples who have been robbed, must lose the habits of mind which have characterized them up to now. If need be the native can accept a compromise with colonialism, but never a surrender of principle . . .

The nationalist militant who had fled from the town in disgust at the demagogic and reformist manoeuvres of the leaders there, disappointed by political life, discovers in real action a new form of political activity which in no way resembles the old. These politics are the politics of leaders and organizers living inside history who take the lead with their brains and their muscles in the fight for freedom. These politics are national, revolutionary and social and these new facts which the native will now come to know exist only in action. They are the essence of the fight which explodes the old colonial truths and reveals unexpected facets, which brings out new meanings and pinpoints the contradictions camouflaged by these facts. The people engaged in the struggle who because of it command and know these facts, go forward, freed from colonialism and forewarned of all attempts at mystification, inoculated against all national anthems. Violence alone, violence committed by the people, violence organized and educated by its leaders, makes it possible for the masses to understand social truths and gives the key to them. Without that struggle, without that knowledge of the practice of action, there's nothing but a fancy-dress parade and the blare of trumpets. There's nothing save a minimum of readaptation, a few reforms at the top, a flag waving; and down there at the bottom an undivided mass, still living in the Middle Ages, endlessly marking time.

13: Léopold Sédar Senghor

From L. S. Senghor, *Selected Poems*, translated and edited by John Reed and Clive Wake (Oxford University Press, 1964). Reprinted by permission of Atheneum Publishers, U.S.A.

Lord God, forgive white Europe.
It is true Lord, that for four enlightened centuries, she has scattered the
     baying and slaver of her mastiffs over my lands
And the Christians, forsaking Thy light and the gentleness of Thy heart
Have lit their camp fires with my parchments, tortured my disciples,
     deported my doctors and masters of science.
Their powder has crumbled in a flash the pride of *tatas* and hills
And their bullets have gone through the bowels of vast empires like day-
     light, from the Horn of the West to the Eastern Horizon
They have fired the intangible woods like hunting grounds, dragged out
     Ancestors and spirits by their peaceable beards,
And turned their mystery into Sunday distraction for somnambulant
     bourgeois.
Lord, forgive them who turned the Askia into *maquisards,* my princes
     into sergeant-majors
My household servants into 'boys', my peasants into wage-earners, my
     people into a working class.
For Thou must forgive those who have hunted my children like wild
     elephants,
And broken them in with whips, have made them the black hands of those
     whose hands were white.
For Thou must forget those who exported ten millions of my sons in the
     leperhouse of their ships
Who killed two hundred millions of them.
And have made for me a solitary old age in the forest of my nights and
     the savannah of my days.
Lord, the glasses of my eyes grow dim
And lo, the serpent of hatred raises its head in my heart, that serpent
That I believed was dead.

Part II
Nation-building:
Philosophies and
Problems

For African nationalist leaders decolonisation was merely a beginning. They were now fully responsible for their new nation-states, for the operation of economies short of both capital and human resources, for the welfare and well-being of societies characterised by poverty, ignorance, and disease, and for the direction of political entities lacking natural cohesion. The following extracts illustrate some of the attempts by political leaders to meet their problems through the formulation of principles or philosophies. These statements represent in part an identification of the problems of economic, social, and political development; and in part a set of proposals for the solution of these problems.

East and Central African leaders provide more ample material than West Africa, perhaps because the political leaders in this region have enjoyed more stability, and more permanence, than their West African counterparts. Julius Nyerere has made a contribution to African political thought which has probably been influential elsewhere in Africa, as well as in Tanzania. The 'Arusha Declaration', 'Education for Self-Reliance' and 'Socialism and Rural Development' provides a coherent and comprehensive statement of attitudes and intentions: the priority is to be rural development; the guiding principle is to be a socialism rooted in African communal traditions; the means will be found, not only in a careful restructuring of the political and administrative agencies, but in the efforts of the people themselves. Kenneth Kaunda of Zambia expresses similar ideas, and proposes similar actions, with a more overtly humanist emphasis. The Kenyan road to African socialism is more cautiously pragmatic, and has come under criticism from radical elements in Kenya. The differences between Obote's Charter and Seretse Khama's 'Kagisano' illustrate the gulf between the radical and the conventional approaches to African development. A common concern, as many of the extracts show, is with the structure and operation of institutions, particularly political parties and governmental bureaucracies, and the interaction of the two.

The extracts from West African leaders show their preoccupation with the same problems, and a similar concern with socialist solutions. Nkrumah emphasises the need for an ideology as an instrument in the struggle against hostile social and economic forces, and the need to adapt political forms to meet the realities of that struggle.

But promise is not performance; and philosophies are easier to enunciate than to put into practice. Moreover, a proclamation of good principles is not an earnest of good intentions. The extracts from Ochieng and Fanon are both an indictment of existing leaders and an appeal for a more populist approach to political leadership.

A. DOCUMENTS ON TANZANIA

1: Nyerere: Freedom and Development

From J. K. Nyerere, *Freedom and Development* (Government Printer, Dar-es-Salaam, no date). Reprinted in *Freedom and Development* (Oxford University Press, 1973). Copyright retained by the President.
This extract comments on the policy of *Ujamaa* (or 'familyhood') established in Tanzania in 1962.

... What do we mean when we talk of freedom? First, there is national freedom; that is, the ability of the citizens of Tanzania to determine their own future, and to govern themselves without interference from non-Tanzanians. Second, there is freedom from hunger, disease, and poverty. And third, there is personal freedom for the individual; that is, his right to live in dignity and equality with all others, his right to freedom of speech, freedom to participate in the making of all decisions which affect his life, and freedom from arbitrary arrest because he happens to annoy someone in authority – and so on. All these things are aspects of freedom, and the citizens of Tanzania cannot be said to be truly free until all of them are assured.

Yet it is obvious that these things depend on economic and social development. To the extent that our country remains poor, and its people illiterate and without understanding or strength, then our national freedom can be endangered by any foreign power which is better equipped ...

Equally obvious is the fact that freedom from hunger, sickness and poverty depends upon an increase in the wealth and the knowledge available in the community: for a group of people can only consume and use the wealth they have already produced. And even personal freedom becomes more real if it is buttressed by development. A man can defend his rights effectively only when he understands what they are, and knows how to use the constitutional machinery which exists for the defence of those rights – and knowledge of this kind is part of development.

. . . . . .

If the purpose of development is the greater freedom and wellbeing of the people, it cannot result from force . . . Force, and deceitful promises, can in fact, only achieve short-term material goals. They cannot bring strength to a nation or a community, and they cannot provide a basis for the freedom of the people, or security for any individual or group of persons.

There is only one way in which you can cause people to undertake their own development. That is by education and leadership . . . But, although we must give this leadership, the decisions must come from the people themselves, and they themselves must carry out the programmes they have decided upon.

. . . . . .

Discipline must exist in every aspect of our lives. And it must be willingly accepted discipline. For it is an essential part of both freedom and development. The greater freedom which comes from working together, and achieving things by co-operation which none of us could achieve alone, is only possible if there is disciplined acceptance of joint decisions. And this involves the acceptance of lawfully constituted authority . . .

. . . . . .

If we are to live our lives in peace and harmony, and if we are to achieve our ambitions of improving the conditions under which we live, we must have both freedom and discipline. For freedom without discipline is anarchy: discipline without freedom is tyranny.

. . . . . .

It is particularly important that we should now understand the connection between freedom, development, and discipline, because our national policy of creating socialist villages throughout the rural areas depends upon it. For we have known for a very long time that development had to go on in the rural areas, and that this required co-operative activities by the people . . .

When we tried to promote rural development in the past, we sometimes spent huge sums of money on establishing a Settlement, and supplying it with modern equipment, and social services, as well as often providing it with a management hierarchy . . . All too often, we persuaded people to go to new settlements by promising them that they could quickly grow rich there, or that Government would give them services and equipment which they could not hope to receive either in the towns or in their traditional farming places. In very few cases was any ideology involved; we thought and talked in terms of greatly increased output, and of things being provided for the settlers.

What we were doing, in fact, was thinking of development in terms of things, and not of people ... As a result, there have been very many cases where heavy capital investment has resulted in no increase in output – where the investment has been wasted. And in most of the officially sponsored or supported schemes, the majority of people who went to settle lost their enthusiasm, and either left the scheme altogether, or failed to carry out the orders of the outsiders who were put in charge – and who were not themselves involved in the success or failure of the project.

It is important, therefore, to realize that the policy of *Ujamaa Vijijini* is not intended to be merely a revival of the old settlement schemes under another name. The Ujamaa village is a new conception, based on the post-Arusha Declaration understanding that what we need to develop is people, not things, and that people can only develop themselves ...

Ujamaa villages are intended to be socialist organizations created by the people, and governed by those who live and work in them. They cannot be created from outside, nor governed from outside. No one can be forced into an Ujamaa village, and no official – at any level – can go and tell the members of an Ujamaa village what they should do together, and what they should continue to do as individual farmers ...

......

It is important that these things should be thoroughly understood. It is also important that the people should not be persuaded to start an Ujamaa village by promises of the things which will be given to them if they do so. A group of people must decide to start an Ujamaa village because they have understood that only through this method can they live and develop in dignity and freedom, receiving the full benefits of their co-operative endeavour ...

Unless the purpose and socialist ideology of an Ujamaa village is understood by the members from the beginning – at least to some extent – it will not survive the early difficulties. For no-one can guarantee that there will not be a crop failure in the first or second year – there might be a drought or floods. And the greater self-discipline which is necessary when working in a community will only be forthcoming if the people understand what they are doing and why ...

The fact that people cannot be forced into Ujamaa villages, nor told how to run them, does not mean that Government and TANU have just to sit back and hope that people will be inspired to create them on their own.

To get Ujamaa villages established, and to help them to succeed, education and leadership are required. These are the things which TANU has to provide. [TANU = Tanganyika African National Union, Nyerere's ruling political party, and the only one permitted.]

2: The Arusha Declaration

Extracts from the Arusha Declaration and TANU's Policy on Socialism and Self-Reliance (Dar-es-Salaam, 1967). Copyright retained by the President.
The Arusha Declaration, a document setting out Tanzania's broad policy on socialist development, was drafted by Nyerere in 1967, and adopted by TANU in the same year.

PART ONE: THE TANU "CREED"

THE POLICY OF TANU IS TO BUILD A SOCIALIST STATE. THE PRINCIPLES OF SOCIALISM ARE LAID DOWN IN THE TANU CONSTITUTION, AND THEY ARE AS FOLLOWS:-

Whereas TANU believes:

(a) That all human beings are equal;

(b) That every individual has a right to dignity and respect;

(c) That every citizen is an integral part of the Nation and has the right to taken an equal part in Government at local, regional and national level;

(d) That every citizen has the right to freedom of expression, of movement, of religious belief and of association within the context of the law;

(e) That every individual has the right to receive from society protection of his life and of property held according to law;

(f) That every individual has the right to receive a just return for his labour;

(g) That all citizens together possess all the natural resources of the country in trust for their descendants;

(h) That in order to ensure economic justice the State must have effective control over the principal means of production; and

(i) That it is the responsibility of the State to intervene actively in the economic life of the Nation so as to ensure the well-being of all citizens and so as to prevent the exploitation of one person by another or one group by another, and so as to prevent the accumulation of wealth to an extent which is inconsistent with the existence of a classless society.

Now, THEREFORE, the principal aims and objects of TANU shall be as follows:

(a) To consolidate and maintain the independence of this country and the freedom of its people;

(b) To safeguard the inherent dignity of the individual in accordance with the Universal Declaration of Human Rights;

(c) To ensure that this country shall be governed by a democratic socialist government of the people;

(d) To co-operate with all political parties in Africa engaged in the liberation of all Africa;

(e) To see that the Government mobilizes all the resources of this country towards the elimination of poverty, ignorance and disease;

(f) To see that the Government actively assists in the formation and maintenance of co-operative organizations;

(g) To see that wherever possible the Government itself directly participates in the economic development of this country;

(h) To see that the Government gives equal opportunity to all men and women irrespective of race, religion or status;

(i) To see that the Government eradicates all types of exploitation, intimidation, discrimination, bribery and corruption;

(j) To see that the Government exercises effective control over the principal means of production and pursues policies which facilitate the way to collective ownership of the resources of this country;

(k) To see that the Government co-operates with other States in Africa in bringing about African Unity;

(l) To see that the Government works tirelessly towards world peace and security through the United Nations Organization.

PART TWO: THE POLICY OF SOCIALISM

(a) *Absence of Exploitation:*

A true Socialist State is one in which all people are workers and in which neither Capitalism nor Feudalism exist. It does not have two classes of people: a lower class consisting of people who work for their living, and an upper class consisting of those who live on other people's labour. In a true Socialist State no person exploits another, but everybody who is able to work does so and gets a fair income for his labour, and incomes do not differ substantially.

In a true Socialist State it is only the following categories of people who can live on other people's labour: children, the aged, cripples and those for whom the State at any one time cannot provide with employment.

Tanzania is a State of Peasants and Workers, but it is not yet a socialist State. It still has elements of Capitalism and Feudalism and their temptations. These elements could expand and entrench themselves.

(b) *Major Means of Production to be under the Control of Peasants and Workers:*
The way to build and maintain socialism is to ensure that the major means of production are under the control and ownership of the Peasants and the Workers themselves through their Government and their Co-operatives. It is also necessary to ensure that the ruling party is a Party of Peasants and Workers.

These major means of production are: the land; forests; mineral resources; water; oil and electricity; communications; transport; banks; insurance; import and export trade; wholesale business; the steel, machine tool, arms, motor-car, cement and fertilizer factories; the textile industry; and any other big industry upon which a large section of the population depend for their living, or which provides essential components for other industries; large plantations, especially those which produce raw materials.

Some of these instruments of production are already under the control and ownership of the people's Government.

(c) *Democracy:*
A state is not socialist simply because all, or all the major, means of production are controlled and owned by the Government. It is necessary for the Government to be elected and led by the Peasants and Workers. If the racist Governments of Rhodesia and South Africa were to bring the major means of production in these countries under their control and direction, this would entrench Exploitation. It would not bring about Socialism. There cannot be true Socialism without Democracy.

(d) *Socialism is an Ideology:*
Socialism is an Ideology. It can only be implemented by people who firmly believe in its principles and are prepared to put them into practice. A true member of TANU is a socialist, and his compatriots, that is his fellow believers in this political and economic faith, are all those in Africa

69

or elsewhere in the world who fight for the rights of the peasants and workers. The first duty of a TANU member, and especially of a TANU leader, is to live by these principles in his day-to-day life. In particular a TANU leader should never live on another's labour, neither should he have capitalist or feudalist tendencies.

PART THREE: THE POLICY OF SELF-RELIANCE

We are at War:

TANU is involved in a war against poverty and oppression in our country; this struggle is aimed at moving the people of Tanzania (and the people of Africa as a whole) from a state of poverty to a state of prosperity.

We have been oppressed a great deal, we have been exploited a great deal and we have been disregarded a great deal. It is our weakness that has led to our being oppressed, exploited and disregarded. We now intend to bring about a revolution which will ensure that we are never again victims of these things.

A poor man does not use Money as a Weapon:

But it is obvious that in the past we have chosen the wrong weapon for our struggle, because we choose money as our weapon. We are trying to overcome our economic weakness by using the weapons of the economically strong – weapons which in fact we do not possess. By our thoughts, words and actions it appears as if we have come to the conclusion that without money we cannot bring about the revolution we are aiming at. It is as if we have said, "Money is the basis of development. Without money there can be no development".

. . . . . .

When it is said that Government has no money, what does this mean? It means that people of Tanzania have insufficient money. The people pay taxes out of the very little wealth they have; it is from these taxes that the Government meets its recurrent and development expenditure. When we call on the Government to spend more money on development projects, we are asking the Government to use more money. And if the Government does not have any more, the only way it can do this is to increase its revenue through extra taxation.

. . . . . .

What of external Aid?

One way we employ to try to escape the need for increased taxation for development purposes is to put emphasis on money coming from outside Tanzania.

. . . . . .

70

It is stupid to rely on money as the major instrument of development when we know only too well that our country is poor. It is equally stupid, indeed it is even more stupid, for us to imagine that we shall rid ourselves of our poverty through foreign financial assistance rather than our own financial resources. It is stupid for two reasons.

Firstly, we shall not get the money. It is true that there are countries which can, and which would like to help us. But there is no country in the world which is prepared to give us loans or gifts, or establish industries, to the extent that we would be able to achieve all our development targets. There are many needy countries in the world. And even if all the prosperous nations were willing to help the needy countries, the assistance would still not suffice. But prosperous nations are not willing to give all they could. Even in these prosperous nations, the rich do not willingly give money to the Government to relieve want.

. . . . . .

Gifts and Loans Will Endanger Our Independence

Secondly, even if it were possible for us to get enough money for our needs from external sources, is this what we really want? Independence means self-reliance. Independence cannot be real if a nation depends upon gifts and loans from another for its development. Even if there was a nation, or nations, prepared to give us all the money we need for our development, it would be improper for us to accept such assistance without asking ourselves how this would affect our independence and our very survival as a nation. Gifts which start off or stimulate our own efforts are useful gifts. But gifts which weaken our own efforts should not be accepted without asking ourselves a number of questions . . .

How can we depend upon gifts, loans and investments from foreign countries and foreign companies without endangering our independence? The English people have a proverb which says: "He who pays the piper calls the tune". How can we depend upon foreign Governments and Companies for the major part of our development without giving to those Governments and countries a great part of our freedom to act as we please? The truth is that we cannot.

Let us therefore always remember the following. We have made a mistake to choose money, something which we do not have, to be our major instrument of development. We are mistaken when we imagine that we shall get money from foreign countries, firstly, because to say the truth we cannot get enough money for our development and, secondly, because even if we could get it such complete dependence on outside help would have endangered our independence and the other policies of our country.

. . . . . .

71

Let Us be Concerned About the Peasant Farmer

Our emphasis on money and industries has made us concentrate on urban development. We recognize that we do not have enough money to bring the kind of development to each village which would benefit everybody. We also know that we cannot establish an industry in each village and through this means effect a rise in the real incomes of the people. For these reasons we spend most of our money in the urban areas and our industries are established in towns.

. . . . . .

This fact should always be borne in mind, for there are various forms of exploitation. We must not forget that people who live in towns can possibly become the exploiters of those who live in the rural areas. All our big hospitals are in towns and they benefit only a small section of the people of Tanzania. Yet if we have built them with loans from outside Tanzania, it is the overseas sale of the peasants' produce which provides the foreign exchange for repayment. Those who do not get the benefit of the hospitals thus carry the major responsibility for paying for them.

. . . . . .

Although when we talk of exploitation we usually think of capitalists, we should not forget that there are many fish in the sea. They eat each other. The large ones eat the small ones, and the small ones eat those who are even smaller. There are two possible ways of dividing the people in our country. We can put the capitalists and feudalists on one side, and the peasants and workers on the other. But we can also divide the people into urban dwellers on one side, and those who live in the rural areas on the other. If we are not careful we might get to the position where the real exploitation in Tanzania is that of the town dwellers exploiting the peasants.

The People and Agriculture

The development of a country is brought about by people, not by money. Money, and the wealth it represents, is the result and not the basis of development. The four prerequisites of development are different; they are (i) People; (ii) Land; (iii) Good policies; (iv) Good leadership. Our country has more than ten million people and its area is more than 362,000 square miles . . .

Agriculture is the Basis of Development

A great part of Tanzania's land is fertile and gets sufficient rains. Our country can produce various crops for home consumption and for export.

We can produce food crops (which can be exported if we produce in large quantities) such as maize, rice, wheat, beans, groundnuts, etc. And

72

we can produce such cash crops as sisal, cotton, coffee, tobacco, pyrethrum, tea, etc. Our land is also good for grazing cattle, goats, sheep, and for raising chickens, etc.; we can get plenty of fish from our rivers, lakes and from the sea. All of our farmers are in areas which can produce two or three or even more of the food and cash crops enumerated above and each farmer could increase his production so as to get more food or more money. And because the main aim of development is to get more food, and more money for our other needs, our purpose must be to increase production of these agricultural crops. This is in fact the only road through which we can develop our country – in other words, only by increasing our production of these things can we get more food and more money for every Tanzanian.

The Conditions of Development

(a) *Hard Work:*

Everybody wants development; but not everybody understands and accepts the basic requirements for development. The biggest requirement is hard work. Let us go to the villages and talk to our people and see whether or not it is possible for them to work harder.

. . . . . .

(b) *Intelligence:*

The second condition of development is the use of INTELLIGENCE. Unintelligent hard work would not bring the same good results as the two combined. Using a big hoe instead of a small one; using a plough pulled by oxen instead of an ordinary hoe; the use of fertilizers; the use of insecticides; knowing the right crop for a particular season or soil; choosing good seeds for planting; knowing the right time for planting, weeding, etc.; all these things show the use of knowledge and intelligence. And all of them combined with hard work to produce more and better results.

. . . . . .

Hard Work is the Root of Development

Some Plan projects which depend on money are going on well, but there are many which have stopped and others which might never be fulfilled because of lack of money. Yet still we talk about money and our search for money increases and takes nearly all our energies. We should not lessen our efforts to get the money we really need, but it would be more appropriate for us to spend time in the villages showing the people how to bring about development through their own efforts, rather than going on so many long and expensive journeys abroad in search of development

73

money. This is the real way to bring development to everybody in the country.

. . . . . .

From now on we shall stand upright and walk forward on our feet rather than look at this problem upside down. Industries will come and money will come but their foundation is THE PEOPLE and their HARD WORK, especially in AGRICULTURE. This is the meaning of self-reliance. Our emphasis should therefore be on:

(a) The Land and Agriculture
(b) The People
(c) The Policy of Socialism and Self-Reliance, and
(d) Good Leadership.

(a) *The Land:*

Because the economy of Tanzania depends and will continue to depend on agriculture and animal husbandry, Tanzanians can live well without depending on help from outside if they use their land properly. Land is the basis of human life and all Tanzanians should use it as a valuable investment for future development. Because the land belongs to the Nation, the Government has to see to it that it is used for the benefit of the whole nation and not for the benefit of one individual or just a few people.

It is the responsibility of TANU to see that the country produces enough food, enough cash crops for export. It is the responsibility of the Government and the Co-operative Societies to see to it that our people get the necessary tools, training and leadership in modern methods of agriculture.

(b) *The People:*

In order properly to implement the policy of self-reliance, the people have to be taught the meaning of self-reliance and its practice. They must become self-sufficient in food, serviceable clothes and good housing.

In our country work should be something to be proud of, and laziness, drunkenness and idleness should be things to be ashamed of. And for the defence of our Nation, it is necessary for us to be on guard against internal stooges who could be used by external enemies who aim to destroy us. The people should always be ready to defend their Nation when they are called upon to do so.

(c) *Good Policies:*

The principles of our policy of self-reliance go hand in hand with our policy on Socialism. In order to prevent exploitation it is necessary for everybody to work and to live on his own labour. And in order to distribute the national wealth fairly, it is necessary for everybody to work to the maximum of his ability. Nobody should go and stay for a long time with his relative, doing no work, because in doing so he will be exploiting his relative. Likewise, nobody should be allowed to loiter in towns or villages without doing work which would enable him to be self-reliant without exploiting his relatives.

TANU believes that everybody who loves his Nation has a duty to serve it by co-operating with his fellows in building the country for the benefit of all the people of Tanzania. In order to maintain our independence and our people's freedom we ought to be self-reliant in every possible way and avoid depending upon other countries for assistance. If every individual is self-reliant the ten-house cell will be self-reliant; if all the cells are self-reliant the whole ward will be self-reliant; and if the wards are self-reliant the District will be self-reliant. If the Districts are self-reliant, then the Region is self-reliant, and if the Regions are self-reliant, then the whole Nation is self-reliant and this is our aim.

(d) *Good Leadership:*

TANU realizes the importance of good leadership. The problem is that we have not prepared proper plans for the training of leaders. The Party Headquarters is now called upon to prepare specific plans for the training of leaders from the national level down to the leaders of the ten-house cells, so that all may understand our political and economic policies. Leaders must be a good example to the rest of the people through their actions and in their own lives.

. . . . . .

PART FIVE: THE ARUSHA RESOLUTION

Therefore, the National Executive Committee, meeting in the Community Centre at Arusha from 26.1.67 to 29.1.67, resolves:-

A. The Leadership

1. Every TANU and Government leader must be either a Peasant or a Worker, and should in no way be associated with the practices of Capitalism or Feudalism.
2. No TANU or Government leader should hold shares in any Company.
3. No TANU or Government leader should hold Directorships in any privately-owned enterprises.
4. No TANU or Government leader should receive two or more salaries.
5. No TANU or Government leader should own houses which he rents to others.

6. For the purposes of this Resolution the term "leader" should comprise the following: Members of the TANU National Executive Committee; Ministers, Members of Parliament, Senior Officials of Organizations affiliated to TANU, Senior Officials of Para-Statal Organizations, all those appointed or elected under any clause of the TANU Constitution, Councillors, and Civil Servants in high and middle cadres. (In this context "leader" means a man, or a man and his wife; a woman, or a woman and her husband).

B. The Government and Other Institutions

1. Congratulates the Government for the steps it has taken so far in the implementation of the policy of Socialism.
2. Calls upon the Government to take further steps in the implementation of our policy of Socialism as described in Part Two of this document without waiting for a Presidential Commission on Socialism.
3. Calls upon the Government to put emphasis, when preparing its development plans, on the ability of this country to implement the plans rather than depending on foreign loans and grants as has been done in the current Five-Year Development Plan. The National Executive Committee also resolves that the Plan should be amended so as to make it fit in with the policy of self-reliance.
4. Calls upon the Government to take action designed to ensure that the incomes of workers in the private sector are not very different from the incomes of workers in the public sector.
5. Calls upon the Government to put great emphasis on actions which will raise the standard of living of the peasants, and the rural community.

......

Appendix II Socialism is not Racialism

The Arusha Declaration and the actions relating to public ownership which we took last week were all concerned with ensuring that we can build Socialism in our country. The nationalisation and the taking of a controlling interest in many firms were a necessary part of our determination to organise our society in such a way that our efforts benefit all our people and that there is no exploitation of one man by another.

Yet these actions do not in themselves create socialism. They are necessary to it, but as the Arusha Declaration states, they could also be the basis for fascism – in other words, for the oppressive extreme of capitalism. For the words with which I began my pamphlet *Ujamaa* in 1962 remain valid; socialism is an attitude of mind. The basis of socialism is a belief in the oneness of man and the common historical destiny of mankind. Its basis, in other words, is human equality.

Acceptance of this principle is absolutely fundamental to socialism. The justification of socialism is Man; not the State, not the flag. Socialism is not for the benefit of black men, nor brown men, nor white men, nor yellow men. The purpose of socialism is the service of man, regardless of colour, size, shape, skill, ability or anything else. And the economic institutions of socialism, such as those we are now creating in accordance with the Arusha Declaration, are intended to serve man in our society. Where the majority of the people in a particular society are black, then most of those who benefit from socialism there will be black. But it has nothing to do with their blackness; only with their humanity.

. . . . . .

The Arusha Declaration talks of Men, and their beliefs. It talks of socialism and capitalism, of socialists and capitalists. It does not talk about racial groups or nationalities. On the contrary, it says that all those who stand for the interests of the workers and peasants, anywhere in the world, are our friends. This means that we must judge the character and ability of each individual, not put each person into a pre-arranged category or race or national origin and judge them accordingly. Certainly no one can be a socialist unless he at least tries to do this. For if the actions taken under the Arusha Declaration are to mean anything to our people then we must accept this basic oneness of man. What matters now is that we should succeed in the work we have undertaken. The colour or origin of the man who is working to that end does not matter in the very least. And each of us must fight, in himself, the racialist habits of thought which were part of our inheritance from colonialism.

It is not an easy thing to overcome such habits. But we have always known that it is necessary, and that racialism is evil. We fought our independence campaign on that basis. And the equality of man is the first item in the TANU Creed. For in our constitution we say "TANU believes (a) That all human beings are equal; (b) That every individual has a right to dignity and respect".

If we are to succeed in building a socialist state in this country it is essential that every citizen, and especially every TANU leader, should live up to that doctrine. Let us always remember two things. We have dedicated ourselves to build a socialist society in Tanzania. And, Socialism and Racialism are incompatible.

3: Nyerere: Education for Self-Reliance

Extracts from J. K. Nyerere, *Education for Self-Reliance* (Government Printer, Dar-es-Salaam, 1967). Reprinted in *Freedom and Socialism* (Oxford University Pres, 1968). Copyright retained by the President.
This policy statement was written by Nyerere in March 1967, and is intended to supplement the Arusha Declaration.

It is now time that we looked again at the justification for a poor society like ours spending almost 20 per cent of its Government revenue on providing education for its children and young people, and began to consider what that education should be doing. For in our circumstances it is impossible to devote Shs. 147,330,000 every year on education for some of our children (while others go without) unless its result has a proportionate relevance to the society we are trying to create.

The educational systems in different kinds of societies in the world have been, and are, very different in organization and in content. They are different because the societies providing the education are different, and because education, whether it be formal or informal, has a purpose. That purpose is to transmit from one generation to the next the accumulated wisdom and knowledge of the society, and to prepare the young people for their future membership of the society and their active participation in its maintenance or development.

. . . . . .

The fact that pre-colonial Africa did not have "schools" – except for short periods of initiation in some tribes – did not mean that the children were not educated. They learned by living and doing. In the homes and on the farms they were taught the skills of the society, and the behaviour expected of its members. They learned the kind of grasses which were suitable for which purposes, the work which had to be done on the crops, or the care which had to be given to animals, by joining with their elders in this work. They learned the tribal history and the tribe's relationship with other tribes and with the spirits, by listening to the stories of the elders. Through these means, and by the custom of sharing to which young people were taught to conform, the values of the society were transmitted. Education was thus "informal": every adult was a teacher to a greater or lesser degree. But this lack of formality did not mean that there was no education, nor did it affect its importance to the society. Indeed, it may have made the education more directly relevant to the society in which the child was growing up.

. . . . . .

78

Colonial Education in Tanzania and the Inheritance of the New State
The education provided by the colonial government in the two countries
which now form Tanzania had a different purpose. It was not designed to
prepare young people for the service of their own country; instead, it was
motivated by a desire to inculcate the values of the colonial society and to
train individuals for the service of the colonial state. In these countries the
State interest in education therefore stemmed from the need for local
clerks and junior officials; on top of that, various religious groups were
interested in spreading literacy and other education as part of their
evangelical work.

. . . . . .

The independent state of Tanzania in fact inherited a system of
education which was in many respects both inadequate and inappropriate
for the new state. It was, however, its inadequacy which was most
immediately obvious. So little education had been provided that in
December 1961, we had too few people with the necessary educational
qualifications even to man the administration of government as it was
then, much less undertake the big economic and social development work
which was essential. Neither was the school population in 1961 large
enough to allow for any expectation that this situation would be speedily
corrected. On top of that, education was based upon race, whereas the
whole moral case of the independence movement had been based upon a
rejection of racial distinctions.

Action since Independence
The three most glaring faults of the educational inheritance have already
been tackled. First, the racial distinctions within education were
abolished. Complete integration of the separate racial systems was
introduced very soon after independence, and discrimination on grounds
of religion was also brought to an end. A child in Tanzania can now
secure admittance to any Government or Government-aided school in this
country without regard to his race or religion and without fear that he will
be subject to religious indoctrination as the price of learning.

. . . . . .

The third action we have taken is to make the education provided in all
our schools much more Tanzanian in content. No longer do our children
simply learn British and European history. Faster than would have been
thought possible, our University College and other institutions are
providing materials on the history of Africa and making these available to
our teachers. Our national songs and dances are once again being learned
by our children; our national language has been given the importance in
our curriculum which it needs and deserves. Also, civics classes taken by

Tanzanians are beginning to give the secondary school pupils an understanding of the organization and aims of our young state. In these and other ways changes have been introduced to make our educational system more relevant to our needs.

. . . . . .

What Kind of Society are we trying to build?

Only when we are clear about the kind of society we are trying to build can be design our educational service to serve our goals. But this is not now a problem in Tanzania. Although we do not claim to have drawn up a blueprint of the future, the values and objectives of our society have been stated many times. We have said that we want to create a socialist society which is based on three principles: equality and respect for human dignity; sharing of the resources which are produced by our efforts; work by everyone and exploitation by none. We have set out these ideas clearly in the National Ethic; and in the Arusha Declaration and earlier documents we have outlined the principles and policies we intend to follow. We have also said on many occasions that our objective is greater African unity, and that we shall work for this objective while in the meantime defending the absolute integrity and sovereignty of the United Republic. Most often of all, our Government and people have stressed the equality of all citizens, and our determination that economic, political, and social policies shall be deliberately designed to make a reality of that equality in all spheres of life. We are, in other words, committed to a socialist future and one in which the people will themselves determine the policies pursued by a Government which is responsible to them.

It is obvious, however, that if we are to make progress towards these goals, we in Tanzania must accept the realities of our present position, internally and externally, and then work to change these realities into something more in accord with our desires. And the truth is that our United Republic has at present a poor, undeveloped, and agricultural economy. We have very little capital to invest in big factories or modern machines; we are short of people with skill and experience. What we do have is land in abundance and people who are willing to work hard for their own improvement. It is the use of these latter resources which will decide whether we reach our total goals or not. If we use these resources in a spirit of self-reliance as the basis for development, then we shall make progress slowly but surely. And it will then be real progress, affecting the lives of the masses, not just having spectacular show-pieces in the towns while the rest of the people of Tanzania live in their present poverty.

Pursuing this path means that Tanzania will continue to have a predominantly rural economy for a long time to come. And as it is in the rural areas that people live and work, so it is in the rural areas that life must be improved. This is not to say that we shall have no industries and factories in the near future. We have some now and they will continue to expand. But it would be grossly unrealistic to imagine that in the near future more than a small proportion of our people will live in towns and work in modern industrial enterprises. It is therefore the villages which must be made into places where people live a good life; it is in the rural areas that people must be able to find their material well-being and their satisfactions.

This improvement in village life will not, however, come automatically. It will come only if we pursue a deliberate policy of using the resources we have – our man-power and our land – to the best advantage. This means people working hard, intelligently, and together; in other words, working in co-operation. Our people in the rural areas, as well as their Government, must organize themselves co-operatively and work for themselves through working for the community of which they are members. Our village life as well as our state organization, must be based on the principles of socialism and that equality in work and return which is part of it.

This is what our educational system has to encourage. It has to foster the social goals of living together, and working together, for the common good. It has to prepare our young people to play a dynamic and constructive part in the development of a society in which all members share fairly in the good or bad fortune of the group, and in which progress is measured in terms of human well-being, not prestige buildings, cars, or other such things, whether privately or publicly owned. Our education must therefore inculcate a sense of commitment to the total community, and help the pupils to accept the values appropriate to our kind of future, not those appropriate to our colonial past.

This means that the educational system of Tanzania must emphasize co-operative endeavour, not individual advancement; it must stress concepts of equality and the responsibility to give service which goes with any special ability, whether it be in carpentry, in animal husbandry, or in academic pursuits. And, in particular, our education must counteract the temptation to intellectual arrogance; for this leads to the well-educated despising those whose abilities are non-academic or who have no special abilities but are just human beings. Such arrogance has no place in a society of equal citizens.

It is however, not only in relation to social values that our educational system has a task to do. It must also prepare young people for the work they will be called upon to do in the society which exists in Tanzania – a rural society where improvement will depend largely upon the efforts of the people in agriculture and in village development. This does not mean that education in Tanzania should be designed just to produce passive agricultural workers of different levels of skill who simply carry out plans or directions received from above. It must produce good farmers; it has also to prepare people for their responsibilities as free workers and citizens in a free and democratic society, albeit a largely rural society. They have to be able to think for themselves, to make judgements on all the issues affecting them; they have to be able to interpret the decisions made through the democratic institutions of our society, and to implement them in the light of the peculiar local circumstances where they happen to live.

It would thus be a gross misinterpretation of our needs to suggest that the educational system should be designed to produce robots, who work hard but never question what the leaders in Government or TANU are doing and saying. For the people are, and must be, Government and TANU. Our Government and our Party must always be responsible to the people, and must always consist of representatives − spokesmen and servants of the people. The education provided must therefore encourage the development in each citizen of three things: an enquiring mind, an ability to learn from what others do, and reject or adapt it to his own needs; and a basic confidence in his own position as a free and equal member of the society, who values others and is valued by them for what he does and not for what he obtains.

These things are important for both the vocational and the social aspects of education. However much agriculture a young person learns, he will not find a book which will give him all the answers to all the detailed problems he will come across on his own farm. He will have to learn the basic principles of modern knowledge in agriculture, and then adapt them to solve his own problems. Similarly, the free citizens of Tanzania will have to judge social issues for themselves; there neither is, nor will be, a political "holy book" which purports to give all the answers to all the social, political and economic problems which will face our country in the future. There will be philosophies and policies approved by our society which citizens should consider and apply in the light of their own thinking and experience. But the educational system of Tanzania would not be serving the interests of a democratic socialist society if it tried to stop people from thinking about the teachings, policies or the beliefs of leaders, either past or present. Only free people conscious of their worth and their equality can build a free society.

Some salient features of the existing Educational System
These are very different purposes from those which are promoted by our existing educational arrangements. For there are four basic elements in the

present system which prevent, or at least discourage, the integration of the pupils into the society they will enter, and which do encourage attitudes of inequality, intellectual arrogance and intense individualism among the young people who go through our schools.

First, the most central thing about the education we are at present providing is that it is basically an elitist education designed to meet the interests and needs of a very small proportion of those who enter the school system.

In other words, the education now provided is designed for the few who are intellectually stronger than their fellows; it induces among those who succeed a feeling of superiority, and leaves the majority of the others hankering after something they will never obtain. It induces a feeling of inferiority among the majority, and can thus not produce either the egalitarian society we should build, nor the attitudes of mind which are conductive to an egalitarian society. On the contrary, it induces the growth of a class structure in our country.

Equally important is the second point; the fact that Tanzania's education is such as to divorce its participants from the society it is supposed to be preparing them for. This is particularly true of secondary schools, which are inevitably almost entirely boarding schools; but to some extent, and despite recent modifications in the curriculum, it is true of primary schools too. We take children from their parents at the age of 7 years, and for up to $7\frac{1}{2}$ hours a day we teach them certain basic academic skills. In recent years we have tried to relate these skills, at least in theory, to the life which the children see around them. But the school is always separate; it is not part of the society. It is a place children go to and which they and their parents hope will make it unnecessary for them to become farmers and continue living in the villages.

The few who go to secondary schools are taken many miles away from their homes; they live in an enclave, having permission to go into the town for recreation, but not relating the work of either town or country to their real life – which is lived in the school compound. Later a few people go to university. If they are lucky enough to enter Dar es Salaam University College they live in comfortable quarters, feed well, and study hard for their Degree. When they have been successful in obtaining it, they know immediately that they will receive a salary of something like £660 per annum. That is what they have been aiming for; it is what they have been encouraged to aim for. They may also have the desire to serve the community, but their idea of service is related to status and the salary which a university education is expected to confer upon its recipient. The salary and the status have become a right automatically conferred by the Degree.

It is wrong of us to criticize the young people for these attitudes. The new university graduate has spent the larger part of his life separated and apart from the masses of Tanzania; his parents may be poor, but he has never fully shared that poverty. He does not really know what it is like to live as a poor peasant. He will be more at home in the world of the educated than he is among his own parents. Only during vacations has he spent time at home, and even then he will often find that his parents and relatives support his own conception of his difference, and regard it as wrong that he should live and work as the ordinary person he really is. For the truth is that many of the people of Tanzania have come to regard education as meaning that a man is too precious for the rough and hard life which the masses of our people still live.

The third point is that our present system encourages school pupils in the idea that all knowledge which is worth while is acquired from books or from "educated people" – meaning those who have been through a formal education. The knowledge and wisdom of other old people is despised, and they themselves regarded as being ignorant and of no account . . .

. . . Everything we do stresses book learning, and under-estimates the value to our society of traditional knowledge and the wisdom which is often acquired by intelligent men and women as they experience life, even without their being able to read at all.

The same thing applies in relation to agricultural knowledge. Our farmers have been on the land for a long time. The methods they use are the result of long experience in the struggle for nature; even the rules and taboos they honour have a basis in reason. It is not enough to abuse a traditional farmer as old-fashioned; we must try to understand why he is doing certain things, and not just assume he is stupid. But this does not mean that his methods are sufficient for the future.

. . . Again, therefore, our young people have to learn both a practical respect for the knowledge of the old "uneducated" farmer, and an understanding of new methods and the reason for them.

. . . . . .

Finally, and in some ways most importantly, our young and poor nation is taking out of productive work some of its healthiest and strongest young men and women. Not only do they fail to contribute to that increase in output which is so urgent for our nation; they themselves consume the output of the older and often weaker people.

. . . . . .

Yet it is easy to say that our primary and secondary schools must prepare young people for the realities and needs of Tanzania; to do it requires a radical change, not only in the education system but also in many existing community attitudes. In particular, it requires that examinations should be down-graded in Government and public esteem. We have to recognize that although they have certain advantages – for example, in reducing the dangers of nepotism and tribalism in a selection process – they also have severe disadvantages too. As a general rule they assess a person's ability to learn facts and present them on demand within a time period. They do not always succeed in assessing a power to reason, and they certainly do not assess character or willingness to serve.

. . . . . .

Most important of all is that we should change the things we demand of our schools. We should not determine the type of things children are taught in primary schools by the things a doctor, engineer, teacher, economist, or administrator need to know. Most of our pupils will never be any of these things. We should determine the type of things taught in the primary schools by the things which the boy or girl ought to know – that is, the skills he ought to acquire and the values he ought to cherish if he, or she, is to live happily and well in a socialist and predominantly rural society, and contribute to the improvement of life there. Our sights must be on the majority; it is they we must be aiming at in determining the curriculum and syllabus. Those most suitable for further education will still become obvious, and they will not suffer. For the purpose is not to provide an inferior education to that given at present. The purpose is to provide a different education – one realistically designed to fulfil the common purposes of education in the particular society of Tanzania. The same thing must be true at post-primary schools. The object of the teaching must be the provision of knowledge, skills and attitudes which will serve the student when he or she lives and works in a developing and changing socialist state; it must not be aimed at university entrance.

Alongside this change in the approach to the curriculum there must be a parallel and integrated change in the way our schools are run, so as to make them and their inhabitants a real part of our society and our economy. Schools must, in fact, become communities – and communities which practise the precept of self-reliance. The teachers, workers, and pupils together must be the members of a social unit in the same way as parents, relatives, and children are the family social unit. There must be the same kind of relationship between pupils and teachers within the school comminity as there is between children and parents in the village. And the former community must realize, just as the latter do, that their life and well-being depend upon the production of wealth – by farming or other activities. This means that all schools, but especially secondary schools and other forms of higher education, must contribute to their own upkeep; they must be economic communities, as well as social and educational communities. Each school should have, as an integral part of it, a farm or workshop which provides the food eaten by the community, and makes some contribution to the total national income.

. . . . . .

Conclusion

The education provided by Tanzania for the students of Tanzania must serve the purposes of Tanzania. It must encourage the growth of the socialist values we aspire to. It must encourage the development of a proud, independent, and free citizenry which relies upon itself for its own development, and which knows the advantages and the problems of co-operation. It must ensure that the educated know themselves to be an integral part of the nation and recognize the responsibility to give greater service the greater the opportunities they have had.

This is not only a matter of school organization and curriculum. Social values are formed by family, school, and society – by the total environment in which a child develops. But it is no use our educational system stressing values and knowledge appropriate to the past or to the citizens in other countries; it is wrong if it even contributes to the continuation of those inequalities and privileges which still exist in our society because of our inheritance. Let our students be educated to be members and servants of the kind of just and egalitarian future to which this country aspires.

4: Nyerere: Socialism and Rural Development

Extracts from J. K. Nyerere, *Socialism and Rural Development* (Government Printer, Dar-es-Salaam, 1967). Reprinted in *Freedom and Socialism*.
This further policy document elaborating the themes of the Arusha Declaration on African socialism was written by Nyerere in September 1967.

The traditional African family lived according to the basic principles of *ujamaa*. Its members did this unconsciously, and without any conception of what they were doing in political terms. They lived together and worked together because that was how they understood life, and how they reinforced each other against the difficulties they had to contend with ... The family members thought of themselves as one, and all their language and behaviour emphasized their unity. The basic goods of life were "our food", "our land" "our cattle". And identity was established in terms of relationships; mother and father of so-and-so; daughter of so-and-so; wife of such and such a person. They lived together and they worked together; and the result of their joint labour was the property of the family as a whole.

The assumptions of Traditional Ujamaa living

This pattern of living was made possible because of three basic assumptions of traditional life. These assumptions were not questioned, or even thought about; but the whole of society was both based upon them, and designed to uphold them. They permeated the customs, manners, and education of the people. And although they were not always honoured by every individual continued to be judged by them.

The first of these basic assumptions, or principles of life, I have sometimes described as "love", but that word is so often used to imply a deep personal affection that it can give a false impression. A better word is perhaps "respect" . . .

While the first principle of the *ujamaa* unit related to persons, the second related to property. It was that all the basic goods were held in common, and shared among all members of the unit . . .

Inequalities existed, but they were tempered by comparable family or social responsibilities, and they could never become gross and offensive to the social equality which was at the basis of the communal life.

Finally, and as a necessary third principle, was the fact that everyone had an obligation to work. The work done by different people was different, but no-one was exempt. Every member of the family, and every guest who shared in the right to eat and have shelter, took it for granted that he had to join in whatever work had to be done. Only by the universal acceptance of this principle was the continuation of the other two made possible.

The inadequacies of the Traditional System

But although these three principles were at the base of the traditional practice of *ujamaa*, the result was not the kind of life which we really wish to see existing throughout Tanzania. Quite apart from personal failures to live up to the ideals and principles of the social system (and traditional Africa was no more composed of unselfish and hardworking angels than any other part of the world), there were two basic factors which prevented traditional society from full flowering.

. . . . . .

The first of these was that, although every individual was joined to his fellows by human respect, there was, in most parts of Tanzania, an acceptance of one human inequality. Although we try to hide the fact, and despite the exaggeration which our critics have frequently indulged in, it is true that the women in traditional society were regarded as having a place in the community which was not only different, but was also to some extent inferior.

The other aspect of traditional life which we have to break away from is its poverty. Certainly there was an attractive degree of economic equality, but it was equality at a low level. The equality is good, but the level can be raised. For there was nothing inherent in the traditional system which caused this poverty; it was the result of two things only. The first was ignorance, and the second was the scale of operations. Both of these can be corrected without affecting the validity and applicability of the three principles of mutual respect, sharing of joint production, and work by all. These principles were, and are, the foundation of human society, of real practical human equality, and of peace between members of a society. They can also be a basis of economic development if modern knowledge and modern techniques of production are used.

. . . . . .

The Objective

This is the objective of socialism in Tanzania. To build a society in which all members have equal rights and equal opportunities; in which all can live at peace with his neighbours without suffering or imposing injustice, being exploited, or exploiting; and in which all have a gradually increasing basic level of material welfare before any individual lives in luxury.

To create this kind of nation we must build on the firm foundations of the three principles of the *ujamaa* family. But we must add to these principles the knowledge and the instruments necessary for the defeat of the poverty which existed in traditional African society. In other words, we must add those elements which allow for increased output per worker, and which make a man's efforts yield more satisfactions to him. We must take our traditional system, correct its shortcomings, and adapt to its service the things we can learn from the technologically developed societies of other continents.

Tanzania as it has been developing

In recent years this is not what has been happening. Our society, our economy, and the dominant ambitions of our own people are all very different now from what they were before the colonial era. There has been a general acceptance of the social attitudes and ideas of our colonial masters. We have got rid of the foreign government, but we have not yet rid ourselves of the individualistic social attitudes which they represented and taught. For it was from these overseas contacts that we developed the ideas that the way to the comfort and prosperity which everyone wants is through selfishness and individual advancement. And, of course, under a capitalist type of system it is quite true that for a few individuals great wealth and comfort is possible. In even the poorest societies – that is, those societies where the total wealth produced and available in the community is very low – a few individuals can be very wealthy, if others are even poorer than they need be. If you abandon the idea and the goal of equality, and allow the clever and fortunate to exploit the others, then the glittering prizes of material success will be attractive to all, and the temptations of individualism will be further increased. No-one likes to be exploited, but all of us are tempted by opportunities to exploit others.

. . . . . .

Thus we still have in this country a predominantly peasant society in which farmers work for themselves and their families, and are helped and protected from exploitation by co-operative marketing arrangements. Yet the present trend is away from the extended family production and social unity, and towards the development of a class system in the rural areas. It is this kind of development which would be inconsistent with the growth of a socialist Tanzania in which all citizens could be assured of human dignity and equality, and in which all were able to have a decent and constantly improving life for themselves and their children.

Tanzania as it must develop

For the foreseeable future the vast majority of our people will continue to spend their lives in the rural areas and continue to work on the land. The land is the only basis for Tanzania's development; we have no other. Therefore, if our rural life is not based on the principles of socialism our country will not be socialist, regardless of how we organize our industrial sector, and regardless of our commercial and political arrangements. Tanzanian socialism must be firmly based on the land and its workers . . .

If we are to succeed in this, certain things are essential. The first of these is hard work by our people. There is no substitute for this, especially as we do not have large accumulations of capital which can be invested in agricultural labour-saving devices or in increased productivity. We have to increase the amount we produce from our land, and we shall have to do it by the use of our own hands and our own brains . . .

Not only this, there must also be an efficient and democratic system of local government, so that our people make their own decisions on the things which affect them directly, and so that they are able to recognize their own control over community decisions and their own responsibility for carrying them out. Yet this local control has to be organized in such a manner that the nation is united and working together for common needs,

89

and for the maximum development of our whole society.

. . . . . .

We shall be unable to fulfil these objectives if we continue to produce as individuals for individual profit. Certainly a man who is working for himself and for his own profit will not suffer from exploitation in this employment. But neither will he make much progress. It is not long before an individual, working alone, reaches the limit of his powers. Only by working together can men overcome that limitation.

. . . . . .

The principles upon which the traditional extended family was based must be reactivated. We can start with extended family villages, but they will not remain family communities, and they must certainly be larger communities than was traditionally the case. Also, modern knowledge must be applied by these communities and to them; and the barriers which previously existed between different groups must be broken down, so that they co-operate in the achievement of major tasks. But the basis of rural life in Tanzania must be the practice of co-operation in its widest sense – in living, in working, and in distribution, and all with an acceptance of the absolute equality of all men and women.

. . . . . .

Ujamaa Agriculture

In a socialist Tanzania then, our agricultural organization would be predominantly that of co-operative living and working for the good of all. This means that most of our farming would be done by groups of people who live as a community and work as a community. They would live together in a village; they would farm together; market together; and undertake the provision of local services and small local requirements as a community. Their community would be the traditional family group, or any other group of people living according to *ujamaa* principles, large enough to take account of modern methods and the twentieth century needs of man. The land this community farmed would be called "our land" by all the members; the crops they produced on that land would be "our crops"; it would be "our shop" which provided individual members with the day-to-day necessities from outside; "our workshop" which made the bricks from which houses and other buildings were constructed, and so on.

Such living and working in communities could transform our lives in Tanzania. We would not automatically become wealthy, although we could all become a little richer than we are now. But most important of all, any increase in the amount of wealth we produce under this system would be "ours"; it would not belong just to one or two individuals, but to all

90

those whose work had produced it. At the same time we should have strengthened our traditional equality and our traditional security.

Ujamaa Socialism in practice

A nation of such village communities would be a socialist nation. For the essential element in them would be the equality of all members of the community, and the members' self-government in all matters which concerned only their own affairs.

......

How do we get to this position? – Persuasion not Force

It is one thing to argue the advantages of this type of rural organization; the question is how can we move from our present position to make it into a reality? The farmers in Tanzania, like those elsewhere in the world, have learnt to be cautious about new ideas however attractive they may sound; only experience will convince them, and experience can only be gained by beginning.

Yet socialist communities cannot be established by compulsion. It may be possible – and sometimes necessary – to insist on all farmers in a given area growing a certain acreage of a particular crop until they realize that this brings them a more secure living, and then do not have to be forced to cultivate it. But living together and working together for the good of all is not just a question of crop output. It depends on a willingness to co-operate, and an understanding of the different kind of life which can be obtained by the participants if they work hard together. Viable socialist communities can only be established with willing members; the task of leadership and of Government is not to try and force this kind of development, but to explain, encourage, and participate . . .

It would also be unwise to expect that established farmers will be convinced by words – however persuasive. The farmers will have to see for themselves the advantage of working together and living together before they trust their entire future to this organization of life. In particular, before giving up their individual plots of land they will wish to see that the system of working together really benefits everyone. Groups of young men may be willing to experiment and this should be welcomed; we must encourage such young people. But what we are really aiming at is balanced communities where young and old are all involved together. Progress may thus be quite slow at the beginning, yet that is no reason for surrendering the goal. The man who creeps forward inch by inch may well arrive at his destination, when the man who jumps without being able to see the other side may well fall and cripple himself.

......

Conclusion

What is here being proposed is that we in Tanzania should move from being a nation of individual peasant producers who are gradually adopting the incentives and the ethics of the capitalist system. Instead we should gradually become a nation of *ujamaa* villages where the people co-operate directly in small groups and where these small groups co-operate together for joint enterprises. This can be done. We already have groups of people who are trying to operate this system in many parts of our country. We must encourage them and encourage others to adopt this way of life too. It is not a question of forcing our people to change their habits. It is a question of providing leadership. It is a question of education. And it is a question of all of us together making a reality of the principles of equality and freedom which are enshrined in our policy of Tanzanian socialism.

5: TANU Guidelines on the Tanzanian Revolution

Extracts from 'Mwongozo Wa Tanu', TANU Guidelines on Guiding, Consolidating and Advancing the Revolution of Tanzania, and of Africa. Published in *The African Review*, Vol. 1, No. 4 (April 1972).

1. Today our African continent is a hot-bed of the liberation struggle. This struggle between those who have for centuries been exploiting Africa's natural resources and using the people of this continent as their tools and as their slaves, and the people of Africa who have, after realising their weakness and exploitation, decided to engage in the struggle to liberate themselves.

It is both a bitter and continuing struggle: at times it is a silent one, occasionally it explodes like gun-powder, at other times the successes and gains achieved by the people slip away . . .

This is why our Party has the duty to spell out the aims of the Tanzanian and the African revolution, and to identify the enemies of this revolution, in order to set out policies and strategies which will enable us to safeguard, consolidate and further our revolution.

2. Revolutions are quick social changes, changes which wrest from the minority the power they exploited for their own benefit (and that of external exploiters) and put it in the hands of the majority so that they can promote their own well-being. The opposite of a revolution is a counter-revolution that is, quick and sudden changes which wrest power from the

majority and hand it over to the minority with the aim of stopping the progress of the masses.

3. The greatest aim of the African revolution is to liberate the African. This liberation is not sent from heaven, it is achieved by combating exploitation, colonialism and imperialism. Nor is liberation brought by specialists or experts. We who are being humiliated, exploited and oppressed are the experts of this liberation. There is no nation in the world which can teach the Africans how to liberate themselves. The duty of liberating ourselves lies with us, and the necessary expertise will be obtained during the struggle itself.

4. Furthermore, the present situation in Africa shows that there is no people in any African state which has achieved the stage of total liberation. Africa is still a continent of people suffering from the weakness inherent in being exploited and humiliated. That is why revolutionary political parties in independent African countries, such as TANU, are still in fact Liberation Movements.

. . . . . .

7. For Tanzania it must be understood that the imperialist enemies we are confronting are British imperialism, Portuguese colonialism, the racism and apartheid of South Africa and Rhodesia. For historical, geographical and political reasons these imperialists will be ready to attack us whenever they have an opportunity . . .

. . . . . .

10. We Tanzanians value our national independence because it is from that point that our liberation, and our aspirations for a liberation struggle in conjunction with other African people, begin. For this reason, we have the duty to take all necessary steps to enable us to guard our independence in order to further our revolution and thus make Tanzania a true example of the African revolution.

Politics

The Party

11. The responsibility of the Party is to lead the masses, and their various institutions, in the effort to safeguard national independence and to advance the liberation of the African. The duty of a socialist party is to guide all activities of the masses. The Government, parastatals, national organizations, etc., are instruments for implementing the Party's policies. Our short history of independence reveals problems that may arise when a Party does not guide its instruments. The time has now come for the Party to take the reins and lead all the people's activities.

12. The first task of the leadership is to spell out the national goal. This is

understood and the Party has already fulfilled this duty. Our aim is to build socialism in Tanzania. But to attain this objective the Party must offer policies and guidelines concerning different aspects of the people's activities. The Party has already given guidelines on socialism in rural areas, education for self-reliance, etc. There is still the need to clarify the Party's policies on other matters, such as housing, workers, money and loan policies, etc.

13. But the charting of objectives and policies does not by itself constitute good leadership. Leadership also means organising the people. It is the Party which decides on the structure of government, various institutions, the army, etc. In addition, the Party should provide guidelines on work methods and attitudes, and decision-making.

The truth is that we have not only inherited a colonial governmental structure but also adopted colonial working habits and leadership methods. For example, we have inherited in the government, industries and other institutions the habit in which one man gives the orders and the rest just obey them. If you do not involve the people in work plans, the result is to make them feel a national institution is not theirs, and consequently workers adopt the habits of hired employees. The Party has a duty to emphasise its leadership on this issue.

14. In addition to organising the people, leadership involves supervising the implementation of the Party's policy. Ways must be found to ensure that the Party actively supervises the activities and the running of its implementing agencies. Leadership also entails reviewing the results of implementation. It is the Party's duty to ensure that it assesses the effects of the policy implementation undertaken by its agencies. This is the only way to establish whether people participate in devising solutions to their problems in offices, institutions, the army, villages, industries, etc.

15. Together with the issue of involving the people in solving their problems, there is also the question of the habits of leaders in their work and in day-to-day life.

There must be a deliberate effort to build equality between the leaders and those they lead. For a Tanzanian leader it must be forbidden to be arrogant, extravagant, contemptuous and oppressive. The Tanzanian leader has to be a person who respects people, scorns ostentation and who is not a tyrant. He should epitomise heroism, bravery, and be a champion of justice and equality.

Similarly, the Party has the responsibility to fight the vindictiveness of some of its agents; such actions do not promote Socialism but drive a wedge between the Party and the Government on the one side and the people on the other.

16. There are presently some leaders who do not fulfil these conditions. They disregard and cleverly avoid the leadership code. The time has come for the Party to supervise the conduct and the bearing of the leaders.

Defence and Security

'And for the defence of our nation, it is necessary for us to be on guard against internal stooges who could be used by external enemies who aim to destroy us.'

(Arusha Declaration)

21. The basis of Tanzania's development is the people themselves – every Tanzanian – in particular each patriot and each socialist. Tanzania's defence and security depend on Tanzanians themselves – every Tanzanian, in particular each patriot, each socialist.

. . . . . .

23. Our Party was not forced to fight a liberation war. It was a Liberation Movement without a Liberation Army. But since 1964 we have been building the Tanzania People's Defence Forces. And just as TANU is still a Liberation Movement, the Tanzania People's Defence Force is the Liberation Army of the people of Tanzania.

TANU's relations with T.P.D.F. should be those of a People's Party and a People's Army. It is up to TANU to ensure that the people's Army is the army for both the liberation and the defence of the people. It is TANU's responsibility to ensure that the army's main task in peacetime is to enable the people to safeguard their independence and their policy of socialism and self-reliance.

. . . . . .

25. Political education must make the people aware of our national enemies and the strategies they employ to subvert our policies, our independence, our economy and our culture. To enable the people to confront the enemy, it is necessary to make them aware of the enemy's strength in all spheres, such as their army, their commercial enterprise, their life and habits, and the way these conflict with our convictions and aspirations.

26. In order that they be able to oppose our enemies, the people must know that it is they who are the nation's shield. This means that defence and security matters must be replaced in the hands of the people themselves. We do not have the means to establish large permanent armies to guard the whole country. Our army must be the people's army, used in teaching the people how to defend themselves in their localities and to enable them to report on matters of national security. Therefore it is imperative to start training a militia for the whole country. Since the

militia will spread through the country, in co-operation with the regular army, they will have the duty to defend our territorial borders, our air space and to expose traitors and enemies, all in co-operation with our regular army.

The Party leads the Army

27. The registration of the militia and the army must be scrutinised very carefully and supervised by the Party. Ensuring co-operation between the army and the militia, and providing for political education to both, must be a prime responsibility of the Party. The Party must establish a sub-committee of the Central Committee to look into defence and security.

Progress of the People

28. For a people who have been slaves or have been oppressed, exploited and humiliated by colonialism or capitalism, 'development' means 'liberation'. Any action that gives them more control of their own affairs is an action for development, even if it does not offer them better health or more bread. Any action that reduces their say in determining their own affairs or running their own lives is not development and retards them even if the action brings them a little better health and a little more bread.

To us development means both the elimination of oppression, exploitation, enslavement and humiliation, and the promotion of our independence and human dignity. Therefore, in considering the development of our nation and in preparing development plans, our main emphasis at all times should be the development of people and not of things. If development is to benefit the people, the people must participate in considering, planning and implementing their development plans.

The duty of our Party is not to urge the people to implement plans which have been decided upon by a few experts and leaders. The duty of our Party is to ensure that the leaders and experts implement the plans that have been agreed upon by the people themselves. When the people's decision requires information which is only available to the leaders and the experts, it will be the duty of leaders and experts to make such information available to the people. But it is not correct for leaders and experts to usurp the people's right to decide on an issue just because they have the expertise.

29. In order that the people shall be enthusiastic in the defence of their country, it is of first importance for the TANU Government to place a lot of emphasis on improving their conditions.

96

6: Nyerere: Decentralisation

J. K. Nyerere, *Decentralisation* (Dar-es-Salaam, 1972). Reprinted in *Freedom and Development* (Oxford University Press, 1973). Copyright retained by the President. A policy document which clearly aims to rationalise and improve Tanzanian government administration, and which may be, in part, the result of a survey of governmental institutions commissioned from the international management consultants, McKinsey & Co.

The purpose of both the Arusha Declaration and of Mwongozo was to give the people power over their own lives and their own development. We have made great progress in seizing power from the hands of capitalists and traditionalists, but we must face the fact that, to the mass of the people, power is still something wielded by others – even if on their behalf.

Thus it has gradually become obvious that, in order to make a reality of our policies of socialism and self-reliance, the planning and control of development in this country must be exercised at local level to a much greater extent than at present. Our nation is too large for the people at the centre in Dar-es-Salaam always to understand local problems or to sense their urgency. When all the power remains at the centre, therefore, local problems can remain, and fester, while local people who are aware of them are prevented from using their intitiative in finding solutions. Similarly it is sometimes difficult for local people to respond with enthusiasm to a call for development work which may be to their benefit, but which has been decided upon and planned by an authority hundreds of miles away.

. . . . . .

For all these and many other reasons, it is necessary that we should reorganise the administration of Government so as to make it more appropriate to our goal of socialist development. We have to work out a system which gives more local freedom for both decision and action on matters which are primarily of local impact, within a framework which ensures that the national policies of socialism and self-reliance are followed everywhere. The system must enable the Central Government to give guidance and assistance to local people, as well as to check on their work, while it reduces the amount of red tape and bureaucracy which is at present in danger of strangling our people's enthusiasm. Also, it must be possible for help to be given to areas with special difficulties or special needs, and the system must ensure the maximum use of scarce resources. Finally, projects which are of national importance must remain under national control, even though they may be situated in one particular area – a decision which does not preclude greater delegation of authority to the responsible officers on the spot.

Power Decentralised

The Government's proposals have been worked out with these objectives in mind.

It is proposed that, in general, Regions and Districts should plan and implement local development activities as well as administer local affairs with the very minimum of interference from Dar-es-Salaam. This will mean, for example, that a very large proportion of agricultural programmes will be made the direct responsibility of the Districts and Regions.

. . . . . .

To ensure that national objectives and priorities are adhered to, and that the policy of a gradual equalisation of well-being between different Regions can be implemented, broad general policy guidelines will be issued within the framework of which the local bodies must make their decisions. The Central Government, in addition to setting this framework and giving technical assistance where required, will also be responsible for inspecting the performance achieved. But otherwise, in the matters for which they are responsible, the Regions and Districts will be free to make their own decisions about priorities and methods of work.

In order that these heavy responsibilities may be carried out effectively, big changes are necessary in the traditional structure of Government. For we have at the same time to deal with the problems which arise from duplication of effort – combined with confusion – at the local level. In other words, we have to decentralise the control and decision-making now exercised from Dar-es-Salaam, and also to centralise local control, decision-making and responsibility.

Therefore it is proposed that single strong Regional and District organisations will be set up to cover all the rural areas. (Urban and other Town Councils will continue as at present for the time being.) The present system of rural local government will be abolished, as will the present practice of each Ministry having its own officers working in Regions and Districts.

New Development Councils and Committees

The abolition of the present system of local government does not mean the abolition of local representation. On the contrary, the purpose of the new system is to increase the people's participation in decision-making, and it will therefore demand that the powers and responsibilities of local representatives are increased, even although they will cease to employ and pay their own local personnel.

. . . . . .

Central Government Changes

  If this decentralisation is to be effective at the same time as the nation continues to go forward in unity, the Central Government organisation also has to be changed in many respects.

  In political terms these changes have already been made with the appointment of a Prime Minister, and the appointment of very senior people as Regional Comissioners. Many administrative changes, however, will have to be put into effect gradually. But over time there should be a reduction in the administration carried out from the centre, and therefore in the number of staff in certain Ministries who work in Dar-es-Salaam. This will be effected by dispersal of staff to Districts and, to a lesser extent, to Regions.

  Further, the staff who remain at the headquarters of those Ministries which are directly affected by the decentralisation will, in most cases, have a new type of job to do. Instead of trying to control every detail throughout the country, their job will be to prepare general guidelines, to inspect work being done, and to answer requests for help from the Regions and Districts.

. . . . . .

  In addition, if these proposals are worked through properly, the mass of the people will find that this is easier for them to practice self-reliance in their own development, and to take part in decision-making which directly affects them. Further, they will find it less difficult to call to account those public servants who are responsible for local activities of Government. For if a villager has a problem now, he is liable to be pushed from the District Council to the Area Commissioner's Office, from there to the Region, and from there to Dar-es-Salaam, where he – or his letter – will wander between one office and another. But if this new system works properly, the villager should be able to go straight to the District Office and find the person responsible for the subject he is interested in.

  There is, however, one danger which must be guarded against. The transfer of power to the Regions and Districts must not also mean transfer of a rigid and bureaucratic system from Dar-es-Salaam to lower levels. Nor is it the intention of these proposals to create new local tyrants in the persons of the Regional and District Development Directors.

  These officers will have overall responsibility; but the Decentralisation exercise is based on the principle that more and more people must be trusted with responsibility – that is its whole purpose. We are trying to eradicate the thicket of red tape and the tyranny of "the proper channels", not to plant them out all over the country.

. . . . . .

There is one further point which must be emphasised. If we are to succeed in reducing the amount of bureaucracy and in making a reality of local control, the system of financial control which now operates will have to be changed. Greater trust will have to be placed in people actually doing the development work – that is, those building the bridges, the schools, the dispensaries, etc., and those who are responsible for the development of a District. You cannot give people discretion without trusting them to use the people's money for the people's purposes. Decentralisation means trusting people. The system of financial control and of payments must be simplified, although the details of how this will be done still have to be worked out. But it is important to realise now that, as greater trust is being placed on different officers, so greater penalties will be, and must be, imposed on those who abuse this trust... Our money must be properly used for the nation's purposes, and those who would divert it to their personal needs must be prevented, and if not prevented then caught and very severely punished. But because a few people are untrustworthy, we must not behave as if everybody is untrustworthy.

TANU

All these proposals refer to Government re-organisation. But their success will depend upon TANU accepting enlarged responsibility for initiating *ujamaa* villages and other co-operative activities. Further, because the District Development Councils will refer their draft development proposals to the District Executive Committee of TANU for approval, the Party at this level will also have new responsibilities. For in these matters they will act in the same manner as the National Executive Committee does to Government development proposals. That is to say, the Party District Executive Committee will consider the policies being implemented by the proposed Plan, not the detailed projects.
. . . . . .
From this it is obvious that the decentralisation proposals will provide a new opportunity for local TANU leadership, as well as local Government leadership. For in addition to their new formal responsibilities, the TANU Branches throughout the rural areas could, and should, make themselves into the active arm of the people, so as to ensure that every advantage is taken of this increased local responsibility. The necessary strengthening of the relevant departments of TANU is now under consideration by the NEC. (National Executive Committee)
. . . . . .
And in fact, this decentralised system should increase the reality of democracy in our society because it brings power closer to the people –

they will be in real contact with those persons in Government and TANU who have responsibility for development in their area. Indeed, it will be one of the functions of TANU, and of the members of the Development Committees, to hold frequent meetings to consult with the people, to answer their questions, and to explain. For this purpose they will be able to call upon the Development Directors and the Functional Officers at District level to explain problems and opportunities. (Indeed, the officials should themselves ask for such meetings). Thus, local democracy will become more real, even as the institutions of development will become more efficient.

B. DOCUMENTS ON ZAMBIA

7: Kaunda: Humanism in Zambia

Extracts from K. Kaunda, *Humanism: a Guide to the Nation* (Government Printer, Lusaka, 1967).
A broad policy statement, written by the President of Zambia, Kenneth Kaunda, and expounded to the National Council of UNIP (The United National Independence Party) on 26 April 1967. The conference was also attended by leading civil servants, army officers, and police officers.

Preamble

The art of colonisation, if it is to succeed, means a coloniser sees to it that the victim is not only colonised politically, but also economically and culturally. This being the case, the act of political independence forms but the first part of the process of decolonisation. This process is a very long one.

Perhaps it is not possible to complete it in one generation, for it does not only require careful thought and planning, but also a lot of material, human and otherwise, to bring it about.

In many ways it is even more difficult than the attainment of political independence. All the same, time does come for leaders of any given revolution, if they know what they are doing, to think of starting to remould their society.

For only by so doing would they profit from the wisdom and values of their forefathers.

Of course, it would be wrong to do this with closed minds, for while there is plenty of good that Africa is justly proud of in its set-up of a mutual aid society – a society in which people worked co-operatively and

101

collectively without losing the identity of the individual for whose benefit and in whose name all was done – one has got to understand and appreciate that the powerful forces from the West which have been aggressively shattering in their individualistic, competitive and possessive approach, have had serious and grave consequences on the African society.

Now during the hazardous road to political independence, we recognised the fact that Africa was going to be one of the biggest, if not the biggest battleground for this century's ideological battles. As is well known, the present-day ideological differences are based on certain economic and political theories and practices. Putting it very simply, one would say it was a question of who owned or controlled the means of creating and distributing wealth in any given nation.

In other words, is it the State or individuals who are to own the means of creating wealth, or is it both, and if it is both, in what proportions? After this, how fair is the distribution of this wealth and, indeed, what methods are used to distribute it in any given nation?

This is a key point, for if the distribution of wealth is not done properly, it might lead to the creation of classes in society and the much-valued humanist approach that is traditional and inherent in our African society would have suffered a final blow. If this happened the world as a whole, and Africa in particular, would be all the poorer by it. For you would then have the "haves" and the "have-nots". Politically you would be creating room for opposing parties based on "the oppressed" and "the oppressor" concept which again would not be in keeping with the society described above; a society in which the Chief as an elected or appointed leader of the people held national property like land in trust for the people, and he was fully aware that he was responsible to them. He knew, too, that his continuing to be their head depended on his people's will.

The African society was progressive and human. The present generation with its responsibilities of taking care of the past traditions, remoulding the present to prepare for the future generations, would do well to bear this in mind in all its political, economic, social and cultural activities.

The question we must now address ourselves to is, in what respect and how much will it be necessary to change our traditional African society and reconstruct it as it emerges from a non-money to a money status. We will have to take into consideration the impact the use of money has made on our society. Economists will tell us that the use of money pre-supposes exchange and exchange pre-supposes specialisation and these three are inseparably linked in a self-generating process. It is a well-known fact that as the money economy expands, such as it is fast doing in Zambia,

Government is being forced to push people to become more and more specialised in various fields; and as the people become more and more specialised, they are becoming more and more effective in their fields and all other factors being equal, the money economy will expand.

. . . . . .

Whatever changes take place in our society, whatever sacrifices are made or are urged on individuals to make, by the Party and Government, in our task of fighting to preserve the Man-centred society, we must remember that it is people above ideology; Man above institutions. We must continuously refuse to slavishly tie men to anything. Society is there because of Man. We choose the hard way of continually experimenting on our generally agreed path, ready to learn from anyone from any part of the world according to our agreed principles. In other words, whatever we undertake to do we have got to remember that it is Man that is the centre of all human activity.

. . . . . .

[The] *high valuation of MAN and respect for human dignity which is a legacy of our tradition should not be lost in the new Africa. However "modern" and "advanced" in a Western sense this young nation of Zambia may become, we are fiercely determined that this humanism will not be obscured. African society has always been man-centred. Indeed, this is as it should be otherwise why is a house built? Not to give man shelter and security? Why make a chair at all? Why build a factory? Why do you want a State ranch? For what else would there be need to grow food? Why is the fishing industry there? We can go on asking these questions. The simple and yet difficult answer is "MAN". Simple in the sense that it is clear all human activity centres around MAN. Difficult, too, because man has not yet understood his own importance. And yet we can say with justification and without any sense of false pride that the African way of life with its many problems has less setbacks towards the achievement of an ideal society. We in Zambia intend to do everything in our power to keep our society man-centred. For it is in this that what might be described as African civilisation is embodied and indeed if modern Africa has anything to contribute to this troubled world, it is in this direction that it should.*

. . . . . .

Now and in Future

One has strong fears that although leaders preached the importance of man before independence and have continued to do so after it, this and its true meaning has not begun to permeate the rank and file of the Party, Civil Service, the Police, our Army and the general public to any

103

appreciable extent. The question is how can we begin to inject this into the bloodstream of the nation?

The fact that (and this is not, repeat not, to glorify the past but rather to humbly try to learn from it for the good of the present and the future) our ancestors were able to achieve a society in which social and political order was tight and effective calls for some examination on our part of how they have achieved this.

This, of course, did not come about by making high sounding declarations in the form of ideologies, etc. It came about by a carefully worked out order and discipline which everybody in society was required to follow. The teaching of their own values and the imparting of knowledge and wisdom by the elders to the youth of the community was part and parcel of this carefully worked out order and discipline. So that we see that the elders in the community used each day very carefully. Early in the morning they would rise to go either cultivating, hunting or fishing; if they were a cattle-rearing people – grazing cattle; or any other economic activities. In the evenings they would pool their experiences of the day while at their communal eating places or, indeed, as often the case, while beer would be taken, which was strictly speaking an affair for the old people, while the young men sat around deeply interested in the knowledge and wisdom that was being imparted, knowing only too well that tomorrow it would be their turn. Is this social harmony possible? Frankly, the answer is "Yes"; it is a question of how we organise society in the face of those shattering and aggressive forces already referred to – (from both the West and the East).

In spite of this, care must be taken that we do not over-stress or over-emphasise the importance of preserving our past society at the expense of the material development of our people. This, in fact, is the crucial point; how do we preserve what is good in our traditions, and at the same time allow ourselves to benefit from the science and the technology of our friends from both the West and the East. We refuse to be dogmatic about anything. That is, this Party and Government is not given to the art of drawing fixed lines somewhere between any two end choices. We choose to be constantly looking for and devising new ways by which to encourage the hastening of material advance while ensuring that the principles of traditional Man-centred society are preserved.

. . . . . .

Clause IV: Party Objects

(a) to (l) to be set on the Justifying board.

(a) To achieve African democratic socialism for Zambia, raise the stan-
    dard of living of the people and generally strive to make the people of

Zambia contented and happy. (*This is being realised beyond all doubt.*)

(b) To ensure acceptance of the principles of equal opportunity for all peoples in all aspects of life including wages of workers, social, health and educational facilities. (*We shall continue to tackle this programme vigorously.*)

(c) To co-operate with any movement or organisation for the improvement of workers' conditions and to secure the most equitable production and distribution of the wealth of the country in the best interests of the people. (*We have done a lot, but much more still remains to be done.*)

(d) To co-operate locally and internationally with all African Nationalist Movements and Parties which work for complete eradication of all forms of colonialism, imperialism, racialism and discriminatory laws and to fight for African Unity. (*This is our cardinal programme. We shall not rest until it is accomplished.*)

(e) To abolish all forms of discrimination and segregation based on colour, tribe, clan and creed and to maintain, protect and promote understanding and unity among the people of Zambia by removing individualism, tribalism and provincialism. (*These rank among deadly vices! !*)

(f) To promote and support worthy African customs and cultures. (*On this, the rest of the world has a lot to learn from us.*)

(g) To protect and promote trade, industry and agriculture in the interests of the people by legislation and to protect the interests of commercial traders and help them in their progressive business and schemes. (*We are vigorous on this programme, because it gives economic opportunities.*)

(h) To run and establish newsletters, newspaper or magazines in order to advance the aims and objects of the Party. (*We have comprehensive plans afoot.*)

(i) To organise and maintain in the country and in Parliament increased membership and support for the United National Independence Party. (*We are doing this with renewed vigour.*)

(j) To give effect to the principles approved from time to time by the Party Conference, the National Council or by the Central Committee.

(k) To ensure that freedom of speech, worship and freedom of the Press shall not be infringed and that the people of Zambia shall be free to think, speak, write, assemble, work and trade in accordance with the laws of the country. (*We are working to achieve this.*)

105

(l)　To carry on any other activities which to the Central Committee may seem conducive to the aims and objects of the Party and to do such other things as are incidental to the attainment of the above objects.

. . . . . .

The next question we must deal with now is the second in Part One. How far have we gone in the direction of attaining humanism in Zambia? To understand this let us outline precisely what this means in political, economic, social and cultural terms. Zambia can say with pride that its humanism is original, based very much on the importance of Man. In this case the State cares for Man, the Person. He, in return, as an individual will, or at least is expected to, care for his neighbour and thereby caring for the State. The oft declared principles of non-tribalism, non-racialism, no discrimination based on religion and creed is very much part of the principles embodied in the importance of the Common Man.

Land

Land, obviously, must remain the property of the State today. This in no way departs from our heritage. Land was never bought. It came to belong to individuals through usage and the passing of time. Even then the chief and the elders had overall control although, as is already pointed out, this was done on behalf of all the people.

On the other hand, Zambia's birth has come at a time when some of our fellow-men founded homes here through a capitalist system or capitalist governments. These have bought some land. It is their way of life. As is clear, we do not necessarily agree with it.

This affects us in two ways. The first is the human side of it and the second is the impact of what might be termed the price tag system of our society.

As regards the first point, we as a Government have promised that this State will not interfere with the property of individuals and we cannot go back on this at all unless, of course, as has been provided in the law of the land, this land property was not being exploited. What we can never agree to here is absentee landlordism.

. . . . . .

It is true to say that once people realized that no one would tamper with their land for years and years to come they would feel that certain. In other words, the incentive to develop to the full would not be there. One feels strongly, however, that land cannot be made and does not grow. From this one hopes the sacredness our ancestors attached to it (that is land) – so much so that they could not think of selling or buying it – will be understood and appreciated. It is, after all, the greatest material gift to man from God. When you come to think of it, it is a source of man's life and its sacredness can only continue to be if all of it is held by the State for the good of all.

......

Agricultural

Government is here again determined to fulfil the Party's promises to the country. The objective is to make the agricultural sector as productive and as profitable as the mining industry – only more permanent. To this extent, it is the intention to carry out the agrarian revolution to the best of our ability by making every village in Zambia and every individual in it productive on the land, as well as in secondary industries based on agriculture.

In this respect there will be again, as in industries, participation by –

A. Government;
B. Co-operatives (various types);
C. Private enterprise;
D. Ordinary village units which may or may not be co-operatively worked.

To give examples:

A. 1. State ranches.
   2. State farms around which might be developed co-operative units which eventually might take over State farms. In some cases State farms are intended to continue with their own production and will also continue to be the pivot of development in those areas by helping new farms and unions of co-operatives around them with some sort of extension services.
   3. State farms used as demonstration centres.

B. 1. Co-operative farms collectively worked.
   2. Co-operative farms individually worked but marketing done co-operatively and where in some cases equipment might be bought and owned jointly.

While dealing with the issue of co-operatives it should be pointed out that in many ways the development of humanism in Zambia will depend on how successful we are in organising people's co-operatives. We must avoid the pitfalls into which others have fallen. We must never allow co-operatives to grow into just another group of exploiters. Co-operators have got to work themselves and not to employ other people.

......

It is a sad legacy that we have inherited and which should be remedied as quickly as possible, that the poorest of the poor, that is the villager, or

107

the peasant, suffers most in terms of cost of living. If it were not for the fact that our people grow their own food we would have been in trouble already. What is required now is to organise ourselves in such a way that Government, through the Zambia National Wholesale Corporation, should help stamp out the sad exploitation of the peasant paying twice as much for what a worker in town gets more cheaply. *This is important.* The trend at the moment is to penalise the poorest of the poor by making them poorer. There is a world wide call in rich nations to help poor nations. A Socialist Government such as ours should within its limited means begin implementing this call at the national level wherever possible.

. . . . . .

PROGRAMME FOR CONSOLIDATION OF HUMANISM IN ZAMBIA

Part One: The Role of the Party

(a) The Party must strive relentlessly to establish in Zambia a true socialist state, based on the principles outlined in the preceding chapters.

(b) The Party must transform Zambia to become progressively a country in which there is equality and respect for human dignity.

(c) The Party must be vigilant about development of capitalist tendencies in Zambia; progressively the Party should work towards the elimination of privileges and inequalities among citizens.

(d) The Party must encourage HARD WORK, SELF-RELIANCE and CO-OPERATIVE EFFORT which form the basis of the Zambian way of life.

(e) The Party must encourage the revival of Zambian arts and crafts, acceptable customs and the development of national culture without thereby entrenching either provincialism or tribalism.

(f) No person, whatever his race, religion or colour can become a member of the Party unless he is prepared to accept the principles of Zambian Humanism.

Part Two: The Role of Party Leaders

(a) All Party leaders, that is all members of the Central Committee, Ministers, Members of Parliament and all officials, must openly declare their support for the principles of Zambian Humanism.

(b) All Party leaders must work actively to promote the accepted principles of Zambian Humanism.

(c) All Party leaders must abandon any practices or privileges which conform to capitalistic principles and not to the declared principles of Zambian Humanism.

Part Three: Land

(a) Land must remain the property of the State.

(b) In future, no person will be allowed to own land in perpetuity or to possess an exclusive interest in the land in perpetuity.

(c) The State may rent land to various users on behalf of the people.

Part Four: Industrial and Agricultural Development

(a) The policy of the Party outlined in Chapter III in relation to Industrial and Agricultural Development in Zambia will continue.

(b) The Party will place greatest emphasis on co-operative effort, especially in respect of agricultural development, although members of co-operative societies formed to promote industrial projects should be increased progressively.

(c) The Party's policy of encouraging private enterprise, within the framework of accepted Government policy, will continue.

(d) The Party will devise targets for industrial and agricultural production in order to provide the much-needed national incentive and to encourage realistic planning.

(e) The Party accepts that a rapid and widespread improvement of living standards of Zambians depends upon *maximum* utilisation of land for agricultural purposes and *hard work*.

Part Five: Co-operation and Development

(a) Success in establishing a true humanist state will depend on co-operation between the Party leaders and leaders of persons in all walks of life in Zambia.

(b) Therefore, there is a need to establish rapidly a college in Zambia where the principles of Zambian Humanism can be studied and understood by all persons concerned with the promotion of development.

(c) The Party should encourage the formation of Village Productivity Councils, wherever possible.

(d) In schools, students should be taught the importance of collective effort in the context of principles of Zambian Humanism.

(e) Wherever possible, school authorities must encourage school children to maintain school gardens.

8: Kaunda: The Mulungushi Declaration

Extracts from K. Kaunda, *Zambia's Economic Revolution: The Mulungushi Declaration* (Government Printer, Lusaka, 1968).
This address by the President to the National Council of UNIP, 19 April 1968, was intended as an economic programme by which Humanism would be implemented.

PART I. INTRODUCTION

Several times before, I have declared in very clear terms that political independence without matching economic independence is meaningless. It is economic independence that brings in its wake social, cultural and scientific progress of man. No doubt political independence is the key, but only the key to the house we must build.

. . . . . .

Now, we in Zambia are becoming known for our fearlessness in exposing our weaknesses and difficulties in human relations, especially politically. The time has now come for us to analyse and expose our weaknesses and difficulties in the field of economic development. Of course, we will do more than just expose our weakness and difficulties.

This National Council, and I hope all others to come, must pay more attention to the country's economic development than has been the case hitherto. We have, I am afraid, tended to see politics first instead of seeing MAN first in everything that we do. We must always remember that we fought and won independence for the sake of MAN, not for the sake of politics.

. . . . . .

All this that I have said is important because if we are going to implement Humanism successfully, then let us remember that we have got to plan to serve the interests of MAN. All our institutions must be geared to serve the interests of the common man. This is an important point and I will repeat it in another way. If we are true humanists then whatever institutions we create must be geared towards fulfilling our commitments to the common man. Basically this means providing adequate food, adequate clothing and adequate shelter for all our people in Zambia and *not* just a few of them.

. . . . . .

Work and Profit Motive

The accumulation of property immediately reminds one of 'there is nothing for nothing'. In other words, to accumulate something we must work. The word 'work' reminds us of the 'profit motive', which is inherent in every human society. The profit motive taken to excess leads us on to the road of capitalism. On the other hand, whatever man does consciously or unconsciously has a strong element of profit motive. This, however, it should be pointed out, could be 'profit motive' in the interest of society as a whole or 'profit motive' in the interest of an individual.

. . . . . .

We cannot declare ourselves in favour of private enterprise, and forbid Zambians from participating in the private sector. It is important to

110

remember, however, that as humanists we cannot allow Zambians to develop into capitalists at all and here is where a serious problem arises. In the final analysis, all this boils down to one major point. Our society through its institutions – its man-made institutions – must fight with all it has at its disposal against the exploitation of man by man in whatever field.

There is yet another field in which we must work hard. And this is generating interest in our people so that they can look at the economic development of the country as the most important cornerstone of nation-building. One must add that once interest is so generated we have also to work hard to keep it there.

Let it be emphasised, however, that the more we interest our people in this particular field the more they will be exposed to dangers I have referred to already – those of becoming a money-centred society. Wealth, like knowledge or any other instrument of service to man we can think of, becomes an instrument of oppression and suppression if we do not handle it properly. Very often we discuss the problem of distributing wealth equally among our people. There are many reasons why this is important. Major among these, however, are that we want each one of our four million people to live a fuller life and, secondly, wealth that is concentrated in the hands of a few people is a danger to any society in that those in whose hands wealth was centred would become exploiters of their fellow men in more than one way and this is no good both for those whom they exploit as well as for themselves.

Any form of exploitation of one man by another is to be fought in Zambia; we hope not only by this generation but also by generations to come. Why do we feel so strongly about this? Before our political independence the combination of political and economic exploitation of so many racial groups by the dominant one made Zambia a very sad country to live in. In this particular field life is no longer so. The people's Parliament has continually been passing revolutionary measures to change this. We will continue to make these efforts as time goes on.

Humanism: Need for Hard Work and Self-reliance

Now, as I have said before, we must open the economic stream to Zambian participation. We have no choice but to swim in this stream so that we can learn by doing. For Zambians, that wealth, like knowledge or any other instrument of service to man, must be acquired before it can be used. In this respect I am emphasising two points: the need for self-reliance and hard work and the need for us to strike an equilibrium so that our society is not destroyed by the upsurge in our people of the instinct to accumulate more and more wealth so that in the end it is done at the expense of the importance of man.

111

We must be careful. The society we are determined to build is one in which, through every individual's maximum contribution to the national whole, we shall provide for each and every one of us, in the shortest possible time, a fuller life. What do we mean by a fuller life and how does this come about? Putting it briefly, this means everyone in society being provided with decent food, decent clothes and decent shelter. These will only come about through the combined efforts of the State on one hand and maximum contribution of each and every individual in any given society to the general whole.

. . . . . .

PART II. AGRICULTURAL SECTOR

Comrades and friends, if we intend to develop Zambia very quickly then we must work very hard at the means of involving all our people in these important economic, social, cultural, scientific and indeed political activities. Without their participation nothing will be achieved. The family tree on which we have got to base our activities to achieve this all-round development of the common man is what we have discussed before.

There is Man the individual; there is Man within the family headed by the head of that family; there is Man within the village headed by the village headman; there is Man within the ward headed by the Ward Councillor; there is Man within the District headed by the Regional Secretary and the District Secretary who are, respectively, Chairman and Secretary of the District Development Committee. Indeed, there is Man within the Province headed by the Minister of State with his Provincial Development Committee; finally, you have Man in the whole country with headquarters in Lusaka.

. . . . . .

If we equate development and progress only with the number of tractors used, with the number of big projects, with a small number of well-looking areas, and with the town only, then we will soon face very big problems: we will not be able to avoid greater unemployment at the end of a year and much more so, at the end of our Four Year Development Plan. Development that is restricted to only a small part of the economic sector, to only a few regions, to only large-scale production, and to only highly capital-intensive techniques is, in my view, no development at all.

These described and often prevailing facts in many countries make it absolutely necessary to follow a different orientation of economic planning. Economic planning must learn to see the virtues of rural development, of small industrialisation; it must realise the potential in utilising human beings where they are and in reaching a self-sustained growth in all the regions and sectors of the economy.

That means that the unutilised potential lying in the unemployed or *under-employed human capital* must be fully grasped and adequate measures and planning methods found to deal with the problem. True development must be orientated to involve people into the development process as much as possible. Let me now come down to earth and discuss Zambia's problems instead of generalising. Zambia's economy, as we all know, is a mixed one, that is, the State, co-operatives and private firms work side by side. We have acknowledged in the past, we do so now, the importance of private capital's participation. It must be emphasised, however, that this co-existence must be a co-ordinated and confident one. It does the country and the economy no good if these agents work against one another as I will point out later.

Agricultural Development: Need to Use Available Resources

We have millions of people living in the rural areas. Give them a chance first to earn a little more than the present subsistence. We have hundreds of thousands of oxen in our villages, which don't cost us money. Let us use them first before we spend millions of Kwacha on more and more tractors. Let us use those things first that we already have before we start crying for more.

The Government is also responsible for providing the required structures to encourage development in our farming sector throughout the country. The whole ... land tenure system must be geared to provide those securities needed to encourage investments to improve the land, required by a modern agriculture. But we must avoid a rigid system, only accompanied by private ownership of the land. I have stated over and over again that the basis of our rural development must start at village level with the approximate 450,000 small family farms in existence. We must provide these thousands of farm units with the means to become an integrated part of our cash economy. It is not our intention to use public funds to create huge, heavily mechanised production units of any sort where a few selected individuals act as shareholders on Government enterprises who, without contributing much in effort, make a good living. If an individual, through hard work and devotion, builds up his small unit to a viable commercial farm, we will be happy to see him emerge, but we will not spend public money to create a few agricultural capitalists. We need commercial farms; we are lucky to have efficient commercial farms, they serve an important purpose in our farming system, but these must rest on the hard work and devotion of the farmers themselves.

......

Need to Involve Women and Youth in Agrarian Revolution

A word on our women's participation in our Agrarian Revolution. Those of us in this country who recall the times of our struggle for our political independence will remember that the attainment of independence might have been delayed without the very active part played by our mothers. If today we want to attain our Agrarian Revolution in record time we must involve our mothers in this field very, very actively indeed. I am glad to say that wherever I have been in the country I have found wonderful response to the call I have made to them; and all I say is, all of us organisers, whether we are politicians or civil servants, must now go flat out to involve our mothers in this very, very important sector of the Zambian economy. I keep reminding you, countrymen, that for the next 50 years or so the majority of our people will simply have to live on the land. We must, therefore, avoid making the errors which other countries, old and young, have made by neglecting their agricultural sector of the economy. I cannot over-emphasise the importance of youth participation in this revolution. Every struggle that is not spearheaded or supported by the youth will not succeed. For one thing, like mothers they are fearless; secondly the future of the country depends very much on how we shape the young ones of today. It is our responsibility, therefore, to show them the way and prepare them to shoulder their responsibilities. I want to repeat this message to all our youth in the country today. Most of you are growing up not knowing what the fight for independence meant, for reading about it in books is not the same as participating in it. A few of you are misled and become scornful of your elders because you have more chances, which have been provided, by the way, for you because of the blood which flowed, because of the sacrifices which these noble sons and daughters of Zambia made so that you should be able to live a fuller life. You will not become leaders simply because you belong to the youth of today. This nation will choose its leaders from among those who are responsible, those who realise, understand and appreciate the importance of man and his position in all things on earth.

. . . . . .

PART III. COMMERCIAL AND INDUSTRIAL SECTOR

Having dealt with the agricultural sector, I will now move on to the commercial and industrial economic activity. Economic activity in this field is dominated by four types of enterprise. These are –

1. State Enterprise;
2. Zambian Private Enterprise;
3. Foreign-controlled Enterprise; and
4. Resident Expatriate Enterprise.

114

First I want to talk about the last mentioned – the Resident Expatriate Enterprise. Economic activity in Zambia is dominated by European and Asian business communities whose members have been residents of this country for many years. Since Independence my Ministers and I have been making repeated appeals to the members of these communities, calling on them to identify themselves with the nation and urging them to Zambianise their businesses as soon as possible. I am very pleased to say that many have responded to our pleas, and have identified themselves with the country by taking up Zambian nationality and by making sincere efforts to train Zambians to skilled and executive positions. There is, however, an appreciably large number of others who have chosen to remain outside the national family. They have kept only one foot in Zambia in order to take advantage of the economic boom created by the Transitional and the First National Development Plans. The other foot they have kept outside Zambia in South Africa, Britain, Europe, India, or wherever they have come from, ready to jump when they have made enough money, or when they think that the country no longer suits them. I am afraid the period of grace is over. These people must now make a final choice. We do not wish to keep them here against their will. We are a proud nation. At the same time it is not fair that we should allow them to make off with the jam and the butter and leave crumbs of dry bread for our people.

Need for Economy to be in Zambian Businessmen's Hands

Comrades, time is now that we must take urgent and vigorous steps to put Zambian business firmly in the hands of the people themselves just as political power is in their hands. This must be done because experience shows that since Independence we have tried to assist the Zambian public with loans as well as know-how in the firm hope that in this way we would establish and build up Zambian entrepreneurship. I regret to report to the nation that this method has been very slow and, I am afraid, it has failed. We can lend very little money to our people and this is mainly for fixed capital development. If they run short of working capital they are unable to obtain credit facilities to see them through. The banks, the insurance companies, the building societies, the hire purchase companies and the other commercial financial institutions have not been very willing to assist the Zambian businessman. So the level of Zambian business has remained low and unless we take firm action now our Zambian businessmen will never catch up with the level of the resident expatriate businessman. These people have access to loan funds from banks, building societies, insurance companies, hire purchase companies, and every financial institution that exists in the country. It is therefore time to take more drastic steps to assist the People's business to bridge the gap that exists between it and the resident expatriate business.

Limiting Local Borrowing by Resident Expatriate Enterprise

As the number one measure, I intend to direct my Minister of Finance to pass an instruction that the local borrowings of expatriate enterprise are to be controlled in the same was as the borrowings of foreign-controlled enterprises are controlled.

Credit Facilities for Zambian Businessmen

Now having done that I hope that the banks, the building societies and the other financial institutions will utilise their excess liquidity to assist Zambian business. I know that so far they have concentrated on helping the people they know and with whom they have dealt for many years. But they must realise that they operate in a free Zambia with Zambian money and they must get to know the Zambian people and the Zambian businessmen in order to be able to assess their ability and credit-worthiness, in the same way as they have learnt to assess expatriate businessmen. After all, let me remind the banks, the building societies, the insurance companies, the hire purchase companies and the other financial institutions once again; they operate in Zambia and they are using Zambian people's money.

. . . . . .

Need for Zambian Enterprise to Develop in Accordance with the Philosophy of Humanism

Humanism recognises the importance of private initiative in the economic development of the Nation. But at the same time, it abhors the exploitation of human beings by other human beings. I shall be watching the development of Zambian enterprise, and at the same time I shall be watching its behaviour — co-operatives, companies, partnerships or individuals alike. If it takes any unfair advantage of the privileged position in which we are putting it; if I see that the prices in Zambian retail shops are higher than those in the expatriate shops; if I hear that Zambian workers are not paid proper wages, if they are not provided with housing; if the contributions to the National Provident Fund and Workmen's Compensation Board are not paid regularly; if I hear that the Zambian businessmen are in any way dishonest with our Tax Department, then the Zambian businessmen will be dealt with very firmly indeed whether they are co-operatives, companies, partnerships, or individuals. I want them to develop so that they can be of service to their fellow human beings. In other words, I do not want them to get rich at the expense of the rest of the nation. Exploitation, whether it is done by people of one racial group against another or done by people of the same racial group against their own kith and kin, is wrong and we will not glorify it here in Zambia by allowing it a place. We are fiercely determined to fight it wherever it shows its ugly head. Even as I say this, Comrades, I know that this is not an easy thing to fight. Let me emphasise that I want Zambian businesses to expand and to prosper. But for goodness sake, I do not propose to create Zambian capitalism here. This is incompatible with my conception of Humanism. I want to see the co-operative spirit develop. I want to see the businesses operating as co-operatives or as companies rather than as individuals. If they operate as companies I want to see that when they have achieved success they will give the opportunity to their fellow Zambians to share their profit.

. . . . . .

Mining Companies

A very special place among the foreign-controlled companies operating in Zambia is held by the mining companies. To these I now wish to turn. I am sure they are wondering what their role is in these economic reforms. I do not wish to go into much detail about the mining companies. But there is one step of the greatest importance the Government intends to take and I shall mention it briefly . . .

Amendment of Exchange Control Regulations

This policy will apply not only to the Mining Companies but to all foreign-controlled companies which operate in Zambia whichever field they operate in − commerce, industry, agriculture, etc. From now on the exchange control regulations will be amended to allow them to remit dividends abroad only when those dividends do not exceed 30% of the equity capital of the companies provided that the 30% does not exceed half of their profits. In other words, if they make profits they can send half of them to their shareholders abroad but if that half means that their shareholders abroad are going to get a 100% dividend then they cannot do so because it means that the company is undercapitalised; it means that they brought too little money from overseas and they have borrowed too much locally and therefore they must be made to re-invest it in order to capitalise their companies properly. I am tired of people who bring one Kwacha from overseas and yet want to take out three in the first year and this I intend to stop by these regulations.

Many of the policy decisions which I have announced can be implemented at once; others will require legislation. I am instructing my Ministers to ensure that the necessary Acts and Regulations are enacted into law as speedily as possible.

Need for Loyalty, Hard Work, Sacrifice and Self-reliance

... Countrymen, let each one of you here understand and appreciate and, indeed, through you all our people in the country, that the measures we take today do not mean fat cheques today, tomorrow or the following year. Whatever we reap from these measures must be put together to enable us to push for economic development. Who among us here does not know that the order of nature is that we have got to cultivate, sow and weed before we harvest? At this point in time, we are just cultivating. Planting will be our next step and then, of course, the inevitable weeding and thereafter harvesting and we hope rejoicing. Between this period of ... cultivating and harvesting will be a number of obstacles. The time will come for tightening of belts, as I have said before. State control is completely meaningless without the basic understanding on our part that this is designed to help us hasten the day when each and every Zambian has plenty to eat, decent clothes to wear and a decent shelter to live in. For, I ask again, what is economic activity about? Is it not about MAN? If we understand the depth of this matter every Zambian must decide now what part he is to play in bringing about this goal.

......

Commending Economic Programme to the Nation

Comrade Vice-President, Comrades National Councillors, Guests and Friends; in the name of the Almighty God, our Creator, He who was not mistaken to provide for us His children so much potential, He who continues to bless this our young country in the face of so many enemies and obstacles within as well as outside the country; indeed in the name of the people He has directed that we should serve for a time; in the name of the brave people who fought and sacrificed all that they had so that we should be independent; in the name of the Zambian posterity whose interest it falls to us to safeguard at this particular point in time, I commend to you all this economic programme.

9: Kaunda: After Mulungushi

Extracts from K. Kaunda, *Towards Complete Independence: After Mulungushi* (Government Printer, Lusaka, 1969).
This address to the National Council of UNIP, 11 August 1969, was essentially a progress report, and a further elaboration of economic policy. The extracts selected here illustrate Kaunda's views on the respective roles of rural cooperatives, organised labour, and the 'leadership code'.

IMPORTANCE AND ROLE OF CO-OPERATIVES

I have told you that rural development is a top priority in our future development projects. Co-operatives will play a key role in this exercise. A co-operative approach is most suited to rural development, both as a way of life and also as an instrument for accelerated development.

......

What must be realised by the Party, Government and every member of a co-operative society is that co-operatives must become an effective means of developing rural areas where the majority of our people live:

They must provide more job opportunities for people in our rapidly expanding towns and cities.

They must be a means of bridging the economic gap between the people on the land and the people in our industrial centres.

They must create better opportunities for rural school leavers to make useful lives for themselves as farmers, mechanics and so forth or in providing services to farmers.

They must assist more school leavers in our towns and cities to become established in the industrial trades rather than to pin all their hopes on the professions or service industries.

They must demonstrate in Zambia that they are the most effective form of economic organisation yet devised to develop human resources on a democratic basis.

Indeed they must become a social, economic and a political force for nation building – for the achievement of the objectives which I set out at the beginning of this speech.

The basis of co-operation is self-help, self-reliance, hard work and faithful participation by members in each and every co-operative society. These are also the essential qualities of good citizenship, whether in the local community or the nation at large. This is why membership in co-operatives provides the best training ground for participatory democracy in which we believe in Zambia regardless of race, ethnic divisions or creed. This, indeed, is what we are working for.

......

Co-operatives, therefore must be self-reliant and self-supporting. Government intends to introduce a new and comprehensive Co-operative Societies Act in the near future as the present Co-operative Societies Ordinance is out of date and does not meet our current and future requirements. The new Act will spell out the services to be provided by the Department of Co-operatives for the organisation and the operation of co-operatives, indicate the preparations that are necessary before a society is

119

registered, describe the different kinds of societies that can be organised to meet the economic and social needs of our people, particularly those in the rural areas. The Act will prescribe the kind of examination and supervision which the Department shall provide to protect the interests of member societies and facilitate the establishment of nationwide Co-operative Federations to provide commercial and other services to their members. This Act will provide a framework within which the people can develop the many and varied kinds of co-operative services they need.

. . . . . .

My Party and Government are determined to work for a classless society and the situation is ideal for our success.

Capitalist economies have been described as creating two nations within one – the bourgeoisie and the proletariat; that is, the property owners on the one hand and on the other, the industrial and farm workers who lack their own means of production and hence sell their labour to live – in simpler language, the rich and the poor.

Here in Zambia we also face the danger of creating two nations within one. But not along the capitalist pattern. The important division in our society is not that which exists between trade union labour on the one hand and managers and property owners on the other, but between the urban and rural areas. These are the two nations we are running the danger of creating; these are the two parts of our dualism; urban and rural and not so much between labour and employers.

Yet our system of industrial relations does not reflect this difference from capitalist societies. We still have unions on one side and employers on the other. Now that the largest single employer is the State, this is, to say the least, absurd. The State controls, even if it does not wholly own, the major means of production in the Nation. The State is, however, not an end in itself; it is the trustee of the people. It holds industrial investments, not for its own good, not merely for the good of those directly employed in the State enterprises, but for the benefit of Zambians everywhere. Thus, for a union to push a claim against the State is to push a claim against the people.

I would like to put some facts before you, Comrades. The average income of Zambians in paid employment in this country is already about K750 per annum. This is probably about eight times the income of the subsistence farmer. The gap between the Zambian in paid employment and his brother in the villages is proportionately greater than between the urban Zambian and the expatriate.

At this point it is clear that labour will have a tremendous role and responsibility in the development of Zambia. In my discussion earlier on the role of co-operatives I made it quite clear that, while the Party and

Government are prepared, and will do all they can, to provide facilities to increase the effectiveness of co-operatives particularly in the implementation of economic reforms, their success is in the final analysis entirely dependent upon the members and their approach to co-operative action and the organisation of their work.

These economic reforms together with those enunciated in April, 1968, are intended to increase the control of Zambian workers and their fellow men in the rural areas on their own economy. Now, there is a clear identity of interests between workers and Government. Comrades, we are all workers. Indeed, some of your own leaders in the Party and Government spear-headed the trade union movement and have not lost interest in the development of an effective trade union movement. I believe they still uphold the principles of united action to secure group interests, particularly so if they are men of principle – I believe they are. However, the fact of the matter is there is now no distinction between employer and employee as is often the case in capitalist economies. Government is the greatest employer and we are all its employees, we are all public servants. Government, in turn is a servant of the Party to which we belong.

. . . . . .

These industries, therefore, are for all Zambians and we in Government and Party are merely managers and only for the time being. Under the circumstances the welfare of the workers in industries for example is not for labour unions alone. It is for the Party and Government as well; it is intertwined with the welfare of all other fellow workers in the country. We all have one common and very fundamental commitment – economic self-determination. We want Zambia to stand on her own feet and not to be a beggar amidst plenty. In a world of inter-dependence we want Zambia to be a contributor, not a perpetual bystander waiting for alms from better-organised nations.

Measures are to be introduced which are intended to assist the workers in their new role:

First

Workers' committees, which are to be formed in accordance with a previous decision, are designed to impart a deeper sense of responsibility among all types of workers in the nation . . .

. . . . . .

Third

Workers in industry, like their counterparts elsewhere, will have to be represented on boards of directors. Therefore, this will enable workers' representatives to know and hopefully to understand the problems and prospects of development in their respective spheres of interest.

Fourth

Having secured the interests of the workers in their various fields, it will be their duty, in turn, to ensure that together the management and the workers' representatives set targets in their productive activity – targets which must aim at beating, if possible, those set out in the nation's development plan.

. . . . . .

I also want to address myself at this stage to the *Leaders in the Party* and Government, indeed to leaders in other walks of life. To all these I say, we have done well so far. Politically, there is no doubt that we have come a very long way towards success. But now the championing of our cause lies in what we can do in the economic field. However, the distribution of manpower now has been dictated very much by history. It is obvious that high-calibre, indigenous manpower is very highly concentrated in the political and administrative fields in Government. This is unhealthy and if we continue we are unlikely to make an impact in the shaping of the economic destiny of Zambia. I am aware that if the Zambian private sector had high-calibre manpower which is indigenous and committed to serve and further the interests of Zambia the economic reforms introduced in April last year would have been much more successful.

I find it imperative to say to you that we must revise the distribution of indigenous high-calibre manpower. It is important for us to spread our resources to the economic field. We need brains to run our State enterprises, to make policies which will make our economy more dynamic, stronger and more productive. We must remember that we are now entering a new state of emergency because we are tackling the most sensitive field of our independence and it requires people who are more committed to action than to talking.

It should not, therefore, be surprising to anybody if a Cabinet Minister, or Minister of State, or senior civil servant or a private businessman is directed to give the much needed leadership in some of the new State enterprises. We need patriotic and committed leadership to make political independence a reality.

. . . . . .

This danger of creating Zambian capitalism was brought more forcibly to my attention by a young man who asked me the following question at a meeting I addressed in London in June, 1968: 'There is a small point which puzzles me about the President's attitude towards Zambian business. It seems to me that you are trying to make use of capitalist skills

122

to develop a non-capitalist society. What is going to happen to those budding little capitalists when their businesses get to the point when you want to absorb them into the State? Are you not going to be left with a lot of capitalists around in a non-capitalist society who might prove to be a disruptive element?'

It was a very perceptive question as it raises fundamental issues about Humanism as an ideology. Humanism is not so much the description of society as it is now, but a description of a society we are striving to achieve. For this reason we must be pragmatic and eclectic in our methods. We make no apologies for the fact that Zambia is prepared to draw on the economic systems of both East and West, and harness them to its purpose. We find that the entrepreneur can, in certain sectors of the economy, be of great benefit to Zambia now. If we insist on controlling everything through the State, we shall . . . restrain our development. We do not have the administrative skills in sufficient quantity to be able to develop and control everything centrally. For example, there is a physical limit to the number of industrial projects that can be supervised. It is for this reason that the State concentrates on large-scale industrial development. In the in-between area of the large projects, in the gaps, the small-scale entrepreneurs can often be the most efficient method of development, the most economical in terms of manpower skills. We have every intention of continuing to learn from disparate economic systems.

However, the question posed to me is even more relevant now than it was then. We have now cleared the way for the development of joint enterprises between Zambians and expatriates. We are actually seeking to encourage small- and medium-scale development through entrepreneurs.

The fundamental clash between capitalists and a non-capitalist society seems more likely than ever. No one is more aware of the problem than I. Once you introduce a man to capitalism, he may acquire a taste for it, a taste for accumulating more and more for himself. He may acquire an individualistic approach. Do we not run the risk of opening Pandora's box by letting out and encouraging this element of free capitalism? Will we not find in, say, ten years' time, that capitalism is so entrenched that we are unable to eradicate it? Or more sinister still, will we not find that we have become tainted, and have lost the desire to eradicate it? It is a risk we are taking, but we must create the means to control capitalism, to make it work for us, not against us.

. . . . . .

LEADERSHIP CODE

I also want today to introduce to you the concept of a Leadership Code. All those who are privileged to own their own business, all those in senior positions in the Party and the labour movement, the Civil Service, the Army, the Air Force, the Police, the Statutory Boards, all our University students, I expect them to set an example to the rest of our people:

I do not want to see lavish consumption;

I do not want to see snobbery and intellectual arrogance;

I do not want to see a weakening of family ties and a repudiation of our poorer relatives;

I do not want to see decisions made for self-interest rather than the benefit of the people;

I do not want to see people using wealth or superior education to manipulate decisions in their favour;

I expect people to work hard and live a simple life;

I expect people to save or re-invest;

I expect people to share with their poorer relatives;

I expect people to accept the obligation to share their enterprise with the State, if it so wishes;

I expect people with shareholdings or business interests, which may compromise the carrying out of their duty, to dispose of them;

I expect people to accept adverse decisions, to wait their turn in the queue, to admit that there are more deserving cases.

Humanism is egalitarian. It believes that certain things in life should not be rationed by money or power. It believes that things like education or health should not go to the highest bidder, but that all people have a moral right to equal opportunities.

. . . . . .

The days when we could blame our difficulties on the colonial past and the expatriate community are rapidly passing by. We can no longer pass the buck – the buck has now stopped here in Zambia.

10: Zambia's Second National Development Plan

Extracts from the four-year plan for January 1972– December 1976. Published by the Ministry of Development Planning and National Guidance (Lusaka, December 1971).

... Our deliberate emphasis, in our Second National Development Plan, is on rural development. The objectives in this programme will be mainly to correct the anomaly of lop-sided development that we inherited from the pre-Independence era. It is also necessary to create incomes for rural people in order to generate a large domestic demand. In order to ensure economic and social justice between the rural and urban populations, a conscious effort will be made to multiply and widen the opportunities for all. For us, developing the rural areas is a matter of life and death, though we do not under-estimate the problems involved.

In the field of education, we plan to concentrate on the production of skills – as against general education. This approach will prepare our young population for skilled and semi-skilled jobs. A considerable percentage of the total allocation for education will be directed into technical and vocational education. In order to create more jobs, more cheaply and quickly, emphasis will be placed on the expansion in rural areas of all possible industrial and agricultural activities. Regarding agriculture, it is necessary to secure self-sufficiency in food crops. As a result, we will attend to both agricultural services and to direct production. We are aware that at least 60 per cent of our population grows its own food. Our strategy to encourage food production throughout the country is geared to meet the demand for self-sufficiency in this area. Indeed, we want to see visible development activity wherever there are Zambians. We are for integrated development.

In addition, private and State production schemes will be encouraged. Government will also concentrate on selected Intensive Development Zones throughout the country. Our agricultural strategy in the Second National Development Plan is, therefore, multi-pronged. The approach through Intensive Development Zones does not mean, therefore, that the rest of the rural area is being neglected. Besides, Intensive Development Zones are not urban areas; they are being selected on the strength of their agricultural and general development potential. We are not talking about urbanisation or industrialisation, but about development.

. . . . . .

As a matter of policy, Ministries will endeavour to implement the rural sections of their development programmes first. For instance, rural housing, rural electrification, rural secondary and primary schools, rural telecommunications, rural roads, rural marketing and credit facilities and rural health services should be implemented as a priority before their urban counterpart programmes. Without pursuing this strategy the rural-urban gap will increase further in the next five years instead of narrowing. If we want to increase social justice both in our economy and in society, the strategy is clearly there, and the politicians and planners must enforce it.

. . . . . .

Finally, the whole Plan is MAN-CENTRED. Citizens of this land, through various development or planning committees at various levels, participated significantly in preparing the Second National Development Plan. It was a typical example of participatory democracy. The Plan calls for self-reliance which is one of the most important principles of our national philosophy of Humanism. I hope that our people will participate fully in the implementation of the Plan, as they did in its formulation.

The Plan is a people's plan. It was designed and formulated by the people for their own development. Government is, in a sense, a mere co-ordinator. The emphasis is on rural development because it is the rural areas that are most in need of development. It is in the rural areas where the majority of our people live. This emphasis should give a fresh impetus to the Government's policy of 'Back to the Land'. We believe in people. Our health, education and social programmes are designed to improve the people's performance. There is no substitution for the people's own participation, motivation and hard work for achieving permanent development.

. . . . . .

7. Starting from the stage of development the Zambian economy has reached and in view of the longer-term needs of economic and social development, the following are the main points of strategy of development in the course of the SNDP period:

(a) The expansion of agricultural production as a top priority with the aim to improve income and nutritional standards of population, cut substantially imports of food, expand economically justified exports and provide industrial inputs.

(b) The increase of agricultural output and efficiency of production in the traditional farming sector as the most direct way of contributing to the solution of employment and income distribution problems between urban and rural areas will be particularly emphasised.

(c) Expansion and diversification of industry and mining to enable substantial import substitution through the conversion of local raw materials and particularly those that can be supplied by domestic agriculture and mining.

The expansion of the manufacturing industry should contribute to the improvement of living conditions of the rural population by providing employment for the labour leaving rural areas, and by increasing demand for agricultural products in terms of both raw materials for the processing industry and food for the growing non-agricultural population.

. . . . . .

126

(f) In social infra-structure, the education programme has been designed to respond effectively to the demand of the people for both primary and continuing education, as well as giving special emphasis to secondary, vocational, technical and professional education in the light of our manpower requirements. Health programmes and services will further expand, with priority given to the improvement and extension of services. In housing, high priority will be given to the construction of low-cost housing units to reduce the present backlog. Community development, through involving the people in their own development and self-help schemes, will strive, in coordination with other Government agencies, at improving the level of living of the general population in rural and urban areas. Services with a youth component and special programmes for young people will receive high priority.

(g) The SDNP will initiate comprehensive regional development, based on the principle of participatory democracy, aimed at the reduction of disparities which exist between the various regions and provinces in the country. This aim will be achieved by channelling more investments, in money, material and skills, to rural areas with growth potentials which have not so far benefited appreciably from past development programmes. The concept of Intensive Development Zones will particularly help the process of rural regeneration.

(h) A new administrative and economic infra-structure will be employed to give a fillip to rural development. An Act of Parliament has been passed requiring the establishment of Village Productivity and Ward Development Committees throughout the Republic. The purpose of these Committees is to improve organisation for economic development at the people's level. Improved organisation will lead to the creation of decision-making centres in the rural areas, and therefore provide further administrative decentralisation . . .

11: Kaunda: The Kabwe Declaration

Extracts from K. Kaunda, *A Nation of Equals* (Lusaka, 1972).
This address to the National Council of UNIP, 1 December 1972, discusses the problems of decentralised administration. [The Report of the National Commission on One Party Participatory Democracy in Zambia (October, 1972) and Government's response to it (November 1972), became available to the Editors too late for inclusion.]

127

I have already re-affirmed our decision against any system of political, economic and social organisation which, by its nature and operation, tends to exploit the people. Hence our choice of Humanism as our national philosophy, and democracy as our system of political organisation . . .

So we must achieve the objectives of our policy of decentralisation of political, economic and social power. It is in pursuance of this policy that, since 1969, the instruments for decentralising the political and administrative machinery have been forged and put to the test. We are satisfied with the decentralised system of Government and Party administration because it helps to guarantee that political and administrative authority will not in future be a monopoly of the centre – Lusaka. The system has further widened the scope of leadership of the political and administrative machinery; it has increased the opportunity at provincial and district levels to make decisions more relevant to the needs of the people while at the same time improving the speed in the process of decision-making and communication.

Our task is to improve this system of decentralised administration. Lusaka's authority must be felt less and less as the provincial, district, ward and village Party and Government committees take on more responsibilities and discharge them with competence, efficiency and effectiveness. The more self-government there is in village, ward and district affairs, the more our nation will succeed in establishing genuinely a 'Government of the people, for the people and by the people.'

. . . . . .

The Party and Government will continue to plan and provide technical and financial assistance where necessary, but let it be understood that the primary responsibility of changing the character of village life, of changing the rural and urban areas, rests with the individual, his family and his institution.

I know the big problems we face in the decentralisation of particularly the economy and administration.

. . . . . .

Second: We have the major task of decentralising the economy in favour of the rural areas. The plight of the overwhelming majority of the people in Zambia's rural areas calls for an urgent and positive programme of action. We have an obligation to fight their cause because it is our cause. We must fight the war against hunger, poverty, ignorance and disease which plague the majority of families who are among the most faithful supporters of the Party and Government; these people will in the final analysis be the most reliable defence for Zambia against dictatorship or external aggression. Our task is to embark on a positive programme of rural reconstruction of a magnitude without parallel.

. . . . . .

Third: In order to combat capitalism and work out practical and constructive programmes for decentralising the economy in favour of the rural areas, we need the right instruments. We need an administrative machinery manned by men and women who understand the shortcomings of our social, economic and political systems and who appreciate the Zambian values and Zambian needs. We cannot succeed if our administrators are cynics, or worship systems which sound good in theory but which have in practice failed to meet the basic needs of human development in other countries. We need serious men and women, well equipped and dedicated to Humanism – to equality and social justice. Regrettably the system of administration which we inherited was more geared to support a foreign capitalist society. Our task is to reshape the administration and give it a new direction based on Zambian values and Zambian needs.

. . . . . .

In the light of the foregoing, District Governors, Party and Government officials must, in future, not merely dwell on generalisations in discussing national problems. They must focus the discussions on the specific problems of village/section life – problems of water, food, housing, roads, markets, schools, bridges and so forth. It is the improvement of these that will create material progress and improve the quality of life of the people. Talk about enemies confronting the nation, but always narrow them down to the immediate and important problems facing the village area. Suggest solutions involving the use of local human and material resources in the first instance. Give the people guidance on, for example, the sources of technical and financial assistance where possible and if necessary.

The objective must be to build the capacity and competence of the people to work out their own future using their own initiative and resources. In this way, they can determine their own destiny. This is the way to help them to become a self-reliant and self-managing community.

C. DOCUMENTS ON KENYA

12: African Socialism in Kenya

Extracts from *African Socialism and its Application to Planning in Kenya*, Kenya Government Sessional Paper No. 10 of 1965 (Nairobi, 1965).

PART I–AFRICAN SOCIALISM

. . . . . .

6. The system adopted in Kenya is African Socialism, but the characteristics of the system and the economic mechanisms it implies have never been spelled out fully in an agreed form.

7. In the phrase "African Socialism", the word "African" is not introduced to describe a continent to which a foreign ideology is to be transplanted. It is meant to convey the African roots of a system that is itself African in its characteristics. African Socialism is a term describing an African political and economic system that is positively African not being imported from any country or being a blueprint of any foreign ideology but capable of incorporating useful and compatible techniques from whatever source. The principal conditions the system must satisfy are –

    (i) it must draw on the best of African traditions
   (ii) it must be adaptable to new and rapidly changing circumstances; and
  (iii) it must not rest for its success on a satellite relationship with any other country or group of countries.

African Traditions

8. There are two African traditions which form an essential basis for African Socialism – political democracy and mutual social responsibility. Political democracy implies that each member of society is equal in his political rights and that no individual or group will be permitted to exert undue influence on the policies of the state. The State, therefore, can never become the tool of special interests, catering to the desires of a minority at the expense of the needs of the majority. The State will represent all of the people and will do so impartially and without prejudice.

9. Political democracy in the African traditional sense provided a genuine hedge against the exercise of disproportionate political power by economic power groups. In African society a man was born politically free and equal and his voice and counsel were heard and respected regardless of the economic wealth he possessed. Even where traditional leaders appeared to have greater wealth and hold disproportionate political influence over their tribal or clan community, there were traditional checks and balances including sanctions against any possible abuse of such power. In fact traditional leaders were regarded as trustees whose influence was circumscribed both in customary law and religion. In the traditional African society, an individual needed only to be a mature member of it to participate fully and equally in political affairs. Political

rights did not derive from or relate to economic wealth or status. When this is translated into our modern state it means that to participate in political matters and party activities as an equal, the individual must prove nothing beyond age and citizenship and need take no oath beyond allegiance to country.

10. Political democracy in the African tradition would not, therefore, countenance a party of the elite, stern tests or discriminatory criteria for party membership, degrees of party membership, or first and second class citizens. In African Socialism every member of society is important and equal; every mature citizen can belong to the party without restriction or discrimination; and the party will entertain and accommodate different points of view. African Socialism rests on full, equal and unfettered democracy. Thus African Socialism differs politically from communism because it ensures every mature citizen equal political rights and from capitalism because it prevents the exercise of disproportionate political influence by economic power groups. Another fundamental force in African traditional life was religion which provided a strict moral code for the community. This will be a prominent feature of African Socialism.

11. Mutual social responsibility is an extension of the African family spirit to the nation as a whole, with the hope that ultimately the same spirit can be extended to ever larger areas. It implies a mutual responsibility by society and its members to do their very best for each other with the full knowledge and understanding that if society prospers its members will share in that prosperity and that society cannot prosper without the full co-operation of its members. The State has an obligation to ensure equal opportunities to all its citizens, eliminate exploitation and discrimination, and provide needed social services such as education, medical care and social security.

12. To ensure success in the endeavours of the Government, all citizens must contribute, to the degree they are able, to the rapid development of the economy and society. Every member of African traditional society had a duty to work. This duty was acknowledged and willingly accepted by members because the mechanism for sharing society's benefits, the reciprocal response of society to the individual's contribution, was definite, automatic and universally recognized. But the response of society was not simply a passive one. African society had the power and duty to impose sanctions on those who refused to contribute their fair share of hard work to the common endeavour.

13. Drawing on this background African Socialism expects the members of the modern State to contribute willingly and without stint to the development of the nation. Society in turn, will reward these efforts and at

the same time will take measures against those who refuse to participate in the nation's efforts to grow. Sending needed capital abroad, allowing land to lie idle and undeveloped, misusing the nation's limited resources, and conspicuous consumption when the nation needs savings are examples of anti-social behaviour that African Socialism will not countenance.

14. While the modern economy is more complex than traditional society, the principle remains that to be successful, society and its members must each acknowledge fully and willingly its responsibility to the other. But the movement towards a modern, monetary economy changes the nature of these responsibilities and the mechanisms by which a member contributes to society and society shares benefits among its members. The people must be continually and carefully informed of what society expects of them and how these efforts will promote the welfare of all.

Adaptability

15. African Socialism must be flexible because the problems it will confront and the incomes and desires of the people will change over time, often quickly and substantially. A rigid, doctrinaire system will have little chance for survival. The system must –

(i) make progress toward ultimate objectives;
(ii) solve more immediate problems with efficiency.

16. No matter how pressing immediate problems may be, progress toward ultimate objectives will be the major consideration. In particular, political equality, social justice and human dignity will not be sacrificed to achieve more material ends more quickly. Nor will these objectives be compromised today in the faint hope that by so doing they can be reinstated more fully in some unknown and far distant future.

17. Given the paramount importance of ultimate objectives, African Socialism must also confront and solve efficiently many immediate problems whose nature will change over time. In Kenya today, the pressing problems include the rapid development of agricultural land; laying a basis for accelerated growth of industry; attracting capital, domestically and from abroad while ensuring that it is used in a socially desirable way; modifying the tax structure in the interests of equity and larger revenues; guarding foreign exchange reserves; providing for a fuller participation by Africans in an expanding economy; relieving unemployment; removing idleness; reconciling pressures for expanding welfare schemes with the need to grow rapidly; and conserving our natural resources of land, water and forests. As some of these problems are solved or alleviated others will rise to take their place and the circumstances in which solutions must be found will also have altered. African Socialism

must be prepared to cope with a vast range of problems, some of which cannot even be visualized in the present. A rigid system, however appropriate to present circumstances, will quickly become obsolete.

18. Indeed, we can learn much from history in this regard – both from the history of thought and from the history of practice. In particular, ideologies and the theoretical systems on which they are based are rigid and uncompromising while the development over time of all viable practical systems has been marked by adaptability to change, frequently of substantial proportions. Marxian socialism and laissez-faire capitalism are both theoretical economic organizations designed to ensure the use of resources for the benefit of society. Both settled on the ownership of property as the critical factor in economic organization and advocated rigid systems based in the one case on State ownership and in the other on private ownership. But ownership is not an absolute, indivisible right subject only to complete control or none. Practical systems have demonstrated that the resources of society are best guided into proper uses by a range of sensitive controls each specifically designed for the task to be performed.

. . . . . .

20. Valid as Marx' description was, it bears little similarity to Kenya today. Under colonialism Kenyans did not have political equality or equal economic opportunities, and their property rights were not always respected. Even so, African traditions have no parallel to the European feudal society, its class distinctions, its unrestricted property rights, and its acceptance of exploitation. The historical setting that inspired Marx has no counterpart in independent Kenya.

. . . . . .

Relationships with Other Countries

23. The third conditioning factor is the need to avoid making development in Kenya dependent on a satellite relationship with any country or group of countries. Such a relationship is abhorrent and a violation of the political and economic independence so close to the hearts of the people. Economic non-alignment does not mean a policy of isolation, any more than political non-alignment implies a refusal to participate in world affairs. On the contrary it means a willingness and a desire –

   (i) to borrow technological knowledge and proven economic methods from any country – without commitment;

  (ii) to seek and accept technical and financial assistance from any source – without strings; and

 (iii) to participate fully in world trade – without political domination.

133

24. The ability of Africa to borrow advanced technological knowledge, modern methods of industrial organization and economic techniques of control and guidance from more advanced countries provides the opportunity to leap over many of the hurdles that have restrained development in these modern societies in the past. It means also that African Socialism as a system can profit from the mistakes of others. Unlike many countries that have eliminated many successful economic mechanisms on narrow ideological grounds, Kenya is free to pick and choose those methods that have been proven in practice and are adaptable to Kenya conditions regardless of the ideologies that others may attach to them. Kenya, therefore, is free to choose among other things –

   (i) a wages and incomes policy that recognizes the need for differential incentives as well as an equitable distribution of income;

  (ii) techniques of production that combine efficiencies of scale with diffused ownership;

 (iii) various forms of ownership – State, co-operative, corporate and individual – that are efficient for different sectors or that compete with each other provided only that the form promotes the objectives of Government; and

 (iv) techniques of control that vary with the needs of society and its members
......

THE OPERATING CHARACTERISTICS OF AFRICAN SOCIALISM

Use of Resources

27. To be consistent with the conditions specified, African Socialism must be politically democratic, socially responsible, adaptable and independent. The system itself is based on the further idea that the nation's productive assets must be used in the interest of society and its members.

28. There is some conflict of opinion with regard to the traditional attitude towards rights to land. Some allege that land was essentially communally or tribally owned; others claim that individual rights were the distinguishing feature; still others suggest that ownership did not really exist in any modern context in many African tribes. Undoubtedly these traditions differed substantially from one tribe to another. In every case, however, and in sharp contrast to the European tradition, ownership was not an absolute indivisible bundle of rights. The ultimate right of disposal outside the tribe was essentially tribal and in this land was tribally owned. It must be remembered, however, that the political arrangements within the tribe were such that every mature member of the tribe would have a say in such a decision. Short of this right, others were assigned or allocated to clans,

families and individuals, including the right to transfer and reclaim property within the clan. Rights to use land were, in effect, assigned in perpetuity to various groups within the tribe, subject always, however, and this is significant, to an understanding of African Socialism, to the condition that resources must be properly used and their benefits appropriately distributed, not merely held idle, abused or misused, or the benefits hoarded. The rights normally associated in Europe with ownership as such scarcely mattered.

29. What does emerge with clarity and force and as a single, unifying principle from these discussions of traditional property rights is that land and other productive assets, no matter who owned or managed them, were expected to be used, and used for the general welfare. No individual family or clan could treat productive assets as private property unless the uses to which those assets were put were regarded as consonant with the general welfare. Unlike the traditional European approach to ownership, no person could treat a piece of land as his own with the freedom to use it or not as he chose. It is worth noting that over the past century, the European tradition of absolute ownership has gradually been eroded so that today the right of the State to guide, plan, and even order the uses to which property will be put is universally recognized and unquestioned.

30. These African traditions cannot be carried over indiscriminately to a modern monetary economy. The need to develop and invest requires credit and a credit economy rests heavily on a system of land titles and their registration. The ownership of land must, therefore, be made more definite and explicit if land consolidation and development are to be fully successful. It does not follow, however, that society will also give up its stake in how resources are used. Indeed, it is a fundamental characteristic of African Socialism that society has a duty to plan, guide and control the uses of all productive resources . . .

. . . . . .

Class Problem

36. The sharp class divisions that once existed in Europe have no place in African Socialism and no parallel in African society. No class problem arose in the traditional African society and none exists today among Africans. The class problem in Africa, therefore, is largely one of prevention, in particular –

  (i) to eliminate the risk of foreign economic domination; and
  (ii) to plan development so as to prevent the emergence of antagonistic classes.

135

In addition, Kenya has the special problem of eliminating classes that have arisen largely on the basis of race. This matter of Africanization in Kenya is reserved for discussion in Part II.

37. The class divisions that Marx deplored in Europe a century ago were supported and strengthened by three factors –

    (i) a concentration of economic power;

    (ii) the treatment of private ownership as an absolute, unrestricted right; and

    (iii) the close relationship between economic power and political influence.

The concept of political equality in Africa rules out in principle the use of economic power as a political base. The vigorous implementation of traditional political democracy in the modern setting will eliminate, therefore, one of the critical factors promoting class divisions. The policy of African Socialism to control by various means how productive resources are used eliminates the second of the factors supporting a class system. Without its two supporting allies, the concentration of economic power cannot be the threat it once was, but African Socialism proposes to restrict and guard against this factor as well with regard to both foreign and domestic concentrations.

. . . . . .

Summary

48. The main features of African Socialism include –

    (i) political democracy;

    (ii) mutual social responsibility;

    (iii) various forms of ownership;

    (iv) a range of controls to ensure that property is used in the mutual interests of society and its members;

    (v) diffusion of ownership to avoid concentration of economic power;

    (vi) progressive taxes to ensure an equitable distribution of wealth and income.

Characteristics (i), (ii), (iii) and (iv) are based directly on African traditions and are emphasized time and again in our Constitution and the KANU Manifesto. Taking political democracy first, our Constitution states that, subject to the rights and freedoms of others and for the public interest, "every person in Kenya is entitled to the fundamental rights and freedoms of the individual whatever his race, tribe, place of origin or residence or other local connexions, political opinions, colour, creed or sex." (Page 32) The KANU Manifesto also states "The KANU Government will steadfastly uphold the rule of law and guarantee the position of every citizen according to the Bill of Rights." (Page 18)

49. In the case of mutual social responsibility generally and in the use of property, the following quotes from the KANU Manifesto show the KANU Government's commitment to preserve this most important African Tradition:

"We aim to build a country where men and women are motivated by a sense of service and not driven by a greedy desire for personal gain". (Page 1) "The traditional respect and care for the aged among our people must continue..." (Page 3) "The first aim of (seven years free education) will be to produce good citizens inspired with a desire to serve their fellow men". (Page 4) "We are confident that the dynamic spirit of hard work and self-reliance which will motivate the Government will inspire the people throughout the land to great and still greater efforts for the betterment of their own communities" (Page 13) Moreover, "every individual has a duty to play his part in building national unity. Your duties are not limited to the political sphere. You must endeavour to support social advance." (Page 19.)

50. With regard to the characteristics of various forms of ownership our Constitution says "no property of any description shall be compulsorily taken possession of, and no interest in or right over property of any description shall be compulsorily acquired", except in strictly defined cases where such action would be necessary "to promote the public benefit" – and in the latter case there is guarantee for "prompt payment of full compensation". (Page 35) The KANU Manifesto also says "citizens will have the right to follow the profession and trade of their choosing and to own property according to the law". (Page 18) "We shall welcome both governmental and private investment in Kenya... we shall (also) encourage investors to participate jointly in projects with our own government" (Page 21) In connexion with land, the Manifesto says "every farmer must be sure of his land rights (and to this end) consolidation and the registration of title will be encouraged wherever people desire." (Page 6)

51. Both the Constitution and the KANU Manifesto also emphasize the fourth characteristic of African Socialism – that there must be controls to ensure that property is used in the mutual interest of the society and its members. The KANU Manifesto clearly states that "we believe in a wide measure of governmental control of the economy in the national interest (and) there are many ways of participation without acquiring public ownership" (Page 22); the KANU Government, while encouraging private investment, will ensure that "the undertaking is being directed according

to our national policy and needs . . . ; while we intend following a liberal policy with regard to foreign capital, investments must be made in accordance with Kenya's interests . . . (and) special consideration will be given to local investors but we shall have no time for those who make large profits and then fail to invest them in the country." (Page 21) In connexion with land, the Manifesto says, "the KANU Government will not tolerate holding of large underdeveloped tracts of land by anyone". (Page 8) . . .

. . . . . .

PART II: POLICY CONSIDERATIONS

142. The following policies are representative of the application of African Socialism to planning in Kenya:-

General

(1) The economic, social and political development of Kenya will be guided by and based on African Socialism as defined in this paper.

(2) Controls on use of resources will be selected and designed to promote the African tradition of mutual social responsibility in Kenya's development.

(3) Our development planning will ensure that the public and co-operative sectors grow rapidly to embrace a large enough section of our economy to establish a socialist basis for future development.

(4) The discipline of planning is recognized by ministries and local authorities as necessary to the efficient and co-ordinated mobilization of resources for development.

(5) Planning will be extended to provinces, districts, and municipalities, so as to ensure that in each administrative unit progress towards development is made.

Nationalization

(6) Nationalization, since it does not always lead to additional resources for the economy as a whole, will be used only where the national security is threatened, higher social benefits can be obtained, or productive resources are seriously and clearly being misused, when other means of control are ineffective and financial resources permit, or where a service is vital to the people and must be provided by the Government as a part of its responsibility to the nation.

Africanization

(7) Foreign enterprises will be informed that the aim of the Government is Africanization of the economy, and they should therefore initiate or

138

accelerate training and apprenticeship programmes so that Africanization can be achieved rapidly in all sectors of the economy (if this policy does not secure the required co-operation, suitable legislation to enforce the policy will be considered).

(8) In promoting Africanization, citizenship guarantees as outlined in our Constitution will be recognized and maintained but without prejudice to correction of existing racial imbalances in various sectors of economy.

(9) In planning Africanization schemes, the overwhelming need for higher rates of growth will be kept in mind; thus Africanization will be pursued within the context of growth and expansion and providing Africans mainly with new assets instead of mere transfers.

(10) A system of traders' licensing will be considered to restrict certain types of trade and business to citizens, with a deliberate bias, in the case of new licences, in favour of African applicants.

Welfare Services

(11) The bulk of Government development expenditure will be channelled into directly productive activities in order to establish a foundation for increased and extended welfare services in the future.

(12) Immediate steps will be taken towards family planning education, because the present high rate of population growth makes extensive and intensive provision of social services more expensive, the unemployment problem more intractable, and saving for development harder than need be – thus lowering the rate of economic growth . . .

. . . . . .

Domestic Saving

(18) Banks, insurance companies and other financial institutions will be subjected to greater control, particularly with respect to investment abroad.

(19) A central bank, whether for Kenya or East Africa, will be established without delay.

(20) Business men in Kenya, many of whom are Asian, who have sizeable amounts of liquid assets will be encouraged to invest their savings either in their own enterprises or by making loans to such development agencies as the Industrial and Commercial Development Corporation, and the Kenya Tourist Development Corporation or to the Government itself.

Tax Structure

(21) The tax structure will be reconstructed progressively with a view to raising the levels of Government revenue, domestic savings, and private

investment in the economy; while also eliminating the outflow of funds through investment in foreign countries, modifying the distribution of income and wealth, and influencing the pattern and methods of production and consumption . . .

Self Help

(25) Self-Help schemes will be planned and controlled to ensure that they are consistent with our national development plan and that the manpower and recurrent cost implications of these schemes are reasonable.

Agriculture and Land Tenure

(26) Emphasis will be given to the development of agriculture in former African areas through land consolidation, registration of titles, development loans, co-operatives, and extension services.

(27) A working party will be established immediately to consider and recommend on forms of land tenure throughout the country.

(28) Land management legislation, including punitive measures against those who mismanage farms, misuse loans, default on loans, refuse to join major co-operative farming schemes where these are necessary, or oppose land consolidation, will be introduced and strictly enforced.

(29) Agricultural land will not be sold to non-citizens unless approved by Government.

(30) The organization and functions of marketing boards will be re-examined with a view to consolidating their activities and modifying their functions to promote the welfare of consumers as well as producers.

(31) Priority will be given to producer co-operatives in making future agricultural development loans.

Education, Training and Experience

(34) Control of education (whether general or vocational) and educational institutions (whether communally or individually owned) will be vigorously enforced in order to ensure uniform standards and to relate educational development to the needs and resources of the country . . .

Trade Unions and Employment

(51) Government will assist trade unions to become involved in economic activities such as co-operatives, housing schemes, training schemes, works' discipline and productivity, and in general, to accept their social responsibilities.

(52) In order to avoid abuses of union power, legislation will be introduced providing for compulsory arbitration of major issues not resolved through the regular bargaining process, together with any other

measures that may be needed to prevent strikes.

(53) In the interest of economic stability and good industrial relations, one central organization for all trade unions, and another for all employers, will be established . . .

13: Kenyatta: The One-Party State

(a) Extract from a speech by Jomo Kenyatta to a KANU conference in March 1966. Published in J. Kenyatta, *Suffering Without Bitterness* (East Africa Publishing House, 1968).
(b) Extract from speech by J. Kenyatta, 13 August 1964. From J. Kenyatta, *Suffering Without Bitterness* (East Africa Publishing House, 1968).
Kenya has been a *de facto* one-party state since 10 November 1964, with the voluntary dissolution of the official opposition party, the Kenya African Democratic Union led by Ronald Ngala. The resignation of Vice-President Oginga Odinga on 14 April 1966 and his formation of a new party, the Kenya People's Union, restored a parliamentary opposition; but the KPU was banned in 1969.

(a) In multi-party states the machinery of political parties is largely concerned with defeating opponents at the polls. To this end they are organized throughout the country to keep the headquarters informed of the pulse of the electorate, and to advise what policies and personalities are likely to win votes from the opponents. Between elections there tends to be a lull in party activities throughout the country.

In a one-party state it is necessary to find a completely different role for the party and its machinery. Such a role has not been clearly defined yet for the party since the *de facto* emergence of a one-party state in Kenya. Possibly partly for this reason the party machinery both at the centre and at the branch level has been weakened, discipline from the centre is poor and the mutual exchange of information on policies and reactions between the centre and the branches is inadequate.

The situation has led to much confusion and frustration which if allowed to continue could seriously damage the image of the party and the government in the country. In seeking a role for themselves, for example, elected politicians have pressed to take over the executive control of civil servants in districts. Because of the absence of a forum within the party there have been embarrassing attacks in Parliament on individual Ministers, and on government policies.

The situation is likely to continue until:

(a) the party organization is strengthened at the centre and in the branches by the appointment of full-time officials chosen as much for their organizing ability and administrative competence as for their political strength and reliability; and

(b) the role of the party in the national endeavour is clearly defined in a new constitution, and efficient administrative machinery is established for its operation.

I make these points because I believe that the unsatisfactory relationship which is in danger of developing between the party and the various organs of the Government is due largely to the failure to define the role of the party in the emergence of a one-party state. This state of affairs is avoidable and is not due to inherent flaws in the Constitution of the Republic.

It is not my function to suggest what the Constitution of KANU should be, but since good relations between KANU and the Government depend on an efficient party organization which speaks with one voice throughout the country, I venture to make the following tentative suggestions for administrative reorganization:

(a) The Central Executive should be established and served by full-time officials of high calibre who are given status and pay commensurate with their qualifications and experience and comparable with what they would enjoy in government or commercial employment.

(b) Serious consideration should be given to making branch secretaries full-time employees appointed and paid from headquarters. This might contribute towards getting Central Executive control of the district units of the party. It would also enable civil servants in the districts to be sure of whom to liaise and co-operate with without getting involved in factional wrangles and disputes.

. . . . . .

KANU AND LOCAL GOVERNMENT

A decision has recently been taken to appoint a commission of inquiry into the local government system and opportunity may be taken to prepare ways and means of linking the party machinery with local government machinery. It is at that level that much co-operation can be achieved to the interest of national development.

. . . . . .

KANU AND THE CABINET

There needs to be a clear distinction between the executive and decision-making functions of the Cabinet and the Ministers and the role of the Central Executive as a political body formulating the broad framework of policy objectives within which the government might work. If the executive is strengthened by appointment of competent full-time staff, these people could carry out basic research and investigation necessary for them to prepare memoranda on broad political policy for the Central Executive to consider. In this way the party might be able to pronounce on such issues of policy.

KANU AND PARLIAMENT

In the absence of a well-organized party machinery which is able to inspire and influence the government, the KANU Parliamentary Group has assumed the role of the party watching on the government. A well-organized party should clearly have the role of dealing with matters of general political policy and Members of Parliament themselves should be guided by the general framework of policy laid down by the party which should be in a position to discipline a Member of Parliament who consistently refuses to toe the party line. The Parliamentary Group would then concern itself exclusively with parliamentary business and the welfare of Members.

KANU AND THE CIVIL SERVANTS

There has been some argument that civil servants should be allowed and encouraged to become active members of KANU. The argument is based on the quite tenable ground that in a one-party state the intellectual expertise of civil servants should properly be made available to help in the formulation of party principles and policies and that closer links between the civil service and the party would bring closer understanding of each other and a greater commitment on the part of the civil service to the achievement of the party programmes. But there are dangers in this path which should not be ignored. The government requires the civil service to develop the high degree of professionalism which is necessary to cope with the complexity of modern government. If civil servants were to become active members of the party, there is a danger that in the division of interest between politics and professionalism the efficiency of the service would suffer. It would be only too easy for the situation to develop where civil servants are promoted and appointed on the ground of political zeal rather than professional competence. This would lead to a rapid run-down of the morale and competence of the civil service.

There is also the embarrassment that could easily arise if a civil servant used his official knowledge in the councils of the party to attack or discomfit a Minister. If Ministers are to be able to discharge their responsibilities effectively, it is essential that the processes by which they reach their decisions should remain confidential even from the party. If it were to be otherwise, the party might give the appearance of taking over the functions of the government.

Lastly, it should be noted that there is a one-party state in Kenya by agreement only. There is nothing in the law of the land to prevent new parties being formed. Should this happen, the need for party neutrality of civil servants would become obvious. But consultations at the level of officials of the party and government should be developed.

(b) Be it as it may, my Government is pledged to uphold the four traditional freedoms: the freedom of association, speech, and assembly, and to respect the rule of law and human dignity. In case of genuine complaints citizens have recourse to independent courts of law. In addition, as provided in the Constitution, machinery already exists for a change of government through free elections when the time comes.

One question which is usually posed about one-party States is that they do not offer a conclusive explanation about means of controlling political power. But to assume that the intrinsic desire for power will be eradicated one day is to show a very mistaken view of human nature. The desire and competition for power after power is a healthy thing, as long as there are effective machineries to restrain dictatorial tendencies.

It was never possible – and it will never be – for the human race to exist in a vacuum. In fact, progress in all walks of human life has come about as a result of the conflict of ideas.

It is my considered opinion that the greatest innovation in the political institutions of the world is not the one-party State or the authoritarian regimes. Dictatorships are as old as the hills.

The fascinating innovation in our time is the mass party and the mass party is to be found in both one-party and two-party States. It is the nature of the organisation of mass political parties – which is outside the scope of this paper – that is the real threat to the rule of law and democracy. Consequently, there are two-party States which are tyrannical and dictatorial and one-party States which can be said to be democratic and liberal. In other words, all two-party States are not necessarily democratic and all one-party States are not necessarily authoritarian.

Secondly, those who talk about democracy and individual freedoms must think critically about the position of democracy in the light of scientific and technological advancement – in particular in the light of the advent of mass media in communication and propaganda.

At this stage, however, we have no choice to make. Through the historical process which has taken place since the last century we find ourselves with myriad relevant grounds and conditions for a one-party State. It is inevitable. In our particular situation, practice will have to precede theory. Should relevant grounds for a multi-party State evolve in the future, it is not the intention of my Government to block such a trend through prohibitive legislation.

14: Opposition in Kenya: The Kenya People's Union

Extracts from the Manifesto of the Kenya People's Union (Nairobi, 1966). Reproduced in C. Gertzel (ed.), *Government and Politics in Kenya* (East Africa Publishing House, 1970).

The KPU was formed in 1966 by Oginga Odinga, and constituted a small parliamentary opposition until 1969. In that year, there were riots in Odinga's constituency during a visit by Kenyatta, and eleven people were killed by the police. Odinga was imprisoned (until 1971), and the KPU was banned. Although the KPU drew support from Luo tribal sources, it also represented a more radical strand in Kenyan political attitudes.

The KPU condemns the infringement of Constitutional Rights by the present Government. It will struggle relentlessly to preserve guarantees of individual freedom and the right of political freedom contained in the constitution. The people of Kenya must beware of the gradual attribution of their freedoms and the establishment of a dictatorship. The KPU stands for the Defence of the Constitution.

SOCIALISM

In the mouths of the Government and KANU leaders, "African Socialism" has become a meaningless phrase. What they call African socialism is neither African nor socialism. It is a cloak for the practice of total capitalism. To describe the policies of the present Government as "African Socialism" is an insult to the intelligence of people. The deception is obvious but the leaders of the Government and of KANU do not have the courage to admit that they are fully committed to the Western ideology of capitalism.

The KPU condemns the Government's and KANU capitalist policies:

145

it is opposed to the creation of a small class of rich people while the masses live in poverty. It will pursue truly socialist policies to benefit the *wananchi* [the people, the common man]. It will share out the nation's wealth equitably among the people, extend national control over the means of production and break the foreigners' grip on the economy.

LAND

This has always been and remains one of the most crucial issues in the minds of the *wananchi*. Our people struggled bitterly against colonialism, not merely because it was foreign rule but also because it went beyond that to seize the *wananchi's* very source of livelihood. Land has always been at the very heart of our struggle. Until the land problem is solved, *uhuru* has no meaning. To millions of people, the end of colonialism meant the return of the stolen lands. They have so far waited without satisfaction.

The Government and KANU have betrayed the *wananchi's* expectations. This repudiation of earlier problems over land is the most serious of the string of broken promises since the end of colonial rule. Tens of thousands of starving and landless people are now tasting with bitter irony the "African socialism". In its paper on African socialism and also in the recently published development plan, the Government has clearly stated the abandonment of settlement schemes on the grounds that all the settlement already achieved is "sufficient". But what is the extent of this "sufficiency"? We are told that nearly 35,000 families are now settled on the one million acres of land formerly held by Europeans. The *wananchi* do not agree that this is "sufficient". Having abandoned further settlement on large scale, the Government is abandoning the tens of thousands of landless who have no jobs to go to. The *wananchi* will not tolerate this callousness.

. . . . . .

A radical change in land policy is obviously necessary. The *wananchi* shed their blood to secure it. They will not tolerate the present position. The KPU is fully committed to secure this change, to correct the highly unjust and inequitable present distribution of land. It recognises that the issue is a complex one but it cannot be evaded. The KPU's land programme includes the following measures.

1. Distribution of free land to the needies, including squatters and those who lost their lands in the struggle for independence, either by expropriation or through land consolidation. The KPU recognises that consolidation in areas affected is now an accomplished fact and it would be undesirable to disturb it.

Those who are now owners of consolidated land will be left in undisturbed possession. Compensation will, therefore, take the form of land acquired from European settlers.

2. Settlers who are not citizens cannot be allowed to continue in ownership of vast areas of high potential land. The KPU will take measures to restrict ownership of such land to Kenya citizens.

3. Co-operative farming on land taken over from European settlers will be preferred and encouraged, in line with the socialist policy of the KPU.

4. The KPU will fight for a reduction in the size of farms held by individuals. It believes that this is an absolutely necessary measure. In this way, more land will be made available to the *wananchi*. We do not want a new class of big landlords.

5. Once all farms are reduced to a size consistent with democracy and socialism, all individual owners will be given maximum assistance to develop their holdings.

6. Land consolidation will be promoted but only in a democratic manner according to the wishes of the people. In particular, care will be taken to ensure that individuals do not grasp too much for themselves to the detriment of the rest of the population in these areas. KPU will honour rights of tribes and clans to their land.

. . . . . .

NATIONALIZATION

KPU is committed to enlargement of the public sector of the economy, believing that in so doing, KPU government will be in a position to bring about more rapid economic development and a more equitable distribution of the fruits of the people's labour. This means that the KPU government will have to acquire control of the means by which this can best be brought about. Thus those industries, like the public utilities, whose existence are vital for national economic independence should be nationalized. Where nationalization may not be used, KPU will accept a joint-venture between the government and private entrepreneurs on the understanding that the nation's interest should be paramount. The industries will also serve as a basis for further industrialization and domestic accumulation so vital for economic development. KPU will, however, encourage and provide ever possible assistance to small producers and entrepreneurs, and protect them from exploitation by the big monopolies.

147

(a) KPU is committed to the expansion of the public sector and as such to public ownership of the means of production, distribution and exchange.

(b) Where the interest of the country demands nationalization such as in public utilities, KPU will not hesitate to do so.

(c) In this regard, KPU will endeavour to benefit from the experience of other welfare states such as Britain and the socialist countries.

EMPLOYMENT

Thousands of unemployed people are roaming the streets in search of jobs. What has the Government done to relieve unemployment? The country is supposed to be making "great economic advances". But why are there not enough jobs if the economy is really developing? Is it possible that the dramatic advances made in the amassing of wealth by some members of the Government lead them to think that everybody else is doing equally well? It is not enough to flaunt the "achievements" made to relieve unemployment under the Tripartite Agreement. The Government itself admits that there are fewer people in jobs today than there were in 1960, six years ago. This means that thousands of school-leavers since 1960 are unemployed.

The drastic measures necessary to eliminate unemployment are not being undertaken by the Government. In the towns new industries are not being developed fast enough to employ more people. In the farming areas, because of the Government's land policy, there is not enough land to settle people. It is naïve and foolish to urge people to go "back to the land" when there is no land to go back to. The slogan can be implemented only by the Members of the Government and rich leaders of KANU who advocate it – they have acquired huge farms for themselves.

The KPU believes that there is a close link between unemployment and the land question. The only immediate solution to the problem is more land for the unemployed who are often also the landless. This must be supplemented with the rapid development of industries in the towns, to create more jobs. The KPU will endeavour to relieve the plight of the unemployed.

15: Tom Mboya

Extracts from T. J. Mboya, *The Challenge of Nationhood* (André Deutsch, 1970). These words were written in March 1969, a few months before Mboya was assassinated.

There are so many fields in which the principles of speculative theory have been modified by harsh experience. It was quite understandable that at independence we should start with a brave rush to create our own political, social and economic institutions and attitudes. Our desire was laudable; the difficulties we have experienced mean that we must adjust our tactics of change. Certainly there is no point in change for its own sake. Only if some special institution has meaning for our people or has utility within our special circumstances is it justified.

Look at the political institutions. In most cases we started off with those bequeathed to us by the former colonial powers. This is the system we have been used to working within. We may introduce certain superficial innovations but the principles and so much of the machinery remain the same. It is difficult to break away entirely, to steer a new course, to create institutions which are African yet which are appropriate for modern society. Ease of communication is drawing the people of the world closer together. While we have every right to safeguard our identity it would be foolish and indeed against our own interest to keep ourselves apart just to be different.

There are facts which we have to bear in mind while properly seeking *African* ways. We must not reject the experience of others while devising means of incorporating traditional African attitudes of mutual social responsibility and grassroots democracy in our modern institutions.

Around the time of independence there was much talk of Africa's need for one-party states – not that the idea is exclusively African. Recent events have shown that one-party systems are not necessarily as strong as or as efficacious as some people thought. They are not a protection for the masses against tyranny, nor do they provide a sure protection for any group to maintain its entrenched position in the face of popular dissatisfaction and revolution. At the time of independence few people talked about the role of the armed forces. Yet it is probably true to say that the army has been more significant in post-independence politics in Africa than any other group or institution . . . Various answers have been found to the problems posed by the existence of armed forces. Some countries have deliberately divided their forces, carefully separating the army, the police, armed youth brigades and other services. Some countries bring military leaders into partnership in the political hierarchy. Others think the best way is to integrate the whole of the armed services into the political fabric of the state by making all of them members of the ruling party. Thus there is a search for an arrangement in this new power structure. It is too early to say if these various experiments will succeed. Tensions between social, economic and other interest groups exist in any state. Certainly by bringing all groups into the party you have a framework within which to resolve potential conflicts. But it could be argued too that if the party and the government are one and the same thing you have not solved the problem, merely shifted it. For the time being, however, the important thing is that the problem has been recognised and efforts to find a solution are being made and must continue to be made.

. . . . . .

Where the party is weak the danger arises that the leadership will become increasingly isolated from the people. Instead of the two-way communication channel which a well organised party provides, governments may come to rely increasingly on officials, administrators and even secret police for their knowledge of their own citizens.

A feeling of 'them' versus 'us' arises among the people and the government falls – by democratic means if relatively free elections take place, otherwise by some more violent process.

. . . . . .

So far no African state has satisfactorily solved the question of local authorities. Obviously there is no universal ideal for the correct division of powers and functions between central and local government. In Africa the tendency has generally been towards a consolidation of power at the centre. In some cases this has been done peacefully and without bloodshed. In other cases secessionist movements have asserted themselves, normally on the basis of allegations of ethnic domination, as in tne Sudan and Nigeria. Provided that the state is not too large the more centralised systems seem to be most appropriate, in view of our scarce resources of human skills and the relatively clear-cut needs in social services and similar fields where local government normally operates. The efforts to find a solution to this problem have often been made difficult by the search for national stability through national unity after independence. The people recognise national leadership and do not often even appreciate the functions of the local authorities. They expect the national leaders to be responsible for all matters affecting their welfare. Any attempt by the new central government to lay blame on local governments for failure to provide services is regarded as a political manoeuvre to avoid responsibility. Where a multi-party situation exists opposition parties can use local authorities to fight the party in power. But perhaps the most crucial question is still how to create local authorities that can respond positively to the urgent task of development.

Another crisis to which various solutions have been proposed is that of the position of civil servants. Some countries have brought civil servants right into politics, making many appointments subject to political control and bringing politically appointed officials into parliament itself. Others have opted for a civil service insulated from politics, although even here it should be pointed out that officials such as those in the administration and information services have clear political functions and commitments. The difficulty is that while the government wishes to use civil servants for political purposes it fears that if they become too active they may usurp its own functions. The problem is rendered more acute because the civil service has attracted most of the best educated people in the nation to its ranks. The administrators are generally better educated and have a broader view of the world than local leaders and councillors, or for that matter than most members of parliament.

This is in fact one of the arguments used by those countries who have chosen to draw civil servants into politics and to allow them active political roles. This in turn leads to a problem which is indeed fundamental to the concept of mobilising a one-party state: it assumes that everyone in the country will agree with at least the basic policies of the government and ruling party. Even where a national consensus exists on ideological matters such a system does not necessarily provide for the working out of genuine conflicts between different interests; between producers and consumers, between wage-earners and peasants; between urban and different regions of the country; between those who have adequate land and those who do not; between those who own or control property and those who do not.

The two-party system and even the multi-party system do not provide completely adequate solutions to these conflicts but they do provide a framework within which interests can project their needs. Yet the single-party state can also provide a unified scheme within which differences can be accommodated, especially during times of crisis. What really matters is whether the political system established allows and facilitates effective discussion of various views before final policy is formulated. Without such a practical possibility suppressed pressures eventually and inevitably lead to revolution.

In any state a balance must be struck between individual liberty and coercion; the choices are often much more difficult for a developing country . . .

It is all very well in theory to say that our state of under-development and the existence of a national consensus justify more authoritarian measures. But a government does not operate according to theories. Practical decisions have to be taken every day of the week. A busy minister or official has to take snap decisions on issues where liberty, freedom and individual rights are at stake. Politically speaking it can be argued that we are in such a state of crisis that authoritarian rule is justified. It is said that opposition is a luxury we cannot afford, since it will divert us from the progress whose general direction is widely agreed within the nation.

Yet the danger is that where opposition is given no institutional framework it may find expression in unconstitutional forms . . .

. . . But perhaps the most crucial factor during this period is the role and personality of the men at the top – those who head the governments of the new states. In most cases the head of the government is also the head of the party in power. He is also regarded as the political philosopher for the new nation. It is also true to say that most African states are still under the first generation leadership, i.e. the leadership of the same persons who led these countries during the struggle for independence into freedom . . . It is also true that their personality can be a force for stability and progress even though no practical party organisation or development of new institutions may be taking place at the same time. In such a case the second generation leadership would inherit a framework that is so dependent on personality that it cannot survive the person on whom it depended. This could bring with it a phase of deep political problems – tribalism, personality cult, foreign intervention and even military coups . . .

Perhaps the greatest crisis facing Africa today is the economic one. We face a situation in which millions are undernourished, uneducated, living narrow lives in poor conditions. This alone would be bad enough. What makes it all the more critical is that these same people, our citizens, had high hopes that independence will change everything.

. . . . . .

Agonising choices must be made. However impartially a government may seek to make the choices its motives will be suspected. Under such conditions it is all too easy for a government to become defensive and to fall back upon catch-phrases. Worse still, the government, especially if it is a weak one, could try to respond to the demands of various groups in an uncoordinated fashion. This leads to mismanagement of the economy.

Slogans can be a useful way of explaining policies. But sometimes they are used instead of policies, and then – sooner or later – the leaders are in serious trouble with the people who feel they have been misled or cheated. For example you can tell the ordinary man he must develop through self-reliance; that he must pull himself up by his own bootstraps. This isn't much good for the man who doesn't even have any boots! It's really no good telling the peasant scratching away at the soil to be self-reliant. He's been self-reliant since he was born – that's why he's still scratching away . . . If the slogan is to mean anything that peasant must be *helped* to become self-reliant.

All the same discussion about self-reliance and self-help does serve a useful purpose in reminding us that with independence our fate and future must now be in our own hands. We cannot depend entirely upon external

152

sources of capital, technical assistance, training or whatever it might be. In the final analysis everything which we receive from outside should supplement and facilitate our own efforts. If this is to be the case then it is apparent that agricultural developments must be the basis of our development, for it is here that our under-used human resources can be utilised. We must make sure that our people do not think that development means merely one or two big factories. Nor should they be left with the idea that development is entirely the responsibility of the government. The people's role in development needs to be emphasised at every stage. There are psychological and sociological aspects of development which need further study if we are fully to make use of the vast human potential of our countries. Self-help and self-reliance are noble ideas yet paradoxically guidance and planning are just as necessary here as anywhere else if they are to be effective. Indeed, lack of direction from above may lead to wasted effort and quickly to disenchantment. With leadership self-help is a means of rallying the people and creating enthusiasm to face the challenges of development. Without effective leadership the concepts themselves will be discredited – to our future embarrassment.

16: The Kenyan Bureaucracy

Extracts from the Ndegwa Report, titled *The Kenya Republic: Report of the Commission of Inquiry (Public Service Structure and Remuneration Commission), 1970–1* (Government Printer, Nairobi, May 1971).

THE CHALLENGE OF THE 1970's

5. The complexity of modern society and the extent of government involvement in "managing prosperity" have destroyed the old conception of the Civil Service as essentially a transmitter of impulses received from the Cabinet. Nowadays the Service is also expected to be skilled in the management of a complicated government machine, working at high pressure in a rapidly-changing environment; and also a creative force constantly reappraising the problems confronting society, and enabling it to solve them by designing new solutions. The political parties and other organizations continue to play their part in developing policy, but problem-identification and problem-solving under conditions of rapid change have in our view become critical functions of a modern Civil Service, making the difference sometimes between a country's success or

failure in preserving its prosperity and values and even the substance of its independence. In Kenya, the old conventional view is even less appropriate. There is one overwhelmingly dominant political party which, experience has shown, does not itself formulate new policies; other organizations which could contribute to policy-formulation are relatively few and weak; and the dependence of the economy on government activity for ensuring rapid growth is even more marked than in industrialized societies. We therefore consider it to be not only inevitable but essential that the Civil Service should be called upon to assume even greater responsibility for managing the economy, and for identifying and solving national problems.

6. We realize however, there is more to it than that. In an industrialized society the task of the Service is still ultimately adaptive. That is to say, it has to enable the country to respond effectively to changes that are occurring at an ever-increasing rate as a result of technological innovation and associated social changes. In doing this, it also tries to mould the future and achieve definite goals, but on the whole the rate of change, the dynamic element in society, is provided by forces within the private sector, at least to a very large extent. Government may deliberately foster or channel change, but it can usually rely on dynamic responses from industry, from local authorities, from merchants, from investors, and so on, who command both expertise and capital resources for exploiting new opportunities. In a developing country like Kenya the problem is often very different. It is often to induce people to want to do new things, and nearly always to discover the minimum "mix" of resources that must be supplied by government to make it possible for them to do new things once they want to. In other words, the dynamic element must very often spring from the government – i.e. from the Civil Service. A good Civil Service in a developing country must, therefore, have the capacity to identify and solve specific kinds of problems – problems of inducing and sustaining social and economic change in addition to the already formidable task of efficient management of the services for which it is now responsible. This means that it must be highly change-oriented; it must reward initiative and experimentation; it must have a high concern for cost-effectiveness and a routine habit of evaluating all ongoing programmes; it must be prepared to compromise between unified central control and the need for flexibility, variety and a degree of autonomy in field organizations charged with implementing policy; it must be extremely strong on action, time-sequences, logistics, and clearly defined goals; and at the same time it must retain a clear consciousness of its role as the servant, not the master, of the public, if its efforts to induce change are not to be self-defeating. This implies that at all costs it must ensure a

154

powerful upward flow of information and frank critical analysis from its staff in the field. We recognize that these ideals are not easy to interpret or implement, but we must stress that they clearly distinguish a "development administration" from both the old-fashioned concept of administration as the passive executor of party policies, and also the more modern concept of a managerial and problem-solving administration in an industrial state.

. . . . . .

27. During our inquiries we have found that the political basis has given rise to some degree of misunderstanding. We think it necessary to clarify this as well as we can, bearing in mind that in political, as distinct from legal matters, an element of discretion and an area of judgment cannot be dispensed with. We deal first of all with the relation between Civil Servants and political Ministers. Ministers are appointed by the President to advise him in the Government of Kenya; they are also collectively responsible to the National Assembly for acts done under the authority of the President, Vice-President or Ministers. The President may also make them responsible for the administration of particular government departments. It follows from this that the Civil Servants in Ministries take their instructions from their Ministers, who bear the President's authority. A Minister may not, of course, instruct a Civil Servant to do anything unconstitutional or illegal. Furthermore there are important areas of administration, not involving policy, which are expressly assigned by law or by internal regulation to Civil Servants. For instance the Exchequer and Audit Act makes the Accounting Officer of each Ministry personally responsible for authorizing all expenditures, and all matters relating to the personal careers of individual officers are expressly entrusted to Permanent Secretaries and their equivalents, not to Ministers. But subject to these qualifications, Civil Servants are there to carry out the instructions of the Government.

28. A more problematic area concerns the relations between Civil Servants and the political parties. At one time Civil Servants were permitted to join political parties but this was later found to be contrary to the interests of the public in that it was capable of leading to discriminatory treatment of members of the public on party lines in matters where Civil Servants should use their discretion with complete impartiality. In our view the rule that Civil Servants should not be members of any political party must be maintained in any country which does not have a *de jure* one-party system. This does not mean that Civil Servants may be indifferent to party policies in performing their duties. They have a duty, on the contrary, to promote actively and publicly the policies of the constitutionally elected President and his government,

which is a party government. In matters where they have discretion and where legitimate party interests are involved they must give precedence to those of the party in office. What counts as a "legitimate" interest is not always easy to define. Some areas of administrative discretion have been the subject of Presidential rulings. In others Civil Servants must be guided by the spirit of such rulings and their ultimate sense of responsibility for the welfare of the public. The support which the Civil Servant is thus expected to give to the party in power is subject to two main provisos. One is that this support must not include administering the provisions of the law in such a way as to discriminate between members of the public on the basis of their party affiliations. The other is that they owe their support to the central leadership of the party, and above all to its President, who is also the President of the Republic; where the Civil Servant is in doubt about the validity of the claim made on his support by any other party leader, he is responsible for exercising his own judgment on the matter.

Private Interests

29. We must at this point deal with a matter on which we feel bound to comment. It concerns the integrity with which the public services as a whole and the individuals comprised within them carry out their duties. The nation is entitled to expect that these duties should be discharged efficiently, honestly and fairly as between one citizen or groups of citizens and another. It is essential if confidence in the Government is to remain unimpaired and if its good name is to be preserved that this should be so. We consider it self-evident that public servants must therefore use the power which is vested in them and the information which comes into their possession with scrupulous care and in such a way that they further and safeguard the interests of the community as a whole. In other fields self-help has become a beneficial national characteristic; we consider that in the present context self-discipline has an equally important role.

. . . . . .

31. With the above considerations in mind we suggest there are certain general principles which should be observed in the conduct of Government business of all types and with which Ministers, Members of Parliament and all public servants would wish to associate themselves. We consider that all those who serve the Republic –

    (i) should give it their undivided loyalty wherever and whenever it has a claim on their services;

    (ii) should not subordinate their duties to their private interests nor put themselves in a position where there is conflict between their duty to the State and their private interests;

    (iii) should not outside their official duties be associated with any financial or other activities in circumstances where there could be suspicion that their official position or official information available to them was being turned to their private gain or that of their associates;

(iv) should not engage in any occupation or business which might prejudice their status as members of a public service or bring any such service into disrepute; and finally

(v) should at all times maintain the professional and ethical standards which the nation expects of them in transacting Government business with efficiency, integrity and impartiality.

. . . . . .

38. Furthermore there is a need to give new content to the ideal of nation-building which provided the most general impetus for the Civil Service immediately after independence. This is, of course, a problem of motivation and as such is easier to formulate than to solve. The immediate needs of the nation in 1964 were so pressing and so apparent that Civil Servants generally, and especially senior officials, did not need a very detailed exposition of the meaning of nation-building before committing themselves to work long hours at high pressure in the service of that ideal. Today, however, there are signs that the atmosphere of those years is wearing off and that a fresh definition of the vocation of the Civil Servant is required. To some extent this is a matter for the political leadership, assisted by the senior Civil Service, to give a lead on a number of important policy issues so that the shape of the society which the Civil Service is called upon to help build is better clarified. But it is also a matter for the Civil Service itself. In the long run, the only lasting and reliable motivation for a Civil Servant is the professional satisfaction of a job well done. We are concerned that the establishment of fully professional standards for a development-oriented Civil Service has so far barely begun. There has been a clear shift of the focus of interest towards development but speaking generally, the working day of the average Civil Servant, the procedures he follows and the tasks he undertakes, have not been subjected to systematic reappraisal in the light of modern knowledge of the nature of the development process. Neither has there been much experimentation with new techniques or new systems of organization.

D. SELECTED AFRICAN DOCUMENTS

17: Uganda: The Common Man's Charter

This Charter was adopted by the Annual Delegates' Conference of the Uganda People's Congress on 24 October 1969. It set out the basic principles of a socialist policy which the government intended to adopt. Shortly after the UPC had adopted this Charter, it decided that Uganda should become a one-party state, with the UPC as the only party. The leader of the UPC, Milton Obote, probably drafted the Charter. Obote was overthrown by a military *coup*, led by General Idi Amin, in November 1971; political parties were subsequently banned.

We hereby commit ourselves to create in Uganda conditions of full security, justice, equality, liberty and welfare for all sons and daughters of the Republic of Uganda and for the realisation of those goals we have adopted the Move to the Left Strategy herein laid down as initial steps.

We subscribe fully to Uganda always being a Republic and have adopted this Charter so that the implementation of this Strategy prevents effectively any one person or group of persons from being masters of all or a section of the people of Uganda, and ensures that all citizens of Uganda become truly masters of their own destiny.

We reject, both in theory and in practice, that Uganda as a whole or any part of it should be the domain of any person, of feudalism, of Capitalism, of vested interests of one kind or another, of foreign influence or of foreigners. We further reject exploitation of material and human resources for the benefit of a few.

We reject, both in theory and in practice, isolationism in regard to one part of Uganda towards another, or in regard to Uganda as a whole to the East African Community in particular, and Africa in general.

Recognising that the roots of the U.P.C. have always been in the people right from its formation, and realising that the Party has always commanded us that whatever is done in Uganda must be done for the benefit of all, we hereby re-affirm our acceptance of the U.P.C. constitution which we set out below in full:

"(i) To build the Republic of Uganda as one country with one people, one Parliament and one Government;

(ii) To defend the Independence and Sovereignty of Uganda and maintain peace and tranquillity, and to preserve the Republican Constitution of Uganda;

(iii) To organise the Party to enable the people to participate in framing the destiny of our country;

158

(iv) To fight relentlessly against Poverty, Ignorance, Disease, Colonialism, Neo-Colonialism, Imperialism and Apartheid;

(v) To plan Uganda's Economic Development in such a way that the Government, through Parastatal Bodies, the Co-operative Movements, Private Companies, Individuals in Industry, Commerce and Agriculture, will effectively contribute to increased production to raise the standard of living in the Country;

(vi) To protect without discrimination based on race, colour, sect or religion every person lawfully living in Uganda and enable him to enjoy the fundamental rights and freedom of the individual, that is to say:

(a) Life, Liberty, Security of the person and Protection of the Law;

(b) Freedom of Conscience, of expression and association;

(c) Protection of Privacy of his home, property and from deprivation of property without compensation.

(vii) To ensure that no citizen of Uganda will enjoy any special privilege, status or title by virtue of birth, descent or heredity;

(viii) To ensure that in the enjoyment of the rights and freedoms no person shall be allowed to prejudice the right and freedoms of others and the interests of the State;

(ix) To support organisations, whether international or otherwise, whose aims, objects and aspirations are consistent with those of the Party."

. . . . . .

To move to the Left is the creation of a new political culture and a new way of life, whereby the people of Uganda as a whole – their welfare and their voice in the National Government and in other local authorities – are paramount. It is, therefore, both anti-feudalism and anti-capitalism.

12. In 1968, the U.P.C. Delegates' Conference passed the following resolution on the important matter of nation-building:

"NOTE with deep satisfaction the liquidation of anti-national and feudal forces, and the introduction of the Republican Constitution;

THANK the leaders of the Party and the government on initiating the revolution for economic, social and political justice;

RECOGNISE that the most important task confronting the Party and the Government today is that of nation-building;

RESOLVE that its entire human and material resources be committed in that task of nation-building;

DIRECT that the National Council of the Party do examine ways and means for active involvement of all institutions, State and private, in joint endeavour with the Party to achieve and serve a nation united and one."

13. We have no doubt whatsoever about the high priority which must be given to nation-building, and we are fully aware that there may be many people in this country who are either uninformed or misguided, who have not yet come to appreciate the importance of nation-building. We, therefore, consider it our responsibility to enlighten the people about the necessity of all the institutions in this country and the people as a whole being actively involved in the joint endeavour to serve the Nation.

. . . . . .

20. We recognise that ours is a society in transition. We want to bring out our considered assessment of the present situation as the starting point for our adoption of the Move to the Left Strategy set out in this Charter. Uganda is a country which is already independent politically. It is that status that makes it the responsibility of the people of Uganda to shape their destiny. Before the 9th October, 1962, the people of Uganda did not have that responsibility or power. The sixty-nine years of colonial rule, during which an alien way of life was not only planted but also took root, resulted in the phenomenon of developing our human and material resources to bear the imprint of this factor in our society. What was planted in Uganda during the era of British protectorate appeared in the eyes and minds of our people as the final word in perfection regarding the development of our material resources and human relationships. Consequently, both before and after Independence, our people have been living in a society in which an alien way life has been embedded. The result has been that most of our people do not look in to the country for ideas to make life better in Uganda, but always look elsewhere to import ideas which may be perfectly suitable in some other society but certainly unfitting in a society like ours. The more we pursue that course, the more we artificially organise our society, our material resources and human relationship, and the more we perpetuate a foreign way of life in our country.

21. We cannot afford to build two nations within the territorial boundaries of Uganda: one rich, educated, African in appearance but mentally foreign, and the other, which constitutes the majority of the population, poor and illiterate. We do not consider that all aspects of the African traditional life are acceptable as socialistic now. We do not, for instance, accept that belonging to a tribe should make a citizen a tool to be exploited by and used for the benefit of tribal leaders. Similarly, we do not accept that feudalism, though not inherently something peculiar to Africa or to Uganda, is a way of life which must not be disturbed because it has

160

been in practice for centuries. With this background, we are convinced that Uganda has to choose between two alternatives. We either perpetuate what we inherited, in which case we will build on a most irrational system of production and distribution of wealth based on alien methods, or we adopt a programme of action based on the realities of our country. The choice adopted in this Charter is the latter. We must move away from the ways of the past to the avenues of reality, and reject travelling along a road where the signpost reads: "Right of admittance is belief in the survival of the fittest." To us, every citizen of Uganda must survive and we are convinced that Uganda has to move to the Left as a unit. Conditions must be created to enable the fruits of Independence to reach each and every citizen without some citizens enjoying privileged positions of living on the sweat of their fellow citizens.

22. The emergence and growth of a privileged group in our society, together with the open possibilities of the group assuming the powers of the feudal elements, are not matters of theory and cannot be disregarded with a wave of the hand . . .

23. We identify two circumstances in which the emergence of a privileged class can find comfort and growth. First, there is our education system which aims at producing citizens whose attitude to the uneducated and to their way of life leads them to think of themselves as the masters and the uneducated as their servants. Secondly, the opportunities for self-employment in modern commerce and industry and to gain employment in Government and in other sectors of the economy are mainly open to the educated few; but instead of these educated few doing everything possible within their powers for the less educated, a tendency is developing where whoever is in business or in Government looks to his immediate family and not to the country as a whole in opening these opportunities. The existence of these circumstances could lead to actual situations of corruption, nepotism and abuse of responsibility.

24. The ordinary citizen of Uganda associates economic development of this country with a rise in his private real income. This income may accrue to him from self-employment, i.e., farming, fishing, cattle-keeping, or paid employment. What is of crucial importance to the ordinary citizen is that Government should provide him with certain social services free and that his income should rise faster than the cost of living, so that he can afford more goods and services for his own use. But there are also three other major dimensions of economic development which must concern our Government. These are the distribution of the national income, the structure of the economy and the creation of institutions conducive to further development and consistent with the Socialist Strategy outlined in this Charter.

25. Let us begin with the examination of the distribution of income in our country. It is obvious that for development to take place there should be a rise in the average income per head (per capita income). This can only occur if the rate of growth of national income exceeds the rate of population growth. For this reason our Government must always place great emphasis on the fast rate of growth of the economy and the national income. Indeed, increased production and wealth is one of the three major goals of the current Plan ("Work for Progress") 1966–7. We are fully convinced that this emphasis is not misplaced, since raising the standard of living of the Common Man in Uganda must be the major aim of our Government. It is possible, however, for the overall rate of growth to rise without affecting large masses of the population. This is a danger that we must guard against. We must not, either because of inertia, corruption, or academic love for the principle of the theory of free enterprise, fail to take bold corrective measures against this danger.

26. There is also the danger that economic development could be unevenly distributed as between regions of the country. The fact is that there is no automatic mechanism within our economic system to ensure an equitable distribution of the national income among persons, groups of persons or regions. We need only to stretch our eyes not to the distant future but to the years immediately ahead of us, taking into account the fact of our present expanding economy, to recognise that if no new strategy is adopted now, inequalities in the distribution of income will change dramatically the status of millions of our people, and might result in our having two nations – one fabulously rich and living on the sweat of the other, and the other living in abject poverty – both living in one country. In such a situation political power will be in the hands of the rich and the maximum the Government will do for the poor will be paternalism, where the lot of the masses will be not only to serve the well-to-do, but to be thankful on their knees when opportunity arises to eat the crumbs from the high table.

. . . . . .

29. The heart of the Move to the Left can be simply stated. It is both political and economic. It is the basic belief of the Uganda People's Congress that political power must be vested in the majority of the people and not the minority. It is also the fundamental belief of the Uganda People's Congress that economic power should be vested in the majority and not in the minority, as is the case at present. It is, therefore, our firm resolution that political and economic power must be vested in the majority.

30. The structure of Uganda's economy is characterised by: an excessive dependence on agriculture as a source of income, employment and foreign

exchange; a heavy dependence on exports based on two major export crops; heavy dependence on imports, particularly of manufactured products; and the limited participation of Ugandans in the modern industrial and commercial sectors of the economy. It has therefore been the policy of the Party to diversify the economy to make it less dependent on foreign trade, to promote the participation of citizens in all sectors of the economy, and the Move to the Left is intended to intensify these efforts through collective ownership, viz. Co-operatives and State enterprises.

......

38. In our Move to the Left Strategy, we affirm that the guiding economic principle will be that the means of production and distribution must be in the hands of the people as a whole. The fulfilment of this principle may involve nationalisation of enterprises privately owned ... The Party therefore directs the Government to work along these lines.

......

40. In this Charter we lay emphasis first on the people being given massive education in operating and establishing institutions controlled, not by individuals, but by the people collectively. This massive education should aim at reorientating the attitudes of the people towards co-operation in the management of economic institutions, and away from individual and private enrichment. We therefore direct the Government to give education to the people to acquire new attitudes in the management of our economy where collective exploitation of our resources to the benefit of all will take the place of individual and private enterprise aimed at enriching a few.

41. We must move in accordance with the principles of democracy. That is the way that brings human progress. Ideas must be generated and sifted, and citizens – educated or not – must be able to think for themselves, learn to work together, and to participate in the processes of governing themselves.

42. The Move to the Left involves government by discussion. This Charter and the principles enunciated herein should be widely disseminated through mass media of communication, and discussed by study groups and individuals all over the country.

43. Principles are a good thing but they are no substitute for hard work. The success of the Charter demands full commitment of leaders to its realisation, acceptance by the mass of the population, and hard work by all.

44. The adoption of the Charter provides an opportunity to the Common Man for the realisation of the full fruits of his labour and of social justice.

18: Seretse Khama: Kagisano – A Policy for Harmony

Extracts from an address delivered by Sir Seretse Khama, President of Botswana, to the Eleventh Annual Conference of the Botswana Democratic Party at Francistown, 1 April 1972.

... I have often said that the greatest threat to progress in Africa comes not from the military might of the minority regimes but from weaknesses within our own societies which our enemies seek to exploit. Thus our principal contribution must be the defence of our independence by the only means available to us – the defence and development of non-racialism and social justice for all. We must build a society in which all our citizens, irrespective of race, tribe or occupation, can fulfil themselves to the greatest possible extent, where they can live in peace and uphold the ideals enshrined in the Setswana concept *kagisano* – unity, peace, harmony and a sense of community.

There are those who accuse us of having no guiding principles. Others fear that we are falling under the influence of alien beliefs. This accusation and these fears are typical of those who believe that Africa, including Botswana, can only shape its development in terms of beliefs and policies which have been conceived in different circumstances in far-away lands. Such beliefs and policies may be perfectly suitable for the countries and continents in which they have developed, but they can have little meaning for the majority of Botswana. In saying this I do not mean we should ignore the experiences of others. Indeed we should seek to learn from these experiences and there is no reason to reject whatever is constructive and humane in many different systems and creeds. But our aspirations, our goals, our policies, our principles must be identified and expressed in terms which our people understand. This means that we must build them on the foundations provided by Botswana's culture and by Botswana's values and traditions.

This we have done. We have recognised that the stable and sustained development of Botswana must be guided by national principles. These principles have been put forward by our Party and widely accepted by our nation. I do not need to expound them to this audience, but I will restate them briefly once again: *Puso ya batho ka batho* – democracy; *ditiro tsa ditlhabololo* – development; *boipelego* – self-reliance; and *popagano ya sechaba* – unity. If we implement these principles as they should be implemented we shall achieve *kagisano*.

......

164

What are the roots of *kagisano*? It is not anything new. Everybody here knows what it means. Its application to our national policy is the logical outgrowth of our national principles. It has always been an essential part of life. It has always been part of our custom that members of a family should help each other face and overcome the problems of life. The well known proverb *kgetse ya tsie e kgonwa ka go tshwaraganelwa* accurately sums up our approach to national policy and to life in general. What we are trying to do in the new Botswana is in fact nothing new. We are simply applying a well-established value, applied in the family, the ward and the tribe to the wider concept of nationhood.

For it must not be seen as a static concept. I said at last year's Conference at Maun, that the Batswana are sometimes complacent about the peace we have enjoyed for so long, and that the calm of the last fifty years or so could be likened to that of a stagnant pool. But we are no longer standing still. We are moving and our society is changing. Mines are opening, towns are growing, our country as a whole is becoming more prosperous, changes are taking place within our rural communities. Therefore to preserve *kagisano* will require constant thought and constant effort.

But I am optimistic that this thought and this effort will be forthcoming. We have one great advantage which was denied some of our brothers elsewhere in Africa. We are often tempted to compare the stagnation of much of the colonial period with the activity which has taken place since self-government. We are sometimes tempted to speak of colonial neglect. But while we regret the human waste caused by the absence of educational opportunity in the pre-independence period, perhaps we should also be thankful that the first major developments in Botswana have come at a time when the Batswana were in control of their own destinies. For in the last five years we have been laying our own foundations and we have had the responsibility of seeing that they were well laid. We have accepted with gratitude the assistance of the many friendly countries which have provided us with aid. But it has been aid provided for development programmes which we have been able to plan in accordance with *our* own values and *our* own priorities. And as we become more and more self-reliant in trained manpower, these values and these priorities will be further clarified and asserted.

And above all our belief in *kagisano* must be asserted. And there are other beliefs which we must reject. Those are the beliefs which are based on the idea that men, or groups of men, must inevitably struggle against each other. Such beliefs assert that, rather than uniting to overcome common problems, men must be divided, and set one against the other.

Thus there are beliefs which are based on the idea that certain groups

165

are faced with an inevitable and irreconcilable conflict of interest – that, for example, there must be an inevitable and irreconcilable struggle between the rich and the poor. Some would argue that, in our circumstances, new leaders must arise within our communities who will inevitably come into conflict with traditional authorities. Again some would argue that, if workers are organised in trade unions, they must inevitably struggle against those who employ them, rather than meet together to identify mutual interests and to consider the common good. Others point to the emergence of a new group in the towns – public servants, for example, with comparatively well-paid posts, and say that their interests must inevitably conflict with those of the poorer people in the rural areas. Men who hold beliefs based on the inevitability of conflict argue that these differences can be resolved only by the triumph of one dominant group. The most extreme of such beliefs argue that such differences can be resolved only by bloodshed, violence and civil strife. Such dangers do exist in societies where rapid change is taking place, but we believe that these dangers and conflicts are not inevitable and can be avoided if we assert and apply in practice our belief in *kagisano*.

And when I speak of *kagisano* and the importance of retaining the positive values of our traditional societies, do not think that these are values held only by the peoples of Botswana. Such values exist or existed in most if not all African societies. Above all, I do not want you to think of these traditional values as belonging to the tribal past and therefore of no validity or usefulness in a modern state. But at the same time I do not want to convey a picture of our tribal past as the Garden of Eden before Eve tasted the forbidden fruit, as a Paradise Lost, which cannot be regained, or which will not survive the strains and tensions which inevitably accompany development and the growth of new communities. For there have always been strains and tensions in tribal societies – for example, ignorance, superstition, poverty and inequality.

. . . to maintain *kagisano* we must, as far as possible see that everyone in our country lifts themselves up together. Our object is primarily to level up not down. And, while there are inequalities in our societies today which are obvious, and which must be corrected by the effective application of revenues derived from the use to which we put our national resources, we must not make the mistake of thinking that all our problems will be solved if we were simply to divide up among all the people what little wealth we have. As Rural Development in Botswana makes clear, emphasis on equality must not lead us into assuming that there is a national crock of gold waiting to be divided up among allcomers – deserving and undeserving. No-one should think that the living standards of all the population can be raised by redistributing the assets of the few people who are relatively well-off, though such people must be prepared for sacrifices. We are above all a poor country and our most pressing problem is to use all our national resources – men, money, minerals, the land – to promote development and see that its benefits are justly distributed.

19: The Dakar Colloquium on African Socialism

Extracts from papers delivered at the colloquium, in Dakar, Senegal, 3–8 December 1962. Published in *Africa Report*, Vol. VIII (May 1963).
The conference was dominated by the French-speaking African countries. Extracts quoted below are from L. S. Senghor (President, Senegal); Seydou Kouyate (then Minister of Planning, Mali); Maurice Adoum (Chad), and Mamadou Dia (then Prime Minister, Senegal).

It is clear that our socialism can no longer be exactly like that of Marx and Engels which was elaborated about a hundred years ago according to the scientific methods and the circumstances of the nineteenth century and of Western Europe . . . Our African socialism, then, will be elaborated not in the dependence but in the autonomy of our thought, and it will choose the most scientific, up-to-date, and, above all, the most efficient methods and institutions and techniques of the Western world and elsewhere. But in the final analysis, they will be efficient only if adapted to the African situation as it is, above all to our geography, history, culture and psychology. Our separation in this way from the Marxist theory after it has been assimilated is all the more necessary as Marx and Engels were not anticolonialist. The latter defended slavery in ancient times and the former British colonialism in India in the name of history!
. . . . . .

It is clear that agricultural development conditions all other development even in the so-called 'developed countries'. Marx did not understand this; Lenin began to understand it; Mao Tse-Tung has understood it perfectly . . .

We will take care not to forget that a plan of economic and social development is made by men and for men; it is not governed by haphazard development. Its implementation requires first and foremost the conscious will of men and consequently their moral and technical training. This truth is Marx's principal discovery although too many 'Marxists' forget about it these days and put greater trust in machines and techniques rather than men.
. . . . . .

167

But it is not only a question of training 'able minds' and skilled technicians – from the worker and the farmer to the engineer. It is rather a matter of training conscientious citizens with a will to change their collective situation: men with a taste for work well done and for creative innovation; above all, men with a sense of common interest. Rather than the utilization of the most efficient techniques, socialism is a sense of community which is a return to Africanism. It involves a merciless struggle against social dishonesty and injustice: excessively high salaries, embezzlement of public funds, illicit trading and bribery. Again, it is a moral alertness which must be maintained from the lowest level to the highest, particularly at the highest. How can this be done? By strict control exercised by the dominant or single party which will positively stimulate both the urban and rural masses . . .
(L. S. Senghor in the opening address)

On the purely economic level, to develop these countries is first and foremost to make it possible for the rural majority, in the context of urgencies, to rise up to the level of productivity required by present needs and the scale of the objectives; to be truly integrated in the stream of centuries. In other words, the first step of operation 'Renovation' is the modernization of agriculture – the sector which provides for the national revenue. The vast majority of our populations are closely linked with agriculture, and it is on agriculture that nearly all of our real economic activities rest. The modernization of agriculture constitutes the first move toward meaningful development.

The modernization of agriculture is not merely a technical, technological problem; it is primarily a psychological human problem, because it calls for a true renovation of the rural sector. Aside from a few places where plantation economy dominates, our peasant population, and this has been said and repeated, lives on a subsistence economy, an economy of auto-consumption where man produces mainly for his sustenance; where he struggles to achieve some sort of balance with misery with the little he produces; an idling life which fits so little with the exigencies of the modern world, in relation to which such a life seems marginal. Thus, an internal need must be created for a better life – in short, the will to break away from the present situation. The starting point of the problem is, therefore, psychological. Modern equipment will not be used much, if at all, if the sense and meaning of its use are not accepted. We must break this equilibrium of deficiency and create new psychological conditions – in short, the new man in the countryside.

. . . . . .

There are, no doubt, many forms of socialism in the world, but that which has the widest applicability and which suggests a global construction stemming from a total vision of the world is the experience of scientific socialism ... Its interpenetration of continents, the rapid spread of its ideas, and its own dynamism entice us not to neglect it. Its precision and the spectacular results of the countries which have adopted it fascinate our youth. It is, therefore, in relation to scientific socialism that we are going to define ourselves. Marxism evokes, immediately, the notion of class, but the attitude which consists of opposing Marxism by citing the absence of classes in Africa is not a solution; it is purely negative. As a matter of fact, our countries are open to foreign private initiative. A proletariat will come about. If classes do not exist today, the workers of tomorrow, born of this private capital, will assume themselves destined to play the historic role of the revolutionary class. The assertion that classes do not exist in Africa is true today, but might not hold true tomorrow ...

We believe that socialist construction cannot be solely the prerogative of the proletariat and that other strata of the population, in given historical conditions, can perfectly well play such a role. We think that socialism can be set up in an industrialized capitalist society, as well as in an agricultural pre-capitalist society.

The aim remains the same, 'a common drive toward the creation of common wealth'. In the still non-industrialized society such as ours, how can we achieve socialism; what are the motivating elements of a socialist construction?

. . . . . .

It must be understood that this socialist option is not at all contrary to religious faith. Our faith in socialism expresses our aspiration for a community whose pillars would be justice, fraternity, and mutual help ...

We can say that the socialist path that we have adopted is based on two fundamental notions: (1) a socialism set up by a movement led by elements not essentially proletarian; and (2) a socialism recognizing spirituality as an integral part of man. As corollary of the first point, we think that socialism can be achieved without a Communist party. As a matter of fact, we believe that the political organization of the people, considered as the driving force of the people, can lead the country in setting up socialism ...

Socialism, however, cannot be a mere economic or socio-economic structure. The goal is man in his material, moral, spiritual, and cultural life. All these edifices have one sole aim: to build a fuller human cadre in order that man can increasingly realize himself.

(Seydou Kouyate, Minister for Development, Mali)

169

But what is socialism? I must admit . . . that I at first was tempted to conclude that the term 'African socialism' was unsuitable, since socialism, being a science, could no more be African than it is Chinese or Russian. On the other hand, African socialism, by its very name, posits the problem of the inevitable adaptation of scientific socialism to African realities . . . The study and assimilation of Marxist theory by our youth will not stand a chance of being applied successfully on the plane of reality as long as this very youth has not taken the trouble, as of now, to acquaint itself more fully with the political, economic, and human realities of Africa. While waiting for the complete Africanization of our secondary and university school programs, it is the responsibility of our school youth of today not to kill tomorrow's Africa by making, due to intellectual sluggishness, a mere copy of the Russian, Chinese, or Polish experiences . . .

The great masters of revolutionary practice, Lenin, Mao Tse-Tung, Tito, Sekou Touré, Fidel Castro, to mention only a few examples, have very well shown us by their concrete experiences that there are many ways to socialism . . . One fact seems certain, and that is the absence over most of the African continent of the notion of class struggle in the Western sense of the term. This means, then, that the scientific socialization of our institutions will inevitably be *progressive* and *peaceful*; the now classical notion of 'dictatorship of the proletariat' must be interpreted in Africa with a great deal of flexibility. It also means that, in the perspective of a socialist evolution, Africa is undoubtedly the continent called to reach more rapidly than others the supreme stage of a classless society where the simple administration of things will substitute for the government of men.

. . . And if our option for socialism means, in the least, an appeal for a common effort (a *sine qua non* condition of its success) I say that the African leaders should from now on mobilize, with vigour, all the modern technical means of information for the political, economic, and cultural education of our peasant masses, in honest, unreserved, and sincere collaboration with all youth.

(Maurice Adoum, Chad)

Having reached independence, the developing countries have adopted planning almost unanimously . . .

Planning is, first of all, the introduction of rationality in economic life. It facilitates its progressive 'demystification'. It requires an increasing knowledge of the economic reality, asking for an increasingly detailed study of the actual functioning of the economy, of the role of its various agents, of the location and behaviour of the decision-making centres. Even if this effort, at first, aims only at the state as an investor or as an economic agent which has many callings, it necessarily brings one to approach the relationship between the state and the other economic agents, interior or exterior, in the same spirit, and, by inescapable progression, to deal with the structure and functioning of the whole economy in rational terms ... Indeed, the plan is the instrument and the centre of all choices ...

Thus, the plan becomes the leading idea around which gather the various popular forces called to participate actively in development. It establishes the bases for new political relations. It leads to the necessary dialogue between the technical élites and the masses, between the government and the citizens.

. . . . . .

Thus, development requires a complete and conscious association of the entire people. It is, before anything else, a collective will for development; for this reason, it can neither be imported from outside nor even imposed from inside by a prevailing ideology. It is therefore essential to organize this association of citizens toward the formulation and realization of the plan. The problem is not to provide the population with cadres to make sure that they follow [a given] course ... On the contrary, what is intended is to make the population aware of the policy of development, to make it live its problems, to make it want the means – first at the level of the village, then by steps to the level of the regional and national needs and realities. This, in Senegal, is the task of *animation*. The goal is to allow the people to take their decisions freely, finally, and in full knowledge of the development questions.

. . . . . .

The shortage of cadres and technicians will constitute for a long time to come the major development bottleneck. In view of this, the danger is real that these cadres, small in number in relation to the needs, will take advantage of their scarcity to get advantages and unjustified standards of living. Thus would come about a privileged class ... not unlike the holders of capital in the capitalist economies. This phenomenon would be unnatural, the more so since the promotion of cadres in our countries is often entirely in the hands of the state.

But, above all, creation of such a privileged and isolated group in the midst of our peoples would progressively make the voluntary participation of the population in development impossible. It is, therefore, important to search for and define the conditions of an active solidarity between the cadres and the entire population. This solidarity must remain alive; its existence is the very foundation of development.

. . . . . .

Our economies are still basically dominated by agriculture. Although we are trying to strengthen the base of our economies, we know very well that development implies industrialization ... This assumes, on the part of the African nations, a policy of denationalization of the great industrial centres and of the essential sectors of production for the benefit of common development.

This assumes, also, the unification of markets and the abolition of customs barriers whose harmful and artificial nature nobody can deny.

......

First, let me say that socialism, for us, is not an end in itself. Socialism does not appear to us to be some sort of prototype to erect at any cost and by all means – that is, even at the sacrifice of some of our fundamental values. For us, the full development of our countries is the sole end of all our efforts, and socialism is nothing but a means to achieve full development. But it is undoubtedly the only one that could be perfectly moulded to suit African exigencies.

I say 'moulded' because socialism is not for us an intangible dogma, a truth revealed to be accepted without changing an iota of it. Socialism is a method of apprehending and understanding social realities, and more precisely economic realities. As such, it is scientific and far from being the prerogative of a given ideology ... As such, it is also basically a method of adaptation to given realities. That is why it gives different answers when applied to different realities.

And since the problem of development presents itself to all countries with data which are not always the same, it is only normal that socialism offers to each a different solution. In Africa, the particularity of both natural and historical data characterized by the direct intervention of European capitalism obviously requires the definition of an African socialism ...

The first step toward the African way of development is the revolutionary rejection of the old structures. Before starting anything, we need the expressed will to replace radically, in its deep logic as well as in its superstructure, the political, economic, and social systems inherited from the old colonial regime ...

It is not enough, as some reformists would like to do, to correct and modify gradually this or that part of the system under the pressure of circumstances. We must conceive, on the contrary, a total mutation which would substitute for the colonial society and trading economy a free society and a development economy. Such a mutation is revolutionary. This does not mean that it calls for the use of blind violence; but it must be inspired by an elaborate conception of national development, by a system of values, in short by an ideology.

......

172

As you know, African development is characterized by an underlying conception of man. Not individualistic man, but *l'homme personnaliste*, who finds his full blossoming in the coherence of a living society, of an organic community. We can, in Africa, rely on the most authentic of our traditional values for achieving such a goal. That is why our way to development leads also to a community-centred socialism; to a socialism not of coercion, but of solidarity, of free adhesion and free co-operation; to a socialism which, after having been the instrument of national liberation, will be that of the liberation of man . . .

The lines are sharp enough and our choice is clear. African socialism is not a label that we can stick to any merchandise. But we don't want our self-assurance to degenerate into a new dogmatism either. Our awareness of having made, in full knowledge, the essential choices allows us to remain concerned with all that pertains to our enterprise. That is why we intend to enrich ourselves with all that we can receive – particularly from Marxism as an analysis of economic realities, and from existentialism as a conception of a new humanism.

(Mamadou Dia, Senegal, closing speech)

20: Ghana: Nkrumah

(a) Extracts from K. Nkrumah, *I Speak of Freedom* (Heinemann Educational Books, 1961). The context of each extract is given after the extract.

(b) Extracts from K. Nkrumah, *Africa Must Unite* (Heinemann Educational Books, 1963).

(c) Extracts from K. Nkrumah, *Consciencism: Philosophy and Ideology for Decolonisation,* 2nd edn (Panaf 1970. First published in 1964).

(a) The government of Ghana has often been criticised by a section of the western press for adopting what they have called 'undemocratic methods'. It would have been more helpful in creating a better understanding if these critics had first carefully considered the reality of our situation. As a new and young government, our first responsibility has been to preserve the independence and security of our state . . . In our case the criticism has been that we have not proceeded in precisely the same way as the old Western democracies . . . In this connection I want to emphasise two fundamental points in relation to our approach to democracy. First, Ghana society is by its own form and tradition fundamentally democratic in character. For centuries our people gave great powers to their chiefs,

173

but only so long as they adhered to the rules and regulations laid down by the people; the moment they deviated from these rules, they were deposed. In our recent history we have inherited a parliamentary system of the Western type which . . . is a subtle and sophisticated type of administration full of balances and checks. This, by its very nature, is a very difficult and cumbersome system to apply to our traditional pattern of government.

I believe that this process will not in any way prejudice our democratic way of life so long as two basic principles are always accepted, namely, universal adult suffrage, which ensures that every adult man and woman has one vote; and regular, free and unfettered elections . . . I have no doubt that in time we in Africa will evolve forms of government rather different from the traditional western pattern but no less democratic in their protection of the individual and his inalienable rights.
(Speech to Indian Council of World Affairs, 26 December 1958)

The Convention People's Party has developed from a small organisation to a nation-wide movement, embracing within its ranks and among its sympathisers the overwhelming majority of our nation. The composition of the Party has become socially quite heterogeneous and there is the danger that our socialist objective may be clouded by opportunistic accommodations and adjustments to petit bourgeois elements in our ranks who are unsympathetic and sometimes even hostile to the social aims to which the party is dedicated.

These aims embrace the creation of a welfare state based upon African socialist principles, adapted to suit Ghanaian conditions, in which all citizens, regardless of class, tribe, colour or creed, shall have equal opportunity, and where there shall be no exploitation of man by man, tribe by tribe, or class by class, our party also seeks to promote and safeguard popular democracy based upon universal suffrage – 'One man, one vote'.
. . . . . .

In our Party all are equal regardless of their race or tribe. All are free to express their views. But once a majority decision is taken, we expect such a decision to be loyally executed, even by those who might have opposed that decision. This we consider and proclaim to be the truest form of *Democratic Centralism* – decisions freely arrived at and loyally executed. This applies from the lowest to the highest level. None is privileged and no one shall escape disciplinary action. For the strength of our Party depends upon its discipline. Up to now there has been too much looseness, and from now on we intend to tighten up on all echelons of the Party, from the Central Committee down to the humblest Branch.
. . . . . .

It is my pleasant duty to tell you that, stimulated by the unselfish gesture of our farmers, the Central Committee of the Convention People's Party has decided that all Party Ministers, Ministerial Secretaries and certain others, shall give up to the nation ten per cent of their salary. We consider it only fair that sacrifices should come from the top as well as from below, since the fruits of our Development Plan will benefit all sections of the community. (Speech to Party members on the Tenth Anniversary of the CPP, 12 June 1959)

(b) For two and a half years of difficult state-building my government took no action to limit the freedom of the press. The opposition was quick to exploit this freedom and soon debased it into licence. Each day, its newspapers came out with screaming headlines about the perfidy of the government. They heaped abuse and libel upon my colleagues and me. They wrote and preached, they called press conferences with local and foreign correspondents, they addressed public meetings all over the country, stigmatizing the government and singling out me and my immediate associates for special attack, abuse and ridicule.

During the struggle for independence we had emphasized the need for national unity for the attainment of freedom, and for the enormous responsibilities of statehood that would follow. These call for a supreme effort on the part of every citizen. How could our people pull their weight with zeal and dedication when it was ceaselessly being drummed into them that their government was unscrupulous, inept and corrupt; that their leaders were venal and power-thirsty, and that the national effort was invoked, not for the greater glory of Ghana but for the personal glory of Kwame Nkrumah? This was not freedom of expression. This was irresponsible licence, and if allowed to continue unbridled, it could have undermined our state, our independence and the people's faith in themselves and their capacities.

. . . . . .

We came to the point where it was obvious that the government must take action if we were to avert the dangers inherent in a false situation. The imposition of any form of press censorship was an idea most repugnant to me, since it ran counter to everything I had always believed in, everything for which I had struggled in my life. Freedom of expression had been one of the essential rights for which I had fought. I had gone to prison for daring to say things the colonial administration had not liked.

. . . We had to face up squarely to the question whether a seedling less developed state, eager to modernise itself in the interests of the community, threatened by the unpatriotic deeds of a minority opposition, could permit itself all the forms which established democracies have taken generations to evolve.

... the building of a new state requires more than the preparation of programmes, the design of plans and the issue of instructions for their implementation. It requires the whole-hearted support and self-identification of the people, and the widest possible response to the call for voluntary service. A war on illiteracy has to be waged; and a country-wide self-help programme of community development arranged, to promote the building of schools, roads, drains, clinics, post offices, houses and community centres.

The effects of self-help schemes, valuable in themselves and the incentive they give to initiative, are, however, local in compass and limited in purpose. Rapid development on a national scale and the attainment of economic independence demand a more intensive and wider application of ability and inventiveness, the speedy acquisition of technical knowledge and skills, a vast acceleration of productivity as a prerequisite to accumulation of savings for re-investment in industrial expansion. In a less developed society there are several impediments to industrialization, quite apart from the lack of requisite capital accumulations, technical skills, scientific knowledge and industrial enterprise, which, unless they are eliminated, will stultify our efforts at advancement. For they have their cumulative effect precisely in the lack of these requisite reserves.

Customs which extol the virtues of extended family allegiance sustain nepotistic practices, and regard the giving and taking of 'presents' as implicit and noble, because they promote the family welfare. They encourage indolence and bribery, they act as a brake upon ability, they discourage that deeper sense of individual responsibility which must be ready in a period of active reconstruction to accept obligation and fulfil trust. Above all, they retard productivity and oppose savings, the crucial factors in the rate of development. Polygamy donates its quota to these retarding influences, while our laws of succession and inheritance stifle the creative and inventive urge.

......

The role of the trade unions, ... in our circumstances, is entirely different from that in a capitalist society where the motive force is the accumulation of private profit. The aims of our trade unions, being identified with those of the government, wed them to active participation in the carrying out of the government's programme. Within the capitalist states, the trade unions play the role of watchdogs for labour against the employers. Even so, they are by no means 'free'. Their leaders are bought off by the sweets of office and often have their secret arrangements with employers. More than that, they have for the most part accepted the ideology of their capitalist class and, through its exposition throughout their extensive forums and the witch-hunting of those who do not conform, have openly identified themselves with that ideology.

In such circumstances there cannot be any talk of freedom. In Ghana, the trade unions are openly associated with the Convention People's Party as one of its wings. They have no need to hide this association behind hypocritical sophistries. They are, in fact, drawing the workers into the implementation of government plans by setting up works councils inside the public enterprises to give effective expression to their national consciousness.

. . . . .

At all stages, we seek the fullest co-operation of the people and their organizations, and in this way, and through public control of the means of production, we hope to evolve the truest kind of democracy within the Aristotelian meaning. By mass consultation we shall associate the people with the running of the nation's affairs, which must then operate in the interests of the people. Moreover, since control of the modern state is linked up with the control of the means of production and distribution, true democracy can only be said to exist when these have passed into the hands of the people. For then the people exercise control of the state through their will as expressed in the direct consultation between government and them. This must surely provide the most concrete and clearest operation of true democracy.

(c) Revolution has two aspects. Revolution is a revolution against an old order; and it is also a contest *for* a new order. The Marxist emphasis on the determining force of the material circumstances of life is correct. But I would like also to give great emphasis to the determining power of ideology. A revolutionary ideology is not merely negative. It is not a mere conceptual refutation of a dying social order, but a positive creative theory, the guiding light of the emerging social order.

The traditional face of Africa includes an attitude towards man which can only be described, in its social manifestation, as being socialist. This arises from the fact that man is regarded in Africa as primarily a spiritual being, a being endowed originally with a certain inward dignity, integrity and value. It stands refreshingly opposed to the Christian idea of the original sin and degradation of man.

This idea of the original value of man imposes duties of a socialist kind upon us. Herein lies the theoretical basis of African communalism. This theoretical basis expressed itself on the social level in terms of institutions such as the clan, underlining the initial quality of all and the responsibility of many for one. In this social situation, it was impossible for classes of a Marxian kind to arise . . .

177

In the traditional African society, no sectional interest could be regarded as supreme; nor did legislative and executive power aid the interests of any particular group. The welfare of the people was supreme.

But colonialism came and changed all this ... For its success, the colonial administration needed a cadre of Africans, who, by being introduced to a certain minimum of European education, became infected with European ideals, which they tacitly accepted as being valid for African societies. Because these African instruments of the colonial administration were seen by all to be closely associated with the new sources of power, they acquired a certain prestige and rank to which they were not entitled by the demands of the harmonious development of their own society.

In addition to them, groups of merchants and traders, lawyers, doctors, politicians and trade unionists emerged, who, armed with skills and levels of affluence which were gratifying to the colonial administration, initiated something parallel to the European middle class ...

. . . . . .

With true independence regained, however, a new harmony needs to be forged, a harmony that will allow the combined presence of traditional Africa, Islamic Africa and Euro-Christian Africa, so that this presence is in tune with the original humanist principles underlying African society. Our society is not the old society, but a new society enlarged by Islamic and Euro-Christian influences. A new emergent ideology is therefore required, an ideology which can solidify in a philosophical statement, but at the same time an ideology which will not abandon the original humanist principles of Africa.

Such a philosophical statement will be born out of the crisis of the African conscience confronted with the three strands of present African society. Such a philosophical statement I propose to name *philosophical consciencism*, for it will give the theoretical basis for an ideology whose aim shall be to contain the African experience of Islamic and Euro-Christian presence as well as the experience of the traditional African society, and, by gestation, employ them for the harmonious growth and development of that society.

. . . . . .

According to philosophical consciencism, ethical rules are not permanent but depend on the stage reached in the historical evolution of a society, so however that cardinal principles of egalitarianism are conserved.

. . . . . .

The cardinal ethical principle of philosophical consciencism is to treat each man as an end in himself and not merely as a means. This is fundamental to all socialist or humanist conceptions of man. It is true that Immanuel Kant also identified this as a cardinal principle of ethics, but whereas he regarded it as an immediate command of reason, we derive it from a materialist viewpoint.

This derivation can be made by way of that egalitarianism which ... is the social reflection of materialism. Egalitarianism is based on the monistic thesis of materialism. Matter is one even in its different manifestations ...

......

It is the basic unity of matter, despite its varying manifestations, which gives rise to egalitarianism. Basically, man is one, for all men have the same basis and arise from the same evolution according to materialism. This is the objective ground of egalitarianism.

......

When a plurality of men exist in society, and it is accepted that each man needs to be treated as an end in himself, not merely as a means, there transpires a transition from ethics to politics. Politics becomes actual, for institutions need to be created to regulate the behaviour and actions of the plurality of men in society in such a way as to conserve the fundamental ethical principle of the initial worthiness of each individual. Philosophical consciencism consequently adumbrates a political theory and a social-political practice which together seek to ensure that the cardinal principles of ethics are effective.

The social-political practice is directed at preventing the emergence or the solidifying of classes, for in the Marxist conception of class structure, there is exploitation and the subjection of class. Exploitation and class subjection are alike contrary to consciencism. By reason of its egalitarian tenet, philosophical consciencism seeks to promote individual development, but in such a way that the conditions of development of all become the conditions of development for each; that is, in such a way that the individual development does not introduce such diversities as to destroy the egalitarian basis. The social-political practice also seeks to co-ordinate social forces in such a way as to mobilize them logistically for the maximum development of society along true egalitarian lines. For this, planned development is essential.

In its political aspect, philosophical consciencism is faced with the realities of colonialism, imperialism, disunity and lack of development. Singly and collectively these four militate against the realisation of a social justice based on ideas of true equality.

21: Ochieng: The African Revolution

Extracts from an article in *Africa*, No. 16 (December 1972). Mr Ochieng is a Lecturer at the University of Nairobi, Kenya.

... What actually has restrained people from enthusiastically embracing the creed of the African Revolution, together with its sister African Socialism, is the conviction that very few African leaders are ready to practise what they preach. The snatching of political independence, it has been realised, did not constitute any meaningful revolution. It is argued in some quarters that even if Africa succeeds in extricating herself from economic dependence no meaningful revolution will have been achieved, especially if colonial and economic structures will simply change hands to a few black exploiters and oppressors. Indeed this is part of the reason why freedom movements in Africa have, in the post-independence period, received very indifferent support because the African masses have learnt through the hard school of experience that the mere replacement of white exploiters and oppressors with their black "cousins" is not worth their sacrifice. People died and sacrified the security of their families to fight for freedom which, they were promised, would radically change their lives. Apart from a few elites who have manned the colonial structures that were inherited at independence the position of the majority of people has in many ways deteriorated from what it was during the colonial period. The number of the unemployed has risen, and the standard of life has fallen. It matters very little to a slum dweller, or to a landless-unemployed, whether or not his nation, or continent, is self-sufficient economically, if the profits of this self-sufficiency will only go to enrich a few privileged and soulless individuals.

... But supposing we had a few committed African revolutionaries what is the nature of their commitment to the welfare of the African individual? Are the just and the natural rights of the individual going to be sacrificed on the altar of a meaningless political and economic independence? Having already been let down by some of our self-seeking nationalists how can we now be sure that we are not being tricked into supporting revolutionary wolves whose ultimate objective ... is not really the welfare of the people but the replacement of those already in positions of authority and influence, without their intending to change existing policies? How many revolutionary councils are ruling African states with no attempt at destroying existing structures and values in order to create a better and different African world?

Everybody in Africa is for the independence, stability and prosperity of the African Continent. But the achievement of these should not be an end in itself. They should not constitute the basis of a political doctrine. Any revolution preached or carried out in Africa, now, must involve and be seen to display a sincere revolution of human values. It is this spiritual change that the majority of the advocates of the African Revolution have not given a sincere and significant emphasis. Nyerere has argued that Socialism is an attitude of the mind. In Africa, even in those parts which we are told are experimenting with Socialism, profit motive and the desire to own property are considered more important than the general welfare of the people. In Tanzania for example, there are those who have jumped onto Mwalimu Nyerere's Socialist band-wagon, not because they believe in it, but because preaching Socialism puts them on the right side of the regime, and therefore gives them a chance to acquire positions of wealth. This, according to certain close observers of Tanzania, will be the undoing of the country's experimentation with Socialism. To most of us, therefore, it will no longer be easy to support a revolution which lays no emphasis on the spiritual revolution of the preachers. Heroics and dramatic words and gestures might provide a platform for temporary crowd pleasing, ego satisfaction, and what have you, but they cannot solve our fundamental problems. Before we make a step beyond our present and sorry positions we will demand to be assured that the advocates of change have shifted their values from a thing-oriented society to a person-oriented society. The revolutionary values will have to be seen to go beyond ... the mere acquisition of complete economic and political independence.

When the revolutionaries talk about change what exactly are they talking about? What kind of society do they wish to create? There are those of us who have been brainwashed by leftist ideas and arguments into believing that once we have destroyed capitalist institutions then the African Revolution will have been achieved. This delusion explains the trendiest preoccupation with doctrinaire socialism by many African intellectuals. It is my feeling that truth is neither in traditional capitalism nor in scientific Socialism. Each of these merely represents a partial truth. We must honestly admit that capitalism has often left an embarrassing gulf between superfluous wealth and abject poverty, has created conditions permitting necessities of life to be taken away from the many to give luxuries to the few, and has encouraged small-hearted men to become cold and conscienceless, so that they are unmoved by suffering and abject poverty around them. On the other hand militant scientific socialism, like the one practised in Communist China, has often reduced men to mere cogs in the wheel of the state. Individuals, the ultimate justification for the existence of any state, have often assumed the role of instruments of production and ambition. Their needs have been defined in terms of food, shelter and clothing. Truly regulated Socialist states have often deprived their people of their inalienable rights. Their "rights" have remained those derived from, and conferred by, the state. Under such conditions the fountains of freedom and humanity have run dry. Restricted are men's liberties of speech, association and their freedom to listen and read. It becomes very difficult to distinguish between human beings and plants.

. . . a genuine and realistic African revolution is the one which demands that our loyalties, as Africans, must also assume a universalist posture. We must accept our citizenship of the world and take note of the fact that some of our problems link us with people who have similar problems in other parts of the world. In the words of Nkrumah, the aim of a truly revolutionary spirit is "to work with other nationalist democratic socialist movements in Africa and other continents with the view to abolishing imperialism, colonialism, racialism, tribalism, and all forms of national and racial oppression and economic inequality among the nations, races and peoples, and to support all action for world peace, progress and justice." This call for a world-wide fellowship that lifts neighbourly concern beyond one's tribe, race, class and nation is in reality a call for an all-embracing and unconditional love for all men.

22: Frantz Fanon: National Consciousness

Extracts from F. Fanon, *The Wretched of the Earth* (Penguin, 1970. First published Paris, 1961).

On Nationalism and National Consciousness

History teaches us clearly that the battle against colonialism does not run straight away along the lines of nationalism. For a very long time the native devotes his energies to ending certain definite abuses: forced labour, corporal punishment, inequality of salaries, limitation of political rights, etc. This fight for democracy against the oppression of mankind will slowly leave the confusion of neo-liberal universalism to emerge, sometimes laboriously, as a claim to nationhood. It so happens that the unpreparedness of the educated classes, the lack of practical links between them and the mass of the people, their laziness, and, let it be said, their cowardice at the decisive moment of the struggle will give rise to tragic mishaps.

National consciousness, instead of being the all-embracing crystallization of the innermost hopes of the whole people, instead of

182

being the immediate and most obvious result of the mobilization of the people, will be in any case only an empty shell, a crude and fragile travesty of what it might have been. The faults that we find in it are quite sufficient explanation of the facility with which, when dealing with young and independent nations, the nation is passed over for the race, and the tribe is preferred to the state. These are the cracks in the edifice which show the process of retrogression that is so harmful and prejudicial to national effort and national unity. We shall see that such retrograde steps with all the weaknesses and serious dangers that they entail are the historic result of the incapacity of the national middle class to rationalize popular action, that it to say their incapacity to see into the reasons for that action.

This traditional weakness, which is almost congenital to the national consciousness of under-developed countries, is not solely the result of the mutilation of the colonized people by the colonial regime. It is also the result of the intellectual laziness of the national middle class, of its spiritual penury, and of the profoundly cosmopolitan mould that its mind is set in . . .

The national economy of the period of independence is not set on a new footing. It is still concerned with the ground-nut harvest, with the cocoa crop and the olive yield. In the same way there is no change in the marketing of basic products, and not a single industry is set up in the country. We go on sending out raw materials; we go on being Europe's small farmers who specialize in unfinished products.

Yet the national middle class constantly demands the nationalization of the economy and of the trading sectors. This is because, from their point of view, nationalization does not mean placing the whole economy at the service of the nation and deciding to satisfy the needs of the nation. For them, nationalization does not mean governing the state with regard to the new social relations whose growth it has been decided to encourage. To them, nationalization quite simply means the transfer into native hands of those unfair advantages which are a legacy of the colonial period.

Since the middle class has neither sufficient material nor intellectual resources (by intellectual resources we mean engineers and technicians) it limits its claims to the taking over of business offices and commercial houses formerly occupied by the settlers. The national bourgeoisie steps into the shoes of the former European settlement: doctors, barristers, traders, commercial travellers, general agents and transport agents. It considers that the dignity of the country and its own welfare require that it should occupy all these posts. From now on it will insist that all the big foreign companies should pass through its hands, whether these companies wish to keep on their connexions with the country, or to open it up. The national middle class discovers its historic mission: that of intermediary.

Seen through its eyes, its mission has nothing to do with transforming the nation; it consists, prosaically, of being the transmission line between the nation and a capitalism, rampant though camouflaged, which today puts on the masque of neo-colonialism . . .

As regards internal affairs and in the sphere of institutions, the national bourgeoisie will give equal proof of its incapacity. In a certain number of under-developed countries the parliamentary game is faked from the beginning. Powerless economically, unable to bring about the existence of coherent social relations, and standing on the principle of its domination as a class, the bourgeoisie chooses the solution that seems to it the easiest, that of the single party. It does not yet have the quiet conscience and the calm that economic power and the control of the state machine alone can give. It does not create a state that reassures the ordinary citizen, but rather one that rouses his anxiety.

The state, which by its strength and discretion ought to inspire confidence and disarm and lull everybody to sleep, on the contrary seeks to impose itself in spectacular fashion. It makes display, it jostles people and bullies them, thus intimating to the citizen that he is in continual danger. The single party is the modern form of the dictatorship of the bourgeoisie, unmasked, unpainted, unscrupulous and cynical.

It is true that such a dictatorship does not go very far. It cannot halt the processes of its own contradictions. Since the bourgeoisie has not the economic means to ensure its domination and to throw a few crumbs to the rest of the country; since, moreover, it is preoccupied with filling its pockets as rapidly as possible but also as prosaically as possible, the country sinks all the more deeply into stagnation. And in order to hide this stagnation and to mask this regression to reassure itself and to give itself something to boast about, the bourgeoisie can find nothing better to do than to erect grandiose buildings in the capital and to lay out money on what are called prestige expenses . . .

The people who for years on end have seen this leader and heard him speak, who from a distance in a kind of dream have followed his contests with the colonial power, spontaneously put their trust in this patriot. Before independence, the leader generally embodies the aspirations of the people for independence, political liberty and national dignity. But as soon as independence is declared, far from embodying in concrete form the needs of the people in what touches bread, land and the restoration of the country to the sacred hands of the people, the leader will reveal his inner purpose: to become the general president of that company of profiteers impatient for their returns which constitutes the national bourgeoisie.

184

In spite of his frequently honest conduct and his sincere declarations, the leader as seen objectively is the fierce defender of these interests, today combined, of the national bourgeoisie and the ex-colonial companies. His honesty, which is his soul's true bent, crumbles away little by little. His contact with the masses is so unreal that he comes to believe that his authority is hated and that the services that he has rendered his country are being called in question. The leader judges the ingratitude of the masses harshly, and every day that passes ranges himself a little more resolutely on the side of the exploiters. He therefore knowingly becomes the aider and abettor of the young bourgeoisie which is plunging into the mire of corruption and pleasure ... The leader, who has behind him a lifetime of political action and devoted patriotism, constitutes a screen between the people and the rapacious bourgeoisie since he stands surety for the ventures of that caste and closes his eyes to their insolence, their mediocrity and their fundamental immorality. He acts as a braking-power on the awakening consciousness of the people. He comes to the aid of the bourgeois caste and hides his manoeuvres from the people, thus becoming the most eager worker in the task of mystifying and bewildering the masses. Every time he speaks to the people he calls to mind his often heroic life, the struggles he has led in the name of the people and the victories in their name he has achieved, thereby intimating clearly to the masses that they ought to go on putting their confidence in him ...

The leader pacifies the people. For years on end after independence has been won, we see him, incapable of urging on the people to a concrete task, unable really to open the future to them or of flinging them into the path of national reconstruction, that is to say, of their own reconstruction; we see him reassessing the history of independence and recalling the sacred unity of the struggle for liberation. The leader, because he refuses to break up the national bourgeoisie, asks the people to fall back into the past and to become drunk on the remembrance of the epoch which led up to independence. The leader, seen objectively, brings the people to a halt and persists in either expelling them from history or preventing them from taking root in it. During the struggle for liberation the leader awakened the people and promised them a forward march, heroic and unmitigated. Today, he uses every means to put them to sleep, and three or four times a year asks them to remember the colonial period and to look back on the long way they have come since then.

Now it must be said that the masses show themselves totally incapable of appreciating the long way they have come. The peasant who goes on scratching out a living from the soil, and the unemployed man who never finds employment do not manage, in spite of public holidays and flags, new and brightly coloured though they may be, to convince themselves that anything has really changed in their lives. The bourgeoisie who are in power vainly increase the number of processions; the masses have no illusions. They are hungry; and the police officers, though now they are Africans, do not serve to reassure them particularly. The masses begin to sulk; they turn away from this nation in which they have been given no place and begin to lose interest in it.

......

There exists inside the new regime, however, an inequality in the acquisition of wealth and in monopolization. Some have a double source of income and demonstrate that they are specialized in opportunism. Privileges multiply and corruption triumphs, while morality declines. Today the vultures are too numerous and too voracious in proportion to the lean spoils of the national wealth. The party, a true instrument of power in the hands of the bourgeoisie, reinforces the machine, and ensures that the people are hemmed in and immobilized. The party helps the government to hold the people down. It becomes more and more clearly anti-democratic, an implement of coercion.

......

In these poor, under-developed countries, where the rule is that the greatest wealth is surrounded by the greatest poverty, the army and the police constitute the pillars of the regime; an army and a police force (another rule which must not be forgotten) which are advised by foreign experts. The strength of the police force and the power of the army are proportionate to the stagnation in which the rest of the nation is sunk. By dint of yearly loans, concessions are snatched up by foreigners; scandals are numerous, ministers grow rich, their wives doll themselves up, the members of parliament feather their nests and there is not a soul down to the simple policeman or the customs officer who does not join in the great procession of corruption ... Such behaviour shows that more or less consciously the national bourgeoisie is playing to lose if the game goes on too long. They guess that the present situation will not last indefinitely but they intend to make the most of it. Such exploitation and such contempt for the state, however, invitably give rise to discontent among the mass of the people. It is in these conditions that the regime becomes harsher. In the absence of a parliament it is the army that becomes the arbiter: but sooner or later it will realize its power and will hold over the government's head the threat of a manifesto ...

The political party in many parts of Africa which are today independent is puffed up in a most dangerous way. In the presence of a member of the party, the people are silent, behave like a flock of sheep and publish panegyrics in praise of the government or the leader. But in the street when evening comes, away from the village, in the cafes or by the river, the bitter disappointment of the people, their despair but also their unceasing anger makes itself heard. The party, instead of welcoming the expression of popular discontentment, instead of taking for its fundamental purpose the free flow of ideas from the people up to the government, forms a screen, and forbids such ideas. The party leaders behave like common sergeant-majors, frequently reminding the people of the need for 'silence in the ranks'. This party which used to call itself the servant of the people, which used to claim that it worked for the full expression of the people's will, as soon as the colonial power puts the country into its control hasten to send the people back to their caves. As far as national unity is concerned the party will also make many mistakes, as for example when the so-called national party behaves as a party based on ethnical differences. It becomes, in fact, the tribe which makes itself into a party. This party which of its own will proclaims that it is a national party, and which claims to speak in the name of the totality of the people, secretly, sometimes even openly organizes an authentic ethnical dictatorship. We no longer see the rise of a bourgeois dictatorship, but a tribal dictatorship. The ministers, the members of the cabinet, the ambassadors and local commissioners are chosen from the same ethnological group as the leader, sometimes directly from his own family. Such regimes of the family sort seem to go back to the old laws of inbreeding, and not anger but shame is felt when we are faced with such stupidity, such an imposture, such intellectual and spiritual poverty. These heads of the government are the true traitors in Africa, for they sell their country to the most terrifying of all its enemies: stupidity . . .

In an under-developed country the party ought to be organized in such fashion that it is not simply content with having contacts with the masses. The party should be the direct expression of the masses. The party is not an administration responsible for transmitting government orders; it is the energetic spokesman and the incorruptible defender of the masses. In order to arrive at this conception of the party, we must above all rid ourselves of the very Western, very bourgeois and therefore contemptuous attitude that the masses are incapable of governing themselves. In fact, experience proves that the masses understand perfectly the most complicated problems . . .

In fact, we often believe with criminal superficiality that to educate the masses politically is to deliver a long political harangue from time to time. We think that it is enough that the leader or one of his lieutenants should speak in a pompous tone about the principal events of the day for them to have fulfilled this bounden duty to educate the masses politically. Now, political education means opening their minds, awakening them, and allowing the birth of their intelligence; as Césaire said, it is 'to invent souls'. To educate the masses politically does not mean, cannot mean making a political speech. What it means is to try, relentlessly and passionately, to teach the masses that everything depends on them; that if we stagnate it is their responsibility, and that if we go forward it is due to them too, that there is no such thing as a demiurge, that there is no famous man who will take the responsibility for everything, but that the demiurge is the people themselves and the magic hands are finally only the hands of the people. In order to put all this into practice, in order really to incarnate the people, we repeat that there must be decentralization in the extreme. The movement from the top to the bottom and from the bottom to the top should be a fixed principle, not through concern for formalism but because simply to respect this principle is the guarantee of salvation. It is from the base that forces mount up which supply the summit with its dynamic, and make it possible dialectically for it to leap ahead. Once again we Algerians have been quick to understand these facts, for no member of the government at the head of any recognized state has had the chance of availing himself of such a mission of salvation. For it is the rank-and-file who are fighting in Algeria, and the rank-and-file know well that without their daily struggle, hard and heroic as it is, the summit would collapse; and in the same way those at the bottom know that without a head and without leadership the base would split apart in incoherence and anarchy. The summit only draws its worth and its strength from the existence of the people at war. Literally, it is the people who freely create a summit for themselves, and not the summit that tolerates the people.

The masses should know that the government and the party are at their service. A deserving people, in other words a people conscious of its dignity, is a people that never forgets these facts. During the colonial occupation the people were told that they must give their lives so that dignity might triumph. But the African peoples quickly came to understand that it was not only the occupying power that threatened their dignity. The African peoples were quick to realize that dignity and sovereignty were exact equivalents, and, in fact, a free people living in dignity is a sovereign people. It is no use demonstrating that the African peoples are childish or weak. A government or a party gets the people it deserves and sooner or later a people gets the government it deserves . . .

Individual experience, because it is national and because it is a link in the chain of national existence, ceases to be individual, limited and shrunken and is enabled to open out into the truth of the nation and of the world. In the same way that during the period of armed struggle each fighter held the fortune of the nation in his hand, so during the period of national construction each citizen ought to continue in his real, everyday activity to associate himself with the whole of the nation, to incarnate the continuous dialectical truth of the nation and to will the triumph of man in his completeness here and now. If the building of a bridge does not enrich the awareness of those who work on it, then that bridge ought not to be built and the citizens can go on swimming across the river or going by boat. The bridge should not be 'parachuted down' from above; it should not be imposed by a deus ex machina upon the social scene; on the contrary it should come from the muscles and the brains of the citizens. Certainly, there may well be need of engineers and architects, sometimes completely foreign engineers and architects; but the local party leaders should be always present, so that the new techniques can make their way into the cerebral desert of the citizen, so that the bridge in whole and in part can be taken up and conceived, and the responsibility for it assumed by the citizen. In this way, and in this way only, everything is possible . . .

It is only when men and women are included on a vast scale in enlightened and fruitful work that form and body are given to that consciousness. Then the flag and the palace where sits the government cease to be the symbols of the nation. The nation deserts these brightly lit, empty shells and takes shelter in the country, where it is given life and dynamic power. The living expression of the nation is the moving consciousness of the whole of the people; it is the coherent, enlightened action of men and women. The collective building up of a destiny is the assumption of responsibility on the historical scale. Otherwise there is anarchy, repression and the resurgence of tribal parties and federalism. The national government, if it wants to be national, ought to govern by the people and for the people, for the outcasts and by the outcasts. No leader, however valuable he may be, can substitute himself for the popular will; and the national government, before concerning itself about international prestige, fill their minds and feast their eyes with human things, and create a prospect that is human because conscious and sovereign men dwell therein.

Part III
Panafricanism

The theme of African unity has dominated political discussion in a continent bedevilled by disunity. Continental unity is seen as a weapon against the forces of imperialism and neo-colonialism, as an instrument in establishing genuine independence, and as a future guarantee of that independence.

Unity is expressed in terms of both practical cooperation, and cultural identity; the extracts in this part illustrate the variety of that expression. The institutions of African unity are well established, and the Organisation of African Unity, while suffering from the defects that trouble all international organisations, is proof of the permanence of the ideal which shapes it. A basic concern of the Organisation has been with decolonisation of the white settler areas of Africa, and evidence of this concern is included in Part IV, as well as here. Other extracts here show that the African leaders' other main concern is with inter-African relations. Regional groupings are a useful forcing-ground for continental unity, and the East African states have for some time been flirting with the idea of federation in their region.

Individuals have made a significant contribution to Panafrican ideas, none more than Nkrumah and Azikiwe in their different styles. Nkrumah, Mamadou Dia, Modibo Keita, and Sekou Touré even made brave attempts to bridge one of the most enduring divisions in the African world, that between French-speaking and English-speaking Africa.

This cultural division emerged clearly in a significant debate in the late 1950s and early 1960s, on the subject of African culture. Senghor's elaboration of the concept of negritude greatly influenced French-speaking Africans, but was coolly received by English-speaking Africans, even when refined into the notion of an 'African personality.' But the importance of cultural identity, particularly as a component of national identity, is constantly emphasised by national political leaders; Fanon and Césaire both give an intellectual underpinning to this concern. Gardiner

190

pleads for an end to that racialism which, in a world of different peoples, is a denial not only of separate cultural existences, but of the common stock of humanity.

A. AFRICAN UNITY: THE INSTITUTIONS

1: The Accra Conference 1958

Extracts from the record of the First Conference of Independent African States, Accra, April 1958. From C. Legum (ed.), *Panafricanism* (Praeger, 1965).
This conference marked the formal beginning of the Panafrican movement as a grouping of African nation-states.

We, the African States assembled here in Accra, in this our first Conference, conscious of our responsibilities to humanity and especially to the peoples of Africa, and desiring to assert our African personality on the side of peace, hereby proclaim and solemnly reaffirm our unswerving loyalty to the Charter of the United Nations, the Universal Declaration of Human Rights and the Declaration of the Asian–African Conference held at Bandung.

We further assert and proclaim the unity among ourselves and our solidarity with the dependent peoples of Africa as well as our friendship with all nations. We resolve to preserve the unity of purpose and action in international affairs which we have forged among ourselves in this historic Conference, to safeguard our hard-won independence, sovereignty and territorial integrity; and to preserve among ourselves the fundamental unity of outlook on foreign policy so that a distinctive African Personality will play its part in co-operation with other peace-loving nations to further the cause of peace.

We pledge ourselves to apply all our endeavours to avoid being committed to any action which might entangle our countries to the detriment of our interests and freedom; to recognise the right of the African peoples to independence and self-determination and to take appropriate steps to hasten the realisation of this right; to affirm the right of the Algerian people to independence and self-determination and to exert all possible effort to hasten the realisation of their independence; to uproot forever the evil of racial discrimination in all its forms wherever it may be found; to persuade the Great Powers to discontinue the production and testing of nuclear and thermo-nuclear weapons; and to reduce conventional weapons.

Furthermore, mindful of the urgent need to raise the living standards of our peoples by developing to the fullest possible advantage the great and varied resources of our lands, we hereby pledge ourselves to co-ordinate our economic planning through a joint economic effort and study the economic potentialities, the technical possibilities and related problems existing in our respective States; to promote co-ordinated industrial planning either through our own individual efforts and/or through co-operation with Specialised Agencies of the United Nations; to take measures to increase trade among our countries by improving communications between our respective countries; and to encourage the investment of foreign capital and skills provided they do not compromise the independence, sovereignty and territorial integrity of our States.

Desirous of mobilising the human resources of our respective countries in furtherance of our social and cultural aspirations, We will endeavour to promote and facilitate the exchange of teachers, professor, students, exhibitions, educational, cultural and scientific material which will improve cultural relations between the African States and inculcate greater knowledge amongst us through such efforts as joint youth festivals, sporting events, etc; We will encourage and strengthen studies of African culture, history and geography in the institutions of learning in the African States; and We will take all measures in our respective countries to ensure that such studies are correctly orientated . . .

RESOLUTIONS

1. Exchange of Views on Foreign Policy

The conference of Independent African States,

Having made the widest exchange of views on all aspects of foreign policy,

Having achieved a unanimity on fundamental aims and principles,

Desiring to pursue a common foreign policy with a view to safeguarding the hard-won independence, sovereignty and territorial integrity of the Participating States,

Deploring the division of the greater part of the world into two antagonistic blocs,

1. Affirms the following fundamental principles:
   A. Unswerving loyalty to and support of the Charter of the United Nations and respect for decisions of the United Nations;
   B. Adherence to the principles enunciated at the Bandung Conference, namely:

(i) Respect for the fundamental human rights and for the purposes and principles of the Charter of the United Nations.

(ii) Respect for the sovereignty and territorial integrity of all nations.

(iii) Recognition of the equality of all races and of the equality of all nations, large and small.

(iv) Abstention from intervention or interference in the internal affairs of another country.

(v) Respect for the right of each nation to defend itself singly or collectively in conformity with the Charter of the United Nations.

(vi) Abstention from the use of arrangements of collective defence to serve the particular interests of any of the big powers. Abstention by any country from exerting pressure on other countries.

(vii) Refraining from acts or threats of aggression or the use of force against the territorial integrity or political independence of any country.

(viii) Settlement of all international disputes by peaceful means such as negotiation, conciliation, arbitration or judicial settlement, as well as other peaceful means of the parties' own choice in conformity with the Charter of the United Nations.

(ix) Promotion of mutual interest and co-operation.

(x) Respect of justice and international obligations.

2. Affirms its conviction that all Participating Governments shall avoid being committed to any action which might entangle them to the detriment of their interest and freedom;

3. Believes that as long as the fundamental unity of outlook on foreign policy is preserved, the Independent African States will be able to assert a distinctive African Personality which will speak with a concerted voice in the cause of Peace in co-operation with other peace-loving nations at the United Nations and other international forums.

2. The Future of the Dependent Territories in Africa

The Conference of Independent African States,

Recognising that the existence of colonialism in any shape or form is a threat to security and independence of the African States and to world peace,

Considering that the problems and the future of dependent territories in Africa are not the exclusive concern of the Colonial Powers but the responsibility of all members of the United Nations and in particular of the Independent African States,

Condemning categorically all colonial systems still enforced in our Continent and which impose arbitrary rule and repression on the people of Africa,

Convinced that a definite date should be set for the attainment of independence by each of the Colonial Territories in accordance with the will of the people of the territories and the provisions of the Charter of the United Nations,

1. Calls upon the Administering Powers to respect the Charter of the United Nations in this regard, and to take rapid steps to implement the provisions of the Charter and the political aspirations of the people, namely self-determination and independence, according to the will of the people;

2. Calls upon the Administering Powers to refrain from repression and arbitrary rule in these territories and to respect all human rights as provided for in the Charter of the United Nations and the Universal Declaration of Human Rights;

3. Calls upon the Administering Powers to bring to an end immediately every form of discrimination in these territories;

4. Recommends that all Participating Governments should give all possible assistance to the dependent people in their struggle to achieve self-determination and independence;

5. Recommends that the Independent African States assembled here should offer facilities for training and educating peoples of the dependent territories; . . .

. . . . . .

11. The Setting up of a Permanent Machinery after the Conference

The Conference of Independent African States,

Firmly convinced that a machinery for consultation and co-operation is essential,

1. Decides to constitute the Permanent Representatives of the Participating Governments at the United Nations as the informal permanent machinery,

(a) for co-ordinating all matters of common concern to the African States,

(b) for examining and making recommendations on concrete practical steps which may be taken to implement the decisions of this and similar future conferences, and

(c) for making preparatory arrangements for future conferences of Independent African States;

2. Agrees that meetings of Foreign Ministers, other Ministers or experts be convened from time to time as and when necessary to study and deal with particular problems of common concern to the African States;

3. Agrees that the Conference of the Independent African States should be held at least once every two years;

. . . . . .

2: The OAU Charter 1963

Extracts from the charter of the Organisation of African Unity, 25 May 1963. From *Basic Documents and Resolutions* (OAU Provisional Secretariat, Addis Ababa, no date).

We, the Heads of African and Malagasy States and Governments assembled in the City of Addis Ababa, Ethiopia;

Convinced that it is the inalienable right of all people to control their own destiny;

Conscious of the fact that freedom, equality, justice and dignity are essential objectives for the achievement of the legitimate aspirations of the African peoples;

Conscious of our responsibility to harness the natural and human resources of our continent for the total advancement of our peoples in spheres of human endeavour;

Inspired by a common determination to promote understanding and collaboration among our States in response to the aspirations of our peoples for brotherhood and solidarity, in a larger unity transcending ethnic and national differences;

Convinced that, in order to translate this determination into a dynamic force in the cause of human progress, conditions for peace and security must be established and maintained;

Determined to safeguard and consolidate the hard-won independence as well as the sovereignty and territorial integrity of our States, and to resist neo-colonialism in all its forms;

Dedicated to the general progress of Africa;

Persuaded that the Charter of the United Nations and the Universal Declaration of Human Rights, to the principles of which we reaffirm our adherence, provide a solid foundation for peaceful and positive co-operation among States;

Desirous that all African and Malagasy States should henceforth unite so that the welfare and well-being of their peoples can be assured;

195

Resolved to reinforce the links between our States by establishing and strengthening common institutions;

Have agreed to the present Charter.

ESTABLISHMENT: ARTICLE 1

The High Contracting Parties do by the present Charter establish an Organisation to be known as the 'Organisation of African and Malagasy States'.

PURPOSES: ARTICLE II

1. The Organisation shall have the following purposes:
    a. To promote the unity and solidarity of the African and Malagasy States.
    b. To co-ordinate and intensify their collaboration and efforts to achieve a better life for the peoples of Africa.
    c. To defend their sovereignty, their territorial integrity and independence.
    d. To eradicate all forms of colonialism from the continent of Africa; and
    e. To promote international co-operation, having due regard to the Charter of the United Nations and the Universal Declaration of Human Rights.
2. To these ends, the Member states shall co-ordinate and harmonise their general policies, especially in the following fields:
    a. Political and diplomatic co-operation
    b. Economic co-operation, including transport and communications.
    c. Educational and cultural co-operation.
    d. Health, sanitation and nutritional co-operation.
    e. Scientific and technical co-operation.
    f. Co-operation for defence and security.

PRINCIPLES: ARTICLE III

The Member States, in pursuit of the purposes stated in Article II, solemnly affirm and declare their adherence to the following principles:

1. The sovereign equality of all African and Malagasy States.
2. Non-interference in the internal affairs of States.
3. Respect for the sovereignty and territorial integrity of each State and for its inalienable right to independent existence.
4. Peaceful settlement of disputes by negotiation, mediation, conciliation or arbitration.
5. Unreserved condemnation, in all its forms, of political assassination as well as of subversive activities on the part of neighbouring States or any

196

other States.

6. Absolute dedication to the total emancipation of the African territories which are still dependent.

7. Affirmation of a policy of non-alignment with regard to all blocs.

MEMBERSHIP: ARTICLE IV

Each independent sovereign African and Malagasy State shall be entitled to become a Member of the Organisation.

RIGHTS AND DUTIES OF MEMBER STATES: ARTICLE V

All Member States shall enjoy equal rights and have equal duties.

ARTICLE VI

The Member States pledge themselves to observe scrupulously the principles enumerated in Article III of the present Charter.

INSTITUTIONS: ARTICLE VII

The Organisation shall accomplish its purposes through the following principal institutions:

1. The Assembly of Heads of State and Government.
2. The Council of Ministers.
3. The General Secretariat.
4. The Commission of Mediation, Conciliation and Arbitration.

THE ASSEMBLY OF HEADS OF STATE AND GOVERNMENT: ARTICLE VIII

The Assembly of Heads of State and Government shall be the supreme organ of the Organisation. It shall, subject to the provisions of this Charter, discuss matters of common concern to all Member States with a view to co-ordinating and harmonising the general policy of the Organisation. It may in addition review the structure, functions and acts of all the organs and any specialized agencies which may be created in accordance with the present Charter.

. . . . . .

THE COUNCIL OF MINISTERS: ARTICLE XII

The Council of Ministers shall consist of Foreign Ministers or such other Ministers as are designated by the Governments of Member States.

The Council of Ministers shall meet at least twice a year. When requested by any Member State and approved by two-thirds of all Member States, it shall meet in extraordinary session.

ARTICLE XIII

The Council of Ministers shall be responsible to the Assembly of Heads of State and Government. It shall be entrusted with the responsibility of preparing conferences of the Assembly.

It shall take cognisance of any matter referred to it by the Assembly. It shall be entrusted with the implementation of the decisions of the Assembly of Heads of State. It shall co-ordinate inter-African co-operation in accordance with the instructions of the Assembly and in conformity with Article II(2) of the present Charter.

ARTICLE XIV

1. Each Member State shall have one vote.

2. All resolutions shall be determined by a two-thirds majority of those members present and voting.

3. Questions of procedure shall require a simple majority. Whether or not a question is one of procedure shall be determined by a simple majority of all Member States present and voting.

4. Two-thirds of the total membership of the Council shall form a quorum for any meeting of the Council . . .

. . . . . .

COMMISSION OF MEDIATION, CONCILIATION AND ARBITRATION: ARTICLE XIX

Member States pledge to settle all disputes among themselves by peaceful means and, to this end, agree to conclude a separate treaty establishing a Commission of Mediation, Conciliation and Arbitration. Said treaty shall be regarded as forming an integral part of the present Charter.

SPECIALISED COMMISSIONS: ARTICLE XX

The Assembly shall establish such Specialised Commissions as it may deem necessary, including the following:

1. Economic and Social Commission.
2. Educational and Cultural Commission.
3. Health, Sanitation and Nutrition Commission.
4. Defence Commission.
5. Scientific, Technical and Research Commission . . .

. . . . . .

AMENDMENT TO THE CHARTER: ARTICLE XXXIII

This Charter may be amended or revised if any Member State makes a written request to the Administrative Secretary-General to that effect;

provided, however, that the proposed amendment is not submitted to the Assembly for consideration until all the Member States have been duly notified of it and a period of one year has elapsed. Such an amendment shall not be effective unless approved by at least two-thirds of all the Member States.

3: OAU Resolution on Border Disputes, July 1964

Resolution by the 1st Assembly of OAU Heads of State, Cairo, July 1964. From *Basic Documents and Resolutions* (OAU Provisional Secretariat).

The Assembly of Heads of State and Government at its First Ordinary Session, held in Cairo, UAR, from 17 to 21 July 1964;

Considering that the frontier problem constitutes a grave and permanent factor of dissension;

Considering all the extra-African manoeuvres aiming at dividing the African States;

Considering that the borders of African States, on the day of their independence, constitute an intangible reality;

Considering the setting up in Lagos of the Committee of Eleven in charge of studying the means of strengthening African Unity;

Considering the necessity of fostering African Unity by all possible means;

Considering the imperious necessity of settling, by peaceful means and within a strictly African framework, all disputes between African States;

Considering that all Member States have pledged, according to Article VI, to scrupulously respect all principles laid down in Article III of the Charter of the Organisation of African Unity;

1. Solemnly reaffirms the strict respect of the principles laid down in Article III paragraph 3 of the Charter of the Organisation of African Unity;

2. Solemnly declares that all Member States pledge themselves to respect the frontiers existing on their achievement of national independence.

4: OAU Resolution on Non-Alignment, February 1964

OAU Council of Ministers, Lagos, 24–9 February 1964, CM/Res. 12 II. From *Basic Documents and Resolutions* (OAU Provisional Secretariat).

199

The Council of Ministers meeting in Lagos, 24–9 February 1964:

. . . . . .

1. *Recommends* to African States the co-ordination of their foreign policies, especially in the non-alignment approach vis-à-vis the existing World Bloc Powers, as an acceptable safeguard for African freedom, stability, and prosperity;

2. *Agrees* to resort to direct consultation among African states in order to put their solemn resolve into practice;

3. *Recommends* the removal of commitments, as soon as possible, which would militate against a consistent policy of non-alignment;

4. *Reaffirms* its determination to give priority to the consolidation of African unity in conformity with the charter, and the reinforcement of Afro-Asian solidarity;

5. *Decides* to maintain direct consultation between Member states of the O.A.U. regarding future international conferences, either as sponsors or participants, in order to preserve a coherent and united position.

5: OAU Resolution on Regional Groupings, August 1963

OAU Council of Ministers, Dakar, Senegal, 10 August 1963. CM/Res. 5(1). From *Basic Documents and Resolutions* (OAU Provisional Secretariat).

Whereas the setting up of the O.A.U. has given rise to great and legitimate hopes amongst African peoples.

Mindful of the will of these peoples to put an end to the division of African states;

Whereas this will was unanimously proclaimed by the Heads of State and Government at the Addis Ababa Conference;

Whereas furthermore regional groupings have favoured the achievement of African Unity and the development of co-operation amongst member states;

Whereas also the charter of the O.A.U. has made provision for economic, cultural, scientific, technical and military specialised institutions in order to strengthen solidarity amongst African peoples and co-operation amongst member states;

Considering therefore the need for regional and sub-regional groupings to evolve with a view to their adaptation to the charter of the O.A.U.;

1. *Takes Note* of the will of member states to implement all means in order to bring about this adaptation;
2. *Recommends* that any regional grouping or sub-grouping be in keeping with the charter of the O.A.U. and meet the following criteria;
   (a) geographical realities and economic, social and cultural factors common to the States;
   (b) co-ordination of economic, social, and cultural activities peculiar to the States concerned;
3. *Suggests* to the African states signatories of agreements in existence before the setting-up of the O.A.U that they henceforth refer to the charter of Addis Ababa;
4. *Invites* all African States desiring to constitute regional groupings or sub-groupings to conform with principles set out above and to contemplate the integration of already existing bodies into the specialised institutions of the O.A.U.;
5. *Requests* member states to deposit the statutes of the said groupings at the seat of the O.A.U. before their entry into force.

6: The 'Good Neighbours' Policy: East and Central Africa

Extracts from the Final Communiqué of the Nairobi meeting of Heads of Government in East and Central Africa, March/April 1966. Published in C. Gertzel (ed.), *Government and Politics in Kenya* (East Africa Publishing House, 1971).

The Heads of States and Government and the representatives of the Governments of Burundi, Congo (Leopoldville), Ethiopia, Kenya, Malawi, Uganda, Rwanda, Somalia, Sudan, Tanzania and Zambia met in Nairobi from 31st March to 2nd April 1966, at the invitation of His Excellency Mzee Jomo Kenyatta, President of the Republic of Kenya.
. . . . . .
It was made clear from the outset that this meeting was not to be regarded as an attempt to form a regional grouping or to usurp the functions of the Organization of African Unity. On the contrary all the countries represented reaffirmed their loyalty and continued support for the Organization of African Unity. They were, however, agreed that recent

201

events in Africa constituted a danger to the cause of African unity and the functioning of the Organization of African Unity. Such events also hamper the efforts of liberating those parts of Africa still under colonial rule.

The meeting considered many matters of mutual concern and common interest. The discussions covered three principal themes:

(a) Promotion of good neighbourly relations.
(b) Strengthening of African Unity.
(c) Decolonization of Africa with special emphasis on the Rhodesian question.

The meeting examined causes of misunderstanding and friction among the neighbouring States in East and Central Africa. It was felt that the improvement of relation among neighbouring states would lead to the strengthening of African unity and that ... most problems of African unity today are in effect difficulties in neighbourly relations. It was therefore concluded that the stability and strengthening of the individual Member States and the improvement of their relations would contribute to the strengthening of the Organization of African Unity itself.

It was agreed that some of the problems causing misunderstanding or friction among neighbours are a legacy of colonialism, while others are the results of new pressures – external or internal – generated after Independence.

The meeting was seriously concerned at the tendency on the part of the Press to exaggerate and distort inter-State problems or incidents, thereby causing unnecessary tension. It was also noted that there was a habit on the part of the Press or individuals and groups to exploit external difficulties, having no regard to the effect on neighbourly relations.

There were exhaustive discussions on the problems created by the refugees. It was noted that in many cases relations between neighbours have been strained as a result of activities of certain refugees who use the host country as a base for subversion and political agitation against their country of origin. In some cases refugees used the host country for the purpose of receiving financial and material aid from external sources.

All States represented, however, noted the United Nations Convention on the Status of Refugees and the humanitarian reasons for accepting refugees including those from Organization of African Unity Member States. It was agreed that each host State take appropriate action to stop refugees, under penalty of expulsion, from using its facilities for subversion and political activities against the country of origin. The host country should keep a watch on the refugees so that they do not settle near the border with their country of origin.

The meeting noted the bilateral efforts made so far to repatriate and rehabilitate refugees and recommended that this should continue.

All the States represented undertook to avoid in future any propaganda campaign by Press, radio or otherwise against a neighbouring State.

It was reaffirmed that good neighbourly relations involved certain principles, which all States accepted unreservedly. Most important among these was the Organization of African Unity doctrine of non-interference in the affairs of other African States. It was agreed that the legitimate interest of each State in the preservation of peace and stability within its borders required a high degree of inter-government co-operation and understanding. It was agreed that each State should take steps necessary to increase this contact and co-operation, and to rebuild mutual trust where this had been damaged in the past. To this end it was agreed that all States represented at the meeting will work together to eliminate border incidents and create machinery for improving neighbourly relations.

. . . . . .

It was felt that all countries represented should support the efforts of the E.C.A. and specialized commissions of the Organization of African Unity, aimed at closer economic relations.

. . . . . .

Finally, the Heads of State and Government agreed to meet informally from time to time, and to discuss problems of mutual interest. The purpose of such meetings would be the fostering of the spirit of brotherhood and neighbourliness through which to strengthen the Organization of African Unity and its institutions.

7: Declaration by the Governments of East Africa, June 1963

From Meetings and Discussions on the Proposed East African Federation (Dar-es-Salaam). Reproduced in D. Rothchild (ed.), *The Politics of Integration* (East Africa Publishing House, 1968).

We, the leaders of the people and governments of East Africa, assembled in Nairobi on June 5, 1963, pledge ourselves to the political federation of East Africa. Our meeting today is motivated by the spirit of Panafricanism, and not by mere selfish regional interest. We are nationalists, and reject tribalism, racialism or inward-looking policies. We believe that the day of decision has come and to all our people we say:-

There is no more room for slogans and words. This is our day of action in the cause of the ideals that we believe in, and the unity and freedom for which we have suffered and sacrificed so much.

Within this spirit of Panafricanism, and following the declaration of African unity at the recent Addis Ababa Conference, practical steps should be taken wherever possible to accelerate the achievement of our common goal.

We believe that the East African Federation can be a practical step towards the goal of Panafrican unity. We hope that our action will help to accelerate the efforts already being made by our brothers throughout the Continent to achieve Panafrican unity.

We share a common past, and are convinced of our common destinies. We have a common history, culture and customs which make our unity both logical and natural. Our futures are inevitably bound together by the identical aspirations and hopes of our peoples, and the need for similar efforts in facing the tasks that lie ahead of each of our free nations. In the past century the hand of imperialism grasped the whole Continent, and in this part of Africa our people found themselves included together in what the colonialists styled "the British sphere of influence". Now that we are once again free, or are on the point of regaining our freedom, we believe the time has come to consolidate our unity and provide it with a constitutional basis.

. . . . . .

Economic planning, the maximum utilisation of manpower and our other resources, the establishment of a central bank and common defence programme, and foreign and diplomatic representation, are areas in which we need to work together. Such an approach would provide greater co-ordination and savings in both scarce capital, facilities for training and manpower. What is more, we would have a total population of more than 25 million people – a formidable force and a vast market to influence economic development at home, attract a greater investment and enhance our prestige and influence abroad. The movement towards popular government and independence in our various countries of recent years has brought forward the issue of political federation once again. The achievement of truly popular governments in each country removes fears of minority or settler domination under federation. We believe a political federation of East Africa is desired by our peoples. There is throughout East Africa a great urge for unity and an appreciation of the significance of federation.

We are aware that local and territorial factors have to be taken into account. We firmly believe that ways can be devised of overcoming any fears, and of surmounting such difficulties. Special attention will be paid to the accommodation of relevant territorial interests in drawing up the constitution of East African Federation.

8: Nyerere's Response

From East African Common Services Organisation, Proceedings of the Central Legislative Assembly Debates, Official Report, Vol. IV, No. 2 (August 10 1965). Published in Rothchild, *Politics of Integration*.

We have no lack of aspiration for unity, nor any absence of understanding about the advantages of it. Throughout our three countries the intellectuals and masses are united on this subject, and no politician would now dare to stand up and oppose East African unity. But we are in danger of treating the will as if it were the deed.

The truth is that we do not in fact have unity in East Africa, and it is now clear that it cannot be achieved as easily as we once hoped and expected. What we do have is such economic integration between our sovereign states that frictions are inevitable in the absence of efficient decision-making machinery. On top of that, we have such close historical connections between our respective nationalist movements that we tend to take each other's understanding for granted.

. . . . . .

In fact, of course, economic co-operation between Kenya, Tanzania and Uganda has never been without its difficulties or its allegations of unfair advantage for one or other country. The present difficulties are by no means the first that East Africa has experienced. They do, however, take place in a different political context than earlier ones . . .

As our three countries obtained their separate independence, the single ultimate authority ceased to exist . . . Instead, the ultimate authority became the three-headed East African Authority, and absolute unanimity of decision between sovereign states had to be obtained on all matters connected with our common services and our common market.

It is important to be clear what this means; if the three leaders cannot agree unanimously on a proposal, then no action is possible at all – unless one or other of us unilaterally breaks the agreements and conventions which are the foundation of our co-operation. In other words, if and while discussion fails to result in agreement or acceptable compromise, then each of our three nations has a veto power in relation to certain developments in the other two. This veto – which can be exercised by failure to answer as well as by an adverse decision – can be ignored; the Authority has no enforcement machinery. But this can only be done at the risk of destroying our whole complex of economic co-operation.

The requirement of unanimity, however, is not easy to achieve despite our great will to co-operate. Each of our three governments is answerable to the people of its own country. Each of them is beset with the urgent needs of one part of the total East African area. In Authority meetings, therefore, each Member can look at the interests of East Africa as a whole only to the extent that these do not conflict fundamentally with the requirements of his own nation's immediate needs. We Members are leaders of democratic governments, and must balance the long-term need for unity with our immediate need for action, in just the same way as we have internally to balance the long-term need for large capital investment against urgent social needs. Ultimately we are not in fact "East African" leaders but leaders of states in East Africa; and regional loyalty has sometimes to come second to our national responsibilities.

. . . . . .

There are many differences in the structure of the common poverty of our three states; in one, urban unemployment is the most pressing problem; in another, the almost complete absence of an industrial sector of the economy. There are differences in the quantity and quality of the educational facilities we each inherited from our colonial past, and differences in the administrative machines. All these, and the many other detailed differences which have resulted from separate colonial histories, mean that each of our territorial governments has to have different priorities of action, and to some extent a different approach to the problems before it. It is therefore inevitable that at any one time there may be genuine clashes of interest, with one nation feeling a positive need to take steps which the others cannot approve . . .

Tanzania believes very strongly that every effort must be made to maintain our economic unity, and our common services. The real security and the real development of our separate territories, as well as the area as a whole, needs unity in East Africa as a preliminary to the unity of the African continent. It is for this reason that we remain so anxious for the establishment of a sovereign federal East African state. Only by such transfer of sovereignty can one authority be established with overall powers in matters of East African concern. We should then have a single voice in the international world; it would be infinitely more difficult for anyone to play us up against each other. In a federation short-term clashes of economic interest could be settled by a body which was responsible to the peoples of the whole area. And this same sovereign body could ensure that each of our particular poverty problems was tackled in co-operation, while at the same time our joint resources were used to tackle the basic underlying problems which are common to us all.

9: The Treaty for East African Co-operation 1967

Extracts from the Treaty for East African Co-operation, Nairobi (Government Printer, 1967).

The Treaty was signed at Kampala on 6 June 1967 by the Governments of Kenya, Uganda, and Tanzania, and came into effect on 1 December 1967.

Whereas the United Republic of Tanzania, the Sovereign State of Uganda and the Republic of Kenya have enjoyed close commercial, industrial, and other ties for many years:

And whereas provision was made by the East Africa (High Commission) Orders in Council 1947 to 1961 for the control and administration of certain matters and services of common interest to the said countries and for that purpose the East Africa High Commission and the East Africa Central Legislative Assembly were thereby established:

And whereas provision was made by the East African Common Services Organization Agreements 1961 to 1966 (upon the revocation of the East Africa (High Commission) Orders in Council 1947 to 1961) for the establishment of the East African Common Services Organization with the East Africa Common Services Authority as its principal executive authority and the Central Legislative Assembly as its legislative body:

And whereas the East African Common Services Organization has, since its establishment, performed on behalf of the said countries common services in accordance with the wishes of the said countries and its Constitution:

And whereas the said countries, while being aware that they have reached different stages of industrial development and resolved to reduce existing industrial imbalances, are resolved and determined to foster and encourage the accelerated and sustained industrial development of all of the said countries:

And whereas the said countries, with a view to strengthening the unity of East Africa, are resolved to abolish certain quantitative restrictions which at present affect trade between them and are desirous of pursuing a policy towards the most favourable development of the freest possible international trade:

And whereas the said countries having regard to the interest of and their desire for the wider unity of Africa are resolved to co-operate with one another and with other African countries in the economic, political and cultural fields:

And whereas the said countries are resolved to act in concert for the establishment of a common market with no restrictions in the long term on trade between such countries:

Now therefore the Government of the United Republic of Tanzania, the Government of the Sovereign State of Uganda and the Government of the Republic of Kenya,

Determined to strengthen their industrial, commercial and other ties and their common services by the establishment of an East African Community and of a Common Market as an integral part thereof, agree as follows:

ARTICLE 1: ESTABLISHMENT AND MEMBERSHIP OF THE COMMUNITY

1. By this Treaty the Contracting Parties establish among themselves an East African Community and, as an integral part of such Community, an East African Common Market.

. . . . . .

3. The members of the Community, in this Treaty referred to as "the Partner States," shall be the United Republic of Tanzania, the Sovereign State of Uganda and the Republic of Kenya.

ARTICLE 2: AIMS OF THE COMMUNITY

1. It shall be the aim of the Community to strengthen and regulate the industrial, commercial and other relations of the Partner States to the end that there shall be accelerated, harmonious and balanced development and sustained expansion of economic activities the benefits whereof shall be equitably shared.

2. For the purposes set out in paragraph 1 of this Article and as hereinafter provided in the particular provisions of this Treaty, the Community shall use its best endeavours to ensure:–

(a) the establishment and maintenance, subject to certain exceptions, of a common customs tariff and a common excise tariff;
(b) the abolition generally of restrictions on trade between Partner States;

208

(c)   the inauguration, in the long term, of a common agricultural policy;

(d)   the establishment of an East African Development Bank in accordance with the Charter contained in Annex VI of this Treaty;

(e)   the retention of freedom of current account payments between the Partner States, and freedom of capital account payments necessary to further the aims of the Community;

(f)   the harmonization, required for the proper functioning of the Common Market, of the monetary policies of the Partner States and in particular consultation in case of any disequilibrium in the balances of payments of the Partner States;

(g)   the operation of services common to the Partner States;

(h)   the co-ordination of economic planning;

(i)   the co-ordination of transport policy;

(j)   the approximation of the commercial laws of the Partner States; and

(k)   such other activities, calculated to further the aims of the Community, as the Partner States may from time to time decide to undertake in common.

B. AFRICAN UNITY: THE LEADERS
10: George Padmore

From G. Padmore, *Panafricanism or Communism?* (Dennis Dobson, London, 1956).
An early Panafricanist, Padmore was at one time a member of the Communist Party, but later rejected Communism, which he felt was merely manipulating Negro discontents. He saw Panafricanism as an ideological alternative for Africa, and was probably a significant influence of Kwame Nkrumah's Panafricanist ideals.

Recognizing the oneness of the struggles of the Coloured World for freedom from alien domination, Panafricanism endorses the conception of an Asian-African front against that racial arrogance which has reached its apogee in the *Herrenvolk* philosophy of *Apartheid*. Panafricanism, moreover, draws considerable inspiration from the struggles of the national freedom movements of the Asian countries, and subscribes to the Gandhian doctrine of non-violence as a means of attaining self-determination and racial equality. It rejects the unbridled system of monopoly capitalism of the West no less than the political and cultural totalitarianism of the East. It identifies itself with the neutral camp, opposed to all forms of oppression and racial chauvinism – white or black – and associates itself with all forces of progress and goodwill, regardless of nationality, race, colour, or creed, working for universal brotherhood, social justice, and peace *for all peoples everywhere.*

Africans, like Asians, have a vested interest in *Peace*, since only in a world ordered and free from violence and war can they hope to create a new life for themselves and make their positive contribution to modern civilization.

Panafricanism recognizes much that is true in the Marxist interpretation of history, since it provides a rational explanation for a good deal that would otherwise be unintelligible. But it nevertheless refuses to accept the pretentious claims of doctrinaire Communism, that it alone has the solution to all the complex racial, tribal, and socio-economic problems facing Africa. It also rejects the Communist intolerance of those who do not subscribe to its ever-changing party line even to the point of liquidating them as 'enemies of the people'. Democracy and brotherhood cannot be built upon intolerance and violence.

In their struggles to attain self-government and self-determination, the younger leaders of Panafricanism have the task of building upon the ideological foundations laid by Dr DuBois, the 'father' of Panafricanism. The problems facing these men are very much more varied and complex than those which beset the founders of the Sierra Leone and Liberian settlements. They are under the necessity to evolve new political means and organizational techniques adapted to African traditions and circumstances. They also have to work out a social philosophy which will integrate and uplift peoples making the transition from primitive tribal forms of society to modern industrialized states with the speed demanded by present-day pressures.

Our criticism of British colonial policy is not in what it professes to stand for – 'self government within the Commonwealth' – but the failure to make good this promise unless actually forced to do so by the colonial peoples. It has always been a case of 'too little and too late'. The result is that the dependent peoples, who would otherwise be Britain's friends and allies, become her implacable enemies. What British colonial policy needs to do today is to make open recognition of awakening African self-awareness, and instil its own acts with boldness and imagination. Deeds and not vague promises are what is wanted.

For their part, the African nationalist leaders must resolve their own internal communal conflicts and tribal differences, so that, having established a democratically elected government, the imperial power will find less danger in passing power to the popularly elected leaders than in withholding it. Once a colonial people have achieved freedom, as the history of the recently emerged Asian nations has so well illustrated, they will know how to defend it against those subversive elements within their midst who seek to make them pawns in the power politics of the cold war belligerents.

In the coming struggle for Africa, the issue, as I have already inferred, will be between Panafricanism and Communism. Imperialism is a discredited system, completely rejected by Africans. As for white colonization, it can maintain itself only with outside military support. The white man in East and Central Africa has forfeited the loyalty and goodwill of the Africans, who no longer have illusions about professions of 'trusteeship' and 'partnership'. These British settlers, to say nothing of the fanatical racialists and rabid defenders of *Apartheid* in South Africa, have made it abundantly clear to the Africans that they regard them merely as hewers of wood and drawers of water in their own countries.

As to Communism, Africans have no reason to be scared of the red bogey as long as their political leaders remain true to the ideals and principles of Panafricanism. For politically, Panafricanism seeks to attainment of the government of Africans by Africans for Africans, with respect for racial and religious minorities who desire to live in Africa on a basis of equality with the black majority. Economically and socially, Panafricanism subscribes to the fundamental objectives of Democratic Socialism, with state control of the basic means of production and distribution. It stands for the liberty of the subject within the law and endorses the Fundamental Declaration of Human Rights, with emphasis upon the Four Freedoms.

The post-war happenings in Asia have shown that forms of government are not of paramount importance to the masses of the people. Their interest is in the satisfaction of their elemental needs. Communism exploits misery, poverty, ignorance and want. The only effective answer to Communism, therefore, is to remove these conditions by satisfying the wants and material needs of the common people, which revolve primarily round food, clothing, and shelter. Any honest, incorruptible government seeking to do this will provide the best guarantee against Communism. Hence, Panafricanism sets out to fulfil the socio-economic mission of Communism under a libertarian political system.

Finally, for Panafricanism, the self-determination of the dependent territories is the prerequisite to the federation of self-governing states on a regional basis, leading ultimately to the creation of a United States of Africa. For there is a growing feeling among politically conscious Africans throughout the continent that their destiny is one, that what happens in one part of Africa to Africans must affect Africans living in other parts. As far back as forty years ago, Dr DuBois, in his book, *The Negro*, pointed out a truth which, if anything, is even more pregnant today. *'There is slowly arising not only a curiously strong brotherhood of Negro blood throughout the world, but the common cause of the darker races against the intolerable assumption and insults of Europeans has already found expression. Most men in the world are coloured. A belief in humanity means a belief in coloured men. The future world will, in all reasonable possibility, be what coloured men make it.'*

This is the inescapable challenge of the second part of the twentieth century.

As long as the African leaders remain true to the people, they have nothing to fear but fear. Destiny is in their own hands. For already they have the powerful moral support of the Asian-African Conference, which declared that 'Colonialism in all its manifestations is an evil which should speedily be brought to an end . . . That the subjection of peoples to alien subjugation, domination and exploitation constitutes a denial of fundamental human rights is contrary to the Charter of the United Nations and is an impediment to the promotion of world peace and co-operation.' [Bandung Conference Declaration, 24 April 1955]

In our struggle for national freedom, human dignity and social redemption, Panafricanism offers an ideological alternative to Communism on the one side and Tribalism on the other. It rejects both white racialism and black chauvinism. It stands for racial co-existence on the basis of absolute equality and respect for human personality.

Panafricanism looks above the narrow confines of class, race, tribe and religion. In other words, it wants equal opportunity for all. Talent to be rewarded on the basis of merit. Its vision stretches beyond the limited frontiers of the nation-state. Its perspective embraces the federation of regional self-governing countries and their ultimate amalgamation into a *United States of Africa*.

In such a Commonwealth, all men, regardless of tribe, race, colour or creed, shall be free and equal. And all the national units comprising the regional federations shall be autonomous in all matters regional, yet united in all matters of common interest to the African Union. This is our vision of the Africa of Tomorrow – the goal of Panafricanism.

11: Kwame Nkrumah

(a) Extracts from K. Nkrumah, *I Speak of Freedom* (Heinemann Educational Books, 1961). The context of each extract is given after the extract.

(b) Extracts from K. Nkrumah, *African Must Unite* (H. E. B., 1963).

(a). . . The colonial powers and their imperialist allies are beginning to advance a new, subtle theory – and a disguised one, at that – to safeguard their position in Africa and to beguile and bamboozle the Africans. They are prepared to grant political independence but, at the same time, they are also planning to continue to dominate the African territories in the economic field by establishing control over the economic life of the newly independent African countries. There is no difference between political imperialism and economic imperialism. By these methods, the enemies of African freedom hope to be able to use the new African states as puppets to continue to dominate Africa, while, at the same time, making the Africans believe that they are, in fact, free and independent.

This new type or concept of independence has been described as 'International Independence' and it is now the new slogan which is being preached in many colonial territories in Africa. Under certain conditions, the colonial powers are prepared even now to grant independence to many of their territories. As independent states, these territories are supposed to acquire international personality and establish diplomatic relations with other states and also have representation in the various international organisations, including the United Nations.

Once this stage has been reached, the devil of colonialism will put all its energies into establishing control over the foreign relations and policies of the new African states, and thus make it difficult or even impossible for the African people to work together to establish a Union of African States. The new policy or concept of 'conditional independence', which the colonial powers are now planning to adopt, is a policy which is intended to create several weak independent states in Africa. These states are designed to be so weak and unstable in the organisation of their national economies and administrations that they will be compelled by internal as well as external pressures to continue to depend upon the colonial powers who have ruled them for several years. The weaker and the less stable an African state is, the easier it is for the colonial power concerned to dominate the affairs and fortunes of the new state, even though it is supposed to have gained independence.

. . . . . .

There is strength in the political unity of our continent and that is why the Convention People's Party, as the vanguard for African liberation, is always against any policy for the balkanisation of Africa into small weak and unstable states. We believe that considerations of mutual security and prosperity of our people demand that all the independent states in Africa

213

should work together to create a Union of African States.
(Speech to public rally, Accra, early 1960)

So deep is our faith in African unity that we have declared our preparedness to surrender the sovereignty of Ghana, in whole or in part, in the interest of a Union of African States and Territories as soon as ever such a union becomes practicable. (Broadcast, 6 March 1960)

(b) An African Common Market, devoted uniquely to African interests, would more efficaciously promote the true requirements of the African states. Such an African Market presupposes a common policy for overseas trade as well as for inter-African trade, and must preserve our right to trade freely anywhere. If it is a good thing for the European buyers to regulate their affairs with their overseas suppliers by combination, then it must be equally good for Africans to do likewise in offering their wares. Besides, an African Common Market that does not concert its policy in regard to its exports seriously reduces its effectiveness, since the mutuality of interest might well be violated by individual actions in regard to the sale of crops common to several of the members. One of the principal objectives of our African Common Market must be to eliminate the competition that presently exists between us, and must continue to do so while any one of us mistakenly shelters under the umbrella of the European Common Market. The cash crops that we produce must be pooled, so that our combined totals will give us a commanding position and, through a united selling policy, enable us to extract better prices. For instance, Ghana and Nigeria between them produce about 50 per cent of the world's cocoa. So far we have been selling against each other, but in uniting our policy, we can beat the undercutting tactics of the buyers who set us one against the other.

The surpluses thus derived from increased revenues resulting from a common selling policy could be placed to realistic development (rejected by the European Development Fund), and give a spurt to fundamental industrialism. The trade now beginning to be developed between us would be stimulated, while a common currency would eliminate the difficulties of exchange as well as the illegitimate dealings which at present rob us of part of our wealth. A common currency, free of links with outside currency zones, would enable us to reserve the foreign exchange made from our export trade for essential imports.

In the same way, the pooled sum of our present individual investments in our similar national projects, if used within an integrated plan, would give greater benefit in mutual development. Indeed, the total integration of the African economy on a continental scale is the only way in which the

214

African states can achieve anything like the levels of the industrialized countries. The idea of African union is not just a sentimental one, emanating from a common experience of colonialism and a desire for young, untried states to come together in the effervescence of their new freedom, though sentiment undoubtedly has its part. The unity of the countries of Africa is an indispensable pre-condition for the speediest and fullest development, not only of the totality of the continent but of the individual countries linked together in the union.

. . . . . .

Any form of economic union negotiated singly between the fully industrialised states of Europe and the newly emergent countries of Africa is bound to retard the industrialization, and therefore, the prosperity and the general economic and cultural development, of these countries. For it will mean that those African states which may be inveigled into joining this union will continue to serve as protected overseas markets for the manufactured goods of their industrialized partners, and sources of cheap raw materials. The subsidy which they will receive in return for assuming these obligations will be small compared with the losses which they will suffer from perpetuating their colonial status, losses which are to be measured not only in terms of their own retarded economic, technical and cultural development, but in the harm which they do the peoples of Africa as a whole. The question must be raised as to where this subsidy comes from. It is difficult to believe that it is a purely altruistic contribution made by the European members of the Market to the cause of African well-being. Such subsidy must, in fact, come out of the trading profits made from forcing down the prices of primary products bought from the African countries and raising the cost of the finished goods they are obliged to take in exchange. It is also included in the cost of the projects which constitute the subsidy, a good part of which returns to the European contributors in the form of payments for materials, services, salaries, and banking commissions and interest.

. . . . . .

The three basic aims of Ghana's foreign policy are African independence, African unity, and the maintenance of world peace through a policy of positive neutrality and non-alignment. The first two aims are inextricably bound together, since until we are free from foreign domination we cannot be completely united. Yet united action is essential if we are to achieve full independence. The third aim is closely associated with the other two. Living as we do under the constant threat of universal destruction, the more unaligned nations there are, the wider the non-committed area of the world, the better the chances of human survival. By moral force, if not by material strength, the non-aligned nations must exert

215

their influence to save the world from ultimate disaster. The unity of Africa and the strength it would gather from continental integration of its economic and industrial development, supported by a united policy of non-alignment, could have a most powerful effect for world peace.

I do not believe it is possible for a state, in the world today, to secure its safety by withdrawing from international affairs and refusing to take a stand on issues which affect peace and war. This would be to follow a policy of negative neutralism which is tantamount to a fatal belief that war between the great powers would bring misery and destruction only to those who participated in it. Since war, if it comes, is likely to destroy most of us, whether we are participants or not, whether or not we are the cause of it, negative neutralism is no shield at all. It is completely impotent and even dangrous.

12: Nnamdi Azikiwe

Extract from 'The Future of Panafricanism', *Présence Africaine,* Vol. 12, No. 40(1962).
Text of an address in London, August 1961, when Azikiwe was Governor-General of Nigeria.

I would prefer to be very broad in my use of the words 'Africa' and 'African' ... unless we accept a broad definition of terms, there can be no worthy future for Africanism. That being the case, I would like to speak of the peoples of Africa in general terms to include all the races inhabiting that continent and embracing all the linguistic and cultural groups who are domiciled therein.

. . . . . .

It would be useless to define 'Panafricanism' exclusively in racial or linguistic terms, since the obvious solution would be parochial. And chauvinism, by whatever name it is identified, has always been a disintegrating factor in human society at all known times of human history ...

Panafricanism in action has proved the existence of deep-seated fears which exist in the minds of certain African leaders in some African States. The Principles of Monrovia demonstrate the nature of these fears, to wit: the right of African States to equality of sovereignty irrespective of size and population; the right of each African State to self-determination and existence; the right of any African State to federate or confederate with another African State; respect for the principle of non-interference in the internal and domestic affairs of African States *inter se* and the inviolability of the territorial integrity of each African State . . .

. . . it is essential that we . . . examine the primary [problems of Panafricanism]. First, the inhabitants of the African continent are not racially homogeneous. . .

Secondly, the existence of various linguistic groups in Africa has intensified the problem of communication and human understanding . . .

Thirdly, the impact of various cultures on African society has created basic problems of social unity . . .

. . . . . .

If the anthropological problems are basic, then the sociological are complex since they affect the economic, political and constitutional aspects of the lives of those concerned. Economically, the existence of tariff walls and barriers has tended to alienate rather than draw closer the relations of those who should be good neighbours. High competitive markets have led to cut-throat methods of bargaining and distribution. The use of separate currencies as legal tender has accentuated social differences. With separate road, railway, aviation and communication systems, Africans have become estranged from one another.

The political issues are even more confounding. Granted that political union is desirable, the question arises whether it should be in the form of a federation or a confederation. If the former, should it be a tight or a loose one? In any case sovereignty must be surrendered in part or in whole, in which case it will be desirable to know whether it is intended to surrender internal or external sovereignty or both? In this context, we cannot overlook the struggle for hegemony as indeed has been the case in the last few years. Hand in glove with the struggle for hegemony goes the manoeuvre for the control of the armed forces for the effective implementation of policy.

The constitutional implications of Panafricanism present to its builders a challenge to create a heaven on earth for African humanity. Therefore, the powers of the executive must be clearly defined, bearing in mind that in most of the progressive States of the world, Heads of States exercise powers formally and Heads of Governments formulate policy and do the actual governing. Nevertheless, the vogue is to accept the supremacy of the legislature, as a forum for airing the views of the electorate and strengthening the hand of the executive.

Panafricanists must also guarantee the independence of the judiciary, not necessarily by stratifying judges as a select and privileged elite but by ensuring that they shall perform their functions without fear or favour and at the same time be responsible to the people for their actions and

217

behaviour. To obtain maximum efficiency in the machinery of administration, the civil service must be insulated from partisan politics. As for the people themselves, their fundamental rights must be guaranteed and entrenched in any document or instrument creating any association of African States.

......

An African federation or confederation, either on a regional or continental basis, has many blessings for the continent of Africa and its inhabitants. Politically, it will raise the prestige of African States in the councils of the world; it will make Africa a bastion of democracy, and it will revive the stature of man by guaranteeing to African citizens the fundamental rights of man. From a military point of view, such a concert of States will protect the people of Africa not only from external aggression and internal commotion, but also it would safeguard the whole of Africa by a system of collective security. Economically, by abrogating discriminatory tariffs, we create a free trade area over the entire continent and thereby expand the economy of all African countries involved, thereby raising living standards and ensuring economic security for African workers. Socially, it will restore the dignity of the human being in Africa.

13: Mamadou Dia

Extracts from M. Dia, *The African Nations and World Solidarity* (Praeger, 1961). These extracts are from the Epilogue, written after the collapse of the Mali Federation (of Senegal and Soudan) in August 1960.

We were hoping to present Mali as an example of inter-African solidarity, a living testimonial to international co-operation. Since the rupture of the Federation on the night of August 19–20, 1960, we have been compelled to renounce this ambition ... We take consolation in being able ... to offer our readers a critique of the model of solidarity that we were proposing to the world. Our fundamental option can only be strengthened thereby.

The issue here is not the theory of solidarity nor the need for African unity. Nor is the policy of large groupings contradicted by the events. At most, one can claim that the rupture of Mali refutes our theories on the formation of the African nation and our theses on the process of setting up large economic complexes. It clearly indicates the failure of the ways and means that we preferred, as well as the schemata of historical evolution that we favoured. Theoretically, a federation presupposes the existence of two or more states, with distinct personalities. In fact, by reinforcing the central power, the federation tends to stifle the personality of the states that compose it . . .

. . . By the very nature of things, the centralizing tendency, gaining strength as the institutions are set up, will triumph over constitutional rules and the partners' repeated avowals to respect affiliated entities. As is always the case in like circumstances, the central power, concentrated in the hands of one of the partners, soon becomes a terrible instrument of domination, weighing heavily on the territory of the state where it is located – in this instance, on the territory of Senegal. The theoretically bipartite character of the Mali government could not check this evolution, which was in the logic of history.

Inasmuch as the thesis of the installation of a chief executive distinct from the prime minister prevailed against the thesis of a concentration of powers, we could hope that the danger of absorption of one state by the other – of Senegal by the Sudan – was finally eliminated, because of the apparatus of the federal state. This underestimated the strength of the centralizing tendency, the greed for power that secretly gnaws at many African leaders, even when they call themselves democrats . . .

. . . our error has been that in our fight against Balkanization, we failed to consider the precolonial fact that is territorialism. Our mistake has been our failure to pay sufficient attention in our analyses to this phenomenon, a fruit of colonialism and sociopolitical fact that a theory of unity – no matter how praiseworthy or attractive – cannot abolish. We allowed ourselves to be lured by the mirage of the most intellectually satisfying construction. Taking our ideal for a reality, we thought we had only to condemn territorialism and its natural product, micronationalism, to overcome them and assure the success of our chimerical undertaking.

14: Modibo Keita

Extracts from Modibo Keita, 'The Foreign Policy of Mali', *International Affairs,* Vol. 37, No. 4 (October 1961).
This article reproduces a speech given in London in June 1961, by the President of Mali.

. . . We have come to the conclusion that when certain European countries afford help to the developing countries they often make such aid conditional, even if only by implication, on political options in their favour. Let me explain. When certain nations grant aid, whether to countries of Africa, Asia, or America, they are surprised that the receiving countries do not follow their policy in international affairs; on the other hand, we have noted ... that the countries of the Eastern bloc, whatever may be their reasons, unreservedly support the peoples struggling for liberation from the colonial yoke. When one tells a slave, even if secretly one wants to free him in order to subject him to another domination, when one tells him as he lies bound and struggling to be free, 'I will help you to win your liberty, I will help you to be yourself, to be a man', then the slave will not bother to ask himself what the future behaviour of his helper is likely to be. He will only see the immediate help that is being offered. This is the reality which must be taken into consideration, and which should cause the Great Powers of Europe and America to give more thought to their policy towards colonial peoples, who are struggling for their freedom from the foreign yoke.

......

... We are convinced that the States of Africa will never be independent, in the full sense of the word, if they remain small States, more or less opposed one to another, each having its own policy, its own economy, each taking no account of the policy of the others.

Our Constitution therefore provides for a total or partial abandonment of sovereignty in favour of a grouping of African States, but such an abandonment of sovereignty demands an identity of views with our fellow-States. One cannot build a complete whole with contradictions. Certain common viewpoints on international policy and on economic policy are absolutely necessary, together with an understanding of the contradictions contained in economic planning, and the necessity for each State to consider its economy within the framework of one large African economy, if it is to constitute an entity with the other States ... Nevertheless the Republic of Mali has decided to co-operate in all fields with all the African States, whatever may be their political, economic, or social set-up. This means however that we envisage a political organization in co-operation with the other African States only in so far as they have identity of views with us in the field of international policy and also in the field of internal economic policy.

......

The Republic of Mali, as a young country in process of development, desires peace and wants to play her part in establishing peaceful relations between the different countries of the world. She therefore supports all proposals for general and genuine disarmament. Moreover, having suffered from colonial domination, she unreservedly supports all peoples struggling to be free from a foreign yoke. She has aligned herself with the policy of positive neutralism, which finds its best expression in co-operation with all countries, with no exceptions . . .

. . . Mali has signed trade agreements and agreements for economic co-operation with countries belonging to both blocs. This policy in international affairs must not be confused with 'équilibrisme', with a political balancing act which takes up no fundamental position and which aligns itself now with one, now with the other of the two blocs according to circumstances.

. . . If our policy then coincides with that of the Eastern or the Western bloc. this is entirely a matter of chance and not the result of calculation. A balancing 'équilibriste' policy causes a country to lose its entire personality. It can be blackmailed by both blocs. It becomes simply an instrument to be used. This I consider dangerous both for the country itself and for the Great Powers.

15: Sekou Touré

Extracts from Sekou Touré, 'Africa's Future and the World', *Foreign Affairs,* Vol. 41, No. 1 (October 1962). Copyright 1962 by Council on Foreign Relations, Inc.
As President of Guinea, Sekou Touré took Guinea into a political federation with Ghana and Mali in 1960, and into the 'Casablanca' group of 1961 (a group which favoured rapid movement towards continental union). Both groups were disbanded with the formation of the Organisation of African Unity in 1963.

Subjective interpretations are at the root of one of the profound misconceptions that prevent a true understanding of Africa's problems and the concerns and activities of her peoples. For the interpretations made by foreign "specialists" in African affairs are as a rule based on the conditions of their own social milieu, and thus take little account of the specific conditions of the various African societies. If the problems of Africa are to be understood, analysed and solved, we must take into consideration the historical, economic, social, moral and cultural conditions which shape Africa's particular identity in the world − elements of the African evolution, in which total emancipation of the African peoples remains the main objective.

. . . . . .

It is vain, then, to hope that Africa will evolve according to any specific form which might be imposed upon her contrary to her own wishes or understanding. She will evolve within her own authentic framework and in accordance with her own personality until her economic conditions lose their particular characteristics and become normal. It is futile to talk of "protecting" Africa, or to give her alms which will salve the conscience of some, blunt temporarily the awareness of others, and perpetuate inequalities between peoples by maintaining differences in their living conditions. And it is futile also to try to trace any one path that Africa must follow. Africa must be left free to follow her own historical path, starting from the imperatives of her destiny and taking into account the requirements of a fraternal and united world.

In other words, it is a question of affirming our "Africanity", that is to say our personality, without attempting to dress it up in Western or Eastern costume. What must be constructed harmoniously and rapidly is an Africa that is authentically African. Africa has her own needs, concepts and customs. She does not seek to deck herself out in borrowed clothing that does not fit.

This destiny, while presupposing the total disappearance of colonialism, the liquidation of imperialism and the establishment of a society free from privileges, also opens new and inspiring perspectives of justice, progress and universal peace. Need we recall that by holding onto their present privileges and technical superiority the highly developed nations are depriving themselves of the creative talent and productive capacities of hundreds of millions of people in the underdeveloped nations? . . .

. . . . . .

Compared to other continents, Africa is relatively retarded. But to what is this backwardness attributable? To some natural inequality between black man and white? No, for there are black men who by their culture have an intrinsic value superior to that of certain white men. Hence in so far as individual capacities are concerned, there is no such thing as intellectual inequality among men whatever their colour or race. Inequality exists solely in living conditions, in the accidents of history, that is to say in the political, economic and social conditions that have dictated, and still dictate, the levels of development in different parts of the world. This is true of the political situation within a nation in which political considerations have hampered national development (as in European countries like Spain, Portugal and Greece). It is true of the economic and social situation where foreign intervention has resulted in exploitation and social oppression (as in any country subjected to direct or indirect foreign rule).

. . . . . .

When we analyze the ills that have beset the African, indeed the whole black race, we are obliged to admit at once that economic factors are what

222

have favored slavery, the deportation of our populations, racial discrimination, colonization and, today, neo-colonialism. Africa has been exploited and oppressed for economic motives; her legitimate desire for rehabilitation – social, moral, cultural – must be fulfilled by her economic development.

......

Colonialism's greatest misdeed was to have tried to strip us of our responsibility in conducting our own affairs and convince us that our civilisation was nothing less than savagery, thus giving us complexes which led to our being branded as irresponsible and lacking in self-confidence. Our greatest victory, then, will not be the one we are winning over colonialism by securing independence but the victory over ourselves by freeing ourselves from the complexes of colonialism, proudly expressing Africa's authentic values and thoroughly identifying ourselves with them. Thus the African peoples will become fully conscious of their equality with other peoples.

......

We know that we must rebuild Africa. To win and proclaim a nation's independence but keep its old structures is to plough a field but not sow it with grain for a harvest. Africa's political independence is a means which must be used to create and develop the new African economy. Our continent possesses tremendous reserves of raw materials and they, together with its potential sources of power, give it excellent conditions for industrialization. This is why, though it would be unrealistic and irrational to think of associating the African nations with the European Common Market, or any other form of economic monopoly, it is to be hoped that an African common market will be organized which eventually can cooperate on a basis of equality and solidarity with other economic zones.

African unity is no more a goal in itself than was independence. It simply is a means of development, a force of inter-African cooperation. It is indispensable because of the unjust nature of the relationship between the underdeveloped African nations and the economically strong nations. The equality of this relationship must be improved in order to overcome the social inequalities and differentiations in the present levels of development throughout the world. The highly developed nations have economic relations among themselves either of cooperation or of competition. But their relations with the undeveloped nations are those of exploitation, of economic domination. The direct colonial exploitation of former days is being succeeded by exploitation by international monopolies, and this has a tendency to become permanent. Paradoxically, it is the underdeveloped nations, exporting raw materials and crude products, which contribute an important share of the costs and the social

223

improvements from which workers in the fully developed countries benefit.
. . . . . .

The African nations are realizing that in order to solve their urgent social problems they must speed up the transformation of their trade economy; and if this is to be done through industrialization, it cannot be done within the limits of our national micro-economies. But unconditional integration into a multi-national market consisting of highly developed and underdeveloped nations negates the possibility of industrial development in advance; it could only be the association of horse and rider. If they are to complement each other economically, the development of all associated nations must be carried out according to their united needs and common interests ... The leaders of the European Economic Community seem not to be aware of all this, at least as far as Africa is concerned, and make no secret of their desire to achieve a political community of Europe which cannot be reconciled with Africa's desire for political independence; Africa remains as grimly hostile as ever to the division of Africa which began with the Congress of Berlin in 1885.

The unity so much desired by all Africans will not be achieved around any one man or any one nation, but around a concrete program, however minimal. The rules of the union must favour and reinforce generally accepted concepts: equality of all nations, large or small; fraternal solidarity in their relationships; the common use of certain resources; and respect for the character and institutions of each state. Not only must there be no interference in the internal affairs of any state by another, but each must help to solve the other's problems. If we do not rapidly achieve such a framework of solidarity, permitting the peaceful evolution of our countries, we risk seeing the cold war enter Africa and divide the African states into antagonistic forces and blocs, jeopardising their whole future in common.
. . . . . .

Some have claimed to see political antagonisms in the formation of various African groupings. Actually these were the first concrete manifestations of unity, and were inspired by human and historical necessity. Skepticism notwithstanding, this tendency towards unity will increase. Political choices which do not correspond to the needs and aspirations of our peoples – and it is important that this be understood – will inevitably fail.
. . . . . .

To attempt to interpret Africa's behaviour in capitalist or Communist terms is to neglect the fundamental fact that Africa's present condition corresponds neither to the given facts of capitalism nor to those in the building of Communism.

224

Africa's way is the way of peaceful revolution, in which the morality of an action counts much more than its form and conditions. That some believe socialism corresponds best to the aims of the African revolution, while others suppose it is preferable, despite the lack of national capital, to espouse capitalist principles – these considerations will not in the last analysis prevent our peoples from deciding their own fate. It is they who are called on to make the sacrifices and the creative efforts necessary to ensure Africa's development. Their awareness is sufficiently keen to enable them to choose the way they want to go.

C. AFRICAN UNITY AND AFRICAN CULTURE

16: The First Congress of Negro Writers and Artists, Paris, 1956

Extracts from the Congress resolutions, published in C. Legum (ed.), *Panafricanism* (Praeger, 1965). Reprinted by permission of Phaidon Press.
The theme of this Congress was 'The Crisis of Negro Culture', and a predominant *Motif* was Aimé Césaire's concept of 'negritude', the uniqueness of black culture.

Whereas the Conference has shown that there is a profound interest in the work undertaken during its sessions in regard to various Negro cultures which have often been ignored, under-estimated or sometimes destroyed;

Whereas there has been made evident the urgent necessity to rediscover the historical truth and revalue Negro cultures; these truths, often misrepresented and denied, being partly responsible for provoking a crisis in Negro culture and in the manner in which that culture relates to World culture;

We recommend that artists, writers, scholars, theologians, thinkers and technicians participate in the historic task of unearthing, rehabilitating and developing those cultures so as to facilitate their being integrated into the general body of world culture.

We Negro writers, artists and intellectuals of various political ideologies and religious creeds have felt a need to meet at this crucial stage in the evolution of mankind in order to examine objectively our several views on culture and to probe those cultures with a full consciousness of

225

our responsibilities – first, before our own respective peoples, second, before colonial people and those living under conditions of racial oppression, and, third, before all free men of good will.

We deem it unworthy of genuine intellectuals to hesitate to take a stand regarding fundamental problems, for such hesitations serve injustice and error.

Jointly we have weighed our cultural heritages and have studied how they have been affected by social and general conditions of racialism and colonialism.

We maintain that the growth of culture is dependent on the termination of such shameful practices in this twentieth century as colonialism, the oppression of weaker peoples and racialism.

We affirm that all peoples should be placed in a position where they can learn their own national cultural values (history, language, literature, etc.) and enjoy the benefits of education within the framework of their own culture.

This conference regrets the involuntary absence of a delegation from South Africa.

This conference is pleased to take due notice of recent advances made throughout the world, advances which imply a general abolition of the colonial system, as well as the final and universal liquidation of racialism.

This Conference invites all Negro intellectuals to unite their efforts in securing effective respect for the Rights of Man, whatever his colour may be, and for all peoples and all nations whatsoever.

This Conference urges Negro intellectuals and all justice-loving men to struggle to create the practical conditions for the revival and the growth of Negro cultures.

Paying tribute to the cultures of all lands and with due appreciation of their several contributions to the progress of Civilisation, the Conference urges all Negro intellectuals to defend, illustrate and publicise throughout the world the national values of their own peoples.

We Negro writers and artists proclaim our fellowship with all men and expect from them, for our people, a similar fellowship.

At the request of several members of Congress the officers have undertaken the responsibility of setting up an International Association of Negro Men of Culture.

17: The Second Congress of Negro Writers and Artists, Rome, 1959

(a) Extracts from the Congress resolutions, published in Legum, *Panafricanism*.
At this Congress, internal conflicts made themselves felt, particularly between the English-speaking and French-speaking representatives.

(b) The Marxist motion in the last part of the extract was issued separately by a splinter group, and reflects political divisions within this cultural assembly.

(a) The Negro Writers and Artists, ... reassert their conviction:

1. That political independence and economic liberation are the essential conditions for the cultural advance of the under-developed countries in general and the Negro-African countries in particular.

2. That every effort towards the regrouping of countries or nations artificially divided by imperialism, every realisation of fundamental solidarity and every determination towards unity are advantageous and profitable for restoring the equilibrium of the world and for the revitalisation of culture.

3. That every effort towards the personification and enrichment of national culture, and every effort to implant Negro men of culture in their own civilisation, constitute in fact, progress towards universalisation and are a contribution towards the civilisation of mankind.

The Congress therefore, recommends the Negro Writers and Artists to regard it as their essential task and sacred mission to bring their cultural activity within the scope of the great movement for the liberation of their individual peoples, without losing sight of the solidarity which should unite all individuals and peoples who are struggling for the liquidation of colonisation and its consequences as well as all those who are fighting throughout the world for progress and liberty.

. . . . . .

In view of all the reasons and considerations set out above, the Commission on Literature calls the attention of the Delegates of the Second Congress of Negro Writers and Artists to the following projects which should be instituted in the various Negro States:

1. The institution in each independent country of a strict and rigorous plan for the fight against illiteracy, inspired both by the most modern techniques already in use, and the original peculiarities of the country in question.

2. An increase in the number of fundamentally decentralised popular libraries, and the use of films and sound-recordings.

227

3. The institution of African Cultural Research Centres; these Centres, which would be responsible for working out practical plans, would be in close contact with the International Organisations, and with other nations.

4. The translation into autochthonous languages, wherever possible, of representative works of Negro writers in the French, English, Portuguese, Spanish, etc. languages.

5. The exchange of translations between the various cultural areas (French, English, Spanish, Italian and Portuguese) of Africa and the other countries of African population. Negro writers should not necessarily adopt the contradictions between the various Western cultures emanating from the nations which have dominated the Negro world.

6. The creation of national organisations for aid to writers. Such organisations already exist in various forms in Ghana and Guinea.

7. The Commission proposes the creation of effective aid to young writers within the Society of African Culture itself.

8. The Commission recommends the Society of African Culture to arrange cultural meetings with the writers of all countries.

9. Finally, the Commission hopes that the Congress will call the attention of the Governments of Negro States to the need to support and encourage the creation of theatrical schools along the lines set out above.

The Commission on literature hopes that Negro-African writers will work to define their common language, their common manner of using words and ideas and of reacting to them. The desire for an ordered language expressing coherent cultures is embodied, among other things, in work within a national reality from which the flagrant disorder specifically inherent in the colonial situation will be banished. This language, transcending the various languages used, transcending the legitimate forms of national cultures, will thus contribute towards strengthening the unity of the Negro peoples, and will furnish their writers with a working tool.

The Commission also finally recognises that this contribution to the progress of the Negro-African peoples cannot fail additionally to strengthen the universal brotherhood of mankind. The Commission had endeavoured to carry out its work bearing constantly in mind this brotherhood and the generosity of spirit which it implies.

Resolution of the Commission on Philosophy

Considering the dominant part played by philosophic reflection in the elaboration of culture,

Considering that until now the West has claimed a monopoly of philosophic reflection so that philosophic enterprise no longer seems conceivable outside the framework of the categories forged by the West,

Considering that the philosophic effort of traditional Africa has always been reflected in vital attitudes and has never had purely conceptual aims,

The Commission declares:

1. That for the African philosopher, philosophy can never consist in reducing the African reality to Western systems;

2. That the African philosopher must base his inquiries upon the fundamental certainty that the Western philosophic approach is not the only possible one; and therefore,

1. Urges that the African philosopher should learn from the traditions, tales, myths and proverbs of his people, so as to draw from them the laws of a true African wisdom complementary to the other forms of human wisdom and to bring out the specific categories of African thought.

2. Calls upon the African philosopher, faced by the totalitarian or egocentric philosophers of the West, to divest himself of a possible inferiority complex, which might prevent him from starting from his African being to judge the foreign contribution.

It calls upon the philosopher to transcend any attitude of withdrawal into himself and his traditions so as to bring out, in true communication with all philosophies, the true universal values.

It is highly desirable that the modern African philosopher should preserve the unitary vision of cosmic reality which characterises the wisdom of traditional Africa.

(b) Motion by a Group of Marxists

We, African Marxists,

Recognise that the evolution of Societies, the steady improvement of technique, recent discoveries, and the consequent emergence of new economic links and new social relationships make the enrichment and effective broadening of Marxism both possible and desirable.

The analyses of Western society worked out by Marx, although linked to the interpretation of a specific system of production, namely capitalism, enabled Marx to describe the feudal (pre-capitalist) forms of society, forms whose equivalent can be found today in the regions which are commonly called underdeveloped.

The economic situation with which Marx found himself faced at the time when he was explaining the laws which govern society led him to advocate certain forms of action.

It is nevertheless clear that in the particular case of underdeveloped countries and, more precisely in the case of Africa, the original forms of struggle take on specific dimensions; already at grips with colonialism, African leaders must further take into account their need to promote a programme of technical modernisation with the maximum speed and efficiency

African Marxists, in their reflections and in their practice, must look strictly, not only at general economic problems, but also and especially at the facts of economic underdevelopment and the cultural configurations proper to their regions.

African Marxists must also draw inspiration from current experiments in other underdeveloped countries which have already attained independence.

In consequence, considering that,

1. The cultural references in Marx's thought are nearly all drawn from Western experience,

2. The economic situation of the Western proletariat cannot be strictly indentified with that of the underdeveloped people,

3. A doctrine is all the more universal so far as, on the one hand, it takes into account all the experience, historic, economic, etc., and the diversity of the cultural genius of peoples, and on the other hand, its application is controlled by a really representative authority.

We invite African Marxists to develop their doctrine on the basis of the real history, aspirations and economic situation of their peoples and to build and found it on the authority of their own culture.

18: Léopold Sédar Senghor: Negritude

(a) Extracts from L. S. Senghor, 'Negritude and African Socialism' in K. Kirkwood (ed.), *St. Antony's Papers, No. 15, African Affairs* (Chatto & Windus, 1963). Copyright Léopold Sédar Senghor 1963.

(b) Extracts from L.S. Senghor, *On African Socialism*, ed. Mercer Cook (Praeger, 1964). Copyright Léopold Sédar Senghor 1964.

Although Césaire formulated the concept of negritude, its fullest elaboration came from Senghor, and this concept is commonly associated with him.

(a) The French forced us to seek the essence of Negritude when they enforced their policy of assimilation and thus deepened our despair ... Early on, we had become aware within ourselves that assimilation was a failure; we could assimilate mathematics or the French language, but we could never strip off our black skins nor root out our black souls. And so we set out on a fervent quest for the Holy Grail, which was our *Collective Soul*.

And we came upon it . . . Its whereabouts was pointed out to us by that handful of free-lance thinkers – writers, artists, ethnologists, and pre-historians – who bring about cultural revolutions in France . . .

What did we learn from all those writers, artists and teachers? They taught us that the early years of colonisation and especially, even before colonisation, the *slave-trade,* had ravaged black Africa like a bush fire, wiping out images and values in one vast carnage. That negroid civilisation had flourished in the Upper Paleolithic Age, and that the Neolithic Revolution could not be explained without them. That their roots retained their vigour, and would one day produce new grass and green branches . . . I must admit that this revelation went to our heads, and set us well on the way to racialism. Soldiers in the cause of Negritude, the Senegalese light infantry, we unsheathed our native knives and stormed the values of Europe, which we summed up in the threefold expression: discursive reason, technical skill, and a trading economy. In other words, *Capitalism.*

I ought at this point . . . to define Negritude. Well, Negritude is *the whole complex of civilised values – cultural, economic, social and political – which characterise the black peoples,* or, more precisely, the Negro-African world. All these values are essentially informed by intuitive reason. Because this sentient reason, the reason which comes to grips, expresses itself emotionally, through that self-surrender, that coalescence of subject and object; through myths, by which I mean the archetypal images of the collective Soul, above all through primordial rhythms, synchronised with those of the Cosmos. In other words, the sense of communion, the gift of myth-making, the gift of rhythm, such are the essential elements of Negritude, which you will find indelibly stamped on all the works and activities of the black man.

. . . . . .

. . . Today, our Negritude no longer expresses itself as opposition to European values, but as a *complement* to them. Henceforth, its militants will be concerned, as I have often said, *not to be assimilated, but to assimilate.* They will use European values to arouse the slumbering values of Negritude . . .

. . . . . .

. . . among the values of Europe, we had no intention, we still have no intention, of retaining Capitalism, not in its nineteenth-century form at least. Of course, private Capitalism was, in its early days, one of the factors of progress, just as Feudalism was in its time, and even Colonisation. For the backwardness of black Africa for example, has been caused less by colonisation than by the Slave Trade, which in three centuries carried off some two hundred million victims, *black hosts.*

Capitalism, then, thanks to the accumulation of financial resources and its development of the means of production, was a factor of progress for Europe and also for Africa.

Today it is an out-of-date social and economic system – like Feudalism, like Colonisation. And, I would like to add, like the Imperialism in which it found its expression. Why? Because, if, with its specialisations, the collectivisation of work constitutes a critical step towards *Socialisation,* the defence, or, more exactly, the extension of private property does not lead in this direction. Just as serious is the alienation, in the material realm and the realm of the spirit, of which Capitalism is guilty. Because Capitalism works only for the well-being of a minority. Because, whenever State intervention and working-class pressure have forced it to reform itself, it has conceded only the minimum standard of living, when no less than the maximum would do. Because it holds out no prospect of a *fuller being* beyond material *well-being.* That is why, under the capitalist system, the political, cultural and spiritual liberties, which are so often quoted, are enjoyed only in theory: on the surface. They are not *lived.*

It is because private Capitalism finds it repugnant – or, more precisely, finds it impossible – to transcend its material bounds, it is because of its transformation into colonialist Imperialism, that we were converted, after much hesitation, to Socialism . . .

But our Socialism is not that of Europe. It is neither atheistic Communism nor, quite, the Democratic Socialism of the Second International of the Labour Party for example. We have modestly called it the *African Mode of Socialism* . . .

. . . . . .

. . . we have decided to borrow from the [non-African] socialist experiments – both theoretical and practical – only certain elements, certain scientific and technical values, which we have grafted like scions on to the wild stock of Negritude. For this latter, as a complex of civilised values, is traditionally *socialist* in character. In this sense, our Negro-African society is a classless society, which is not the same as saying that it has no hierarchy or division of labour. It is a *community-based society,* in which the hierarchy – and therefore power – is founded on spiritual and democratic values: on the law of primogeniture and election; in which decisions of all kinds are deliberated in a *Palaver,* after the ancestral gods have been consulted; in which work is shared out among the sexes and among technico-professional groups based on religion. A community-based society, *communal,* not collectivist.

Thus, in the working out of our African Mode of Socialism, the problem is not how to put an end to the exploitation of man by his fellow, but to prevent its ever happening, by bringing political and economic democracy back to life; our problem is not how to satisfy spiritual, that is cultural needs, but how to keep the fervour of the black soul alive. It is a question, once again, of modernising our values by borrowing from European Socialism its science and technical skill, above all its spirit of Progress.

(b) As for Marxian humanism, ... I wish first of all to recall its strength and its weakness. Its strength is that, starting from concrete facts, it elaborated the sociological realities which the analysis of European society in the mid-nineteenth century revealed: the priority of the economic factor and the class struggle. Its strength is also that it pointed out and renewed the notion of alienation. Its weakness is that it did not carry the economic analysis far enough: it neglected statistics, albeit the embryonic statistics then existing. Its weakness lies above all in the fact that, as Marx proceeded in his writing of *Capital*, he increasingly stressed materialism and determinism, praxis and means, to the detriment of dialectics and ethics – in a word, to the detriment of man and his freedom. I shall no longer say, as I did in my Report, to the detriment of philosophical thought; for, rejecting the spirit of his Philosophical Works, Marx surreptitiously and paradoxically reintroduced metaphysics, an atheistic metaphysics in which mind is sacrificed to matter, freedom to the determined, man to things. This is no doubt what Engels called Marx's "subjective whims".

What should be our attitude as Negro Africans to this de-humanized humanism, to this deterministic subjectivism that negates the truly concrete subjective emotion?
......
... I answer first, that we should not betray its fruitful contributions when faithfulness to it can only lead to lucid transcendence. But West Africans are prone to betray it in both theory and practice, through blind allegiance.

In theory, one betrays Marx by using Marxian dialectic as it stands, without changing a comma. For this is reasoning twice in abstraction, the surest way to miss reality. We must not tire of repeating: dialectical materialism is born of history and geography; it was born in the nineteenth century in Western Europe. Conceived in that milieu, it was essentially designed to analyse and transform it. Marx often affirmed this. The proof is that today, in those same countries, scientists and philosophers, writers and artists, while assimilating Marx's methodological contributions, have gone beyond, shaded, and enriched them to penetrate realities no longer of the nineteenth but of the twentieth century.

233

And what of Asian or African realities? The Israelis, like the Chinese have been able to find their Asian road to socialism adapted to the spirit and realities of their native soil. Theirs are exemplary efforts to inspire us. West African realities are those of underdeveloped countries – peasant countries here, cattle countries there – once feudalistic, but traditionally classless and with no wage-earning sector. They are community countries where the group holds priority over the individual; they are, especially, religious countries, unselfish countries, where money is not King. Though dialectical materialism can help in analysing our societies, it cannot fully interpret them . . .

We should betray Marx by applying his method like a veneer to West African realities. We would betray him even more if we were to apply but not integrate European political, economic, social, and cultural organisations here, whether that of West or East, of liberal parliamentarianism or "peoples' democracy". This would strangely betray Man, as well as Negro-African – I mean Negro-Berber – humanism . . .

How can one fail to realise that, in these conditions, alienation, far from being corrected, will be singularly aggravated? For the alienation of the Negro-Berber does not stem from Negro-Berber capitalism, nor even from European capitalism. Nor does it stem from the class struggle. Rather, it results from the domination of one country over another – or rather, of one ethnic group over another. Here, political and cultural domination, colored by racism, is fused with economic domination.

Man is not without a country, nor is he without a color or a history, a fatherland or a civilisation. It is West African man, our neighbor, exactly defined in time and space. He is Malian, Mauritanian, Eburnian, Wolof, Targui, Songhai, Hausa, Fon, or Mossi. He is a man of flesh and blood, nourished on milk, millet, rice and yams. He is a man humiliated for centuries, less perhaps in his nudity and hunger than in his skin and civilisation, in his dignity.

19: Alioune Diop: The African Personality

From the American Society of African Culture (ed.), *Panafricanism Reconsidered* (University of California Press, 1962). Reprinted by permission of the Regents of the University of California. Extracts from an address to the Third Annual Conference of the American Society for African Culture, held in Philadelphia, 1960.
The American Society of African Culture was established as a result of the 1956 Congress of Negro Writers and Artists, and the 1960 Conference resumed

the earlier debates on negritude and African culture. Diop, founding father of the 1956 Congress, and of the cultural journal *Présence Africaine,* here attempted to reconcile conflicting views of negritude through the concept of 'the African personality'.

Panafricanism was launched here and was of an essentially intellectual nature. Many years after its birth, the African peoples and their leaders – some of their leaders – took hold of Panafricanism and made an elaborate doctrine of it, adapted to our aspirations and our situation. Each country or each cultural region has its terminology; in France, we invented negritude (negro-ness); in the Anglo-Saxon countries, they invented Panafricanism; and together, we launched another expression with the same perspective, the African personality ... We are not children, we are adults; and it might even be said that we have nothing to learn from the Western culture for which we could not find an equivalent in our own cultures. The only misfortune is that these cultures are based on institutions, on an economy, and on a political freedom which are shaken and frustrated by colonialism. But we are convinced that our cultures are as organic, as deserving of respect and as rich as Western culture – and we have the advantage over Westerners here, for we have for the most part experienced that culture in all its dimensions.

The African personality is manifested in various disciplines and also in the political field. Dr. Ki-Zerbo said that the thinking African should not accept the pure and simple transference of the teachings of Marxist Communism into Africa, for the very simple reason that Karl Marx lived in and belonged to another era and environment, and that his concepts, whatever his genius, can apply only to the society he knew – and at the present no one could contend that the economic situation of Africa is the same as that of nineteenth-century Europe.

It is certain that if we cannot go backward, that is, return to primitivism, we can, with confidence in our personal genius, elaborate a political way of life that is our own and which will assure us more security and dynamism and will permit an easier collaboration with other countries. I am thinking now of certain experiments that are at present being made in Africa, particularly West Africa. I am thinking of that tendency which is more and more clearly emerging among political leaders, to let the people speak – those people who have so often been ridiculed and considered less mature and less responsible than children. The political leaders are manifesting their confidence in these people, and more and more it is not just national problems, but international ones as well they feel it their duty to explain, provided the people are organised.

We have on many occasions witnessed their reflection, their deliberation, and their formulation of solutions adapted to their aspirations – solutions that add to the dignity of their community.

There is no problem of an economic, a political, or a cultural nature that the African peoples, organised in a certain way, cannot deliberate upon and for which they are not capable of finding an appropriate solution ... But our color does not isolate us; we do not withdraw into ourselves. The African personality, on the contrary, is an effort to permit us to join others on the universal level and to truly build – taking into account all conditions, necessary ideas, concepts – institutions necessary for the definition of a new justice, which this time will be a justice for all, for all cultures and all peoples.

20: Ezekiel Mphahlele: Negritude and Culture

(a) Extracts from E. Mphahlele, *The African Image* (Faber & Faber, 1962). Reprinted by permission of Praeger Publishers, Inc. Copyright Praeger.
(b) Extracts from an interview by Cosmos Pieterse in D. Duerden & C. Pieterse (ed.), *African Writers Talking* (Heinemann Educational Books, 1972). Reprinted by permission of the Africana Publishing Company, a Division of Holmes & Meier Publishers, Inc.

(a) Beyond the focus on freedom from colonialism in certain countries and fascist white rule in others, and the emergence into nationhood of others, the only thing that can really be said to be capable of expressing an African Personality lies in those areas of cultural activity that are concerned with education and the arts. And this requires no slogan at all ...

Throughout Negro Africa the content of education will have to outgrow colonial origins of whatever brand. The African artist, because he must needs deal with African themes, rhythms and idiom cannot but express an African personality. There need be no *mystique* about it.

It is significant that it is not the African in British-settled territories – a product of 'indirect rule' and one that has been left in his cultural habitat – who readily reaches out for his traditional past. It is rather the assimilated African, who has absorbed French culture, who is now passionately wanting to recapture his past. In his poetry he extols his ancestors, ancestral masks, African wood carvings and bronze art and tries to recover the moorings of his oral literature; he clearly feels he has come to a dead-end in European culture, and is still not readily accepted as an organic part of French society, for all the assimilation he has been through . . .

If there is any negritude in the black man's art in South Africa, it is because we *are* African. If a writer's tone is healthy, he is bound to express the African in him. Stripped of Senghor's philosophic musings, the African traits he speaks of can be taken for granted: they are social anthropology. We who grew up and were educated in Africa do not find anything new in them. Simply because we respond intensely to situations is no reason why we should think non-Africans are incapable of doing so, or that we are the only section of the human race who are full of passionate intensity . . . In my struggle to overcome the artistic difficulty that arises when one is angry most of the time and when one's sense of values is continually being challenged by the ruling class, I have never thought of calling my negritude to my aid, except when writing protest material. But is this not elementary – shall I call it 'underdoggery'? – that Senghor is talking about? Even he must know, however, that his philosophy will contain his art only up to a point: it won't chain his art for long. He must know that his negritude can at best be an attitude, a pose, where his art is concerned, just as it was a pose in my protest writing.

(b). . . I still think that in the African context, negritude has overplayed itself and that negritude, purely as a cultural front against colonialism and while culture, is now something that has succeeded in what it set out to do, and now that the African is independent, and now that the African should be able to make his own choice, what he should adopt and what he should reject, I don't think that negritude is necessary. Again, we begin to realise now that the beginnings of negritude were after all in the Caribbean and in the Western Hemisphere generally, so negritude proper was an expression, the outcry of an aliented people, people who couldn't go back to Africa and recapture their African roots because they were complete exiles, and this is why negritude found its most poignant expression in this area: it was a natural beginning for negritude. But how different with the African: an African who feels alienated can always go back to Africa if he wants to, and if he has a mind to it; he can go back and recapture his roots and the *can* because, after all, a good deal of Africa is still very traditional, and all he needs to do is go back to his people and make the contact again, while the negro in America and the negro in the Caribbean could not do that. So we begin to realize, all the more now, that it is a Western Hemisphere negro phenomenon more than an African one. Because now, and I'm beginning to sympathize more and more with the American negro, because there is in their expression of Black Power a negritude, because they are culturally in a state of siege, they are besieged by a formidable white culture which is threatening to suck them in, on its own terms; and the African is not in this situation at all. He is not in a state of siege . . .

. . . . . .

[Negritude] . . . romanticizes the past, it is a yearning for the past, and a past which has gone, which has long gone.

21: K. A. Busia: Negritude

Extracts from K. A. Busia, *The Challenge of Africa* (1962). Reprinted by permission of Phaidon Press.

There is, at the present time, a quest by Africans for unity and co-operation on a wider scale than has hitherto been possible. Consequently, attempts have been made to find bases for unity in conceptual formulations. The most prominent of these attempts have given expression to the concepts of African personality and Negritude.

. . . . . .

The concept of national character is an abstraction serving, in any given instance, to embody a set of culturally regular traits. The concept of African personality belongs in the same category as that of national character; it too is an abstraction embodying a set of culturally regular traits said to be exhibited by nationals who have been integrated into shared social tradition. But the difficulty becomes at once apparent. What is the shared social tradition with reference to which the abstraction of an African personality is conceived? Where does it prevail? In the whole continent? In parts of the continent? Which parts? In terms of culture, . . . there is not one social tradition; there are different social traditions. And there are different nationalities.

The concept of African personality is of recent origin and is really an expression of political aspirations. In a negative sense, it is a reaction to colonialism. It is a protest against European domination and the crude biological theories that have been used in efforts to justify European imperialism. In this sense, . . . the concept is an expression of nationalism . . .

The concept is also a reaction against the disdain that has been shown for African cultures and the stunting they have suffered under European domination, and against the enthronement, conscious and unconscious, of the culture of imperialist countries. In this sense, the concept of African

238

personality is a claim to and an assertion of cultural freedom . . .

And more, the concept of African personality is an arbitrary focusing of common sentiments in an emotional appeal for the unity of African states . . .

In the last analysis, the concept of African personality is a political myth; but for that reason it can have a strong emotional appeal and profound social consequences. There have already been extravagant abuses of the concept. It has been appealed to to justify undemocratic practices and ruthless steps towards the establishment of one-party rule, and to excuse such patent injustices as the arbitrary arrest of political figures and their imprisonment without trial. Blatant aggressiveness has been defended as the projection of the African personality. But these clear aberrations are not necessarily inherent in the concept, either as a protest against colonialism or as a defense of cultural freedom.

The concept of Negritude represents a philosophical approach, although it, too, is a revolt against imperialism. In particular, it is a revolt against the French policy toward African cultures, a policy that has completely ignored them, on the assumption that, because French culture represents a 'higher' civilization, the best thing would be for France's African subjects to adopt the culture of their rulers. The concept of Negritude has thus been promulgated by African intellectuals of former French colonies – principally, by Alioune Diop and Léopold Sédar Senghor.

Senghor's approach is in line with the concept of national character as explained above. He sees Negritude as a pair of common psychic traits possessed by the Negro African – 'his heightened sensibility and his strong emotional quality'. 'Emotion is Negro'. The concept of Negritude may be regarded as a convenient abstraction, a conceptual tool for researchers who are trying to find common cultural traits that will distinguish the Negro African from other races. But 'heightened sensibility' and 'strong emotional quality' – those cannot be claimed as the exclusive possessions of Negro Africans, nor as qualities embodied in every Negro African irrespective of his cultural heritage and social experience. The essential problem of the concept is that race and culture do not necessarily go together . . . Historical circumstances have put Negro Africans into different cultures, and the personality traits conditioned by these cultures cannot be assumed to be identical. Even if they were, it should be noted that the concept of Negritude would express values common to only one of the races of Africa. For not all Africans are Negro Africans.

Diop conceives of Negritude as the values that are the 'vindication of the dignity of persons of African descent'. His position is understandable against the background of French colonial policy. And all 'persons of African descent' are not Negroes.

The concept of Negritude thus requires further clarification and refinement. It can, however, be seen as a *quest* for the 'vindication of the dignity of persons of African descent', as a quest of Africans for recognition as equals in a world-wide brotherhood of man.

22: L. Vambe: African Characteristics

Extracts from L. Vambe *An Ill-Fated People* (Heinemann, 1972). Reprinted by permission of the University of Pittsburgh Press.

Although we are on the surface a loquacious and a gregarious people, we are essentially a secretive, inordinately jealous and individualistic race. It sounds an outrageous thing to say, but it is nevertheless basically true. Unhappily, jealousy and secretiveness do not go with co-operation and progress ... The view of inventors and discoverers in the Western World, that humanity should profit by their knowledge, was not generally entertained by their African equivalents. The most they did was to pass on what they knew to one person in the family; he too would then use his art for the benefit of himself and of his patients, but most certainly not for society as a whole. Consequently, until the aggressive white man arrived on the African scene, the peoples of Africa as a whole had not reached a stage where they were involved in a conscious and deliberate effort to amass and preserve their knowledge for the benefit of posterity in all Africa. Colonialism, like all adversities in the life of any people, forced Africans to recognise their common interests, especially in the political field.

Yet it is still true to say that this inward-looking tradition holds the black people in shackles today. Admittedly, African countries are showing a greater sense of awareness of the need for unity and co-operation. But their attempts in this direction are fraught with suspicion and qualifications that make progress painfully slow. Indeed, outside the circle of the very small number of politicians and educated Africans who have a cosmopolitan outlook, you cannot avoid observing that tribalism and narrow nationalism have become much stronger forces in independent Africa than they were under colonial rule. In the struggle against colonialism many African leaders used to boast that when freedom was achieved a man's black skin would be an adequate passport for him to move. live and work in any African-governed country. But in many African countries, 'foreign' Africans find it harder to be admitted, let alone to live and work, than white persons. To the arbitrary boundaries made by the colonial powers have been added passport and visa regulations, residence and work permits and other requirements which are enforced so inflexibly that the concept of African 'brotherhood' sounds more mythical than real. Black Africa is one of the areas of the world which have suffered most from 'brain-drain'. Thousands of expensively trained and educated Africans are living and working in Europe and America because outside their actual places of birth they are regarded as 'foreigners' in another African country. Nobody in responsible African circles is seriously concerned with this phenomenon because it is not regarded as a problem. But to me it is a tragedy so great that I am often overcome by despair at the apparent inability of my people to pinpoint their priorities and so make their continent one of the greatest of human creativity and unity in the world.

. . . . . .

I am always amused as well as saddened when I read that in some African countries a group of people, usually young party-organizers who tend to be easily carried away by the fervour of patriotism, have issued a directive, asking all their supporters to go back to their African culture. I feel this way because these no doubt well-meaning advocates of negritude remind me of my tribal elders who undertook the same cultural crusade. I cannot help thinking that . . . these people are running away from reality, for the collective will of their followers, simply stated, is to catch up with the rest of the world, economically, politically, educationally and culturally. To stem this silent, but nevertheless raging human emotional current, which is quite consistent with the African national wish for self-fulfilment, is something that nobody who respects the right of any people to evolve as they wish should attempt to do. My experience in . . . Southern Rhodesia and elsewhere in Africa has taught me to realize that few Africans are prepared to live by ideals alone.

23: James Ngugi: National Culture

From J. Ngugi (ed.), *Homecoming* (Heinemann Educational Books, 1972). Extracts from an essay, 'Toward a National Culture'. Published in the U.S. by Lawrence Hill and Co., New York/Westport.

We need to see Africa's cultural history in three broad phases: Africa before white conquest, Africa under colonial domination, and today's

Africa striving to find its true self-image. To do this is to indicate the obvious: that the pressures, inside and outside, at the different stages of her growing up have changed Africa's cultural needs and outlook. Yesterday, for instance, there were many ethnic groups, each with a distinct cohesive culture: today, these groups are trying to form nations within wider, more inclusive boundaries of geography and politics. Hence we should examine the role of culture in our time within the new horizons, themselves made hazy by the often conflicting calls of the tribe, the nation, Panafrica, and even the third World.

Yet too often, as in the statement under discussion, we talk of African culture as if it were a static commodity which can and should be rescued from the ruins and shrines of yesterday, and projected on to a modern stage to be viewed by Africa's children, who, long lost in the labyrinth of foreign paths in an unknown forest, are now thirsty and hungry for the wholesome food of their forefathers. No living culture is ever static. Collectively, human beings struggle to master their physical environment and in the process create a social one. A change in the physical environment, or, more accurately, a change in the nature of their struggle, will alter their institutions and hence their mode of life and thought. Their new mode of life and thought may in turn affect their institutions and general environment. It is a dialectical process. A profound change in a people's economy, or in their dwelling-place, through trade and migration, will make people organize themselves differently to meet the new set of circumstances ... Alioune Diop declared at the first World Conference of Negro Writers and Artists in Paris: "There is this scandalous allegation of peoples without culture. While it is true that those who were really responsible for colonization knowingly fabricated this myth, it is none the less surprising that generations of cultural and spiritual authorities have conceded that men could live in a community without culture." Because he knew that this 'scandalous allegation' was also embodied in European books, especially fiction, on Africa, the African writer tied to answer by asserting in the books he wrote that Africa had a culture as good as any. The Negritude movement was a cultural phenomenon with a political facet. It was generally realized that a community deprived of its political liberty would find it dfficult to recreate an image of its past and confidently look towards the future.

The realization was general, at times vague. The belief has persisted, among most African intellectuals, artists and politicians, that 'cultural liberation is an essential condition for political liberation'. And since they think of culture only in terms of dances, jungle drums and folk-lore, they think it enough if they assert the need for the revival of these things. But it is wrong to think of culture as prior to politics. Political and economic liberation are the essential condition for cultural liberation, for the true release of a people's creative spirit and imagination. It is when people are involved in the active work of destroying an inhibitive social structure and building a new one that they begin to see themselves. They are born again . . .

Today, after regaining their independence, most African countries are committed to developing a distinctive national culture. In some cases, they have even set up agencies to promote it. Yet little has been done to translate this commitment into action. This, in part, is due to wrong attitudes towards culture. There are people, honest people, who confuse culture with irrelevant traditionalism; it is surely not possible to lift traditional structures and cultures intact into modern Africa. A meaningful culture is the one born out of the present hopes and especially the hopes of an impoverished peasantry, and that of the growing body of urban workers. There are still other people who believe that you can somehow maintain colonial, economic, and other social institutions and graft on them an African culture. We have seen that colonial institutions can only produce a colonial mentality . . .

If we are to achieve true national cultures we must recognize our situation. That means we must thoroughly examine our social and economic structures and see if they are truly geared to meeting the needs and releasing the energy of the masses. We must in fact wholly Africanize and socialize our political and economic life. We must break with capitalism, whose imperialistic stage — that of colonialism and neo-colonialism — has done so much harm to Africa and dwarfed our total creative spirit. Capitalism can only produce anti-human culture, or a culture that is only an expression of sectional, warring interests. African culture used to be most communal when and where economic life and the means of production were communally organized and controlled. Any ideal, any vision, is nothing unless it is given institutional forms and solid economic bases.

24: Aimé Césaire: Culture and Political Leadership

Extracts from A. Césaire, 'The Political Thought of Sekou Touré', *Présence Africaine*, No. 29 (1960). Translated from the French by the Editors.

It is a fact that black Africa, at the time that it entered modern history, had the luck to find worthy political cadres, that is, leaders who, as if with a machete, knew how to cut a pathway for Africa through the jungle of events.

In this respect, one cannot overemphasize that their essential merit is to have known in time how to break off all allegiance to the European sectors; to have been careful not to make their politics a mere part of metropolitan politics; in a word, to have exposed, at the right time, the trap of assimilation.

That is the collective merit of the present generation of African leaders. But it is not to belittle their particular merit . . . to say that the President of the young Republic of Guinea, Sekou Touré, was during this last period *"l'homme africain décisif"*. 'As for us, we have a basic and indispensable need, that of our dignity. But there is no dignity without liberty. We prefer poverty in freedom to affluence in slavery.' In any case, the man who uttered this historical phrase, and who without bloodshed won independence for his country, is an exceptional man.

. . . . . .

People make many mistakes about him. Some of his French admirers claim, with satisfaction: "He is a product of our culture." Others, the reactionaries: "Beware of him, he is a product of Prague and Moscow." The truth, it seems to me, is quite different. One only has to look at his style: self-abandonment and self-control, vehemence and wisdom, particularism and humanism, he has created the African political style. But it is Africa and its age-old history that have taught him all this. It is precisely here that lies his strength and the secret of his success.

. . . . . .

|His| thought would be incomprehensible if it were not seen in the colonial context in which it developed, and which, in turn, conditioned it.

If 'the empire' means depersonalization, slow sinking into anonymity, the move to becoming a nation can only mean, for a community, the awakening of individuality.

From here derives the importance, the double importance, of which Sekou Touré is so conscious, that of culture: culture which, on the one hand, lifts the individual to the level of universal consciousness of his community, and on the other hand, in an opposing way, sets apart this very community from other communities from which it excludes and protects itself: 'We have, we think, our own message to deliver, our own human resources to contribute to those of modern society, the values characteristic of our own civilisation to add to the values of other civilisations.'

We know how, on this principle, Sekou Touré is cautious – and with him the Guineans. The colonial regime left them with a strong sense of themselves, as well as with a phobia: that of being a "satellite" or an "extension": Sekou Touré proclaims this with pride:

'Africa could not agree, at the risk of losing her self-respect, to let her civilisation and her own structure become an organic extension of any state system or ideological system.' . . .

. . . . . .

'Independence is the means chosen by the Party to destroy the structure of the colonial system. When we say "decolonization", we mean destroying the habits, the conceptions and the ways of the colonial system. We mean replacing them *with formulae which are Guinean, thought out by the people of Guinea, adapted to the conditions, the means, and the aspirations of the people of Guinea.'* A nice idea with which to educate people.

But from where does one start? From Africa, of course:

'Each must return to the cultural and moral springs of Africa, reintegrate his own conscience, readapt, in his thoughts and actions, to the values and conditions and interests of Africa.'

To arrive where?

Again, of course, in Africa.

And the ways and means will also come from Africa. For example, Sekou Touré would say that the economy must 'rediscover its African personality'. Law must be built upon the 'African personality'. Always the same word and always the same fundamental claim: Africa . . .

Africa is therefore posed not only as a principle, but also as a result; not only as object but as subject, that is, as a dynamic force, and a progressive self-realization . . .

To define [the] Guinean state, this African state, Sekou Touré uses a neologism: 'communocracy'. The word is explicit in itself: the state of Guinea, . . . like any state, would be above the individuals but at the same time created by the individuals. This is what is emphasized: the active co-operation of all, the product of the people imposed upon the people; the product under which the individual disappears but at the same time rediscovers himself fully, for the first time.

. . . If the transition from the colonial regime to independence means the transition from irresponsibility to total responsibility, then it is necessary to have a psychological transformation which will change the 'inferior' man into the 'liberated' man.

'The true political leaders of Africa', Sekou Touré maintains, 'can only be men committed, fundamentally committed, to the struggle against all the forms and forces of the depersonalization of African culture . . . For decolonization is not only liberation from *colonialism,* it must necessarily go on to mean the total liberation of the "colonial mind". Colonization, in

245

order that it can enjoy any amount of security, always needs to create and sustain a psychological climate favourable to its justification. It is for this reason that the national fight for liberation is not complete unless, having broken away from the colonial apparatus, the country is conscious of the negative values which have been knowingly injected into its life, its thought and its traditions.'

And finally, it is a political necessity, for the Africanization of action is a condition of its efficacy:

'Our unceasing efforts will lead to a discovery of our own paths of development if we want our emancipation and evolution to take place without our personality being altered. *Each time we choose a solution authentically African in its nature and conception, we shall solve our problems without any trouble, for all who participate will be neither disorientated nor surprised by what they will have to achieve;* they will grasp, without any difficulty, the correct way of working, acting or thinking. Our own specific qualities will be fully utilized and in the end we shall have hastened our historical evolution.'

......

It is significant that, with him, choice is never an ideological choice: if one presses him to define his position with regard to socialism, his answer is ready and he avoids the question ... 'Your question', he will reply, 'presupposes that we have defined what you call "African socialism" and that we base our political orientation and principles of action upon this definition. Not at all. Outsiders expect us to adopt some definite political system and to attempt, willy-nilly, to let it govern our political activities and our realities. We have a very different conception. We start from our realities and, depending on our ends and means, we establish a programme of action in the development of which we use anything that will help it along and increase its efficacy ...'

......

'Society is not made for principles, for a philosophy, for a doctrine, or for a given science, but on the contrary, science, philosophy and the principles of action must be determined for the people and as functions of the realities of the people. Instead of applying society to science, it is more suitable to apply science to society. And the Marxism which was used to mobilize the African populations, in particular the working class, and to guide this working class towards success, had been modified, thus excluding those characteristics which did not correspond to African reality.'

Thus speaks Sekou Touré. For this reason, one can purport that he is attempting not to "Marxise" Africa, but to "Africanise" Marxism: 'In Marxism, the principles of organisation, of democracy, of control, etc., all

246

that is concrete and that concerns the life of given movements, finds the perfect means to adapt to the present conditions of Africa. *But we would have failed – it is written – had we been entrenched in abstract philosophy.* I maintain that we are not interested in philosophy. We have concrete needs.'

Abstraction is the mother of sclerosis, of the mind as well as of the heart. When one starts simplifying human problems, the chances are that one will end up by crushing man ... Bringing Marxism down from its starry heights of principles to the level of flesh and blood, [Sekou Touré] humanises it and among the people he democratises it: 'Africa is essentially "communocratic" ', he remarks, 'collective life and social solidarity create among the people a degree of humanism that many might envy.'

25: Frantz Fanon: On National Culture

From F. Fanon, *The Wretched of the Earth* (Penguin, 1967).
These extracts are from a statement made to the second Congress of Negro Writers and Artists, Rome 1959.

The native intellectual who decides to give battle to colonial lies fights on the field of the whole continent. The past is given back its value. Culture, extracted from the past to be displayed in all its splendour, is not necessarily that of his own country. Colonialism, which has not bothered to put too fine a point on its efforts, has never ceased to maintain that the Negro is a savage; and for the colonist, the Negro was neither an Angolan nor a Nigerian, for he simply spoke of 'the Negro'. For colonialism, this vast continent was the haunt of savages, a country riddled with superstitions and fanaticism, destined for contempt, weighed down by the curse of God, a country of cannibals – in short, the Negro's country. Colonialism's condemnation is continental in its scope. The contention by colonialism that the darkest night of humanity lay over pre-colonial history concerns the whole of the African continent. The efforts of the native to rehabilitate himself and to escape from the claws of colonialism are logically inscribed from the same point of view as that of colonialism. The native intellectual who has gone far beyond the domains of Western culture and who has got it into his head to proclaim the existence of another culture never does so in the name of Angola or of Dahomey. The culture which is affirmed is African culture. The Negro, never so much a

247

Negro as since he has been dominated by the whites, when he decides to prove that he has a culure and to behave like a cultured person, comes to realize that history points out a well-defined path to him: he must demonstrate that a Negro culture exists.

And it is only too true that those who are most responsible for this racialization of thought, or at least for the first movement towards that thought, are and remain those Europeans who have never ceased to set up white culture to fill the gap left by the absence of other cultures. Colonialism did not dream of wasting its time in denying the existence of one national culture after another. Therefore the reply of the colonized peoples will be straight away continental in its breadth. In Africa, the native literature of the last twenty years is not a national literature but a Negro literature. The concept of Negro-ism, for example, was the emotional if not the logical antithesis of that insult which the white man flung at humanity. This rush of Negro-ism against the white man's contempt showed itself in certain spheres to be the one idea capable of lifting interdictions and anathemas. Because the new Guinean or Kenyan intellectuals found themselves above all up against a general ostracism and delivered to the combined contempt of their overlords, their reaction was to sing praises in admiration of each other. The unconditional affirmation of African culture has succeeded the unconditional affirmation of European culture. On the whole, the poets of Negro-ism oppose the idea of an old Europe to a young Africa, tiresome reasoning to lyricism, oppressive logic to high-stepping nature, and on one side stiffness, ceremony, etiquette and scepticism, while on the other frankness, liveliness, liberty and – why not? – luxuriance: but also irresponsibility.

The poets of Negro-ism will not stop at the limits of the continent. From America, black voices will take up the hymn with fuller unison. The 'black world' will see the light and Busia from Ghana, Birago Diop from Senegal, Hampate Ba from the Sudan and Saint-Clair Drake from Chicago will not hesitate to assert the existence of common ties and a motive power that is identical . . .

We must not therefore be content with delving into the past of a people in order to find coherent elements which will counteract colonialism's attempts to falsify and harm. We must work and fight with the same rhythm as the people to construct the future and to prepare the ground where vigorous shoots are already springing up. A national culture is not a folklore, nor an abstract populism that believes it can discover the people's true nature. It is not made up of the inert dregs of gratuitous actions, that is to say actions which are less and less attached to the ever present reality of the people. A national culture is the whole body of efforts made by a people in the sphere of thought to describe, justify and praise the action through which that people has created itself and keeps itself in existence. A national culture in under-developed countries should therefore take its place at the very heart of the struggle for freedom which these countries are carrying on. Men of African cultures who are still fighting in the name of African-Negro culture and who have called many congresses in the name of the unity of that culture should today realize that all their efforts amount to is to make comparisons between coins and sarcophagi.

There is no common destiny to be shared between the national cultures of Senegal and Guinea; but there is a common destiny between the Senegalese and Guinean nations which are both dominated by the same French colonialism. If it is wished that the national culture of Senegal should come to resemble the national culture of Guinea, it is not enough for the rulers of the two peoples to decide to consider their problems – whether the problem of liberation is concerned, or the trade-union questions, or economic difficulties – from similar view-points. And even here there does not seem to be complete identity, for the rhythm of the people and that of their rulers are not the same. There can be no two cultures which are completely identical. To believe that it is possible to create a black culture is to forget that niggers are disappearing, just as those people who brought them into being are seeing the break-up of their economic and cultural supremacy. There will never be such a thing as black culture because there is not a single politician who feels he has a vocation to bring black republics into being. The problem is to get to know the place that these men mean to give their people, the kind of social relations that they decide to set up and the conception that they have of the future of humanity. It is this that counts; everything else is mystification, signifying nothing.

In 1959 the cultured Africans who met at Rome never stopped talking about unity. But one of the people who was loudest in the praise of this cultural unity, Jacques Rabemananjara, is today a minister in the Madagascan government, and as such has decided, with his government, to oppose the Algerian people in the General Assembly of the United Nations. Rabemananjara, if he had been true to himself, ought to have resigned from the government and denounced those men who claim to incarnate the will of the Madagascan people. The ninety thousand dead of Madagascar have not given Rabemananjara authority to oppose the aspirations of the Algerian people in the General Assembly of the United Nations.

It is around the peoples' struggles that African-Negro culture takes on substance, and not around songs, poems or folklore. Senghor, who is also a member of the Society of African Culture and who has worked with us on the question of African culture, is not afraid for his part either to give the order to his delegation to support French proposals on Algeria. Adherence to African-Negro culture and to the cultural unity of Africa is arrived at in the first place by upholding unconditionally the peoples' struggle for freedom. No one can truly wish for the spread of African culture if he does not give practical support to the creation of the conditions necessary to the existence of that culture; in other words, to the liberation of the whole continent . . .

. . . . . .

We believe that the conscious and organized undertaking by a colonized people to re-establish the sovereignty of that nation constitutes the most complete and obvious cultural manifestation that exists. It is not alone the success of the struggle which afterwards gives validity and vigour to culture; culture is not put into cold storage during the conflict. The struggle itself in its development and in its internal progression sends culture along different paths and traces out entirely new ones for it. The struggle for freedom does not give back to the national culture its former value and shapes; this struggle which aims at a fundamentally different set of relations between men cannot leave intact either the form or the content of the people's culture. After the conflict there is not only the disappearance of colonialism but also the disappearance of the colonized man.

This new humanity cannot do otherwise than define a new humanism both for itself and for others. It is prefigured in the objectives and methods of the conflict. A struggle which mobilizes all classes of the people and which expresses their aims and their impatience, which is not afraid to count almost exclusively on the people's support, will of necessity triumph. The value of this type of conflict is that it supplies the maximum of conditions necessary for the development and aims of culture. After national freedom has been obtained in these conditions, there is no such painful cultural indecision which is found in certain countries which are newly independent, because the nation by its manner of coming into being and in the terms of existence exerts a fundamental influence over culture. A nation which is born of the people's concerted action and which embodies the real aspirations of the people while changing the state cannot exist save in the expression of exceptionally rich forms of culture.

The natives who are anxious for the culture of their country and who wish to give to it a universal dimension ought not therefore to place their confidence in the single principle of inevitable, undifferentiated independence written into the consciousness of the people in order to achieve their task. The liberation of the nation is one thing; the methods and popular content of the fight are another. It seems to us that the future of national culture and its riches are equally also part and parcel of the values which have ordained the struggle for freedom.

And now it is time to denounce certain pharisees. National claims, it is here and there stated, are a phase that humanity has left behind. It is the day of great concerted actions, and retarded nationalists ought in consequence to set their mistakes aright. We, however, consider that the mistake, which may have very serious consequences, lies in wishing to skip the national period. If culture is the expression of national consciousness, I will not hesitate to affirm that in the case with which we are dealing it is the national consciousness which is the most elaborate form of culture.

The consciousness of self is not the closing of a door to communication. Philosophic thought teaches us, on the contrary, that it is its guarantee. National consciousness, which is not nationalism, is the only thing that will give us an international dimension. This problem of national consciousness and of national culture takes on in Africa a special dimension. The birth of national consciousness in Africa has a strictly contemporaneous connexion with the African consciousness. The responsibility of the African as regards national culture is also a responsibility with regard to African-Negro culture. The joint responsibility is not the fact of a metaphysical principle but the awareness of a simple rule which wills that every independent nation in an Africa where colonialism is still entrenched is an encircled nation, a nation which is fragile and in permanent danger.

If man is known by his acts, then we will say that the most urgent thing today for the intellectual is to build up his nation. If this building up is true, that is to say if it interprets the manifest will of the people and reveals the eager African peoples, then the building of a nation is of necessity accompanied by the discovery and encouragement of universalizing values. Far from keeping aloof from other nations, therefore, it is national liberation which leads the nation to play its part on the stage of history. It is at the heart of national consciousness that international consciousness lives and grows. And this two-fold emerging is ultimately the source of all culture.

26: Robert Gardiner: Race, Culture, and Community

Extracts from R. Gardiner, *A World of Peoples*, BBC Reith Lectures, 1965 (1966 edition).

Formerly a Ghanaian civil servant, Gardiner has been since 1962 the Executive Secretary of the Economic Commission for Africa.

We all inherit a vast complex of attitudes and prejudices which inform our dealings with people of other races – our race consciousness, if you will. This complex has been created out of all the diverse historical experiences which have made our world what it is. But the largest single influence in this process has been the phenomenon of western European expansionism. From the moment that Columbus discovered, or perhaps rediscovered, America in 1492, Europeans assumed that the resources of the world were theirs, to be exploited, used, and traded . . .

At one time it was believed that non-Europeans under colonial rule should be educated, 'enlightened' and gradually assimilated – a belief that was based on a notion of 'potential' equality. Taken at its face value this may well appear to be a liberal concept. I suggest that it is, rather, an insulting and illiberal one. Humanism values a man for what he is, not for what he may become under a set of arbitrarily chosen stimuli. If the fact of being the creation of God does not confer equality, how can being the creation of man do so? On the other hand, the humanist must reject with equal vehemence any attempt to 'preserve' the non-European or to keep him 'unspoilt', or perpetually confined to his traditional institutions. Real equality demands that people be totally free to decide what parts of their own culture they wish to preserve and what elements of other cultures they desire to assimilate . . .

Different races come to live together in one society as a result of either peaceful immigration or conquest. If the immigrant community has a distinct culture of its own and is large enough to live as a coherent and reasonably self-contained unit, then it tends to retain its separate identity. But where there are enough cultural similarities between the indigenous and the immigrant peoples, and when the two groups are at comparable levels of technological advancement, they tend to settle down side by side, and can eventually come to form an integrated society. Of course there will be divisions within this society, but they will be determined by occupation, wealth and factors other than race.

Where the immigrant race happens both to be culturally different from the indigenous race and to enjoy a certain technological superiority over it, integration seems to be ruled out, and we have the peculiar phenomenon of the so-called parallel society . . .

. . . . . .

The main objectives of parallel societies seem to be first to maintain and if possible increase the distance between the planes on which the

252

communities lie, and secondly to reduce movement of persons from one plane to the other as far as possible. And this means keeping control of as much of the national resources of the country as possible in the hands of the upper economy.

. . . . . .

In short, there can be no doubt that discrimination based upon ideas of race superiority has profoundly affected the internal economic development of African communities, and the same process has had its effect on the economic relationships between African countries and the outside world . . .

. . . . . .

In short, the parallel society's customs, laws and institutions are all informed by the assumption, more or less explicit, that the different races have a certain fixed position in the economy. Under apartheid this assumption is formulated as a philosophy.

. . . To remove the inequalities inherited from past policies the newly independent African countries will have to use the power of the state, which means that the political revolution in parallel societies must be more far-reaching than liberal opinion generally admits. The entire state apparatus must be purged of its built-in inequalities.

Until a semblance of equality has been reached there has to be discrimination in favour of Africans. For instance, special credits and other assistance to African business, special educational opportunities, deliberate Africanization of public employment, introduction of Africans into exclusive residential and farming areas.

It is not enough to aim at equality: people who have been made unequal through past policy cannot merely be treated equally under the new policy. That approach can only perpetuate inequality.

. . . . . .

. . . race relations, like all relationships between people, are not static; and where you have had two forces, that of the material power and material ambition of the rulers and that of the self-esteem of the ruled, in constant conflict, it is inevitable that change must come. It is fortunate for the subject peoples of the world that history has ruled in their favour.

While the struggle between these two forces has been long-drawn-out in some places and less so in others, in every case it seems to have been waged in three identifiable phases. From the point of view of the ruling race these have been the building up of racial power, its consolidation, and finally its dissolution. From the viewpoint of the subject races they are acceptance, questioning, and revolt.

253

Part IV
The Struggle
Goes On

The continuing struggle against colonialism takes place on two fronts. Firstly, it involves those territories still under colonial or settler rule, i.e. Rhodesia, South-West Africa, South Africa and the Portuguese territories of Mozambique, Angola and Guinea–Bissau. Secondly, for independent African countries the struggle continues against neo-colonialism, which is a more subtle and pervasive means of political and economic domination by non-African states.

There are two broadly opposed views on the methods to be used within existing colonial territories. On the one hand, there are those who support violence against the oppressive regimes in these countries. Support for this means of liberation is manifest in the resolutions of the Organisation of African Unity, the Lusaka and Khartoum Conferences, and in the attitudes and actions of individual nationalists such as Mandela of South Africa, Mondlane of Mozambique and Cabral of Guinea–Bissau. It is noticeable that all these supporters of violent means express their regret at having been driven to such extremes.

On the other hand, certain leaders, although opposing apartheid and oppression by minority white regimes, have rejected violence as a means of ending colonial domination. Luthuli, who was President of the South African National Congress and Bishop Muzorewa, President of the Zimbabwe African National Council, both ardent Christians, reject violence intrinsically.

Hastings Banda of Malawi, Sir Seretse Khama of Botswana and Chief Leabua Jonathan of Lesotho also reject violence, but their countries are all situated close to South Africa, Rhodesia and Mozambique, and they are all economically dependent on South Africa. They advocate dialogue and negotiation with the colonial regimes as the only realistic approach.

However, there is a common factor between those leaders who support violence and those who do not: they are all opposed to racialism, including discrimination of blacks against whites.

254

The phenomenon of neo-colonialism is most lucidly analysed by Fanon. It is a danger of which almost all African leaders are aware because they see that their economic dependence on the rich countries makes them vulnerable in international politics. Mamadou Dia typifies the argument that neo-colonialism can only be overcome by inter-African cooperation, especially on the economic front. Nkrumah also recognises that, because neo-colonialism operates on a continental scale, it must be tackled on a continental scale, but he goes further than the advocacy of economic cooperation in proposing a panafrican government to organise an armed revolutionary struggle against both overt colonialism and neo-colonialism.

A. INTERNATIONAL ORGANISATIONS

1: OAU Resolutions, Addis Ababa, 1963

Extracts from resolutions adopted by the Summit meeting of Independent African States, Addis Ababa, 1963. From *Basic Documents and Resolutions* (OAU Provisional Secretariat).

The Summit Conference of Independent African States meeting in Addis Ababa, Ethiopia, from 22 May to 25 May 1963;

Having considered all aspects of the question of decolonisation;

Unanimously convinced of the imperious and urgent necessity of co-ordinating and intensifying their efforts to accelerate the unconditional attainment of national independence by all African territories still under foreign domination;

Reaffirming that it is the duty of all African Independent States to support dependent people in Africa in their struggle for freedom and independence;

Noting with deep concern that most of the remaining dependent territories in Africa are dominated by foreign settlers;

Convinced that the colonial powers by their forcible imposition of the settlers to control the governments and administration of those territories are thus establishing colonial bases in the heart of Africa;

Have agreed unanimously to concert and co-ordinate their efforts and action in this field, and to this end have decided on the following measures:

1. Declares that the forcible imposition by the colonial powers of the

settlers to control the governments and administration of the dependent territories is a flagrant violation of the inalienable rights of the legitimate inhabitants of the territories concerned;

2. Invites the colonial powers to take the necessary measures for the immediate application of the Declaration of the Granting of Independence to Colonial Countries and Peoples; and insists that their determination to maintain colonies or semi-colonies in Africa constitutes a menace to the peace of the continent;

3. Invites further the colonial powers, particularly the United Kingdom, with regard to Southern Rhodesia, not to transfer the powers and attributes of sovereignty to foreign minority governments imposed on African peoples by the use of force and under cover of racial legislation; transfer of power to settler minorities would amount to a violation of the provision of United Nations resolution 1514 (XV) on independence;

4. Reaffirms its support of African nationalists of Southern Rhodesia and solemnly declares that if power in Southern Rhodesia were to be usurped by a racial white minority government, Member States of the Conference would lend their effective moral and practical support to any legitimate measures which the African nationalist leaders may devise for the purpose of recovering such power and restoring it to the African majority; the Conference also undertakes henceforth to concert the efforts of its Members to take such measures as the situation demands against any State according recognition to the minority government;

5. Reaffirms further, that the territory of South-West Africa is an African territory under international mandate and that any attempt by the Republic of South Africa to annex it would be regarded as an act of aggression; Reaffirms also its determination to render all necessary support to the second phase of the South-West Africa case before the International Court of Justice; Reaffirms further the inalienable right of the people of South-West Africa to self-determination and independence;

6. Intervenes expressly with the great powers so that they cease without exception to lend direct or indirect support or assistance to all those colonialist governments which might use such assistance to suppress African national liberation movements, particularly the Portuguese Government which is conducting a real war of genocide in Africa; Informs the allies of colonial powers that they must choose between their friendship for the African peoples and their support of powers that oppress African peoples;

7. Decides to send a delegation of Ministers of Foreign Affairs to speak on behalf of all African States at the meeting of the Security Council which will be called to examine the report of the United Nations Committee of 24 on the situation in African territories under Portuguese

domination; (The Conference has decided the members of the Delegation to be: Liberia, Tunisia, Madagascar and Sierra Leone);

8. Decides further the breaking off of diplomatic and consular relations between all African States and the Governments of Portugal and South Africa so long as they persist in their present attitude towards decolonisation;

9. Asks for an effective boycott of the foreign trade of Portugal and South Africa by:

(a) prohibiting the import of goods from those two countries;
(b) closing African ports and airports to their ships and planes;
(c) forbidding the planes of those two countries to overfly the territories of all African States;

10. Earnestly invites all national liberation movements to co-ordinate their efforts by establishing common action fronts wherever necessary so as to strengthen the effectiveness of their struggle and the national use of the concerted assistance given them;

11. Establishes a co-ordinating committee consisting of Algeria, Ethiopia, Guinea, Congo (Leopoldville), Nigeria, Senegal, Tanganyika, United Arab Republic and Uganda, with Headquarters in Dar-es-Salaam, Tanganyika, responsible for harmonising the assistance from African States, and for managing the Special Fund to be set up for that purpose;

12. Establishes a Special Fund to be raised by voluntary contribution of Member States for the current year, the deadline for such contribution being 15 July 1963; Requests the Co-ordinating Committee to propose the necessary fund for the Council of Ministers so as to supply the necessary practical and financial aid to the various African national liberation movements;

13. Appoints the day of 25 May 1963 as African Liberation Day so as to organise popular demonstrations on that day to disseminate the recommendations of the Summit Conference and to collect sums over and above the national contributions for the special fund; (this year it will be the opening day of the 18th Session of the UN);

14. Decides to receive on the territories of independent African States, nationalists from liberation movements in order to give them training in all sectors, and afford young people all the assistance they need for their education and vocational training;

15. Decides further to promote, in each State, the transition of material aid and the establishment of a body of volunteers in various fields, with a view to providing the various African national liberation movements with the assistance they need in various sectors.

APARTHEID AND RACIAL DISCRIMINATION

Having considered all aspects of the questions of apartheid and racial discrimination;

Unanimously convinced of the imperious and urgent necessity of co-ordinating and intensifying their efforts to put an end to the South African Government's criminal policy of apartheid and wipe out racial discrimination in all its forms;

Have agreed unanimously to concert and co-ordinate their efforts and action in this field, and to this end have decided on the following measures:

1. To grant scholarships, educational facilities and possibilities of employment in African Government service to refugees from South Africa;

2. To support the recommendations presented to the Security Council and the General Assembly by the special Committee of the United Nations on the apartheid policies of the South African Government;

3. To despatch a delegation of Foreign Ministers to inform the Security Council of the explosive situation existing in South Africa; (The Conference has decided the members of the Delegation to be: Liberia, Tunisia, Madagascar and Sierra Leone);

4. To co-ordinate concerted measures of sanction against the Government of South Africa;

5. Appeals to all States, and more particularly to those which have traditional relations and co-operate with the Government of South Africa, to strictly apply UN resolution 1761 (XVII) of 6 November 1962 concerning apartheid;

6. Appeals to all Governments who still have diplomatic, consular and economic relations with the Government of South Africa to break off those relations and to cease any other form of encouragement for the policy of apartheid;

7. Stresses the great responsibility incurred by the colonial authorities administering territories neighbouring South Africa in the pursuit of the policy of apartheid;

8. Condemns racial discrimination in all its forms in Africa and all over the world;

9. Expresses the deep concern aroused in all African peoples and governments by the measures of racial discrimination taken against communities of African origin living outside the continent and particularly in the United States of America; Expresses appreciation for the efforts of the Federal Government of the United States of America to put an end to these intolerable malpractices which are likely seriously to deteriorate relations between the African peoples and governments on the one hand and the people and government of the United States of America on the other.

2: OAU Resolutions, Rabat, 1972

Selected resolutions adopted by the 19th Ordinary Session of the Council of Ministers at Rabat, Morocco, 5–12 June 1972. Published in C. Legum (ed.), *Africa Contemporary Record, 1972–3* (Hollings).
Zimbabwe=Rhodesia; Namibia=South West Africa.

RESOLUTION ON ZIMBABWE

The Council of Ministers: Reaffirming that any attempt to negotiate the future of Zimbabwe with the illegal regime on the basis of independence before majority rule would be in contravention of the inalienable rights of the people of that territory and contrary to the provisions of the UN Charter and of the General Assembly Resolution 1514 (XV);

Recognizing the importance of the continued imposition of political, diplomatic, economic and social sanctions against the illegal Smith regime until that illegal minority racist regime is brought to an end;

1. Pledges to increase its assistance to the people of Zimbabwe in their armed struggle for self-determination and independence;

2. Reaffirms support for the principle that there should be no independence before majority rule in Zimbabwe;

3. Calls upon the Government of the United Kingdom not to transfer or accord, under any circumstances, to the illegal regime any of the powers or attributes of sovereignty, and urges it to promote the country's attainment of independence by a democratic system of Government in accordance with the aspirations of the majority of the population;

4. Urges the United Kingdom, as administering authority, to convene as soon as possible a national constitutional conference in which the genuine political representatives of the people of Zimbabwe would be able to work out a settlement relating to the future of the territory for subsequent endorsement by the people under free and democratic processes;

5. Calls upon the United Kingdom Government to create the conditions necessary to permit the free expression of the right to self-determination, including:

(a) the release of all political prisoners, detainees and restrictees;
(b) the repeal of all repressive discriminatory legislation;
(c) the removal of all restrictions on political activity and the establishment of full democratic freedom and equality of political rights;

6. Further calls on the United Kingdom Government to ensure that in any exercise to ascertain the wishes of the people of Zimbabwe as to their political future, the procedure to be followed will be in accordance with the principle of universal adult suffrage and by secret referendum on the

basis of one-man-one-vote without regard to race, colour or to educational, property or income considerations;

7. Condemns the United Kingdom Government for its failure to take effective measures to bring to an end the illegal regime in Zimbabwe;

RESOLUTION ON THE PORTUGUESE COLONIES

The Council of Ministers: Fully aware of the fact that the complete achievement of African unity requires first of all the total liberation and independence of all the African territories still subjected to foreign domination and exploitation;

Reaffirming the determination and commitment on the part of the independent African States to liberate all the territories under Portuguese domination . . .

Recalling all resolutions on the question of territories under Portuguese domination previously adopted by the OAU . . .

1. Solemnly reaffirms the inalienable right of the people of Angola, Mozambique and Guinea–Bissau to self-determination and independence,

2. Fully supports the legitimate armed struggle of the people of Angola, Mozambique and Guinea–Bissau against colonialist domination and oppression by Portugal for their freedom and independence;

3. Solemnly reaffirms its commitment to pursue the struggle with a view to the total liberation of the territories of Angola, Mozambique and Guinea–Bissau through concerted and practical actions of all kinds and at all levels;

4. Reaffirms that the national liberation movements of the Portuguese colonies are the custodians of the sovereignty of their countries and peoples;

5. Calls upon the international community to recognize the national liberation movements of the Portuguese colonies as the legitimate representatives of their peoples and countries and to discuss problems concerning these peoples and countries only with the respective liberation movements;

. . . . . .

12. Strongly condemns the alliance of Portugal and the minority racialist regimes of South Africa and Rhodesia aimed at perpetuating colonialism, oppression and racial discrimination in this part of Africa.

13. Urges the Governments of OAU member-States to implement vigorously the provisions of the Resolution adopted by OAU and to cease maintaining relations with Portugal;

. . . . . .

19. Encourages all the liberation movements of Angola, Mozambique

and Guinea–Bissau to intensify the struggle against Portuguese colonialism and for national independence;

20. Decides to increase assistance to the liberation movements of Angola, Mozambique and Guinea–Bissau in conformity with the recommendations of the Liberation Committee, and

21. Further invites the Governments of OAU Member States to strengthen and increase their moral and material support for the liberation struggle being waged by the valiant freedom-fighters of Angola, Mozambique and Guinea–Bissau against Portuguese domination.

. . . . . .

RESOLUTION ON NAMIBIA

The Council of Ministers: Recalling its previous resolutions on Namibia,

1. Reaffirms the inalienable right of the people of Namibia to freedom and independence in one *entity*, in conformity with UN General Assembly Resolution 1514 (XV),

2. Reiterates its solidarity and full support to the people of Namibia in their just struggle to regain their freedom and independence,

3. Reaffirms further that the administration of the territory of Namibia is the direct responsibility of the UN and that this responsibility includes the obligation to support, promote and protect the rights of the peoples of Namibia as well as the national unity and the territorial integrity of the territory in accordance with the UN resolutions,

4. Condemns all actions by South Africa designed to destroy the unity and territorial integrity of Namibia such as the establishment of Bantustans and declares that the OAU will oppose any action detrimental to the national unity and the territorial integrity of Namibia,

5. Condemns any support and assistance given to South Africa which enables it to continue its illegal occupation of the territory or entrench its authority.

RESOLUTION ON THE REPORT OF THE CO-ORDINATING COMMITTEE FOR THE LIBERATION OF AFRICA

The Council of Ministers: Having examined the report of the Co-ordinating Committee for the Liberation of Africa on the activities of the various Liberation Movements and having studied the development of the armed struggle on all fronts and combat zones,

Noting with satisfaction the progress made by the various Liberation Movements actively engaged in the armed struggle, particularly in Guinea–Bissau, Mozambique, Angola and Namibia, which constitute a major development of far-reaching military, political and social impact on

261

the evolution of the armed liberation struggle,

Mindful of the fact that the total liberation of the African Continent from foreign domination, occupation and the eradication of all forms of colonialism and racial discrimination remain the principal objective and constant preoccupation of the OAU . . .

Reiterating the urgent necessity for Liberation Movements fighting within the same territory to close ranks and form a united front for mobilizing the masses inside the territory and intensifying the armed struggle,

Realizing that the present evolution of the armed struggle necessitates increased material and financial assistance to liberation movements particularly in territories where the struggle has reached an advanced stage, and taking into account the requests and needs of various Liberation Movements,

Aware of the importance of publicity and information to alert and enlighten world public opinion in order to further support the liberation movements and isolate the colonial and racist regimes,

1. Takes note of the report of the co-ordinating committee for the Liberation of Africa;

2. Commends those movements which are actively and effectively engaged in the liberation struggle especially the PAIGC, FRELIMO, MPLA and SWAPO for the important results so far achieved;

3. Strongly condemns the Portuguese aggression against the territorial integrity of OAU Member States namely the People's Republic of the Congo, Republic of Guinea, Senegal, Tanzania and Zambia;

4. Reaffirms that any aggression against any Member State is considered an aggression against all OAU Members;

5. Recommends to the Ninth Ordinary Session of the Assembly of Heads of State and Government:

(i) That concrete assistance be rendered to the above-mentioned Member States in order to strengthen their defences;
(ii) That OAU member-States should endeavour to earmark national military units or war material to be put at the disposal of countries requesting such assistance;

6. Takes note of the efforts exerted by the Liberation Committee to bring about unity between the Liberation Movements fighting in Zimbabwe, and directs the Committee to pursue its efforts to bring about a unified Zimbabwe military organization under one single command and one single political organization;

7. Recommends that the representatives of recognized Liberation

Movements participate as observers in the deliberations of OAU organs on matter of decolonization; or any other matter which may be in the interest of their territories;

8. Requests the Co-ordinating Committee for the Liberation of Africa to continue granting assistance to movements struggling for independence and self-determination in the Comoros and the so-called French Somaliland (Djibouti) and Seychelles;

9. Endorses the recommendations of the Liberation Committee for voluntary additional material and financial assistance to the liberation struggle; and to that end:

(a) Decides to submit the relevant document of the report of the Liberation Committee on additional material and financial assistance to the Assembly of Heads of State and Government CM/430/ Rev. I Annex (III) meeting at its Ninth Ordinary Session;

(b) Recommends that a pledging meeting be held during the Ninth Ordinary Session in which Member States may be invited to pledge such assistance;

(c) Appeals once more to Member States to honour in full their obligations towards the liberation struggle by paying without delay all their arrears and contributions to the Special Fund of the Co-ordinating Committee for the Liberation of Africa;

10. Approves the terms and conditions of service of the military experts employed by the Co-ordinating Committee for the Liberaion of Africa.

RECOMMENDATIONS ON SPECIAL MEASURES TO BE ADOPTED ON DECOLONIZATION AND THE STRUGGLE AGAINST APARTHEID AND RACIAL DISCRIMINATION

The Council of Ministers:

1. Reaffirms all its previous resolutions on Decolonization.

2. Calls upon member-States to take the necessary steps to deny landing and other facilities to aircraft proceeding to or coming from South Africa and Rhodesia.

3. Recommends in order to strengthen the means of defence of certain African States, that member-States apply themselves to making available to those States who request them, units, modern military equipment and military assistance, pending the setting up of the Executive Secretariat of Defence.

4. Considers that assistance given to the colonial and racist regimes in particular military assistance increases tension and endangers international peace and security and contravenes the obligations of UN

Member States according to the UN Charter by assisting the aggressor against the aggressed.

5. Considers that the repeated acts of aggression against independent African States are intended to prevent them from helping or supporting the liberation struggle and declares that such acts of aggression against any African State constitute an aggression against the whole of Africa.

6. Proclaims that the liberation of the African soil cannot, under any circumstances, be the subject of concessions or bargaining.

3: The Khartoum Conference, 1969

Extracts from a report by Yusef Dadoo, member of the South African National Congress delegation; published in *Etudes Congolaises* (April-June 1969). Translated from the French by the Editors.
This Conference on the liberation of African colonial territories was jointly sponsored by the World Council for Peace and the Afro-Asian Peoples' Solidarity Organisation (AAPSO). These are non-governmental political organisations which are generally much more radical than governmental organisations.

This conference, jointly sponsored by the Organization for the Solidarity of the Afro-Asian Peoples and the World Council for Peace, collaborating with the six original movements of national liberation by armed struggle, was attended by representatives and experts from more than fifty countries as well as by a certain number of international organizations . . .

It was a sad reflection on the political situation existing on the African continent that independent Africa was very poorly represented in spite of the persistent efforts made by those in charge of the conference. But there were delegations from Nigeria, Senegal, Sierra Leone, Somalia and Madagascar.

Recognizing the importance of international action in support of the struggle, the most important leaders of the six national liberation movements came to the conference in person to present a realistic and direct report on the situation in their respective countries, the progress they have achieved on various fronts and the state of affairs in the liberated regions.

Portuguese Colonies: powerful delegations from Guinea–Bissau, Angola and Mozambique were led by Amilcar Cabral of the PAIGC (Partido Africano da Independencia de Guinè y do Cabo Verde), Agostinho Neto, of MPLA (Movimento Popular de Libertaçâo de

Angola) and Edouard Mondlane of FRELIMO who has since been unjustly assassinated. They talked of fascist terror and of repressions initiated by the African colonialists against the population. They gave a sparing but encouraging account of the worth and the capabilities of the armed guerilla fighters who, with the help of local inhabitants, were able to make the Portuguese army retreat, and to liberate vast areas of the three territories in question. In Guinea–Bissau, more than two-thirds of the territory has been liberated and the Portuguese troops were driven back and had to take refuge in the towns they had left. In Angola, one-third of the area has been freed and in Mozambique, one-fifth. Approximately 250,000 Portuguese troops are fumbling around in a desperate effort to stop the inflow of freedom fighters.

It was proved, at the conference, that had NATO not supplied Portugal with economic and military aid, the Portuguese colonial administration in Africa would probably have collapsed.

South Africa: the South Africa report was presented in a series of speeches given at the conference by the delegation of the African National Council of South Africa. The report on apartheid ... was given by Robert M. Resha and the others dealt with questions such as the bases of imperialism in South Africa, the power of race and apartheid, political prisoners and the role of women.

These reports showed clearly that South Africa is now a highly imperialist State and that, supported by Great Britain, the United States, West Germany and other powers, she is energetically concerned with regaining the imperialist responsibilities in Africa and that, allied to Smith's regime in Rhodesia and to the fascist regime of Portugal, she constitutes a serious and direct threat to world peace.

As Robert Resha rightly pointed out in his report, the fascist Republic of South Africa 'is vigorously intervening in Zimbabwe to support Smith's illegal regime faced with a people's revolution – that is an act of invasion of what is a so-called British colony. She continues her policy of economic, political and military domination of neighbouring Lesotho, Swaziland and Botswana as far north as Malawi, with the object of infiltrating all independent States of Africa. South Africa has flagrantly threatened Zambia and Tanzania. *South African fascism is as great a threat to the peace, the security and the independence of the African continent as was Hitler's regime thirty years ago.'*

Armed struggle in South Africa: the ANC report, like that of the Zimbabwe African People's Union (ZAPU), also concerned guerila warfare waged in Zimbabwe since 1967 by the military alliance of the ANC and ZAPU.

. . . . . .

Namibia (South-West Africa): the repression of the population by the savage enforcement of apartheid laws in its territory by the fascist regime of South Africa, in flagrant opposition to the UNO, was vigorously condemned in the report of Sam Nujomo, president of SWAPO (South West African People's Organization). The report also concerned the massive abuse of the country's resources and the merciless exploitation of cheap labour carried out by South African and foreign monopolies.

It also concerned the activities of the guerillas hired by the Namibia Liberation Army, the military section of SWAPO, since the beginning of the armed struggle in 1966.

. . . . . .

... the commissions [set up at the conference] submitted three resolutions that were passed unanimously and enthusiastically by the Assembly during the last plenary session.

The Declaration called urgently upon the total solidarity of the democratic forces and proclaimed among other things:

'We are gathered at a time when all the forces of national liberation, enjoying the support of the forces of progress and socialism, challenge the aggressive forces of imperialism, of colonialism, of racism and are winning new battles in the struggle for liberty, independence and social progress.

We are gathered to face the challenge against Africa and humanity of Portuguese colonialism and of the white supremacy regimes of South Africa.

We have decided unanimously that Africa and the world should supply wider effective aid to the African liberation movements which are fighting for the liberty of their people. We ... make the solemn pledge that this Khartoum conference will turn out to be a new step forward that will go down in the history of Africa's struggle for liberty, independence and unity.

The existence of these racist regimes, their aggressive alliance and the aid provided by imperialism in the economic, financial, political and military fields, constitute a major danger for world peace ...

The conference calls upon the progressive, anti-imperialist forces of the whole world to support the armed struggles that have been imposed upon them as the only alternative to slavery in the near future'.

B. SOUTHERN AFRICA

4: The Lusaka Manifesto

Published in *The Times*, 22 May 1969.
The manifesto on relations with South Africa, Rhodesia and Portugal, was signed on 16 April 1969 by fourteen states from East and Central Africa. It was later adopted by the OAU Heads of States (September 1969) and approved by the United Nations General Assembly

1. When the purpose and the basis of States' international policies are misunderstood, there is introduced into the world a new unnecessary disharmony. Disagreements, conflicts of interest, or different assessments of human priorities, which already provoke an excess of tension in the world, disastrously divide mankind at a time when united action is necessary to control modern technology and put it to the service of man. It is for this reason, that discovering widespread misapprehension of our attitudes and purposes in relation to Southern Africa, we the leaders of East and Central African States meeting at Lusaka, 16th April, 1969, have agreed to issue this Manifesto.

2. By this Manifesto we wish to make clear, beyond all shadow of doubt, our acceptance of the belief that all men are equal, and have equal rights to human dignity and respect, regardless of colour, race, religion, or sex. We believe that all men have the right and the duty to participate, as equal members of the society, in their own government. We do not accept that any individual or group has any right to govern any other group of sane adults, without their consent, and we affirm that only the people of a society, acting together as equals, can determine what is, for them a good society and a good social, economic, or political organization.

3. On the basis of these beliefs we do not accept that any one group within a society has the right to rule any society without the continuing consent of all the citizens. We recognize that at any one time there will be, within every society, failures in the implementation of these ideals. We recognize that for the sake of order in human affairs, there may be transitional arrangements while a transformation from group inequalities to individual equality is being effected. But we affirm that without an acceptance of these ideals — without commitment to these principles of human equality and self-determination — there can be no basis for peace and justice in the world.

4. None of us would claim that within our own States we have achieved that perfect social, economic, and political organization which would

ensure a reasonable standard of living for all our people and establish individual security against avoidable hardship or miscarriage of justice. On the contrary, we acknowledge that within our own States the struggle towards human brotherhood and unchallenged human dignity is only beginning. It is on the basis of our commitment to human equality and human dignity, not on the basis of achieved perfection, that we take our stand of hostility towards the colonialism and racial discrimination which is being practised in Southern Africa. It is on the basis of their commitment to these universal principles that we appeal to other members of the human race for support.

5. If the commitment to these principles existed among the States holding power in Southern Africa, any disagreements we might have about the rate of implementation, or about isolated acts of policy, would be matters affecting only our individual relationships with the States concerned. If these commitments existed, our States would not be justified in the expressed and active hostility towards the regimes of Southern Africa such as we have proclaimed and continue to propagate.

6. The truth is, however, that in Mozambique, Angola, Rhodesia, South-West Africa, and the Republic of South Africa, there is an open and continued denial of the principles of human equality and national self-determination. This is not a matter of failure in the implementation of accepted human principles. The effective Administrations in all these territories are not struggling towards these difficult goals. They are fighting the principles; they are deliberately organizing their societies so as to try to destroy the hold of these principles in the minds of men. It is for this reason that we believe the rest of the world must be interested. For the principle of human equality, and all that flows from it, is either universal or it does not exist. The dignity of all men is destroyed when the manhood of any human being is denied.

7. Our objectives in Southern Africa stem from our commitment to this principle of human equality. We are not hostile to the Administrations of these States because they are manned and controlled by white people. We are hostile to them because they are systems of minority control which exist as a result of, and in the pursuance of, doctrines of human inequality. What we are working for is the right of self-determination for the people of those territories. We are working for a rule in those countries which is based on the will of all the people, and an acceptance of the equality of every citizen.

8. Our stand towards Southern Africa thus involves a rejection of racialism, not a reversal of the existing racial domination. We believe that all the peoples who have made their homes in the countries of Southern

Africa are Africans, regardless of the colour of their skins: and we would oppose a racialist majority government which adopted a philosophy of deliberate and permanent discrimination between its citizens on grounds of racial origin. We are not talking racialism when we reject the colonialism and apartheid policies now operating in those areas; we are demanding an opportunity for all the people of these States, working together as equal individual citizens, to work out for themselves the institutions and the system of government under which they will, by general consent, live together and work together to build a harmonious society.

9. As an aftermath of the present policies, it is likely that different groups within these societies will be self-conscious and fearful. The initial political and economic organizations may well take account of these fears, and this group self-consciousness. But how this is to be done must be a matter exclusively for the peoples of the country concerned, working together. No other nation will have a right to interfere in such affairs. All that the rest of the world has a right to demand is just what we are now asserting, that the arrangements within any State which wishes to be accepted into the community of nations must be based on an acceptance of the principles of human dignity and equality.

10. To talk of the liberation of Africa is thus to say two things: First, that the peoples in the territories still under colonial rule shall be free to determine for themselves their own institutions of self-government. Secondly, that the individuals in Southern Africa shall be freed from an environment poisoned by the propaganda of racialism, and given an opportunity to be men – not white men, brown men, yellow men, or black men.

11. Thus the liberation of Africa for which we are struggling does not mean a reverse racialism. Nor is it an aspect of African Imperialism. As far as we are concerned the present boundaries of the States of Southern Africa are the boundaries of what will be free and independent African States. There is no question of our seeking or accepting any alterations to our own boundaries at the expense of these future free African nations.

12. On the objective of liberation as thus defined, we can neither surrender nor compromise. We have always preferred and we still prefer, to achieve it without physical violence. We would prefer to negotiate rather than to destroy, to talk rather than kill. We do not advocate violence; we advocate an end to the violence against human dignity which is now being perpetrated by the oppressors of Africa. If peaceful progress to emancipation were possible, or if changed circumstances were to make it possible in the future, we would urge our brothers in the resistance

movements to use peaceful methods of struggle even at the cost of some compromise on the timing of change. But while peaceful progress is blocked by actions of those at present in power in the States of Southern Africa, we have no choice but to give to the peoples of those territories all the support of which we are capable in their struggle against their oppressors. This is why the signatory states participate in the movement for the liberation of Africa, under the aegis of the Organization of African Unity. However, the obstacle to change is not the same in all the countries of Southern Africa, and it follows therefore, that the possibility of continuing the struggle through peaceful means varies from one country to another.

13. In Mozambique and Angola, and in so-called Portuguese Guinea, the basic problem is not racialism but pretence that Portugal exists in Africa. Portugal is situated in Europe; the fact that it is a dictatorship is a matter for the Portuguese to settle. But no decree of the Portuguese dictator, nor legislation passed by any Parliament in Portugal, can make Africa part of Europe. The only thing which could convert a part of Africa into a constituent unity in a union which also includes a European State would be the freely expressed will of the people of that part of Africa. There is no such popular will in the Portuguese colonies. On the contrary, in the absence of any opportunity to negotiate a road to freedom, the peoples of all three territories have taken up arms against the colonial power. They have done this despite the heavy odds against them, and despite the great suffering they know to be involved.

14. Portugal, as a European State, has naturally its own allies in the context of the ideological conflict between West and East. However, in our context, the effect of this is that Portugal is enabled to use her resources to pursue the most heinous war and degradation of man in Africa. The present Manifesto must, therefore, lay bare the fact that the inhuman commitment of Portugal in Africa and her ruthless subjugation of the people of Mozambique, Angola and the so-called Portuguese Guinea, is not only irrelevant to the ideological conflict of power-politics, but it is also diametrically opposed to the politics, the philosophies and the doctrines practised by her Allies, in the conduct of their own affairs at home. The peoples of Mozambique, Angola, and Portuguese Guinea are not interested in their freedom. They are demanding an acceptance of the principles of independence on the basis of majority rule, and for many years they called for discussions on this issue. Only when their demand for talks was continually ignored did they begin to fight. Even now, if Portugal should change her policy and accept the principle of self-determination, we would urge the Liberation Movements to desist from

their armed struggle and to co-operate in the mechanics of a peaceful transfer of power from Portugal to the peoples of the African territories.

15. The fact that many Portuguese citizens have immigrated to these African countries does not affect this issue. Future immigration policy will be a matter for the independent Governments when these are established. In the meantime we would urge the Liberation Movements to reiterate their statements that all those Portuguese people who have made their homes in Mozambique, Angola, or Portuguese Guinea, and who are willing to give their future loyalty to those States, will be accepted as citizens. And an independent Mozambique, Angola, or Portuguese Guinea may choose to be as friendly with Portugal as Brazil is. That would be the free choice of a free people.

16. In Rhodesia the situation is different in so far as the metropolitan power has acknowledged the colonial status of the territory. Unfortunately, however, it has failed to take adequate measures to reassert its authority against the minority which has seized power with the declared intention of maintaining white domination. The matter cannot rest there. Rhodesia, like the rest of Africa, must be free, and its independence must be on the basis of majority rule. If the colonial power is unwilling or unable to effect such a transfer of power to the people, then the people themselves will have no alternative but to capture it as and when they can. And Africa has no alternative but to support them. The question which remains in Rhodesia is therefore whether Britain will reassert her authority in Rhodesia and then negotiate the peaceful progress to majority rule before independence. In so far as Britain is willing to make this second commitment, Africa will co-operate in her attempts to reassert her authority. This is the method of progress we would prefer; it would involve less suffering for all the people of Rhodesia, both black and white. But until there is some firm evidence that Britain accepts the principle of independence on the basis of majority rule and is prepared to take whatever steps are necessary to make it a reality, then Africa has no choice but to support the struggle for the people's freedom by whatever means are open.

17. Just as a settlement of the Rhodesian problem with a minimum of violence is a British responsibility, so a settlement in South West Africa with a minimum of violence is a United Nations responsibility. By every canon of international law, and by every precedent, South West Africa should by now have been a sovereign, independent State with a Government based on majority rule. South West Africa was a German colony until 1919, just as Tanganyika, Rwanda and Burundi, Togoland, and Cameroon were German colonies.

It was a matter of European politics that when the Mandatory System was established after Germany had been defeated, the administration of South West Africa was given to the white minority Government of South Africa, while the other ex-German colonies in Africa were put into the hands of the British, Belgian, or French Governments. After the Second World War every mandated territory except South West Africa was converted into Trusteeship Territory and has subsequently gained independence. South Africa, on the other hand, has persistently refused to honour even the international obligation it accepted in 1919, and has increasingly applied to South West Africa the inhuman doctrines and organizations of apartheid.

18. The United Nations General Assembly has ruled against this action and in 1966 terminated the Mandate under which South Africa had a legal basis for its occupation and domination of South West Africa. The General Assembly declared that the territory is now the direct responsibility of the United Nations and set up an ad hoc Committee to recommend practical means by which South West Africa would be administered, and the people enabled to exercise self-determination and to achieve independence.

19. Nothing could be clearer than this decision — which no permanent member of the Security Council voted against. Yet, since that time no effective measures have been taken to enforce it. South West Africa remains in the clutches of the most ruthless minority government in Africa. Its people continue to be oppressed and those who advocate even peaceful progress to independence continue to be persecuted. The world has an obligation to use its strength to enforce the decision which all the countries co-operated in making. If they do this there is hope that the change can be effected without great violence. If they fail, then sooner or later the people of South West Africa will take the law into their own hands. The people have been patient beyond belief, but one day their patience will be exhausted. Africa, at least, will then be unable to deny their call for help.

20. The Republic of South Africa is itself an independent Sovereign state and a member of the United Nations. It is more highly developed and richer than any other nation in Africa. On every legal basis its internal affairs are a matter exclusively for the people of South Africa. Yet the purpose of law is people and we assert that the actions of the South African Government are such that the rest of the world has a responsibility to take some action in defence of humanity.

21. There is one thing about South African oppression which distinguishes

it from other oppressive regimes. The apartheid policy adopted by its Government, and supported to a greater or lesser extent by almost all its white citizens, is based on a rejection of man's humanity. A position of privilege or the experience of oppression in the South African society depends on the one thing which it is beyond the power of any man to change. It depends upon a man's colour, his parentage, and his ancestors. If you are black you cannot escape this categorization, nor can you escape it if you are white. If you are a black millionaire and a brilliant political scientist, you are still subject to the pass laws and still excluded from political activity. If you are white, even protests against the system and an attempt to reject segregation, will lead you only to the segregation and the comparative comfort of a white jail. Beliefs, abilities, and behaviour are all irrelevant to a man's status; everything depends upon race. Manhood is irrelevant. The whole system of government and society in South Africa is based on the denial of human equality. And the system is maintained by a ruthless denial of all human rights of the majority of the population and thus, inevitably, of all.

22. These things are known and are regularly condemned in the Councils of the United Nations and elsewhere. But it appears that to many countries international law takes precedence over humanity; therefore no action follows the words. Yet even if international law is held to exclude active assistance to the South African opponents of apartheid, it does not demand that the comfort and support of human and commercial intercourse should be given to a government which rejects the manhood of most of humanity. South Africa should be excluded from the United Nations Agencies, and even from the United Nations itself. It should be ostracized by the world community. It should be isolated from world trade patterns and left to be self-sufficient if it can. The South African Government cannot be allowed both to reject the very concept of mankind's unity, and to benefit by the strength given through friendly international relations. And certainly Africa cannot acquiesce in the maintenance of the present policies against people of African descent.

23. The signatories of this Manifesto assert that the validity of the principles of human equality and dignity extend to the Republic of South Africa just as they extend to the colonial territories of Southern Africa. Before a basis for peaceful development can be established in this continent, these principles must be acknowledged by every nation, and in every State there must be a deliberate attempt to implement them.

24. We re-affirm our commitment to these principles of human equality and human dignity, and to the doctrines of self-determination and non-racialism. We shall work for their extension within our own nations and throughout the continent of Africa.

273

5: Hastings Banda

Extracts from speeches by H. K. Banda, President of Malawi, to the Malawi Parliament, 28 and 31 July 1970. Published by the Department of Information, Blantyre (Malawi, 1970).

Let us take the African point of view. As I understand it, my fellow African leaders are saying this; Britain must not sell arms to South Africa because if she does that then she is helping South Africa to prolong, to continue apartheid, Britain is helping South Africa making it easier for them to defeat the freedom fighters, that if Britain supplies arms to South Africa she will make South Africa much more of a threat to African States north of the Zambezi.

My answer is simply this, to maintain her policy of apartheid, policy of discrimination, South Africa does not need Nimrods, does not need submarines, does not need Buccaneers or anything that you can think of; she is already manufacturing all the necessary arms for internal suppression if you like; she does not need these at all, and therefore I believe Britain, when Britain says they are not doing this to uphold apartheid or to help South Africa to suppress the African himself.

Helping South Africa defeat the freedom fighters, anyone to believe this language, I just do not understand. How nearer have the freedom fighters from Dar-es-Salaam and Lusaka reached South Africa? South Africa is able to defeat freedom fighters now without any assistance from Britain, without anything from Britain. She has been doing it and she is doing it still. Therefore it is not correct to say that the sale of arms to South Africa will make it impossible for the freedom fighters to fight South Africa, it is already impossible for them.

In allowing South African Ministers to visit this country, Honourable Members, in allowing Mr. Vorster himself to visit this country, I personally, the Government and the people of this country are not allowing them because we approve of and support the policy of apartheid. We are not doing this because we are indifferent to the conditions under which our brothers and sisters are living. Far from it. Just the opposite. I made this plain to Mr. Vorster himself, when he was here; I even referred to this in my speech at a Banquet given in Mr. Vorster's honour, quite plainly, that I did not agree with racial discrimination.

I invited Mr. Vorster to visit this country because as I have said so many times in the past in this House, and outside this House, I do not believe in the policy of denunciation; because I do not believe in the policy of boycott and isolation; because I do not believe in the politics and diplomacy of bluff and bluster, Mr. Speaker, Honourable Members. It is for the same reason that I personally and the Government of this country allow the white people of South Africa, men and women, Briton and Afrikaner, to visit, to come here.

In my view, in my honest belief, honest opinion, Mr. Speaker, it is absolutely of no use we the African leaders, North of the Zambezi or farther elsewhere on our continent, the African Continent, denouncing the white people of South Africa, the white people of Rhodesia, white people of Mozambique and Angola, from a distance, thousands of miles away in Addis Ababa, New York, London, Lagos, Singapore; it is no use we African leaders shrieking our heads off, calling for boycott and isolation of the whites in South Africa, whites in Rhodesia, whites in Mozambique and Angola; it is of no use us uttering empty, idle and childish threats at the whites of these countries, which threats, everybody, everyone, including ourselves, knows we are not capable of implementing. No use at all.

6: Seretse Khama

Extracts from a speech by the President of Botswana to a Botswana Democratic Party Conference, 28 March 1970. Published by Government Printer (Botswana, 1970).

But Botswana's dependence on South Africa is great enough already. We have noted South Africa's assurances of friendly intentions towards Botswana and other independent states. We have recently, together with Lesotho and Swaziland, concluded lengthy negotiations with South Africa on the Customs Agreement. These have resulted in a more equitable distribution of the revenues of the Customs Area, and the right to protect our infant industries while retaining access to the South African market. But in these negotiations we have not been seeking aid. Nor do we intend to seek aid from South African official sources. It would not be in the interests of either country to increase Botswana's dependence on South Africa. Instead our aim has been and remains to convert the almost total dependence of the colonial period into a pattern of interdependence.

Yet it cannot be denied that there is a cloud hanging over Southern Africa. The economic prospects of our region could be limitless were it not for the threat posed by racialism and minority rule and the instability and the potential instability to which it must give rise. Botswana endorses as do all independent African states and all but a handful of United

Nations members the Lusaka Manifesto. The Lusaka Manifesto, drawn up a year ago by the heads of state of East and Central Africa, firmly states Africa's preference for the achievement of self-determination through negotiation.

It was in this way that Botswana's independence was achieved and we would wish that the indigenous populations of neighbouring territories could share our experience. Yet the Lusaka Manifesto, although widely proclaimed throughout the world as a moderate and realistic statement has gone unheeded. The consequences of this refusal to consider even the possibility of change in the region will be serious indeed.

. . . . . .

But Botswana cannot allow itself to be used as a springboard for violence against the minority regimes. Our task is to insulate ourselves from the instability their policies provoke. we must preserve our independence while asserting the principles of human freedom and dignity. I should like at the same time to explain Botswana's position on the recent Security Council Resolution on Rhodesia. It must be obvious that while we share the concern over the Rhodesian situation expressed in the Finnish resolution, it will not be possible for us to comply with all the sanctions it calls for. All of you are only too aware that the only railway linking South Africa and Rhodesia goes through Botswana. As I have repeatedly made clear, Botswana has no intention of interfering with that line, on which we depend for the vital imports and exports essential to our development. Nor can we cut off road communications with Rhodesia. Even the reduction of trade with Rhodesia presents great difficulties, because of Rhodesia's capacity to retaliate. An alternative link with South Africa via Beittridge could be built relatively quickly and cheaply, and this would leave the future of the Botswana line at best uncertain.

Yet Botswana has not ignored the United Nations call for sanctions against the Rhodesian regime. Indeed we have supported this policy as the only alternative to conceding defeat. We have called upon member states, who are in a better position to assist in this matter than ourselves, to co-operate in making sanctions more effective. And we ourselves have done all we can within the constraints of our land-locked position, our frail economy and the administrative problems involved. We have prevented the Rhodesians from using their railway to import arms and military supplies. Our airline has long ceased to fly into Rhodesia. We have prevented the import of Rhodesian beer and tobacco. We are determined where possible to limit our dependence on Rhodesia.

7: Leabua Jonathan

Statement by Chief Leabua Jonathan, Prime Minister of Lesotho, before OAU Heads of State, June 1971. Published in Legum, *Africa Contemporary Record, 1971–2.*

This conflict between the white governments and the Organization of African Unity should be of concern to everyone and every government interested in the stability of the African Continent and the avoidance of the unleashing of a racial war whose battlefield will go far beyond the perimeter of the African Coast-line.

In our view this conflict has recently assumed certain sombre dimensions which bring the possibilities of such a war to realization with every decade. The disproportionate military budgets of the white governments in relation to the overall economic demands of the countries they governed; the emergence of liberation movements; the armed clashes which have almost become an everyday affair on the borders of Rhodesia and Mozambique – all constitute warning signs that the possibilities of a racial war are much more serious than mere prophecies of a timid mind ... It is thus from our recognition of what is happening in Southern Africa that we advocate dialogue as an alternative to violence ...

In the heat of the debate about dialogue the essence of this approach has become somewhat blurred. For us dialogue is essentially a direct and practical and joint examination of all peaceful ways to avert racial confrontation in Southern Africa. At the core of such an examination must lie a recognition of the basic inhumanity of racial discrimination and a willingness to remove its manifestations in the Society of Southern Africa. The white governments must accept that racial tensions in Africa are as much against their own interests as racial discrimination is humiliating to every black man. Dialogue cannot succeed without a basic acceptance of the common humanity of man irrespective of his racial or ethnic origins. Neither can dialogue go far unless it is accepted that whites in South Africa belong to Africa as much as any of the citizens of the Member States of the Organization of African Unity. In short our conception of dialogue is practical discussions between the Organization of African Unity and the white governments on the problems of Southern Africa aimed at reaching a modus vivendi to the elimination of the racial tensions and confrontations which have become synonymous with Southern Africa.

We in Lesotho have since independence engaged in neighbourly relations with the government of South Africa. It is however a matter of regret that race has again been a limiting factor to the full development of relations between the black governments in Southern Africa and the white governments. The development of these relations on the widest spectrum as possible would be of immense value to the economic development of Southern Africa.

At the United Nations, in Addis Ababa and at the recent Commonwealth Prime Ministers' Conference I have advocated the acceptance of the Lusaka Manifesto as a basis for dialogue. The Manifesto has been given due recognition by the United Nations at the initiative of the Organization of African Unity but its proposals on negotiation have never been fully explored with the white governments. In my view the Manifesto provides sufficient scope for practical discussions between the Organization of African Unity and the white governments on easing the tensions in Southern Africa . . .

We in Lesotho have pursued a policy of contact with the white government of our neighbouring country. In my capacity as Prime Minister, I was the first African to hold discussions with my counterparts in South Africa. In those discussions it was amply demonstrated that it is possible for people of different races to meet and exchange views in an atmosphere of mutual respect. This in itself is a hopeful indication that dialogue has practical possibilities. I do not pretend that acceptance of dialogue will result in changes of attitudes overnight. At the very least it would indicate that people with a common concern, can apply their minds to solutions of problems irrespective of their racial origins. It could also provide opportunities for a better appreciation of the common humanity of all races. But basically dialogue needs to be tried if only because its success shall have saved the world from racial conflagration.

8: OAU Declaration on Dialogue

OAU Eighth Summit Meeting of Heads of State, Addis Ababa, 21–3 June 1971. Published in Legum, *African Contemporary Record, 1971–2*. Note the reference to the Lusaka Manifesto.

Declaration on the Question of Dialogue

The Council of Ministers of the Organization of African Unity meeting in its 17th Ordinary Session, in Addis Ababa, Ethiopia, from 15 to 19 June 1971, discussed in an atmosphere of utmost cordiality and frankness the question of a proposal for a dialogue with the minority racist regime of South Africa.

The discussions afforded all Members of the Council an opportunity to fully express the views of their respective governments on this important question.

The Council reaffirmed:

1. Their total commitment to the principles and purposes contained in Articles II and III of the Charter of the Organization of African Unity, especially in regard to the eradication of all forms of colonialism from Africa, and the absolute dedication to the total emancipation of the African territories which are still dependent.

2. That the Manifesto on Southern Africa (Lusaka Manifesto) unanimously adopted by the Organization of African Unity and endorsed by the United Nations and the Conference of Non-Aligned States, but rejected by the racist regimes of Southern Africa, is the only objective basis for any meaningful solution to the problems of Apartheid, racial discrimination and Colonialism in Africa.

3. The legitimacy of the struggle being waged by the peoples of Africa to obtain their legitimate rights to independence, freedom, human dignity and equality, and that all Member States of the Organization of African Unity remain totally and unconditionally committed to their struggle.

Moreover, it was agreed that no Member State of the Organization of African Unity would initiate or engage in any type of action that would undermine or abrogate the solemn obligations and undertakings to the commitments contained in the Charter.

It was also agreed that any action to be taken by Member States in regard to the solution of the problems of colonialism, racial discrimination and Apartheid in Africa, must be undertaken within the framework of the Organization of African Unity and in full consultations with the Liberation Movements of the territories concerned.

The Council rejected the idea of any dialogue with the minority racist regime of South Africa which is not designated solely to obtain for the enslaved people of South Africa their legitimate and inherent rights and the elimination of Apartheid in accordance with the Lusaka Manifesto.

The Council of Ministers also considered and agreed that in any case any form of dialogue should appropriately be commenced only between the minority racist regime of South Africa and the people they are oppressing, exploiting and suppressing.

The Council of Ministers, also agreed that the proposal for a dialogue between the independent African States and the racist minority regime of South Africa is a manoeuvre by the regime and its allies to divide African States, confuse world public opinion, relieve South Africa from international ostracism and isolation and obtain an acceptance of the status quo in Southern Africa.

In view of the above considerations the 17th Ordinary Session of the Council of Ministers of the Organization of African Unity emphatically declares that there exists no basis for a meaningful dialogue with the minority racist regime of South Africa. Under these circumstances, the Council reaffirms its determination to continue to render and increase its assistance to the liberation movements until victory is achieved.

9: Albert Luthuli

Extracts from A. Luthuli, *Let My People Go* (Fontana, 1962).
The *Freedom Charter* was produced by a Congress of the People, Johannesburg, 25–6 June 1955. The chief participants were the African National Congress and the South African Indian Congress; Luthuli, President of the ANC, was unable to attend because he had been banned from public meetings by the Government.

... our children have been born, with the whole of their generation, into the midst of the triumph of prejudice. Young Africans know from infancy upwards – and the point here is that they know nothing else – that their strivings after civilised values will not, in the present order, ever earn for them recognition as sane and responsible civilised beings.

The argument behind the idea that we Africans need a two-thousand-year apprenticeship has occasionally been uttered, though never very coherently. It goes like this: 'It has taken us two thousand years to reach our present civilised state. A hundred years ago the natives were barbarians. It will take them two thousand years to catch up with where we are now, and they will not be civilised until then'.

It is pure nonsense, of course. The argument does not arise from a survey of history, it arises from the urge to justify a course already chosen. The conclusion ('No rights for two thousand years') is there before the argument begins. An uncritical assumption ('Whites are civilised') is there too ... The argument assumes that, whereas whites can take up where the last generation left off, Africans cannot encounter and absorb anything in the present – they must go back and take each step of the road from the beginning, as though nothing that has happened during the last two thousand years can affect them.

......

Men so manifestly insecure as South Africa's rulers cannot afford to stop short of absolute power ...

280

One of the deep-seated intentions of [Bantu] education is to erase all African leadership . . .

The ethnic grouping principle in education and throughout other spheres of life is significant. Africans were very painfully beginning to shed themselves of purely tribal allegiances. Even in the most backward areas they are beginning to see themselves as part of a larger African community, and many made the step of expressing allegiance to South Africa as a whole, and to the family of mankind.

But the Nationalists and their fellow-travellers start off with the principle of disunity. Where bonds have formed, they must be broken. The only allegiance they recognise is allegiance to disunity, apartheid. Now not only in education but throughout our lives, ethnic grouping must apply.

. . . . . .

It is true, I believe, that tribal organisation is outmoded, and that the traditional rule by chiefs retards my people – a fact of which the Nationalists are not slow to take advantage. The wiser and more courageous of the chiefs recognise this, and refuse either to obstruct the political leaders of the people or to become Government catspaws – but it is becoming progressively harder for them to stand aside or to rule in the traditional way, because of the pressures which the Nationalist Government brings to bear on them. Chiefs find themselves caught between the interests of their people and the commands of the Government, and the weaker ones go down. Nevertheless, loyalty to the institution of the chieftainship persists. It would take a few years more of Nationalist rule to undermine it far enough to bring it tumbling down. Meanwhile many Africans are caught in a real dilemma – our impulse is to be loyal to our chiefs, but we know full well that the Nationalists are turning more and more of them into their puppets . . .

We are subjected to intensive wooing by both East and West. But what we want now is to be ourselves, to retain our personality, and to let our soul, long buffeted by the old scramble for Africa, grow free. African leaders must be wary of the material enticement of her people. We do not live by bread alone, however alluring the sight of bread may be to the hungry . . .

I do not find myself among those people who tend to reduce all human affairs to questions of economics and economic pressures. None the less, the basic point at issue in South Africa is the question of ownership. Because the races inhabiting the country disagree fundamentally on the answer to this question, the whole controversy is hopelessly tangled with racial factors, and on both sides these racial distinctions have become an unavoidable part of the struggle. One cannot separate the issue of race from the argument about ownership at present, because one race insists on exclusive ownership. Who owns South Africa?

With the exception of a small group of black nationalists who have learned their politics from Dr. Verwoerd's and General Smuts' parties, *the great majority of Africans* reply that the country now belongs to fourteen million people of different races – it is jointly owned by all its inhabitants, quite regardless of their colour. This view, which I adhere to without qualification, demands that people be regarded primarily as people. As far as culture and habits of life are concerned, they may differ as radically as they wish. But when it comes to participation in ownership and government, race must be made wholly irrelevant.

With the exception of a small number of voices crying in the wilderness, the overwhelming majority of whites reply that South Africa is exclusively owned by three million whites . . .

The business of [the African National] Congress is not deliberation and legislation. Its business is to right the total exclusion of the African from the management of South Africa, to give direction to the forces of liberation, to harness peacefully the growing resistance to continued oppression, and, by various non-violent means, to demand the redress of injustice . . .

One of the major purposes of Congress, right at the beginning, was to overcome the divisions and disunities between tribes and . . . to develop African unity . . . Our oppressors have done all in their power to retain and emphasise minor allegiances. In spite of this, although we have not won the battle for unity, we have gained much ground, and increasing oppression of all Africans by white supremacists is one of our strongest allies in this battle . . .

[The] Programme of Action is a milestone in Congress history. It represents a fundamental change of policy and method. Underlying it was the refusal to be content for ever with leavings from white South Africa's table – stated uncompromisingly and finally.

The challenge was to be on fundamentals, we were no longer interested in ameliorations and petty adjustments. There was no longer any doubt in our mind that without the vote we are helpless . . .

The Programme of Action adopted in 1949 stressed new methods. Representations were done with. Demonstrations on a countrywide scale, strike action, and civil disobedience were to replace words . . . we agreed to concentrate mainly on non-violent disobedience. This disobedience was not directed against law. It was directed against all those particular discriminatory laws, from the Act of Union onwards, which were not informed by morality.

. . . . . .

282

For myself I am not a Communist. Communism seems to me to be a mixture of a false theory of society linked on to a false 'religion' ... In politics I tend towards the outlook of British Labour, with some important modifications.

There are Communists in the South African resistance, and I co-operate with them. The Congress stand is this: our primary concern is liberation, and we are not going to be side-tracked by ideological clashes and witch hunts. Nobody in Congress may use the organisation to further any aims but those of Congress. When I co-operate with Communists in Congress affairs I am not co-operating with Communism ...

It has naturally crossed our minds to wonder whether anything but indiscriminate bloodshed and violence will make any impression; so impervious do they [The Nationalists] seem. It will do neither them nor us any good, and if they get it, it will not be from Congress. It will be simply the result of unendurable provocation, of trading for too long on a patience which has its limits. If the whites continue as at present, nobody will give the signal for mass violence. Nobody will need to ...

It is a tragedy that the great majority of South African whites are determined to permit no peaceful evolution. They have for so long refused to adapt themselves, and insisted that all adaptation shall come from us, that they seem incapable now of anything but rigidity. It is this attitude which is likely to make difficult, if not impossible, bargaining and compromise. Each new challenge leads to a further hardening of heart.

Such obduracy is doubly criminal in view of the persistent good will of Africans. The whites cannot or will not see that it is there. The trouble is that they credit us with their own ambitions. They mislead themselves by believing that we too have master-race aspirations. And since they see things in those terms, they terrify themselves into an attitude which knows only two alternatives – dominate or perish. For us, we do not desire to dominate but to share as between brethren, basing our hierarchy on ability, not colour. That is our offer. And we shall not consent to perish. Let them never cherish that foolhardy illusion, for all their guns and Saracens.

. . . . . .

THE FREEDOM CHARTER

We the People of South Africa, declare for all our country and the world to know:

> that South Africa belongs to all who live in it, black and white, and that no government can justly claim authority unless it is based on the will of all the people;
> that our people have been robbed of their birthright to land, liberty and

peace by a form of government founded on injustice and inequality;

that our country will never be prosperous or free until all our people live in brotherhood, enjoying equal rights and opportunities;

that only a democratic state, based on the will of all the people, can secure to all their birthright without distinction of colour, race, sex or belief;

And therefore we, the People of South Africa, black and white together – equals, countrymen and brothers – adopt this Freedom Charter. And we pledge ourselves to strive together sparing neither strength nor courage, until the democratic changes here set out have been won.

The People Shall Govern!

Every man and woman shall have the right to vote for and to stand as a candidate for all bodies which make laws;

All people shall be entitled to take part in the administration of the country;

The rights of the people shall be the same, regardless of race, colour or sex;

All bodies of minority rule, advisory boards, councils and authorities shall be replaced by democratic organs of self-goverment.

All National Groups Shall Have Equal Rights!

There shall be equal status in the bodies of state, in the courts and in the schools for all national groups and races;

All people shall have equal right to use their own languages, and to develop their own folk culture and customs;

All national groups shall be protected by law against insults to their race and national pride;

The preaching and practice of national, race or colour discrimination and contempt shall be a punishable crime;

All apartheid laws and practices shall be set aside.

The People Shall Share in the Country's Wealth!

The national wealth of our country, the heritage of all South Africans, shall be restored to the people;

The mineral wealth beneath the soil, the banks and monopoly industry shall be transferred to the ownership of the people as a whole;

All other industry and trade shall be controlled to assist the well-being of the people;

All people shall have equal rights to trade where they choose, to manufacture and to enter all trades, crafts and professions.

The Land Shall be Shared Among Those Who Work It!

Restriction of land ownership on a racial basis shall be needed, and all the land redivided amongst those who work it, to banish famine and land hunger;

The State shall help the peasants with implements, seed, tractors and dams to save the soil and assist the tillers;

Freedom of movement shall be guaranteed to all who work on the land;

All shall have the right to occupy land wherever they choose;

People shall not be robbed of their cattle, and forced labour and farm prisons shall be abolished.

All Shall Be Equal Before the Law!

No one shall be imprisoned, deported or restricted without a fair trial;

No one shall be condemned by the order of any Government official;

The courts shall be representative of all the people;

Imprisonment shall be only for serious crimes against the people, and shall aim at re-education, not vengeance;

The police force and army shall be open to all on an equal basis and shall be the helpers and protectors of the people;

All laws which discriminate on grounds of race, colour or belief shall be repealed.

All Shall Enjoy Equal Human Rights!

The law shall guarantee to all their right to speak, to organise, to meet together, to publish, to preach, to worship, and to educate their children;

The privacy of the house from police raids shall be protected by law;

All shall be free to travel without restriction from countryside to town, from province to province, and from South Africa abroad;

Pass laws, permits and all other laws restricting these freedoms shall be abolished.

There Shall be Work and Security!

All who work shall be free to form trade unions, to elect their officers and to make wage agreements with their employers;

The State shall recognise the right and duty of all to work, and to draw full unemployment benefits;

Men and women of all races shall receive equal pay for equal work;

There shall be a forty-hour working week, a national minimum wage, paid annual leave, and sick leave for all workers, and maternity leave on full pay for all working mothers;

Miners, domestic workers, farm workers and civil servants shall have the same rights as all others who work;

Child labour, compound labour, the tot system and contract labour shall be abolished.

The Doors of Learning and of Culture Shall be Opened!

The Government shall discover, develop and encourage national talent for the enhancement of our cultural life;

All the cultural treasures of mankind shall be open to all, by free exchange of books, ideas and contact with other lands;

The aim of education shall be to teach the youth to love their people and their culture, to honour human brotherhood, liberty and peace;

Education shall be free, compulsory, universal and equal for all children;

Higher education and technical training shall be opened to all by means of state allowances and scholarships awarded on the basis of merit;

Adult illiteracy shall be ended by a mass state education plan;

Teachers shall have all the rights of other citizens;

The colour bar in cultural life, in sport and in education shall be abolished.

There Shall be Houses, Security and Comfort!

All people shall have the right to live where they choose, to be decently housed, and to bring up their families in comfort and security;

Unused housing space shall be made available to the people;

Rents and prices shall be lowered, food plentiful and no one shall go hungry;

A preventive health scheme shall be run by the State;

Free medical care and hospitalisation shall be provided for all, with special care for mothers and young children;

Slums shall be demolished, and new suburbs built where all have transport, roads, lighting, playing fields, crèches and social centres;

The aged, the orphans, the disabled and the sick shall be cared for by the State;

Rest, leisure and recreation shall be the right of all;

Fenced locations and ghettos shall be abolished and laws which break up families shall be repealed.

There Shall be Peace and Friendship!

South Africa shall be a fully independent state, which respects the rights and sovereignty of all nations;

South Africa shall strive to maintain world peace and the settlement of all international disputes by negotiation – not war;

Peace and friendship amongst all our people shall be secured by upholding the equal rights, opportunities and status of all;

The people of the protectorates – Basutoland, Bechuanaland and Swaziland – shall be free to decide for themselves their own future;

The rights of all the peoples of Africa to independence and self-government shall be recognised and shall be the basis of close co-operation.

Let all who love their people and their country now say, as we say here: 'THESE FREEDOMS WE WILL FIGHT FOR, SIDE BY SIDE, THROUGHOUT OUR LIVES, UNTIL WE HAVE WON OUR LIBERTY'.

10: Nelson Mandela

Extracts from N. Mandela, *I Am Prepared to Die,* published by Christian Action for the International Defence and Aid Fund, London.
This pamphlet records Mandela's speech in his own defence at the Rivonia Trial, 1964. Accused of planning acts of sabotage against the State, he was found guilty, and sentenced to life imprisonment.

Firstly, we believed that as a result of Government policy, violence by the African people had become inevitable, and that unless responsible leadership was given to canalize and control the feelings of our people, there would be outbreaks of terrorism which would produce an intensity of bitterness and hostility between the various races of this country which is not produced even by war. Secondly, we felt that without violence there would be no way open to the African people to succeed in their struggle against the principle of White supremacy. All lawful modes of expressing opposition to this principle had been closed by legislation, and we were placed in a position in which we had either to accept a permanent state of inferiority, or to defy the Government. We chose to defy the law. We first broke the law in a way which avoided any recourse to violence; when this form was legislated against, and when the Government resorted to a show of force to crush opposition to its policies, only then did we decide to answer violence with violence.

. . . . . .

In 1960, there was the shooting at Sharpeville, which resulted in the proclamation of a State of Emergency and the declaration of A.N.C. as an unlawful organization. My colleagues and I, after careful consideration, decided that we would not obey this decree. The African people were not part of the Government and did not make the laws by which they were governed. We believed in the words of the Universal Declaration of

Human Rights, that "the will of the people shall be the basis of authority of the Government", and for us to accept the banning was equivalent to accepting the silencing of the Africans for all time. The A.N.C. refused to dissolve, but instead went underground.

...... What were we, the leaders of our people to do? Were we to give in to the show of force and the implied threat against future action, or were we to fight it, and if so, how?

We had no doubt that we had to continue the fight. Anything else would have been abject surrender. Our problem was not whether to fight, but was how to continue the fight. We of the A.N.C. had always stood for non-racial democracy, and we shrank from any action which might drive the races further apart than they already were. But the hard facts were that fifty years of non-violence had brought the African people nothing but more and more repressive legislation, and fewer and fewer rights. It may not be easy for this Court to understand, but it is a fact that for a long time the people had been talking of violence – of the day when they would fight the White man and win back their country.

......

As far as the A.N.C. was concerned, it formed a clear view which can be summarized as follows:-

(a) It was a mass political organization with a political function to fulfil. Its members had joined on the express policy of non-violence . . .

(b) Because of all this, it could not and would not undertake violence. This must be stressed. One cannot turn such a body into the small closely-knit organization required for sabotage. Nor would this be politically correct, because it would result in members ceasing to carry out this essential activity; political propaganda and organization. Nor was it permissible to change the whole nature of the organization.

(c) On the other hand, in view of this situation I have described, the A.N.C. was prepared to depart from its 50-year-old policy of non-violence to this extent, that it would no longer disapprove of properly controlled violence. Hence members who undertook such activity would not be subject to disciplinary action by the A.N.C.

Four forms of violence were possible. There is sabotage, there is guerilla warfare, there is terrorism and there is open revolution. We chose to adopt the first method and to exhaust it before taking any other decision.

In the light of our political background the choice was a logical one. Sabotage did not involve loss of life, and it offered the best hope for future race relations. Bitterness would be kept to a minimum and, if the policy bore fruit, democratic government could become a reality. This is what we felt at the time, and this is what we said in our Manifesto (Exhibit AD):-

"We of Umkonto We Sizwe have always sought to achieve liberation without bloodshed and civil clash. We hope, even at this late hour, that our first action will awaken everyone to a realisation of the disastrous situation to which the Nationalist policy is leading. We hope that we will bring the Government and its supporters to their senses before it is too late, so that both the Government and its policies can be changed before matters reach the desperate stage of civil war". [Umkonto We Sizwe was a conspirational group associated with the A.N.C.]

. . . . . .

Attacks on the economic life lines of the country were to be linked with sabotage on Government buildings and other symbols of apartheid. These attacks would serve as a source of inspiration to our people. In addition, they would provide an outlet for those people who were urging the adoption of a stronger line and were fighting back against Government violence.

In addition, if mass action were successfully organized, and mass reprisals taken, we felt that sympathy for our cause would be brought to bear on the South African Government.

Experience convinced us that rebellion would offer the Government limitless opportunities for the indiscriminate slaughter of our people. But it was precisely because the soil of South Africa was already drenched with the blood of innocent Africans that we felt it our duty to make preparations as a long-term undertaking to use force in order to defend ourselves against force. If war were inevitable, we wanted the fight to be conducted on terms most favourable to our people. The fight which held out prospects best for us and the least risk of life to both sides was guerilla warfare. We decided, therefore, in our preparations for the future, to make provision for the possibility of guerilla warfare.

All Whites undergo compulsory military training, but no such training was given to Africans. It was in our view essential to build up a nucleus of trained men who would be able to provide the leadership which would be required if guerilla warfare started. We had to prepare for such a situation before it became too late to make proper preparations. It was also necessary to build up a nucleus of men trained in civil administration and other professions, so that Africans would be equipped to participate in the Government of this country as soon as they were allowed to do so . . .

I started to make a study of the art of war and revolution and, whilst abroad, underwent a course in military training. If there was to be guerilla warfare, I wanted to be able to stand and fight with my people and to

289

share the hazards of war with them. Notes of lectures which I received in Algeria are contained in Exhibit 16, produced in evidence. Summaries of books on guerilla warfare and military strategy have also been produced. I have already admitted that these documents are in my writing, and I acknowledge that I made these studies to equip myself for the role which I might have to play if the struggle drifted into guerilla warfare. I approached this question as every African Nationalist should do. I was completely objective. The Court will see that I attempted to examine all types of authority on the subject – from the East and from the West, going back to the classic work of Clausewitz, and covering such a variety as Mao Tse Tung and Che Guevara on the one hand, and the writings on the Anglo-Boer War on the other . . .

The ideological creed of the A.N.C. is, and always has been, the creed of African Nationalism. It is not the concept of African Nationalism expressed in the cry, "Drive the White man into the sea". The African Nationalism for which the A.N.C. stands, is the concept of freedom and fulfilment for the African people in their own land. The most important political document ever adopted by the A.N.C. is the "Freedom Charter". It is by no means a blueprint for a socialist State. It calls for redistribution, but not nationalization, of land; it provides for nationalization of mines, banks and monopoly industry, because big monopolies are owned by one race only, and without such nationalization racial domination would be perpetuated despite the spread of political power. It would be a hollow gesture to repeal the Gold Law prohibitions against Africans when all gold mines are owned by European companies. In this respect the A.N.C.'s policy corresponds with the old policy of the present Nationalist Party which, for many years, had as part of its programme the nationalization of the Gold Mines, which, at that time, were controlled by foreign capital. Under the Freedom Charter nationalization would take place in an economy based on private enterprise. The realization of the Freedom Charter would open up fresh fields for a prosperous African population of all classes, including the middle class. The A.N.C. has never at any period of its history advocated a revolutionary change in the economic structure of the country, nor has it, to the best of my recollection, ever condemned capitalist society.

As far as the Communist Party is concerned, and if I understand its policy correctly, it stands for the establishment of a State based on the principles of Marxism, although it is prepared to work for the Freedom Charter, as a short-term solution to the problems created by White supremacy, it regards the Freedom Charter as the beginning, and not the end, of its programme.

The A.N.C., unlike the Communist Party, admitted Africans only as members. Its chief goal was, and is, for the African people to win unity and full political rights. The Communist Party's main aim, on the other hand, was to remove the capitalists and to replace them with a working-class Government. The Communist Party sought to emphasize class distinctions whilst the A.N.C. seeks to harmonize them. This is a vital distinction.

It is true that there has often been close co-operation between the A.N.C. and the Communist Party. But co-operation is merely proof of a common goal – in this case the removal of White supremacy – and it is not proof of a complete community of interests . . .

It is perhaps difficult for White South Africans, with an ingrained prejudice against Communism, to understand why experienced African politicians so readily accept Communists as their friends. But to us the reason is obvious. Theoretical differences amongst those fighting against oppression is a luxury we cannot afford at this stage. What is more, for many decades Communists were the only political group in South Africa who were prepared to treat Africans as human beings and their equals; who were prepared to eat with us, talk with us, live with us and work with us. They were the only political group which was prepared to work with the Africans for the attainment of political rights and a stake in society. Because of this, there are many Africans who, today, tend to equate freedom with Communism. They are supported in this belief by a legislature which brands all exponents of democratic government and African freedom as Communists and bans many of them (who are Communists) under the Suppression of Communism Act. Although I have never been a member of the Communist Party, I myself have been named under that pernicious Act because of the role I played in the Defiance Campaign. I have also been banned and imprisoned under that Act . . .

Today I am attracted by the idea of a classless society, an attraction which springs in part from Marxist reading and, in part, from my admiration of the structure and organization of early African societies in this country. The land, then the main means of production, belonged to the tribe. There were no rich or poor and there was no exploitation.

It is true, as I have already stated, that I have been influenced by Marxist thought. But this is also true of many of the leaders of the new independent States. Such widely different persons as Gandhi, Nehru, Nkrumah and Nasser all acknowledge this fact. We all accept the need for some form of Socialism to enable our people to catch up with the advanced countries of this world and to overcome their legacy of extreme poverty. But this does not mean we are Marxists.

Indeed, for my own part, I believe that it is open to debate whether the Communist Party has any specific role to play at this particular stage of our political struggle. The basic task at the present moment is the removal of race discrimination and the attainment of democratic rights on the basis of the Freedom Charter. Insofar as that Party furthers this task, I welcome its assistance. I realize that it is one of the means by which people of all races can be drawn into our struggle.

From my reading of Marxist literature and from conversations with Marxists, I have gained the impression that Communists regard the parliamentary system of the West as undemocratic and reactionary. But, on the contrary, I am an admirer of such a system.

The Magna Carta, the Petition of Rights and the Bill of Rights, are documents which are held in veneration by democrats throughout the world.

I have great respect for British political institutions, and for the country's system of justice. I regard the British Parliament as the most democratic institution in the world, and the independence and impartiality of its judiciary never fail to arouse my admiration.

The American Congress, that country's doctrine of separation of powers, as well as the independence of its judiciary, arouse in me similar sentiments.

I have been influenced in my thinking by both West and East. All this has led me to feel that in my search for a political formula, I should be absolutely impartial and objective. I should tie myself to no particular system of society other than of socialism. I must leave myself free to borrow the best from the West and from the East . . .

The Government often answers its critics by saying that Africans in South Africa are economically better off than the inhabitants of the other countries in Africa. I do not know whether this statement is true and doubt whether any comparison can be made without having regard to the cost of living index in such countries. But even if it is true, as far as the African people are concerned it is irrelevant. Our complaint is not that we are poor by comparison with people in other countries, but that we are poor by comparison with the White people in our own country, and that we are prevented by legislation from altering this imbalance.

The lack of human dignity experienced by Africans is the direct result of the policy of White supremacy. White supremacy implies Black inferiority. Legislation designed to preserve White supremacy entrenches this notion. Menial tasks in South Africa are invariably performed by Africans. When anything has to be carried or cleaned the White man will look around for an African to do it for him, whether the African is employed by him or not. Because of this sort of attitude, Whites tend to regard Africans as a separate breed. They do not look upon them as people with families of their own; they do not realize that they have

292

emotions – that they fall in love like White people do; that they want to be with their wives and children like White people want to be with theirs; that they want to earn enough money to support their families properly, to feed and clothe them and send them to school. And what "houseboy" or "garden-boy" or labourer can ever hope to do this?

Africans want to be paid a living wage. Africans want to perform work which they are capable of doing and not work which the Government declares them capable of. Africans want to be allowed to live where they obtain work, and not be endorsed out of an area because they were not born there. Africans want to be allowed to own land in places where they work, and not be obliged to live in rented houses which they can never call their own. Africans want to be part of the general population, and not confined to living in their own ghettos. African men want to have their wives and children to live with them where they work, and not be forced into an unnatural existence in men's hostels. African women want to be with their men folk and not be left permanently widowed in the reserves. Africans want to be allowed out after 11 o'clock at night and not to be confined to their rooms like little children. Africans want to be allowed to travel in their own country and to seek work where they want to and not where the Labour Bureau tells them to. Africans want a just share in the whole of South Africa; they want security and a stake in society.

Above all, we want equal political rights, because without them our disabilities will be permanent. I know this sounds revolutionary to the Whites in this country, because the majority of voters will be Africans. This makes the White man fear democracy.

But this fear cannot be allowed to stand in the way of the only solution which will guarantee racial harmony and freedom for all. It is not true that the enfranchisement of all will result in racial domination. Political division, based on colour, is entirely artificial and, when it disappears, so will the domination of one colour group by another. The A.N.C. has spent half a century fighting against racialism. When it triumphs it will not change that policy.

This then is what the A.N.C. is fighting. Their struggle is a truly national one. It is a struggle of the African people, inspired by their own suffering and their own experience. It is a struggle for the right to live.

During my lifetime I have dedicated myself to this struggle of the African people. I have fought against White domination, and I have fought against Black domination. I have cherished the ideal of a democratic and free society in which all persons live together in harmony and with equal opportunities. It is an ideal which I hope to live for and to achieve. But if needs be, it is an ideal for which I am prepared to die.

11: L. Vambe

Extracts from L. Vambe, *An Ill-fated People: Zimbabwe before and after Rhodes* (Heinemann, 1972).
Vambe was a black Rhodesian journalist, and at one time a public relations officer for the Central African Federation.

There is fear in all of us, fear that either drives us to irrational aggression or makes us merely stand still in paralytic helplessness. In my experience, the fear that we Africans had for the Europeans was of the latter kind and, I venture to suggest, perhaps largely accounts for the prolonged state of subjection of the Southern Rhodesian Africans. To say that this is a sad reflection on the black people of the country, as most people outside Rhodesia tend to do, would be an over-simplification of this issue. This total, helpless fear did not exist in the Africans of my country before 1896. But after being utterly defeated on the field of battle, and subjected to every form of control, subtle and violent, the entire African population lapsed into a state in which the passive instinct of self-preservation became predominant: this contributed as much to UDI as the arrogance and dementia of the Rhodesian Front Party. What I find dangerous and abhorrent now is the attitude of the autocratic white minority, who after so many years of silent obedience from the Africans, are so sure of themselves that they think they can hold power indefinitely . . .

I saw no point in any white-made laws, least of all in our duty to obey them. We had our own and they were good enough for us. They were sensible, human and democratic, but not a single one of them involved extorting money, grain, cattle or labour for the benefit of some self-appointed clique in the tribe.

. . . . . .

Almost up to the Unilateral Declaration of Independence in 1965 the official line on the history of Southern Rhodesia fostered the belief that the Shona people throughout Zimbabwe were hapless victims of Ndebele savagery, from which they were gratefully delivered by white men. Successive Southern Rhodesian governments have claimed that the white man's coming brought salvation to the primitive indigenous population of this part of the world. White rule, they went on, had conferred on us a freedom and a future which we would otherwise have not had as subjects of the blood-thirsty Ndebele, who were intent on exterminating my people . . .

But the facts I was told by the VaShawasha elders relating to their attitude towards and relationship with the Ndebele and the white settlers differ widely from most accounts that have been put forward to rationalize minority rule in Southern Rhodesia from 1890 onwards. The VaShawasha were not filled with gratitude for their supposed 'deliverance'. On the contrary, they never stopped emphasizing that the occupation of their country was the biggest disaster and curse in the entire history of their national life in Zimbabwe . . .

My people soon learned that to the white man's voracious appetite for land was added the need for black labour. It was a big shock, a bigger shock than the others they experienced so far. The concept of hired labour was completely unknown to my people, and this innovation cut right across the most sensitive area of what the Shona understood by personal freedom. It was bad enough that the Europeans were taking their land, but by demanding their labour as well they were stripping the Shona of the last vestige of the little freedom that they still possessed. This brought about a much more direct personal confrontation between black men and white men than before, for apart from wishing to maintain some personal independence, the Shona could not in any case see any reason for selling their labour to anyone, least of all to white men whom they now detested heartily. Their traditional economic system was rooted in agriculture, which protected the individual from any of the humiliating stigmas associated with the master-and-servant relationship of the Rhodesian way of life. They had little need for money, and were unlikely to want to work for it under a white master. They had enough food of their own, they had enough meat, adequate shelter and warmth and, of course, they felt they had the freedom not to want most things of white origin. They thought they had a right not to do what they regarded as irksome and purposeless. And they were convinced that most things European were irksome and purposeless, particularly work that went on from sunrise to sunset, from Monday to Saturday, season to season and from year to year. Such a mode of existence was singularly barren and reduced human beings to the level of cattle or donkeys, as my elders used to say. So they did not respond to the white man's call for their services . . .

Certainly, to the Africans of Southern Rhodesia, like myself, who are condemned from the cradle to the grave to live by the racial system of white rule in that country, it seems that the difference between Hitler and white Rhodesia is one of degree and not of kind. However, I believe that if the situations were reversed and Africans, either in Rhodesia or Zambia, treated their white fellow citizens as black people are treated in Rhodesia, the problem would be seen by the outside world exactly for what it is and has been since the day the Pioneer Column raised the Union Jack at Fort Salisbury on September 12, 1890 . . .

Seen from the African point of view, there was a conspiracy in the general role of the Church in Southern Rhodesia. For the Church, like the rest of the white society of which it was an appendage, did not recognize nor care to understand many of the values in the traditional institutions of the VaShawasha. It took the attitude that it knew what was best for the African people and in all spiritual matters expected them to follow like sheep without giving so much as a hint that it understood their difficult position. Thus the old traditionalists were roundly condemned as children of darkness because they clung to their own beliefs and practices. In turn these people wondered why it was so difficult for the priests to appreciate the simple fact that if, for instance, they gave up their wives the tribe would be landed with insecure women, particularly the old ones, who had passed the stage at which they could raise their own crops and fend for themselves.

. . . . . .

But the arid, cruel background of Southern Rhodesia did not provide conditions in which wisdom and foresight in both the Church and the State might develop. The whole organization of the country rather engendered a spirit of arrogance and blindness in those who held power, be they of the Church or the State. The results of this unfortunate situation are evident in the present-day Rhodesia, where the Church has not been able to do anything more effective than denounce the system in angry pastoral letters. That this kind of episcopal protest has had no visible influence on the bulk of the Catholic and Protestant European supporters of the Rhodesian Front regime is so apparent that it needs no elaboration. So debased have our European fellow men in Southern Rhodesia become that some of them have even stooped to denouncing the bishop for siding with the Africans. So corrupted are they that some of them are even reported to have found a Christian justification for racial segregation.

I am not questioning the motives of the Church, nor saying that it deliberately set out to destroy the freedom and dignity of the African people. As a product of Church education, I know better than to deny that on the whole the Christian Churches had the best intentions in carrying out their joint mission among the African people in Southern Rhodesia. But because the Church is an institution organized and represented by white men, it was, unhappily, inevitable that it reflected the interests of the white system within which it operated.

12: The Zimbabwe African National Council

Extracts from the pamphlet by E. Mlambo, *No Future Without Us* (no date).
The ZANC was formed in December 1971 to represent African opposition to

the Anglo–Rhodesian settlement proposals of 1971. Mlambo is the London representative of the ZANC. The context of each extract is given after the extract.

The Anglo-Rhodesian proposals for a settlement have been critically studied, analysed and found to be a vicious and subtle device for the recognition of UDI by the British Government. These proposals are a constitutional 'rape' of Africans by both the Rhodesian and the British Governments, which is tantamount to a sellout of the African Majority of this country to a perpetual oppression and domination by the privileged white minority. The simple fact that a racist Rhodesian Government has accepted them is a measuring stick pointing to their dangerousness for Africans.

The sensible African people of this country deplore and condemn the manner in which the British Government conducted the negotiations that resulted in the constitutional proposals now before the country. It is sad that the African leaders were excluded from the talks until after Her Majesty's Government had reached an agreement with the Rhodesian Government.

. . . . . .

As a result, responsibility and patriotism have challengingly compelled us to organize ourselves into a body that represents the voice and will of the silent African Majority throughout the country.

This National organization shall be called the African National Council (or ANC) . . .

The ANC aims and objectives are:

1. To call our people to realise the essential power of unity now. And move on as one people for the sake of achieving our ultimate goal of freedom.
2. To explain, advise and expose the dangerous implications that would result if we accepted the Anglo-Rhodesian constitutional settlement proposals.
3. To raise funds for the promotion of the organization. It is a temporary body to execute the task before us.

. . . .

Following the views we have advanced above and the details of the analysis of the proposals, . . . we are convinced beyond doubt that acceptance of these proposals by Africans would be a betrayal of the Africans, dead, living and yet to be born. We cannot be vendors of our own heritage and rights. Therefore, the African's responsible answer should be an *emphatic 'No'*.

. . . . . .

297

Remember whether we are poor or rich, educated or non-educated, chiefs or not, civil servants or not, whether we dwell in the King's domain or not we are all condemned as BLACK PEOPLE. We must, and it is a big million dollar *must*, be united and work for a common good – *Independence*. It must be realized with grave concern that our enemies have thrived and continue to capitalize upon our disunity and apathy. (Extracts from ANC press release, December 1971, entitled 'The ANC Says No')

. . . . . .

Mr. Smith became the leader of the Rhodesian Front because he was prepared to stop at nothing to ensure that Rhodesia would remain a country ruled *by* the whites, and *for* the whites, for as long as the rule of the gun permits. The principles of the Rhodesia Front are Apartheid principles. There is no question of Apartheid drifting to Rhodesia. *It is already there.* Does this British government really think that the Africans of Rhodesia are so naive, are so stupid as to believe that Mr. Smith will ever allow the Africans the basic human right to rule themselves? Does this government think that we are children who can be fooled by such a blatant lie? I assure you we are not children, we are not fooled – we are grown men and, by God, we have dignity.

. . . . . .

. . . we reject these proposals not because anyone has threatened or intimidated us into rejection. We reject them IN SPITE OF a system of intimidation which surrounds the life of every African from the cradle to the grave – and tells him that the white people are superior to him, and nothing they propose for him can be rejected. The right to decide how and where and why one should live is surely basic to this problem. Rhodesian whites believe that they alone are competent to govern us, and if we don't agree to this we must be intimidated into agreement. Today, once again, *we reject the myth of our inferiority, we reject this intimidation.* Whether that intimidation comes from the District Commissioner, who in our intimidatory system is free to take away a man's land or cattle at his own discretion; whether it is from the policeman who has the power to stop any African on the street and demand his pass – *we reject it.*

Whether that intimidation is by a cabinet minister, who without explanation or reason can take away a man's or a woman's freedom for any length of time from one hour to fifteen years – *we reject it.*

Whether it is the intimidation of Municipal Authorities in the townships, who can take away a man's home and throw him and his family onto the street, without explanation – *we reject it.*

Whether it is the intimidation of the employer, who can sack his workers without reason, knowing that that man and his family will starve – *we reject it.*

We reject a policy and a regime that can justify the murder of 31 unarmed human beings on the streets of Gwelo, Salisbury and Umtali and the arrest of the Todds and the Chinamanos, and over 250 people whose only crime is to stand up for their dignity and to ask the world simply to treat them as human beings.

We reject the intimidation of a government of thugs. Above all, my brothers and sisters, WE REJECT INJUSTICE AND DEMAND OUR FREEDOM. (Extracts from a speech by Bishop Muzorewa, National Chairman of the ANC, Trafalgar Square, London, February 1972)

......

1. This Council [i.e. the ANC] believes in the power of the unity of the African masses in the imperative need for the opposition of those elements or forces which seek to sow the seeds of division among our people. Divided we will remain slaves and strangers in the land of our birth. United, though we may suffer, we shall toil, but with dignity, until we are free. We should, therefore, be warned that our worst enemies are those who seek to divide us and those who labour to keep us in perpetual oppression, be they black or white.

2. *We* believe in the invincibility of numbers of the masses of men and women of goodwill in Rhodesia and that the African National Council is truly a grass-roots organization in its very scope, membership and spirit.

3. *We* believe in a government that will establish and promote the sanctity and practice of the essential human freedom of conscience, of expression, association, religion, assembly and movement of all people irrespective of colour, race or creed.

4. *We* believe in non-racialism, the universal brotherhood of man under the fatherhood of God. This means forced segregation and forced integration violate the principle of free choice of association.

5. *We* believe in a non-violent, peaceful, orderly but permanent and continuing struggle to be waged within the Law and for the establishment of a constitutional government.

6. *We* believe that true peace and harmony among all people and economic stability of this country can only be assured for all time by the establishment of 'the government of the people, by the people and for the people'.

7. *We* believe that the rights and property of the minority should be protected; we do not, however, believe in the minority's amassing of social, political and economic privileges at the expense of the freedom of the majority.

Declaration

The African National Council solemnly dedicates itself to strive for the realization of those universal human rights conceded to the citizens in all democratic and just societies. This being so,

1. *We* shall not waver or prevaricate in our demand for the creation, in this country, of a just social order; but shall strive to achieve this justice which is long overdue;

2. *We* shall not deviate from our just demand for universal adult suffrage;

3. *We* shall never concede to the fallacy that there is any justification for racial and other forms of discrimination as between one human being against another. Thus, we shall continue to oppose racial bigotry, religious intolerance, class arrogance, the idiocy of tribalism and undeserved economic privileges. And we shall strive to create a nation where black and white can live as children of the One Almighty God.

4. *We* shall never compromise with the sin of greed which is the main characteristic of a minority-controlled economy; but will continue to promote a fair and free participation of each and every citizen of this our motherland – rich in natural resources.

5. *We* shall forever abhor the continued denial, under the pretext of 'preservation of Western Christian civilization', of the masses' demand for legitimate self-determination.

6. *We* shall never support nor respect a system which lays emphasis on Law and Order at the expense of charity, justice and human dignity; but will continue to call upon the conscience of this country to influence the establishment of law and order with justice.

7. *We* shall require and desire nothing less than self-determination.
(Extracts from the African National Council Manifesto, March 1972)

13: The Pearce Commission

Extracts from *Rhodesia: Report of the Commission on Rhodesian opinion under the Chairmanship of the Rt Hon. the Lord Pearce*, Cmd. 4964 (HMSO, London, May 1972). The extracts are (a) evidence from Bishop Muzorewa, National Chairman of ZANC; and (b) evidence from Joshua Nkomo, leader of the banned Zimbabwe African People's Union, who has been detained without trial since 1963.

(a) The African National Council has studied and analysed the Anglo-Rhodesian Settlement Proposals in depth and considered their possible implications if they were accepted and put into force. *The ANC*

300

unhesitatingly rejects these proposals as being unacceptable to the African people of this country who they represent.

. . . . . .

Both before and after UDI the British Government has carried on a dialogue with the Rhodesian authorities to the complete exclusion of the recognised African leaders. The basic demand of the ANC is that no settlement of the Rhodesian problem can be achieved without the active participation by the African people, through the leaders of their choice, in the actual process of negotiation leading to any settlement to be approved by them. The ANC accordingly rejects these proposals which have been arrived at without consultation with the people of Rhodesia. Further, the ANC believes that after the cynical disregard for law represented by UDI, the 1969 so-called 'Republican Constitution' is a high water mark in such lawlessness and can never be made the basis for any settlement. The ANC, on behalf of an overwhelming majority of people in Rhodesia, cannot in any circumstances accept a settlement whose result, directly or indirectly, is the legalisation of UDI and the Republican Constitution. The ANC believes that the present proposals do not amount to any significant amendment of the 1969 Constitution. Unlike previous occasions when the fate of the country was being considered the African people can at least say 'No' to these proposals and attempt to block them even though they have not been consulted during the stages of their negotiation. This is the first and last chance for the African people to pass a verdict on white minority rule. Our rejection of these proposals is unanimous.

. . . . . .

These proposals create three voters, rolls which will have the effect of entrenching and perpetuating racialism. Apart from this, the franchise system is both unjust and undemocratic. The African Higher Roll qualifications are so unfair, taking into account th legal disabilities the African people are subjected to in this country, that no sane and fair to legalise UDI.

These proposals create three voters, rolls which will have the effect of entrenching and perpetuating racialism. Apart from this, the franchise system is both unjust and undemocratic. The African Higher Roll qualifications are so unfair, taking into account the legal disabilities the African people are subjected to in this country, that no sane and fair minded person could accept them. All African soldiers, most African policemen, most teachers, nurses, agricultural demonstrators, ministers of religion and the mass of African workers would never hope to qualify. It is nonsensical to require the possession of immovable property of the value now proposed from the African when, in the terms of the Land Tenure Act and related discriminatory legislation, Africans are debarred from owning land on the same basis as Europeans in more than 90 per cent of Rhodesia.

As to the Lower African Roll, the ANC rejects the qualified franchise thus enshrined, as unjust and undemocratic, especially, no matter how many Africans qualify for inclusion on the Roll the number of seats that they can elect remains constant at 16 seats. The allocation of parliamentary seats in the House of Assembly is unacceptable to the ANC since we cannot accept any arrangements whereby 5,200,000 Africans are granted 16 seats while a mere 250,000 whites are given 50 seats. Nor are the ANC prepared to accept an arrangement which is designated, in its proposals for increases in the number of African seats, to postpone indefinitely the Africans' right to govern themselves. It has been calculated by some experts that majority rule cannot come any earlier than 2035, if then.

The ANC adheres to the view that the Senate, as presently constituted, is undemocratic and racial. Why, for example, should the European members of the House of Assembly enjoy the privilege of constituting themselves as a separate electorate for the purpose of electing the Senate when African members are denied the same right? In any event, the ANC finds it impossible to accept the tribalism and racialism that the present system entrenches.

In principle, the ANC thinks that the inclusion of a Declaration of Rights is a good thing as is the decision to make it justiciable. But the existing oppressive Statute Law is saved by these proposals and will not be affected by the provisions of the Declaration. In view of the limitations which have been imposed as regard the scope and justiciability of the Declaration the ANC is forced to reject this proposal as well.

The ANC believes that the proposal to reduce the period within which a State of Emergency requires renewal misses the point since such an emergency invariably affects the safeguards which the Bill of Rights contains.

The ANC does not regard the safeguards on amendment of the Constitution or review of existing legislation as satisfactory. In particular, the proposed Commission on Racial Discrimination will not be set up until after the test of acceptability is complete. It will not therefore be able to report until long after independence has been granted by the British Parliament. The Commission itself will be nominated by the régime and responsible to it. In these circumstances we think that the proposed Commission will be valueless. This is especially as the Commission will only have advisory powers and will be similar if not identical to the ill-fated Constitutional Council established under the 1961 Constitution.

......

The Settlement Proposals accept the basic provision of the Land Tenure Act. The Commission on Discrimination to be appointed after the granting of legal independence cannot recommend the repeal of the Land Tenure Act. The ANC rejects unreservedly the Land Tenure Act as embodied in the Settlement Proposals because it is blatantly discriminatory, unfair and an incitement to racial animosity among the peoples of this country.

The amount of aid is uncertain. All that is clear is that it will not be more than £5 million per year and will be applied to purposes and projects to be agreed with the Rhodesian Government. The strings attached to the aid are questionable. The principal beneficiaries of the proposed £50 million British aid will be the Rhodesian Government in terms of foreign exchange and the stimulus to white industry. The ANC believes that much of this money will be used on the promotion of 'provincialisation' which is the regime's euphemism for bantustans, and thus reject these proposals as perpetuating and extending an already unjust system.

The undertaking by the Rhodesian Government (to take steps to enable an increasing number of Africans to fit themselves to compete on equal terms with candidates of other races so far as appointments or promotions are concerned) is vague and unsatisfactory. It does not spell out what steps are to be taken in pursuance of the undertaking. It implies that at present Africans have neither the qualifications nor the experience for appointment or promotion in the Public Service. This is not true.

In spite of the régime's claim that promotion is on the basis of merit only, the ANC would especially point out the failure to promote African inspectors of schools to positions of Provincial Education Officers in spite of their high qualifications and long experience; the appointment of young Europeans as District Officers with only Form 1V education instead of African graduates with university degrees; the refusal to amend the Education Act so that all teachers regardless of race can become members of the Public Service; the refusal to allow African nurses to take up appointments in so-called European hospitals in spite of the shortage of nurses in these hospitals. This story is repeated in every Government Department. The ANC cannot trust the Rhodesian Front Government to apply criteria of merit and suitability in filling vacancies in the Public Service. The ANC therefore rejects this section of the proposals as vague and illusory.

It is clear that the proposals as they now stand do not provide a satisfactory arrangement acceptable to the vast majority of people in the country. On behalf of these people, the ANC calls for the Pearce Commission to report the rejection of these terms, which, if accepted, can only serve to perpetuate the existing divisions and injustice in Rhodesia.

. . . . . .

(b) Southern Rhodesia has a population of about five and three-quarter million people. Of these, five and a half million are black indigenous people. The rest of the population is made up of people of European and Asian descent, as well as the coloured people. All the African people and some of the other sections of the population are citizens of this country by birth, and the rest by registration.

We maintain that any decisions that affect the present and future of this country must be made by all the citizens irrespective of their colour, creed or station in life. But, as we observe, since the occupation of this country by Europeans in the mid 1890's all political, economic, financial, administrative and military control has remained an exclusive preserve of the European section of our population, so that the direction the affairs of the country took since then, was, and is still being determined by this section of the population.

. . . . . .

. . . The question to be asked is this. 'Do these proposals attempt to solve all or any of the . . . basic problems of this country?'. To us the answer is an emphatic 'NO!' These proposals are a superficial modification of the 1969 illegal republican constitution, whose main purpose is to entrench, maintain and enforce oppressive and discriminatory practices in the country permanently. Are the African people of this country expected to accept a constitution whose purpose is to entrench half the country (44,948,300 acres) for use by 249,000 people of European descent (including Asian and Coloured people) while $5\frac{1}{2}$ million of them (said to stand a chance of doubling in 20 years), are to share the other half? Are they expected to accept that all the towns in their country that they, together with the other sections of the population built, are to be European areas permanently? NO! This we cannot accept.

We are more than convinced that to allow entrenchment of racial division of land in the constitution of our country in the manner suggested in these proposals is to allow entrenchment of mistrust and conflict. How can we hope to build a united people and nation on a divided foundation?

. . . UDI intervened while there was a constitutional dispute between the African people on one hand and the British and Rhodesian Government on the other. These proposals do not attempt to solve this basic constitutional dispute. If anything, they aggravate the situation. The aim of these proposals, as we see it, is to end the derived dispute between the Rhodesian rebel government and the British Government, leaving the constitutional problem as it affects the majority of the people in a worse position than it was before the declaration of illegal independence. The proposals are an attempt by the British Government to recognise UDI and to get the African people, against whose interests UDI was taken, to endorse it. We cannot agree to this, Lord Pearce. Our answer is an emphatic 'NO!' We reject these proposals in the strongest terms.

Sir Alec Douglas-Home is reported as saying, if the answer is no there will be no further negotiations. This to us is a fatalistic attitude. The African people are not saying no to a genuine settlement of the real problem of their country; they are saying no to proposals, which, if accepted, are bound to make their country a permanent area of conflict. The African people want a settlement that will bring about reconciliation between our peoples; not one that is aimed only at reconciling Britain and the Smith Régime as these proposals do. We expect Britain to respect our stand and call a constitutional conference to discuss the future of our country. No matter how long it may take, Britain, together with white and black citizens, must find the right answer for the sake of our country.

. . . . . .

The so much talked about unimpeded progress to parity and majority rule by Africans is so impeded by . . . legislation that one cannot see how it can ever be achieved.

It is suggested in the proposals that Africans can move towards this goal by increasing their numbers on the African Higher Roll. This can be done by a number of Africans satisfying voters' qualifications . . .

This they can do by either acquiring immovable property of a specified value or income at a specified rate per annum or a combination of four years of secondary education of prescribed standard and a lesser value or rate of the other two.

Let us examine each of these requirements and the prospect of Africans acquiring them in sufficiently large numbers for the purposes of the African Higher Roll under existing legislation and administrative arrangements.

1. *Ownership of farm or land*: African per capita land is about 9 acres. Approximately 95 per cent of this is communal land and therefore cannot be used for qualification purposes. Even if this land was turned to individual ownership its value would be too low for the requirements.

The remaining 5 per cent of African land is made up of purchase area, parks and wild life areas and specially designated land. Of this, land open to individual ownership, i.e. purchase area, amounts to only $3\frac{1}{2}$ million acres as against 38,671,232 acres for Europeans. If divided into 300 acre plots (as many African holdings are), only about 12,000 people would own land. The value of these small farms is far below the required value for the vote unless heavily developed. Those Africans who own some of these small farms have found it almost impossible to raise development funds. The nature and constitution of the Agricultural Finance Corporation is such that small African farmers stand very little chance of financial assistance, if at all.

2. *Ownership of Houses or Buildings*: Ownership of houses or buildings in appreciable numbers can only be achieved in urban areas for obvious reasons . . . all urban areas in this country, according to the Land Tenure Act, are in the European area, and entrenched in the constitution. This being the case, whatever houses or buildings that the African may own, in these areas, is dependent on what European controlled municipal councils may provide under strict government supervision.

It is generally accepted that commerce and industry in any country grows in urban areas; as these areas are European-owned, whatever commercial or industrial undertakings that Africans may carry out are those that individual European municipal councils may allow, and because of the nature of land tenure in these European-owned African townships, it has been found to be almost impossible for financial institutions to extend credit to African businessmen and for building societies to give loans for either dwelling or business premises.

As the position is as stated above, we cannot see how Africans can be able to increase their numbers on the African Higher Roll appreciably by ownership of immovable property of any kind.

3. *Education*: Educational qualification required for combination with either income or immovable property is 'four years secondary education of prescribed standard'. In the first place, European education is free and compulsory; African education is not. Only $12\frac{1}{2}$ per cent of African children passing through primary schools may proceed to four years secondary education, irrespective of the availability of funds for secondary education. In this way the number of Africans with a four year secondary education is kept in check each year as against that of Europeans.

. . . . . .

4. *Income*: The difference between the annual average earnings of Africans and Europeans . . . for the year 1970 shows that the number of Africans earning the required income for the purpose of registering on the African Higher Roll must be very low indeed. The African earning capacity cannot be expected to increase appreciably for a very long time to come for various reasons: Rhodesian traditional prejudice and discrimination, undeclared job reservation, differential educational qualifications which militate against the African school-leaver, European skilled workers' refusal to train African apprentices and different racial pay scales for people doing the same type of work. The examples of this discriminatory practice permeate all sectors of employment in the country, public or private.

. . . . . .

306

Declaration of Rights: Much has been said about the protection of individual rights by the Declaration of Rights as contained in the proposals. But, looking through them, we have discovered that the nature and extent of exceptions in the Declaration of Rights render it ineffectual and of little value to the citizen. It cannot escape our attention that, under the Declaration as it stands in these proposals, courts would not be able to exercise any powers if measures taken against any individual or group of individuals were taken under legislation passed more than ten years before the Declaration of Rights came into force, or any law that was part of the law of Rhodesia before the fixed date. It is quite plain that these provisions are aimed at protecting all oppressive and discriminatory legislation . . .

We submit that with powers contained in, for instance, the Law and Order (Maintenance) Act, the Unlawful Organizations Act etc, an unscrupulous ruling party, dedicated to white supremacy, can render the working of a genuine representative African party impossible in a number of ways and courts would be powerless to intervene.

. . . . . .

Last, but not by any means least, in these proposals, the House of Assembly can renew a state of emergency at intervals of nine months. During this period the Declaration of Rights would be, in a way, suspended. As we have experienced in the last seven years, a government bent on suppressing normal African political activity can declare a state of emergency on the section of the country where its opponents reside and thereby keep them in detention indefinitely . . .

Finally, we would like to emphasise to the Commission, that we unreservedly reject these proposals because they do not satisfy universally accepted conditions of independence and self determination for all our people; they are racial and discriminatory, and we believe that if implemented, they will engender feelings of hostility between black and white citizens of our country and bring about bloodshed and untold human suffering. This must not be allowed to happen.

14: Constitution of the Front for the Liberation of Zimbabwe (FROLIZI)

Published in C. Legum, *Africa Contemporary Record, 1972–3*.
FROLIZI brings together the formerly separate African nationalist movements in Rhodesia, the Zimbabwe African People's Union (ZAPU) led by Joshua

Nkomo, and the Zimbabwe African National Union (ZANU) led by N. Sithole; both leaders are in detention in Rhodesia.

The Front for the Liberation of Zimbabwe, FROLIZI, uniting ZANU and ZAPU, is the Zimbabwe people's political-military instrument for national liberation, dedicated to a protracted revolutionary struggle against the true enemy of Zimbabwe – the capitalist imperialists and the colonial settlers in Zimbabwe.

FROLIZI was formed on 1 October 1971 by militant members of ZANU and ZAPU without bitterness to either of the parties, first and foremost to continue the work of the heroic members of both groups who had given their liberty and, in many noble instances, their lives, for the dignity and freedom of Zimbabwe.

The formation of FROLIZI was due to the imperative of unity among the broad masses of the people of Zimbabwe who have resolved to bury the politics of inter-party rivalry and are now struggling for liberation behind a single banner of total national unity.

Political Programme of FROLIZI

The political programme of FROLIZI shall be as follows:

Article 1: To organize and unite the people of Zimbabwe into a revolutionary combat force aware of its interests, win the broad masses of the people to the armed struggle and to the side of the progressive world outlook, wage a protracted people's war of national liberation until victory is won, achieve total political and economic control of our motherland, establish and consolidate a people's revolutionary army which would protect and defend the people's revolutionary gains, establish a democratic and socialist State, and overthrow all vestiges of colonialism and cut off links with imperialism.

Article 2: To establish and develop an independent socialist economy based upon the policy of national planning and ownership and control of land, capital and all means of production and distribution by the people, and actively work to abolish the distinction between town and country.

Article 3: To establish and protect the people's fundamental right to:

(1) employment and living wages;
(2) free compulsory education and health services;
(3) equal and comradely treatment without regard to ethnic origin, race, sex, age or religion;
(4) freedom of expression, movement, association and assembly;
(5) free election, referendum and recall.

Article 4: To re-establish and develop our culture along revolutionary lines.

Article 5: To establish and develop solidarity with revolutionary movements, organizations and governments in Africa, Asia, South America and elsewhere.

. . . . . .

Organizational Principle

Article 10: Democratic centralism shall be the Front's basic organizational principle. Democratic centralism means that all the leading bodies of the Front shall be elected through revolutionary democratic consultation; and this principle aims at ensuring both centralism and democracy, discipline and freedom. It also means that the individual is subordinate to the organization, the minority to the majority, the lower level to the higher one, and the entire organization to Congress.

Article 11: Members of the Front shall have the right to criticize the organization and its leadership at all levels, provided the criticism is constructive and aimed at building the organization and advance the cause of the revolution. Members who criticize shall be required to come forward with concrete proposals.

Article 12: Decisions of the Front involving policy matters and important national issues shall be reached collectively so as to facilitate the practice of revolutionary democracy and prevent the emergence of personality conflicts, factionalism, sectarianism and internal conspiratorial combinations.

15: Namibia (South-West Africa)

Extracts from the declaration of a conference in Brussels, 26–8 May 1972, organised by the South-West African People's Organisation (SWAPO). Published in C. Legum, *Africa Contemporary Record, 1972–3.*

1. This International Conference takes place at a time when decisive action is needed on the issue of Namibia.

2. South Africa's occupation of the territory is now in its 57th year. During this half century while the old colonial empires have been dissolved, South Africa has entrenched in Namibia a system of colonial-type rule maintained by an apparatus of repression unequalled in race tyranny.

3. This conference recognizes that the principal battleground of the

freedom struggle lies within Namibia. The people of this country have a proud record of resistance to conquest, beginning with the independence wars of the beginning of this century and culminating in the 1966 decision to embark upon armed struggle which opens a new era of confrontation between the people and the occupying power.

4. The outcome of this battle is not in doubt, but in the coming years the struggle will summon the maximum resources of endeavour and sacrifice of the Namibian people. The strike of contract workers has demonstrated the readiness of the people for mass struggle and their capacity to organize under conditions of grim and unrelenting repression. This strike must be seen as an integral and indivisible part of the overall liberation struggle. The regiments of freedom fighters are being drawn from the rank of striking workers, rebellious students, embattled peasants led by the political militants and armed units of SWAPO. This conference accordingly recognizes that the initiatives, methods and conduct of their struggle lie with SWAPO, the authentic voice and fighting organization of the peoples of Namibia.

5. At the same time the world has a unique and special responsibility for the colonial condition of Namibia, for this territory was a ward of the international community which was forcibly and illegally incorporated by the white minority State.

6. The advisory opinion of the International Court of Justice has pronounced the South African occupation illegal. Successive resolutions of the General Assembly and the Security Council have recognized the international status of the territory. The Council of Namibia has been charged with the task of administering the territory in the name of the United Nations. The status of the territory is therefore no longer at issue. The problem of the world body is one of implementation.

. . . . . .

11. In the full knowledge of . . . committed Western support, South Africa has steadily extended its control over Namibia. The Bantustan system is the central part of this strategy. Far from offering the prospect of self-determination and genuine independence, the Bantustans, which constitute a reservoir of cheap forced labour, are intended to dismember the national unity and territorial integrity of the Namibian people and to undermine the forces of resistance.

12. A prime purpose of the Bantustan policy is also to ward off international criticism. This conference denounces the tactic as fraudulent and affirms that Namibia is one and its independence indivisible, and that its national sovereignty is the preserve of all the people.

13. Since the future of Namibia can only be determined by its people, any action that affects the future of Namibia should be with the consent of

SWAPO, all negotiation and dealings with the occupying power must be conducted with their consent and proper participation. Towards this end the conference calls for the recognition of SWAPO as the true and legitimate representative of Namibia and demands that it be accorded formal status in all international forums and institutions concerned with Namibia.

C. THE PORTUGUESE TERRITORIES

16: Amilcar Cabral: Portuguese Guinea

Extracts from A. Cabral, *Revolution in Guinea* (R. Handyside, London, 1972). Reprinted by permission of Stage 1 Publications. The context of each extract is given after the extract.

... the constitutional, political, legal, administrative and judicial status of Guinea, far from that of being a 'province of Portugal' is that of a non-self-governing country, conquered and occupied by force of arms, ruled and administered by a foreign power. The economic, political and social life of the people of Guinea is governed by laws and rules which differ from those applied to the people of Portugal; the people of Guinea have no political rights, they do not help to operate the country's institutions or to draft its laws, which, however, they must obey; they do not elect representatives and cannot invest political and administrative leaders with office or remove them from office; they do not enjoy the most rudimentary human rights or fundamental freedoms. Thus, far from having their own legal identity, the people of Guinea are a colonised and dependent people, whose dignity has been deeply wounded. Neither directly nor indirectly do they decide their present or future fate. Consequently there can be no doubt that the people of Guinea are being deprived of their right to self-determination, a right proclaimed and established for all peoples in the United Nations Charter.

......

... the constitutional, legal, political and administrative situation of Guinea – the laws and practices of Portuguese colonialism – have never given the people of that country an opportunity of fulfilling their aspirations, or of making even gradual headway along the path of freedom and progress, 'within the framework of the Portuguese administration'. Thus there has never been more than one way in which the people of Guinea could attempt to fulfil their aspirations towards liberty and

311

progress, namely, *by a struggle for national liberation*. Despite the particularly difficult conditions confronting them, the people of Guinea, guided by enlightened leaders who at an early stage foresaw the decline and end of the colonial era, roused themselves and in 1953, with courage and enthusiasm, plunged into the struggle for national liberation.

It was the actual internal conditions, the realities of their daily life, which decided the people of Guinea to undertake the struggle for national liberation and for the speedy and total liquidation of Portuguese colonialism. But the struggles and victories of other African peoples against foreign rule and the progress made by mankind in the realms of freedom, human dignity, social justice and international law have played no small part in influencing and strengthening that decision. That is why the fight of Guinea for national liberation is part and parcel of the struggle of the African peoples for the total abolition of foreign rule in Africa – for the final and irrevocable abolition of the colonial system – which is one of the outstanding features of contemporary history. (Extracts from a statement made in Conakry in June 1962 to the UN Special Committee on Territories under Portuguese Administration)

We are not here to ask the UN to send troops to free our countries from the Portuguese colonial yoke. Perhaps we could ask for it, but we do not think it necessary, for we are confident that we will be able to free our countries. We invoke only one right: the right to obtain collaboration and concrete assistance from the UN in order to hasten the liberation of our countries from the colonial yoke and thus to lessen the human and material losses which a long struggle can cause. (Extract from a declaration to the Fourth Commission of the UN General Assembly, December 1962)

Here I should like to broach one key problem, which is of enormous importance for us, as we are a country of peasants, and that is the problem of whether or not the peasantry represents the main revolutionary force. I shall confine myself to my own country, Guinea, where it must be said at once that the peasantry is not a revolutionary force – which may seem strange, particularly as we have based the whole of our armed liberation struggle on the peasantry. A distinction must be drawn between a physical force and a revolutionary force; physically, the peasantry is a great force in Guinea: it is almost the whole of the population, it controls the nation's wealth, it is the peasantry which produces; but we know from experience what trouble we had convincing the peasantry to fight ... The conditions of the peasantry in China were very different: the peasantry had a history of revolt, but this was not the case in Guinea, and so it was not possible for our party militants and propaganda workers to find the same kind of welcome among the peasantry in Guinea for the idea of national liberation as the idea found in China . . .

. . . . . .

. . . On the other hand, the . . . group . . . for which we have not yet found any precise classification (the group of mainly young people recently arrived from the rural areas with contacts in both the urban and the rural areas) gradually comes to make a comparison between the standard of living of their own families and that of the Portuguese; they begin to understand the sacrifices being borne by the Africans. They have proved extremely dynamic in the struggle. Many of these people joined the struggle right from the beginning and it is among this group that we found many of the cadres whom we have since trained.

The importance of this urban experience lies in the fact that it allows comparison: this is the key stimulant required for the awakening of consciousness. It is interesting to note that Algerian nationalism largely sprang up among the emigré workers in France. As far as Guinea is concerned, the idea of the national liberation struggle was born not abroad but in our own country, in a milieu where people were subjected to close and incessant exploitation. Many people say that it is the peasants who carry the burden of exploitation: this may be true, but so far as the struggle is concerned it must be realised that it is not the degree of suffering and hardship involved as such that matters: even extreme suffering in itself does not necessarily produce the *prise de conscience* required for the national liberation struggle. In Guinea the peasants are subjected to a kind of exploitation equivalent to slavery; but even if you try and explain to them that they are being exploited and robbed, it is difficult to convince them by means of an unexperienced explanation of a technico-economic kind that they are the most exploited people; whereas it is easier to convince the workers and the people employed in the towns who earn, say, 10 escudos a day for a job in which a European earns between 30 and 50 that they are being subjected to massive exploitation and injustice, because they can see . . . This is of major importance when considering where the initial idea of the struggle came from.

. . . . . .

. . . In Guinea, as in other countries, the implantation of imperialism by force and the presence of the colonial system considerably altered the historical conditions and aroused a response – the national liberation struggle – which is generally considered a revolutionary trend; but this is something which I think needs further examination. I should like to formulate this question: is the national liberation movement something which has simply emerged from within our country, is it a result of the internal contradictions created by the presence of colonialism, or are there external factors which have determined it? And here we have some reservations; in fact I would even go so far as to ask whether, given the advance of socialism in the world, the national liberation movement is not an imperialist initiative. Is the judicial institution which serves as a reference for the right of all peoples to struggle to free themselves a product of the peoples who are trying to liberate themselves? Was it created by the socialist countries who are our historical associates? It is signed by the imperialist countries, it is the imperialist countries who have recognised the right of all peoples to national independence, so I ask myself whether we may not be considering as an initiative of our people what is in fact an initiative of the enemy? Even Portugal, which is using napalm bombs against our people in Guinea, signed the declaration of the right of all peoples to independence. One may well ask oneself why they were so mad as to do something which goes against their own interests — and whether or not it was partly forced on them, the real point is that they signed it. This is where we think there is something wrong with the simple interpretation of the national liberation movement as a revolutionary trend. The objective of the imperialist countries was to prevent the enlargement of the socialist camp, to liberate the reactionary forces in our countries which were being stifled by colonialism and to enable these forces to ally themselves with the international bourgeoisie. The fundamental objective was to create a bourgeoisie where one did not exist, in order specifically to strengthen the imperialist and the capitalist camp. This rise of the bourgeoisie in the new countries, far from being at all surprising, should be considered absolutely normal, it is something that has to be faced by all those struggling against imperialism. We are therefore faced with the problem of deciding whether to engage in an out and out struggle against the bourgeoisie right from the start or whether to try and make an alliance with the national bourgeoisie, to try to deepen the absolutely necessary contradiction between the national bourgeoisie and the international bourgeoisie which has promoted the national bourgeoisie to the position it holds.

...I think one thing that can be said is this: the revolutionary petty bourgeoisie is honest; i.e. in spite of all the hostile conditions, it remains identified with the fundamental interests of the popular masses. To do this it may have to commit suicide, but it will not lose; by sacrificing itself it can reincarnate itself, but in the condition of workers or peasants. In speaking of honesty I am not trying to establish moral criteria for judging the role of the petty bourgeoisie when it is in power; what I mean by honesty, in a political context, is total commitment and total identification with the toiling masses.

. . . . . .

... Neocolonialism is at work on two fronts – in Europe as well as in the underdeveloped countries. Its current framework in the underdeveloped countries is the policy of aid, and one of the essential aims of this policy is to create a false bourgeoisie to put a brake on the revolution and to enlarge the possibilities of the petty bourgeoisie as a neutraliser of the revolution; at the same time it invests capital in France, Italy, Belgium, England and so on. In our opinion the aim of this is to stimulate the growth of a workers' aristocracy, to enlarge the field of action of the petty bourgeoisie so as to block the revolution. In our opinion it is under this aspect that neocolonialism and the relations between the international working class movement and our movements must be analysed.

If there have ever been any doubts about the close relations between our struggle and the struggle of the international working class movement, neocolonialism has proved that there need not be any. Obviously I don't think it is possible to forge closer relations between the peasantry in Guinea and the working class movement in Europe; what we must do first is try and forge closer links between the peasant movement and the wage-earners' movement in our own country. (Extracts from the text of a seminar on the social structure of Guinea, held in the Frantz Fanon Centre, Treviglio, Milan, 1–3 May 1964)

The ideological deficiency, not to say the total lack of ideology, within the national liberation movements – which is basically due to ignorance of the historical reality which these movements claim to transform – constitutes one of the greatest weaknesses of our struggle against imperialism, if not the greatest weakness of all. We believe, however, that a sufficient number of different experiences has already been accumulated to enable us to define a general line of thought and action with the aim of eliminating this deficiency ...

It is with the intention of making a contribution, however modest, to this debate that we present here our opinion of *the foundations and objectives of national liberation in relation to the social structure*. This opinion is the result of our own experiences of the struggle and of a critical appreciation of the experiences of others. To those who see in it a theoretical character, we would recall that every practice produces a theory, and that if it is true that a revolution can fail even though it be based on perfectly conceived theories, nobody has yet made a successful revolution without a revolutionary theory.

... the socio-economic phenomenon 'class' is created and develops as a function of at least two essential and interdependent variables – the level

315

of productive forces and the pattern of ownership of the means of production. This development takes place slowly, gradually and unevenly, by quantitative and generally imperceptible variations in the fundamental components; once a certain degree of accumulation is reached, this process then leads to a *qualitative jump,* characterised by the appearance of classes and of conflict between them.

......

This leads us to pose the following question: does history begin only with the development of the phenomenon of 'class', and consequently of class struggle? To reply in the affirmative would be to place outside history the whole period of life of human groups from the discovery of hunting, and later of nomadic and sedentary agriculture, to the organisation of herds and the private appropriation of land. It would also be to consider – and this we refuse to accept – that various human groups in Africa, Asia and Latin America were living without history, or outside history, at the time when they were subjected to the yoke of imperialism . . .

Our refusal, based as it is on concrete knowledge of the socio-economic reality of our countries and on the analysis of the process of development of the phenomenon 'class', as we have seen earlier, leads us to conclude that if class struggle is the motive force of history, it is so only in a specific historical period. This means that *before* the class struggle – and necessarily *after* it, since in this world there is no before without an after – one of several factors was and will be the motive force of history. It is not difficult to see that this factor in the history of each human group is the *mode of production* – the level of productive forces and the pattern of ownership – characteristic of that group. Furthermore, as we have seen, classes themselves, class struggle and their subsequent definition, are the result of the development of the productive forces in conjunction with the pattern of ownership of the means of production. It therefore seems correct to conclude that the level of productive forces, the essential determining element in the content and form of class struggle, is the true and permanent motive force of history.

......

The foregoing, and the reality of our times, allow us to state that the history of one human group or of humanity goes through at least three stages. The first is characterised by a low level of productive forces – of man's domination over nature; the mode of production is of a rudimentary character, private appropriation of the means of production does not yet exist, there are no classes, nor, consequently, is there any class struggle. In the second stage, the increased level of productive forces leads to private appropriations of the means of production, progressively complicates the mode of production, provokes conflicts of interests within the socio-economic whole in movement, and makes possible the appearance of the phenomenon 'class' and hence of class struggle, the social expression of the contradiction in the economic field between the mode of production and private appropriation of the means of production. In the third stage, once a certain level of productive forces is reached, the elimination of private appropriation of the means of production is made possible, and is carried out, together with the elimination of the phenomenon 'class', and hence of class struggle; new and hitherto unknown forces in the historical process of the socio-economic whole are then unleashed.

In politico-economic language, the first stage would correspond to the communal agricultural and cattle-raising society, in which the social structure is horizontal, without any state; the second to feudal or assimilated agricultural or agro-industrial bourgeois societies, with a vertical social structure and a state; the third to socialist or communist societies, in which the economy is mainly, if not exclusively, industrial (since agriculture itself becomes a form of industry) and in which the state tends to progressively disappear, or actually disappears, and where the social structure returns to horizontality, at a higher level of productive forces, social relations and appreciation of human values.

. . . . . .

Thus we see that our peoples have their own history regardless of the stage of their economic development. When they were subjected to imperialist domination, the historical process of each of our peoples (or of the human groups of which they are composed) was subjected to the violent action of an external factor. This action – the impact of imperialism on our societies – could not fail to influence the process of development of the productive forces in our countries and the social structures of our countries, as well as the content and form of our national liberation struggles.

But we also see that in the historical context of the development of these struggles, our peoples have the concrete possibility of going from their present situation of exploitation and underdevelopment to a new stage of their historical process which can lead them to a higher form of economic, social and cultural existence.

. . . if we can calmly analyse the imperialist phenomenon, we will not shock anybody by admitting that imperialism – and everything goes to prove that it is in fact the last phase in the evolution of capitalism – has been a historical necessity, a consequence of the impetus given by the productive forces and of the transformations of the means of production in the general context of humanity, considered as one movement, that is to say a necessity like those today of the national liberation of peoples, the

317

destruction of capital and the advent of socialism.

The important thing for our peoples is to know whether imperialism, in its role as capital in action, has fulfilled in our countries its historical mission: the acceleration of the process of development of the productive forces and their transformation in the sense of increasing complexity in the means of production; increasing the differentiation between the classes with the development of the bourgeoisie, and intensifying the class struggle; and appreciably increasing the level of economic, social and cultural life of the peoples.

. . . . . .

On the question of the effects of imperialist domination on the social structure and historical process of our peoples, we should first of all examine the general forms of imperialist domination. There are at least two forms: the first is direct domination, by means of a political power made up of people foreign to the dominated people (armed forces, police, administrative agents and settlers); this is generally called *classical colonialism* or *colonialism*. The second form is indirect domination, by a political power made up mainly or completely of native agents; this is called *neocolonialism*.

In the first case, the social structure of the dominated people, whatever its stage of development, can suffer the following consequences: (a) total destruction, generally accompanied by immediate or gradual elimination of the native population and, consequently, by the substitution of a population from outside; (b) partial destruction, generally accompanied by a greater or lesser influx of population from outside; (c) apparent conservation, conditioned by confining the native society to zones or reserves generally offering no possibilities of living, accompanied by massive implantation of population from outside.

The two latter cases are those which we must consider in the framework of the problematic national liberation, and they are extensively present in Africa. One can say that in either case the influence of imperialism on the historical process of the dominated people produces paralysis, stagnation and even in some cases regression in this process. However this paralysis is not complete. In one sector or another of the socio-economic whole in question, noticeable transformations can be expected, caused by the permanent action of some internal (local) factors or by the action of new factors introduced by the colonial domination, such as the introduction of money and the development of urban centres. Among these transformations we should particularly note, in certain cases, the progressive loss of prestige of the ruling native classes or sectors, the forced or voluntary exodus of part of the peasant population to the urban centres, with the consequent development of new social strata: salaried workers, clerks, employees in commerce and the liberal professions, and an unstable stratum of unemployed. In the countryside there develops, with very varied intensity and always linked to the urban milieu, a stratum made up of small landowners. In the case of neocolonialism, whether the majority of the colonised population is of native or foreign origin, the imperialist action takes the form of creating a local bourgeoisie or pseudo-bourgeoisie, controlled by the ruling class of the dominating country.

. . . . . .

The colonial situation, which does not permit the development of a native pseudo-bourgeoisie and in which the popular masses do not generally reach the necessary level of political consciousness before the advent of the phenomenon of national liberation, offers the petty bourgeoisie the historical opportunity of leading the struggle against foreign domination, since by nature of its objective and subjective position (higher standard of living than that of the masses, more frequent contact with the agents of colonialism, and hence more chances of being humiliated, higher level of education and political awareness, etc.) it is the stratum which most rapidly becomes aware of the need to free itself from foreign domination. This historical responsibility is assumed by the sector of the petty bourgeoisie which, in the colonial context, can be called *revolutionary*, while other sectors retain the doubts characteristic of these classes or ally themselves to colonialism so as to defend, albeit illusorily, their social situation.

The neocolonial situation, which demands the elimination of the native pseudo-bourgeoisie so that national liberation can be attained, also offers the petty bourgeoisie the chance of playing a role of major and even decisive importance in the struggle for the elimination of foreign domination. But in this case, by virtue of the progress made in the social structure, the function of leading the struggle is shared (to a greater or lesser extent) with the more educated sectors of the working classes and even with some elements of the national pseudo-bourgeoisie who are inspired by patriotic sentiments. The role of the sector of the petty bourgeoisie which participates in leading the struggle is all the more important since it is a fact that in the neocolonial situation it is the most suitable sector to assume these functions, both because of the economic and cultural limitations of the working masses, and because of the complexes and limitations of an ideological nature which characterise the sector of the national pseudo-bourgeoisie which supports the struggle. In this case it is important to note that the role with which it is entrusted demands from this sector of the petty bourgeoisie a greater revolutionary consciousness, and the capacity for faithfully interpreting the aspirations of the masses in each phase of the struggle and for identifying themselves more and more with the masses.

But however high the degree of revolutionary consciousness of the sector of the petty bourgeoisie called on to fulfil this historical function, it cannot free itself from one objective reality: the petty bourgeoisie, as a service class (that is to say a class not directly involved in the process of production) does not possess the economic base to guarantee the taking over of power. In fact history has shown that whatever the role — sometimes important — played by individuals coming from the petty bourgeoisie in the process of a revolution, this class has never possessed political control. And it could never possess it, since political control (the state) is based on the economic capacity of the ruling class, and in the conditions of colonial and neocolonial society this capacity is retained by two entities: imperialist capital and the native working classes.

To retain the power which national liberation puts in its hands, the petty bourgeoisie has only one path: to give free rein to its natural tendencies to become more bourgeois, to permit the development of a bureaucratic and intermediary bourgeoisie in the commercial cycle, in order to transform itself into a national pseudo-bourgeoisie, that is to say in order to negate the revolution and necessarily ally itself with imperialist capital. Now all this corresponds to the neo-colonial situation, that is, to the betrayal of the objectives of national liberation. In order not to betray these objectives, the petty bourgeoisie has only one choice: to strengthen its revolutionary consciousness, to reject the temptations of becoming more bourgeois and the natural concerns of its class mentality, to identify itself with the working classes and not to oppose the normal development of the process of revolution. This means that in order to truly fulfil the role in the national liberation struggle, the revolutionary petty bourgeoisie must be capable of committing suicide as a class in order to be reborn as revolutionary workers, completely identified with the deepest aspirations of the people to which they belong.

This alternative — to betray the revolution or to commit suicide as a class — constitutes the dilemma of the petty bourgeoisie in the general framework of the national liberation struggle. The positive solution in favour of the revolution depends on what Fidel Castro recently correctly called *the development of revolutionary consciousness*. (Extracts from Address to the first Tricontinental Conference of the peoples of Asia, Africa and Latin America, Havana, January 1966)

17: Edouardo Mondlane: Mozambique

Extracts from E. Mondlane, *The Struggle For Mozambique* (Penguin, 1969).

At the first Congress of FRELIMO, the aims of the party were defined:

The Congress of FRELIMO –

Having examined the present needs of the struggle against Portuguese colonialism in Mozambique – declares its firm determination to promote the efficient organization of the struggle of the Mozambican people for national liberation, and adopts the following resolutions to be put into immediate execution by the Central Committee of FRELIMO:

1. To develop and consolidate the organizational structure of FRELIMO;·
2. to further the unity of Mozambicans;
3. to achieve maximum utilization of the energies and capacities of each and every member of FRELIMO;
4. to promote and accelerate training of cadres;
5. to employ directly every effort to promote the rapid access of Mozambique to independence;
6. to promote by every method the social and cultural development of the Mozambican woman;
7. to promote at once the literacy of the Mozambican people, creating schools wherever possible;
8. to take the necessary measures towards supplying the needs of the organs of different levels of FRELIMO;
9. to encourage and support the formation and consolidation of trade union, student, youth and women's organizations;
10. to cooperate with the nationalist organizations of the other Portuguese colonies;
11. to cooperate with African nationalist organizations;
12. to cooperate with the nationalist movements of all countries;
13. to obtain funds from organizations which sympathize with the cause of the people of Mozambique, making public appeals;
14. to procure all requirements for self defence and resistance of the Mozambique people;
15. to organize permanent propaganda by all methods in order to mobilize world public opinion in favour of the cause of the Mozambican people;
16. to send delegations to all countries in order to undertake campaigns and public demonstrations of protest against the atrocities com-

321

mitted by the Portuguese colonial administration, as well as to press for the immediate liberation of all nationalists who are inside the Portuguese colonialist prisons;

17. to procure diplomatic, moral and material help for the cause of the Mozambican people from the African states and from all peace and freedom loving people.

These aims could be summarized as consolidation and mobilization; preparation for war; education; diplomacy.

. . . . . .

The need for an armed struggle
Although determined to do everything in our power to try to gain independence by peaceful means, we were already convinced at this stage that a war would be necessary. People more familiar with the policies of other colonial powers have accused us of resorting to violence without due cause. This is partly refuted by the fate met by every type of legal, democratic and reformist activity tried over the preceding forty years.

The character of the government in Portugal itself makes a peaceful solution inherently unlikely. Within Portugal the government has promoted neither sound economic growth nor social well-being, and has gained little international respect. The possession of colonies has helped to conceal these failures: the colonies contribute to the economy; they add to Portugal's consequence in the world, particularly the world of finance; they have provided a national myth of empire which helps discourage any grumbling by a fundamentally dissatisfied population. The government knows how ill it can afford to lose the colonies. For similar reasons it cannot afford to liberalize its control of them: the colonies contribute to the metropolitan economy only because labour is exploited and resources are not ploughed back into local development; the colonies ease the discontent of the Portuguese population only because immigration offers to the poor and uneducated a position of special privilege. Not least, since the fascist government has eliminated democracy within Portugal itself, it can scarcely allow a greater measure of freedom to the supposedly more backward people of its colonies.

Despite all this, attempts were made to use persuasion, encouraged by the acceptance elsewhere of the principle of self-determination. But such efforts were never rewarded with any kind of 'dialogue'. The only reaction to them was prison, censorship, and the strengthening of the PIDE, the secret police. The character of the PIDE is itself an important factor. For it has a strong tradition of violence – its officers were trained by the Gestapo – and it enjoys a considerable measure of autonomy, allowing it

322

to act outside the control of the official law.

This is why political activity in Mozambique has called for the techniques of the 'underground', for secrecy and exile . . .

. . . . . .

The army also has a major part to play in the mobilization and educational campaigns. Militants learn more than just military science. As far as possible they are taught Portuguese and basic literacy, with those who have already had a little education frequently teaching their comrades. Political education is a very important part of their training, and in the course of it they acquire some experience of speaking in public and of working on committees, while also learning the rudiments of political argument and the historical and geographical background of the struggle. Thus the army itself becomes an important agent in the political mobilization and education of the population.

. . . . . .

The New Mozambique

The purpose of our struggle is not only to destroy. It is first and fore-most aimed at building a new Mozambique, where there will be no hunger and where all men will be free and equal. We are fighting with arms in our hands, because in order to build the Mozambique that we want we must first destroy the Portuguese colonial system . . . only after this will we be able to use for ourselves our labour and the wealth of our country . . .

Message from the Central Committee to the Mozambican people for 25 September 1967, the anniversary of the beginning of the struggle.

One of the chief lessons to be drawn from nearly four years of war in Mozambique is that liberation does not consist merely of driving out the Portuguese authority, but also of constructing a new country; and that this construction must be undertaken even while the colonial state is in the process of being destroyed. We realized this in principle before we began fighting, but it is only in the development of the struggle that we have learned quite how rapid and comprehensive civil reconstruction must be. There is no question of making a few provisional arrangements and waiting until we control our whole country before deciding how to govern it. We are having now to evolve structures and make decisions which will set the pattern for the future national government.

One of the first results of the war is the elimination of the colonial state where its repressive forces have disappeared . . .

On the ruins of the colonial state a new type of power is emerging which corresponds to the forces which have brought about the revolution. Before the war two authorities coexisted: the colonial, and that of the traditional

323

chiefdoms subordinated and integrated into the colonial system but retaining nevertheless a certain autonomy. When the colonial power is destroyed by a guerrilla victory in a given area, this leaves an administrative void. The power of tribal chiefs, however, has its origins in the traditional life of the country, and in the past was based on a popular conception of legitimacy, not on force. For the future, this therefore poses potential problems of tribalism and regionalism. In its precolonial form, such traditional government often served its purpose quite well within a limited area, providing an adequate form of organization in the interests of the majority; but even in such cases, limited in its scope and based on a small local unit, it cannot form a satisfactory foundation for the needs of a modern state. In other areas, such power already had an element of feudalism, permitting an exploitation of the peasantry which, masked by metaphysical and religious claims, was accepted. The survival of such systems is obviously a hindrance to the progress of a revolution that aims at social and political equality. The effect of colonialism, moreover, was to pervert all traditional power structures, encouraging or creating authoritarian and elitist elements.

In its session of October 1966, the Central Committee of FRELIMO re-examined the problems of tribalism and regionalism, and vigorously condemned the 'tribalist or regional tendencies shown by certain comrades in the execution of their work, reaffirming solemnly that such attitudes are contrary to the interests of the Mozambican people and impede the successful development of the people's liberation struggle. It emphasizes that the battle against tribalism and regionalism is as important as the battle against colonialism, such a battle being the safeguard of our national unity and our liberty' . . .

Certainly, where the traditional power does not actively uphold the colonial structure or oppose the revolution, the change has to come through positive developments, the emergence of new forms of power, of new political ideas. The main weapon in this struggle is general and political education, achieved through practical experience as well as in meetings, discussions and lessons.

Here again the solution must lie in education and practical organization.

In the liberated areas, the political structure is the party. In the villages, people's militias are created which are dependent on the local party organization and on the military leadership of the zone; their power rests on the nationalist and revolutionary forces. Besides this, economic life is organized so that the producers work in cooperatives under the direction of the local party; this takes away from the chief his traditional role as organizer of the economic life and at the same time puts an end to the exploitation of the peasantry by any privileged group. It should also be stressed that this process is not a 'dictatorship of the party': the party is an open organization, and its members are drawn from the whole population, with the majority being, as is the majority of the population, peasants; its role is to provide a political framework above the local level. There is no deep distinction between party and population: the party is the population engaged in political action.

Public meetings, held through the local party, are an important part of life in the liberated areas. At these, non-party members can hear more about FRELIMO and about the struggle, can voice their opinions, ask questions and enter into discussion. The work of political education, the example and explanations given by the 'responsible' members and the political commissars, and the fact that the struggle is led by elements of the working masses, all go to create conditions for the disappearance of traditional tribal and often semi-feudal power and for its replacement by new forms of power. At the present time the administrative life of villages is being reorganized on the basis of people's committees elected by the whole population, and the way is being prepared for the extension of this system to the district level . . .

Political structure
The emerging political structure follows the characteristic pattern of one party democracy; and FRELIMO, as well as being the driving force behind the liberation struggle, is becoming the government in the liberated areas. The essential structure of the party was formulated in 1962, at the first Congress; but since at that time there was no liberated territory and no possibility of legal political activity in Mozambique, the original pattern was orientated towards underground organization. This structure has subsequently developed to fulfil effectively the function of a legal government in the areas which have come under our control.

The Congress is the supreme organ of FRELIMO and is formed of elected representatives of the people . . . The Congress elected a Central Committee of twenty members and delegated to this committee the total responsibility for directing the liberation struggle. The Central Committee, therefore, combined legislative, judicial and executive powers – a situation which began to create problems as the party grew into the large and complex organization it is now.

One of the first tasks of the Central Committee was to establish a political structure inside Mozambique. Until 1964, all activity had to be clandestine, which meant that still only a small minority of the population, the most politically advanced, could be involved. Once some areas were liberated, however, the party could come into the open there as a public legal body, with membership open to every adult Mozambican. Here, the

325

party provides a coherent structure for mass representation.

The smallest party unit is the cell, which consists of all the members in a particular locality. At the next level is the district council, which consists of representatives elected by the members of all the cells in the district. The district council then elects representatives to the provincial council, and the provincial councils in their turn elect the delegates to the Congress. At each level, decisions are reached through discussion, and if there are irresolvable differences of opinion, the issue is decided by a vote, with the minority held to the majority decision.

As well as contributing to national policy, the local organs of the party have responsibility for local government. The exact structure of this varies from region to region, as existing para-political structures, traditional and modern, have been incorporated in the structure of the liberation movement. In areas where cooperatives have been established, the cooperative committees take over several functions of a local government body, and this system, which is spreading rapidly, is likely to become an important factor in local government of the future. Meanwhile, a variety of systems coexist, each one geared to the specific conditions prevalent in the particular locality.

At the level of the Central Committee, the work of the party both as a liberation force and as a provisional government, was organized into a number of departments . . .

Economic organization
Production is of extreme and immediate importance, since it is necessary for the survival of the population, of the army and of any civilian services. In this context, food is obviously the first need.

With the overthrow of the colonial system, the companies which had imposed the production of cash crops either through plantations or the system of forced cultivation, withdrew. The people were free to organize agriculture as they wished and to concentrate on their own needs. As a result, after the war liberated a region, there was a return to the production of such basic food crops as maize, cassava, millet, beans, and groundnuts. But the war imposed additional demands on food producers. Although the military grow their own food wherever possible, there are inevitably large sections of the army which cannot be self-sufficient; also, to avoid reprisals from the Portuguese, it has been necessary in many areas to evacuate peasants and install them in new villages, where they need to be supplied with food until the first harvest from their new fields; in some areas a part of the crops is regularly destroyed by Portuguese action. Merely to satisfy food requirements over the liberated areas, therefore, it is necessary to produce a surplus.

The people are constantly encouraged to clear more land for cultivation and to grow more food, and this campaign has been so successful that, despite the hazards and upheavals of the war, more land is actually under cultivation today than there was during the colonial administration. Even after the first year of war, more food was being produced than before. Now in some areas, as at Ngazela, 80 per cent of the land cultivated had not previously been productive.

The greatest impetus to production has clearly come from the abolition of the companies, and from the fact that the people now themselves profit from their work. Two other factors are also important. One is the work of the party in advising, encouraging, and explaining the needs of the struggle, and in providing essential pieces of equipment like hoes and pangas. The other, linked with this, is the development of new methods of organization, principally the cooperative. In areas where there had been a cooperative movement before the struggle, the organization reappeared rapidly and spontaneously after the colonial forces had been expelled. In other areas, the idea has been introduced, and party members have had to help the people get them started. Instruction in book-keeping has been a particularly important aspect. Between the liberated areas, there are considerably differences in the stage of development that the cooperative system has reached. In some, all production may be organized collectively; in others, the people work shambas individually, to supply their own family needs, but the village as a whole works other shambas cooperatively, to produce a surplus for the army or other groups unable to produce. In some areas the people have not formed cooperatives at all, mainly because they lack the necessary knowledge of how to organize them and keep the accounts, and in such cases a surplus is produced by a system whereby many of the villagers individually cultivate an extra shamba to produce food for collective needs.

. . . . . .

Education

When FRELIMO was first formed, we gave top priority jointly to two programmes: the military and the educational. We have always attached such great importance to education because, in the first place, it is essential for the development of our struggle, since the involvement and support of the population increase as their understanding of the situation grows; in the second place, a future independent Mozambique will be in very grave need of educated citizens to lead the way in development.

The Portuguese system of education has been hopelessly inadequate, not only because it has involved so very few Africans, but also because the instruction given to those few was so unsuited to the needs of

327

Mozambique. We have had to start working from scratch, not only in providing the structure but in working out the content.

Schooling in most African countries uses a system designed to meet the needs of late nineteenth-century Europe. It is now recognized even in Europe that this system is out of date and that much of it is irrelevant. In Africa, it never did and certainly does not now answer the real needs of the population. All colonial education was designed essentially to produce a small Europeanized elite who would either serve or take over from the colonial government, to preserve its values. Every effort was made to cut these people off from their origins, partly because most Europeans despised every aspect of African culture and partly because the elite would thus present less of a threat to European government. The colonial regimes completely ignored existing indigenous methods of education and acted as if there had been no education at all before the Europeans opened schools . . .

. . . . . .

A new factor is involved: the development of the independent national state. For neither the traditional nor the colonial system of education is designed to fit the needs of this new entity. A new departure is required. But a departure must begin somewhere. We can learn from other cultures, including the European, but we cannot graft them directly to our own. It is for this reason that a certain understanding of our own cultures and our own past is essential. Much of our traditional education is obsolete; but some aspects – the art and some of the moral values, for instance – can help form a basis for the new society we are trying to build. As Jahn put it: 'Only where man feels himself to be heir and successor to the past has he the strength for a new beginning'.

The immediate context within which we are working is that of the national liberation struggle and the accompanying social revolution. It is this which must mould the new aspects of the educational service we are developing. As society is changing with the struggle, so we must be prepared for education to change. In the short run, though, there are urgent practical purposes which must be served: we need educated cadres at all levels and in all disciplines: we need to raise the abysmally low educational level of the general population, to fight illiteracy and ignorance. We must start working on this now with what we have available, and develop our theory and system as we work . . .

. . . . . .

The Second Congress of FRELIMO (1968)

Resolutions on the armed struggle

1. The Portuguese government is a colonialist, fascist government that still

maintains the myth that Mozambique is a Portuguese Province, and, consequently, 'part and parcel of Portugal'. It still does not recognize the right of the Mozambique people to their national independence.

Nationalist demonstrations are violently repressed with massacres, jailings, tortures, assassinations.

Under these conditions, and in order to face all forms of colonialist oppression and repression, the Mozambican people have decided to follow resolutely the way of armed struggle, by fighting a decisive war of independence or death.

. . . . . .

3. Our struggle is a people's struggle. It requires the total participation of all the masses of the people. For this reason it is necessary to intensify the mobilization and the organization of the masses in the liberated zones, as well as in the regions where the armed struggle has not yet started.

The direct participation of all in the armed struggle is, therefore, one of the main objectives of the people's mobilization effort.

In the present phase of our struggle, our main armed forces are made up of the regular guerrilla forces, but the people's militias do also play a very important role. People's militias are part and parcel of the population. They are supplementary to the guerrilla forces and they are fixed in the territory in which they work. All the people – old, young, women and men – who are not part of the guerrillas, must be part of the militias.

People's militias should at the same time satisfy the needs of production, vigilance and defence. In the liberated and semi-liberated zones, people's militias do in particular the following work:

(1) transport of material and the sick;
(2) reconnaissance and patrol of the zones in which they work against the infiltration of enemy troops and agents;
(3) fighting, when the enemy invades the region.
    People's militias do take part in heavy fighting, when that is called for.

The organization of people's militias is an important form of integrating the masses into the armed struggle. In this way, at every place, sufficient and militarily prepared forces are created. People's militias are therefore reserve forces.

4. In order to realize more completely and efficiently the participation of the Mozambican women in the struggle, a women's detachment has been created whose main functions are:

(1) mobilization and organization of the masses;
(2) recruitment of young people of both sexes to be integrated into the armed struggle;

(3) production;

(4) transport of material;

(5) military protection for the populations.

......

7. Our war is essentially a political war, and its direction is defined by the party. The people's army is part and parcel of the party, and its strategic plans are made by the top leadership of the party.

In order to conduct correctly the struggle, all the leaders should be involved in the armed struggle. Only in this way, following the struggle step by step, the leaders can be able to solve all the complex problems arising daily. The people's army performs its task in accordance with the policy defined by FRELIMO.

......

Resolutions on national reconstruction

1. The Second Congress notes that the building of a new life in the liberated zones is a requirement of the struggle for national liberation. The liberated zones shall constitute the material basis for growth of our revolutionary armed struggle for national liberation. In that sense, the growth of production assumes special importance.

It is necessary for us to produce progressively the material goods we need for the growth of our armed struggle. We should promote the development of agriculture, industry, cottage industries, always directing our activities towards the meeting of the interests of our people's revolution.

......

On production and commerce

   (1) Agricultural production shall be developed, such that we may get all we need for food as well as the raw materials for production of soap, fabrics, etc.

   (2) Technical and scientific level of production shall be promoted.

   (3) Defence of agricultural fields shall be more and more consolidated.

   (4) Organization of agricultural, commercial, and industrial cooperatives shall be developed.

On education

   (1) Development of primary schools shall be accelerated.

   (2) Teacher training programme for primary schools shall be developed in order to raise rapidly its numbers and its technical level.

   (3) Intensive literacy campaigns among the masses of the people, men,

woman, old and young people shall be promoted.

(4) Special courses for raising rapidly the level of knowledge of the militants shall be organized.

(5) Young Mozambican women shall be encouraged to complete at least primary school education.

(6) Production centres shall be created at every school place for self-maintenance.

(7) A system shall be established which shall make it possible for the students to interrupt temporarily their studies in order to participate in teaching and literacy campaigns.

(8) It shall be the duty of all Mozambican students to take part, whenever it may be deemed necessary, in the various tasks of the struggle for national liberation.

(9) Development of schools of political training shall be promoted.

D. NEO-COLONIALISM

18: Mamadou Dia

Extracts from M. Dia, *The African Nations and World Solidarity* (Praeger, 1961).

Many speak eloquently of African unity. Many vehemently denounce the divisions instituted by colonial authorities. But no serious, disinterested attempt is made to correct the mistake, to effect realignments inspired by a sincere desire for unity. Instead of horizontal co-operation, many prefer – by opportunism or for reasons of personal propaganda – vertical alliances established in a spirit that aggravates the old divisions by introducing the Cold War among our countries. Beyond the common exaltation, general dissatisfaction, and revolt, we should like to see an effort made to co-ordinate our economies, to synchronize the objectives of economic planning in the various countries – at least in those located in the same economic area, in the same zone of development. We claim to be free of the West, while by the fault of the leaders of African or Asian states, Western ideologies are drawing the economic map of the liberated countries, determining the general orientation of the economic structure, allocating the markets, and establishing trade policy. Never has the presence of the West been exerted so dangerously on countries so violently jealous of their sovereignty. Never has its ascendency been so decisively effective as in this postcolonial period . . .

... the most urgent task for overseas nationalisms is to put an end to foreign occupation, to political domination. The revolution will have as its number one objective the breaking of the political power responsible for economic, social, and cultural dependence, the upsetting of the idols of colonialism – by negotiation if possible, by violence if need be. Its goal will be to confer the nobility of freedom regained, even if it does not bring prosperity, even if this change of moral condition is not accompanied by a transformation of our material condition ...

Since colonial power imposed the domination of foreign capitalism everywhere, there is naturally, in the mind of proletarian nations, complete identification between capitalism and colonialism, between the political system and the economic system ... Thus it is understandable that in rejecting colonialism, the most conscious leaders of the most organized countries reject, at the same time, the capitalist system. One can understand why they prefer the socialist system and look toward socialist experiments. Unfortunately, the question is not so simple, for it seems that colonialism is able to survive any system ...

It would be a fatal error for the nations of the *Tiers-Monde,* especially those just recovering their freedom, to think that the struggle ends with the proclamation of independence ... One cannot warn too strongly against the illusions of nominal independence that would encourage a kind of internal immobility in so far as the old structures are concerned, and a close dependence on relations with the industrialized world.

......

To start the process of development in economies of retarded growth like ours, the first objective must be to suppress structural obstacles that hamper development. Thus one will understand the importance that we attach to the reform of Mali's economic structures inherited from colonial capitalism. It will be vain to hope for a profound change toward a progressive economy – guaranteeing the minimal conditions of life to the nation, creating conditions for a market on a scale to meet our needs – without a bold restructuration incompatible with an exaggerated desire to spare the former capitalist structures. But the inner dynamism, the creative capacity, will not suffice to spark the process of development. We will need investments, poles of development, networks of trade – all of which are items that force us out of our isolation – to proceed to relations with more developed economies. However, we must be careful lest these relations reinforce dependence ...

At the same time, we shall strengthen our ties with the economies of neighbouring sister countries, which – by the market, the network of trade, and the zones and points of development that they offer – are factors of progress not to be neglected ... We shall be realistic enough not to require the abolition of the idea of profit or to dream of an economy founded on the unselfishness of nations. But we shall take care to replace the selfishness of rich nations that have a one-sided conception of development with a truly co-operative spirit that will make development a two-way street on which – in accordance with a law of reciprocity – the related economies, the less developed as well as the more developed, can evolve a perpetual dialogue.

The concept of mutual development . . . provides the solution that will reconcile the conflicting interests of East and West, capitalist and communist, and ward off the structural dangers of imperialism they threaten. This concept will also lessen the threat of violent opposition between rich nations and poor nations. It is necessary to describe its mechanism, its method of application, and its spirit to appreciate its full scope in a world confused by the ineffectiveness of systems that strive so bitterly for hegemony. A group of nations – unequally developed technically and culturally, aware of the unreality of development in the narrow framework of projects territorially limited, with means strictly circumscribed by domestic possibilities – decides rationally and deliberately, by common accord, to undertake a collective experiment of open co-operation. It will be noted at once that the basis of the enterprise is both the mutual consent of the partners freely given, and the determination to pursue the common experiment over a period necessary for its fruition.

The elder, or pilot, nation – France in this instance – places at the disposal of the sister nations seeking development its knowledge, its production and organizational techniques (capital being only one and not the essential one of these), its poles, centers, and axes of development. This participation in the attempted collective experiment involves certain basic requirements for the elder nation. It will not be enough to define its position negatively by proclaiming the abolition of former relationships and a break with all imperialisms. It must positively resolve to contribute to the elaboration of new relationships.

19: Kwame Nkrumah

Extracts from K. Nkrumah, *Handbook of Revolutionary Warfare* (Panaf, 1968). This book was written while Nkrumah was in exile in Guinea, soon after his deposition as President of Ghana by a military *coup* in February 1966.

A number of external factors affect the African situation, and if our liberation struggle is to be placed in correct perspective and we are to KNOW THE ENEMY, the impact of these factors must be fully grasped. First among them is imperialism, for it is mainly against exploitation and poverty that our peoples revolt. It is therefore of paramount importance to set out the strategy of imperialism in clear terms:

1. The means used by the enemy to ensure the continued economic exploitation of our territories.

2. The nature of the attempts made to destroy the liberation movement.

Once the components of the enemy's strategy are determined, we will be in a position to outline the correct strategy for our own struggle in terms of our actual situation and in accordance with our objectives.

Before the Second World War, the world (excluding the USSR, China, etc.) was divided into:

(a) Capitalist states practising orthodox imperialism under the generally known form of imperialism.

(b) Colonial territories which fed the economies of the capitalist imperialist states . . .

However, after the Second World War, serious economic, social and political tensions arose in both spheres.

(a) Inside the capitalist-imperialist states, workers' organizations had become comparatively strong and experienced, and the claims of the working class for a more substantial share of the wealth produced by the capitalist economy could no longer be ignored . . .

(b) While the capitalist system of exploitation was coming to grips with its internal crises, the world's colonised areas were astir with the upsurge of strong liberation movements . . .

Both in the colonial territories and in the metropolitan states, the struggle was being waged against the same enemy: international finance capital under its external and internal forms of exploitation, imperialism and capitalism.

Threatened with disintegration by the double-fisted attack of the working class movement and the liberation movement, capitalism had to launch a series of reforms in order to build a protective armour around the inner workings of its system.

. . . . . .

By way of a solution, capitalism proceeded to introduce not only internal reforms, but external reforms designed to raise the extra money needed for the establishment and maintenance of the welfare state at home. In other words, modern capitalism had come to depend more heavily than before on the exploitation of the material and human resources of the colonial territories. On the external front, therefore, it became necessary for international finance capital to carry out reforms in order to eliminate the deadly threat to its supremacy of the liberation movement.

. . . . . .

The modifications introduced by imperialism in its strategy were expressed:

    (a) through the disappearance of the numerous old-fashioned "colonies" owing exclusive allegiance to a single metropolitan country.

    (b) through the replacement of "national" imperialisms by a "collective" imperialism in which the USA occupies a leading position.

. . . . . .

But as far as the imperialists are concerned the real solution to the problem of continued exploitation through concessions and reform lies in the concept of "sham-independence". *A state can be said to be a neo-colonialist or client state if it is independent de jure and dependent de facto. It is a state where political power lies in the conservative forces of the former colony and where economic power remains under the control of international finance capital.*

. . . . . .

    The pre-requisite of a correct and global strategy to defeat neo-colonialism is the ability to discover and expose the way in which a state becomes neo-colonialist. For although a neo-colonialist state enjoys only sham independence it is to all outward appearances independent, and therefore the very roots of neo-colonialism must be traced back to the struggle for independence in a colonial territory.

    If the liberation movement is firmly established, the colonial power invariably resorts to a "containment" policy in order to stop any further progress, and to deaden its impact. To achieve this objective, the colonial power uses its arsenal of alliances, its network of military bases, economic devices such as corruption, sabotage and blackmail, and equally insidious, the psychological weapon of propaganda with a view to impressing on the masses a number of imperialist dogmas:

    1. That western democracy and the parliamentary system are the only valid ways of governing; that they constitute the only worthwhile model for the training of an indigenous elite by the colonial power.

    2. That capitalism, free enterprise, free competition, etc., are the only economic systems capable of promoting development; that the western powers have mastered the liberal-capitalist technique per-

335

fectly; that the colonial territory should become an economic satellite in its own interest; that there is no reason to put an end to the policy of "co-operation" pursued during the colonial regime; and that any attempt to break away would be dangerous, since the colonial power is always ready to give "aid".

3. That the slightest "lapse" on the part of the leaders of the liberation movement could push the country into the grip of "communism" and of "totalitarian dictatorship".

4. That the carve-up agreed upon by the imperialists during the colonial period is fair and sacred; that it would be unthinkable even to attempt to liberate areas in terms of their common cultural and historical links; that the only acceptable version of "liberation" must apply to the artificial units designed by the imperialists, and hurriedly labelled "nations" in spite of the fact that they are neither culturally unified, nor economically self-sufficient.

As a further justification of its policy, *imperialism usually resorts to all types of propaganda in order to highlight and exploit differences of religion, culture, race, outlook, and of political ideology among the oppressed masses, or between regions which share a long history of mutual commercial and cultural exchange.*

Such methods aim to orientate the leaders of the liberation movements towards a brand of nationalism based on petty-minded and aggressive chauvinism, as well as to steer the liberation movement along a reformist path. The problem of liberation is therefore usually raised in terms of a participation of "good" indigenous elements in the administration of the colonised territory, for instance through a policy of "africanisation" devoid of any fundamental changes in the political, economic and administrative structure of the territory.

The transition to neo-colonialism is marked by a succession of more or less important measures which culminate into a ritual of so-called free elections, mostly organised through methods of intimidation. Local agents, selected by the colonial power as "worthy representatives" are then presented to the people as the champions of national independence, and are immediately given all the superficial attributes of power: a puppet government has been formed.

By the very nature of its essential objective, which is exploitation, neo-colonialism can only flourish in a client state.

. . . . . .

However, *the machinations of the colonial power will fail wherever the leaders of the struggle for independence maintain a clear spirit of vigilance, and cultivate genuinely revolutionary qualities.*

336

Then, and only then, does a truly independent government emerge, dedicated to national reconstruction in the liberated territory, and determined to assist all those engaged in the imperialist struggle.

Such a government is an obstacle barring the advance of neo-colonialism, and such obstacles must be increased because the example of genuine independence is contagious and will help to fortify extensive zones against imperialist aggression.

Faced with genuine independence, imperialism is increasingly compelled to resort to encirclement and subversion in order to overthrow these popular governments, using such weapons as *coups d'etat,* assassination, mutiny within the party, tribal revolt, palace revolutions, and so on, while at the same time strengthening neighbouring puppet regimes to form a political safety belt, a *cordon sanitaire.*

Therefore, the main sphere in which we must strive to defeat neo-colonialist intrigues is within the movement for true independence; that is, within the progressive political party which forms the government. This is particularly true in the one party state which can only function successfully under socialism. Usually, this ruling party is made up of several groups each with its distinct economic and political interests. The relative importance of each group in the party and state machinery will determine the course of development. Imperialist strategy is therefore directed towards bringing into a position of pre-eminence that group which most nearly shares its economic and political views.

. . . . . .

Our objectives are defined by the three political components of our liberation movement:

1. Nationalism
2. Panafricanism
3. Socialism

The three objectives of our struggle stem from our position as peoples in revolt against exploitation in Africa. These objectives are closely inter-related and one cannot be achieved fully without the other. If one of the three components is missing, no territory on our continent can secure genuine freedom or maintain a stable government.

Nationalism
Nationalism is the ideological channel of the anti-colonialist struggle and represents the demand for national independence of colonised peoples. It is a concept most easily grasped by the population of territories where the low level of development of productive forces (and therefore of capitalist implantation), and the absence of indigenous elements in the spheres of political power, are factors that facilitate the formation of a united

337

militant front, one of the primary conditions for a successful liberation movement.

Colonised peoples are not highly differentiated from a social point of view, and are exploited practically without discrimination by the colonial power. Hence the slogan: "the nation must be freed from colonialism" is a universally accepted rallying cry whose influence is heightened by the fact that the agents of colonialism, exploiting the territory from within, are there for everybody to see. It is therefore the people as a whole who revolt and struggle as a "nation-class" against colonial oppression, and who win independence.

The nationalist phase is a necessary step in the liberation struggle, but must never be regarded as the final solution to the problem raised by the economic and political exploitation of our peoples. For nationalism is narrow in its application. It works within the geopolitical framework produced by the colonial powers which culminated in the carve-up agreed upon in 1884 at the Berlin Conference, where today's political maps of Africa were drawn.

. . . . . .

The African "nations" of today, created artificially by foreigners for their own purposes, neither originate from ancient African civilisation, nor do they fit in with our African way of life or habits of exchange. They are not even, for the most part, economically viable. Yet they continue to struggle on, each one separately, in a pathetic and hopeless attempt to make progress, while the real obstacle to their development, imperialism, mainly in its neo-colonialist stage, is operating on a panafrican scale . . .

. . . . . .

It is time that we also planned our economic and political development on a continental scale. The concept of African unity embraces the fundamental needs and characteristics of African civilisation and ideology, and at the same time satisfies all the conditions necessary for an accelerated economic and technological advance. Such maximum development would ensure a rational utilisation of the material resources and human potential of our continent along the lines of an integrated economy, and within complementary sectors of production, eliminating all unnecessary forms of competition, economic alienation and duplication. The idea is not to destroy or dismantle the network of foreign mining complexes and industrial companies throughout Africa, but to take them over and operate them in the sole interest of the African peoples.

. . . . . .

Panafricanism
The limitations of nationalism have already been acknowledged by the

338

most mature leaders of the liberation movement; but wherever the conditions for the transition to a higher ideological level and a wider form of struggle were lacking, the necessary leap could not be made, and nationalism was never transcended.

. . . . . .

African unity therefore implies
1. *That imperialism and foreign oppression should be eradicated in all their forms.*
2. *That neo-colonialism should be recognised and eliminated.*
3. *That the new African nation must develop within a continental framework.*

However, the specific content of the new social order within the developoing African nation remains to be defined.

Socialism
At the core of the concept of African unity lies socialism and the socialist definition of the new African society.
Socialism and African unity are organically complementary.

Socialism implies:

1. Common ownership of the means of production, distribution and exchange. Production is for use and not for profit.
2. Planned methods of production by the state, based on modern industry and agriculture.
3. Political power in the hands of the people, with the entire body of workers possessing the necessary governmental machinery through which to express their needs and aspirations. It is a concept in keeping with the humanist and egalitarian spirit which characterised traditional African society, though it must be applied in a modern context. All are workers; and no person exploits another.
4. Application of scientific methods in all spheres of thought and production.

. . . . . .

Socialism has become a necessity in the platform diction of African political leaders, though not all pursue really socialist policies. We must therefore be on our guard against measures which are declared to be "socialist" but which do not in fact promote economic and social

339

development. An example of muddled thinking about socialism is the attempt made in recent years to suggest the existence of an "African Socialism" peculiar to our continent.

There is only one true socialism and that is scientific socialism, the principles of which are abiding and universal. The only way to achieve it is to devise policies aimed at general socialist goals, which take their form from the concrete, specific circumstances and conditions of a particular country at a definite historical period.

The socialist countries of Africa may differ in the details of their policies. There are different paths to socialism, and adjustments have to be made to suit particular circumstances. But they should not be arbitrarily decided, or subject to vagaries of taste. They must be scientifically explained.

Only under socialism can we reliably accumulate the capital we need for our development, ensure that the gains of investment are applied to the general welfare, and achieve our goal of a free and united continent.

20: Frantz Fanon

Extracts from F. Fanon, *Toward the African Revolution*, translated by H. Chevalier (Pelican, 1970). First published in Paris as *Pour la Révolution Africaine* (Maspero, 1964). Reprinted by permission of the Monthly Review Press. These extracts are from an article written in July 1958 for the Algerian nationalist publication, *El Moudjahid*.

The twentieth century, when the future looks back on it, will not only be remembered as the era of atomic discoveries and interplanetary explorations. The second upheaval of this period, unquestionably, is the conquest by the peoples of the lands that belong to them.

Jostled by the claims for national independence by immense regions, the colonialists have had to loosen their stranglehold. Nevertheless, this phenomenon of liberation, of triumph of national independence, of retreat of colonialism, does not manifest itself in a unique manner. Every former colony has a particular way of achieving independence. Every new sovereign state finds itself practically under the obligation of maintaining definite and preferential relations with the former oppressor.

The parties that lead the struggle against colonialist oppression, at a certain phase of the combat, decide for practical reasons to accept a fragment of independence with the firm intention of arousing the people again within the framework of the fundamental strategy of the total evacuation of the territory and of the effective seizure of all national resources. This style, which has taken form on a succession of occasions, is today well known. On the other hand, there is a whole opposite dialectic which, it seems, has not received sufficient attention.

A FIRST CONDITION: 'THE RIGHTS' OF THE FORMER OCCUPANT

Some decades ago, the colonialist rulers could indefinitely propound the highly civilising intentions of their countries. The concessions, the expropriations, the exploitation of the workers, the great wretchedness of the peoples, were traditionally conjured away and denied. Afterwards, when the time came to withdraw from the territory, the colonialists were forced to discard their masks. In the negotiations on independence, the first matters at issue were the economic interests: banks, monetary areas, research permits, commercial concessions, inviolability of properties stolen from the peasants at the time of the conquest, etc. .... Of civilising, religious, or cultural works, there was no longer any question. The time had come for serious things, and trivialities had to be left behind. Such attitudes were to open the eyes of men struggling in other regions of the world.

The actual rights of the occupant were then perfectly identified. The minority that came from the mother country, the university missions, technical assistance, the friendship affirmed and reaffirmed, were all relegated to a secondary level. The important thing was obviously the real rights that the occupant meant to wrench from the people, as the price for a piece of independence.

The acceptance of a nominal sovereignty and the absolute refusal of real independence – such is the typical reaction of colonialist nations with respect to their former colonies. Neo-colonialism is impregnated with a few ideas which both constitute its force and at the same time prepare its necessary decline.

In the course of the struggle for liberation, things are not clear in the consciousness of the fighting people. Since it is a refusal, at one and the same time, of political nonexistence, of wretchedness, of illiteracy, of the inferiority complex so subtly instilled by oppression, its battle is for a long time undifferentiated. Neo-colonialism takes advantage of this indetermination. Armed with a revolutionary and spectacular good-will, it grants the former colony everything. But in so doing, it wrings from it an economic dependence which becomes an aid and assistance programme.

We have seen that this operation usually triumphs. The novelty of this phase is that it is necessarily brief. This is because it takes the people little time to realize that nothing fundamental has changed. Once the hours of effusion and enthusiasm before the spectacle of the national flag floating in the wind are past, the people rediscovers the first dimension of its requirement: bread, clothing, shelter.

Neo-colonialism, because it proposes to do justice to human dignity in general, addresses itself essentially to the middle class and to the intellectuals of the colonial country.

Today, the people no longer feel their bellies at peace when the colonial country has recognized the values of its elites. The people want things really to change right away. Thus it is that the struggle resumes with renewed violence.

In this second phase, the occupant bristles and unleashes all his forces. What was wrested by bombardments is reconverted into results of free negotiations. The former occupant intervenes, in the name of duty, and once again establishes his war in an independent country.

All the former colonies, from Indonesia to Egypt, without forgetting Panama, which have tried to denounce the agreements wrung from them by force, have found themselves obliged to undergo a new war and sometimes to see their sovereignty again violated and amputated.

The notorious 'rights' of the occupant, the false appeal to a common past, the persistence of a rejuvenated colonial pact, are the permanent bases of an attack directed against national sovereignty.

A SECOND OBSTACLE: THE ZONES OF INFLUENCE

The concern to maintain the former colony in the yoke of economic oppression is obviously not sadism. It is not out of wickedness or ill-will that such an attitude is adopted. It is because the handling of their national riches by the colonized peoples compromises the economic equilibrium of the former occupant. The reconversion of the colonial economy, the industries engaged in processing raw materials from the under-developed territories, the disappearance of the colonial pact, competition with foreign capital, constitute a mortal danger for imperialism.

For countries like Great Britain and France there arises the important question of zones of influence. Unanimous in their decision to stifle the national aspirations of the colonial peoples, these countries wage a gigantic struggle for the seizure of world markets. The economic battles between France, England, and the United States, in the Middle East, in the Far East, and now in Africa, give the measure of imperialist voracity and bestiality. And it is not an exaggeration to say that these battles are the direct cause of the strategies which, still today, shake the newly independent states. In exceptional circumstances, the zones of influence of the pound sterling, of the dollar, and of the franc, are converted and

342

become by a conjurer's trick, the Western world. Today in the Lebanon and in Iraq, if we are to believe M. Malraux, it is *homo occidentalis* who is threatened.

The oil of Iraq has removed all prohibitions and made concrete the true problems. We have only to remember the violent interventions in the West Indian archipelago or in Latin America every time the dictatorships supported by American policy were in danger. The Marines who today are being landed in Beirut are the brothers of those who, periodically, are sent to re-establish 'order' in Haiti, in Costa Rica, in Panama. The United States considers that the two Americas constitute a world governed by the Monroe Doctrine whose application is entrusted to the American forces. The single article of this doctrine stipulates that America belongs to the Americans, in other words the State Department.

Its outlets having proved insufficient, it was inevitable that America would turn to other regions, namely the Far East, the Middle East, and Africa. There ensued a competition between beasts of prey; its creations are: the Eisenhower doctrine against England in the Middle East; support for Ngo Dinh Diem against France in Indochina; Economic Aid Commission in Africa announced by the presidential voyage of Mr. Nixon, against France, England, and Belgium.

Every struggle for national liberation must take zones of influence into account.

. . . . . .

THE PRESTIGE OF THE WEST

And we here touch upon a psychological problem which is perhaps not fundamental but which enters into the framework of the dialectic that is now developing. The West, whose economic system is the standard (and by virtue of that fact oppressive), also prides itself on its humanist superiority. The Western 'model' is being attacked in its essence and in its finality. The Orientals, the Arabs, and the Negroes, today, want to present their plans, want to affirm their values, want to define their relations with the world ... It is no longer true that the promotion of values passes through the screen of the West. It is not true that we must constantly trail behind, follow, depend on someone or other. All the colonial countries that are waging the struggle today must know that the political independence that they will wring from the enemy in exchange for the maintenance of an economic dependency is only a snare and a delusion, that the second phase of total liberation is necessary because required by the popular masses, that this second phase, because it is a capital one, is bound to be hard and waged with iron determination, that, finally, at that stage, it will be necessary to take the world strategy of coalition into

343

account, for the West simultaneously faces a double problem: the communist danger and the coming into being of a third neutral coalition, represented essentially by the underdeveloped countries.

The future of every man today has a relation of close dependency on the rest of the universe. That is why the colonial peoples must redouble their vigilance and their vigour. A new humanism can be achieved only at this price. The wolves must no longer find isolated lambs to prey upon. Imperialism must be blocked in all its attempts to strengthen itself. The peoples demand this; the historic process requires it.

Part V
Political Attitudes
of the Military

Successful and unsuccessful attempts at military *coups* have occurred in a number of independent African states in the past decade. The extracts in this chapter do not by any means relate to all of them, but they illustrate the explicit attitudes of some of the men involved. And these attitudes may be significant, because although military regimes often talk of their intervention as a temporary phenomenon, in practice they rarely have politics once they have made their first dramatic entry.

The main justifications for *coups* are almost invariably given by their perpetrators as widespread dissatisfaction with the political and economic policies of the old regime. The usual claim is that democracy has been stifled, corruption and hypocrisy have been rife, and the economy has been mishandled to the detriment of the masses and to the personal advantage of a small elite. Where an unpopular and corrupt elite has become entrenched to the extent that it is immovable by constitutional means, the military has a duty to remove it, and the power to implement this duty. Both Afrifa and Acheampong, involved in separate Ghanaian *coups,* typify this kind of claim.

An additional explanation for the necessity of the *coup* is that the armed forces were poorly paid and equipped under the old regime, and suffered from political interference. These reasons are cited, for example, by the Ugandan Army which overthrew Obote and by the Ghanaian Army which overthrew Nkrumah.

However, other leaders involved in or affected by military régimes do not regard the assumption of power by the military in such altruistic terms. Nkrumah, after he had been deposed in Ghana, regarded *coups* in Africa as the work of neo-colonialist puppets. Similarly, Ojukwu, when leader of Biafra, regarded the civil war in Nigeria not as a tribal conflict but as neo-colonial aggression, arguing that Nigeria was backed by Britain in an attempt to crush the Biafran secession so that Britain would not lose her oil investments in Biafra. Both Nkrumah and Ojukwu were confident that these *coups,* inspired as they were by neo-colonialists, would eventually enlighten the masses about the dangers of neo-colonialism and capitalism, since the masses would find themselves exploited to an even greater degree.

The stated aims of military leaders centre on attempts to correct the ills for which they criticised the regimes they have supplanted. They inevitably face the same problems that beset the outgoing elites; and Mobutu's manifesto for Zaire is a clear illustration that the solutions offered to the problems of development do not differ substantially from civilian policies.

Note: the military ranks of officers responsible for *coups* change rapidly through self promotion; to avoid inaccuracy, military ranks are not indicated in the following extracts.

1: A. A. Afrifa

Extracts from A. A. Afrifa, *The Ghana Coup* (Frank Cass, 1966).
Written while Afrifa was a Minister in Ghana's National Liberation Council, set up after the military *coup* which ousted Nkrumah on 24 February 1966. Afrifa played a major part in the *coup*, and was later (in 1969) instrumental in the return of Dr. K. A. Busia's civilian government, albeit one with limited powers.

A Coup d'état is the last resort in the range of means whereby an unpopular government may be overthrown. But in our case where there were no constitutional means of offering a political opposition to the one-party government the Armed Forces were automatically made to become the official opposition of the government. This may also be true of other one-party states on the continent of Africa. There is ample justification for our moves on the 23rd February, 1966; and when the operation commenced we had no doubts in our minds as to the justness of our cause. This conviction gave us the additional courage to carry the exercise through at all costs and if the worst came to the worst to fight a civil war and stand our ground until the Nkrumah government was overthrown . . .

. . . . . .

Between 1961 and 1966 the old regime of Kwame Nkrumah had instilled fear into every Ghanaian. There were security men and women everywhere, and no one trusted his friend. Fathers did not trust their sons who had been indoctrinated with Young Pioneer ideas, neither did husbands trust their wives. It was a reign of terror. The Preventive Detention Act was used indiscriminately. The army itself was being infiltrated by the Convention People's Party. It was a painful period. Kwame Nkrumah was strong; there were no constitutional means of getting rid of him.

I have always felt it painful to associate myself with a coup to overthrow a constitutional government, however perverted that constitution may be. Oliver Cromwell was a good general, but he did not take his rightful place in the glorious gallery of British generals because he overthrew a constitutional authority by force of arms. It was painful, therefore, to come to the conclusion that the coup was necessary to save our country and our people. We owed allegiance and loyalty to the Government of Ghana by practice of our profession. But we also owed allegiance to the people of Ghana for their protection and to us it was "Dulce et Decorum est pro Patria Mori" . . .

The declaration of Ghana as a Republican State sharply sealed off democracy which the Constitution apparently sought in the country. It soon became evident that the Constitution did not conform to Ghanaian custom, tradition and culture which permitted a chief who did not listen to the advice of his elders to be destooled. By it, therefore, Kwame Nkrumah's aim of completely dominating the whole country was achieved. He was the only man; the whole of Ghana belonged to him and to him alone; no one had the right to advise him against anything he, as an individual, felt strongly about, and considered "right" for the State.

The opposition was completely smashed, smothered, and stifled out of existence. By law, there was to be only one Party and this was to be the Convention People's Party. No really free elections were to be held. Elections in Ghana under the Consitution meant, as the country was soon to learn, that the Head of State nominated all the candidates who were to be returned unopposed. These candidates became representatives of constituencies in which they had never set foot.

No doubt Ghana's Republican Constitution satisfied Nkrumah's wish. It made the Government of Ghana very strong and thus established in our society the fear of one individual in whom all powers were vested. But it was bound to go wrong. The powers of one man against the powers of seven million inhabitants were made so manifest by the Constitution that it needed a most righteous citizen, a true statesman with a level head, to steer the affairs of the State. Any Head of State with the type of Ghana's Republican Constitution, with the best of will or intention, was bound to misuse his powers to the detriment of the country.

This was the plight of Kwame Nkrumah. In interpreting the Constitution, Kwame Nkrumah and his lieutenants, under the guise of ensuring political calm, worked to consolidate their own future. The Head of State, armed with all his powers, dismissed members of the Armed

Forces and the Judiciary, when and how he liked, every time he suspected a threat to his position, or throne. The Constitution not only permanently established Kwame Nkrumah as the President of Ghana for as long as he lived, but also made it legal for him to remove any threat to his position. It became clear that Kwame Nkrumah was seriously working to become Head of a United Africa, and that he was devising numerous plans which he supposed would lead to the easy achievement of this. Ghana's Republican Constitution provided for the surrender of the sovereignty of Ghana – part or whole – to a Union Government of African States . . .

We had no course left to us. We had no voice. The President used his powers indiscriminately, and acted wickedly towards most of his countrymen.

We all lived in constant fear. We had to find a way out. For sixty-six months we tolerated a Constitution purporting to serve the people, but designed to hero-worship an over-ambitious individual and to create a myth around him. This myth was destroyed on the 24th February 1966 . . .

On my arrival at the Accra Airport from the Congo in 1962, I was to lead the men to Tamale, our destination. I paused for a moment and reflected. Should I throw this troop of three hundred men into Flagstaff House and stop the rot from continuing? Should I not by military action stop Kwame Nkrumah from leading this country towards communism? Should the destruction of individual liberty and the imposition of economic hardship not be ended through a quick and decisive military action? I must confess here that I did not at that time really understand communism in detail and all its implications. But I knew that whatever it was, it took away freedom, and denied the very fundamental liberties which it preached it brought to the people. In the quick moment of decision I was prepared to act. But I did not have the courage to do this, for two reasons. My ammunition supply was limited, and my commanding officer was away in the Congo and did not know what I was contemplating. I knew that if the operation failed he might be executed for a plot in which he had no hand. I was only a Captain, but to me this was immaterial. A corporal with the necessary courage and belief and love for his country can topple corrupt leaders and lead a coup in a just cause. I always feel bitter, every time it occurs to me, that with the vastness of the problems facing Ghana, a military coup was the only course open to rescue our people from tyranny and alien ideologies. A coup in itself is not a good thing; but it is one of the most effective methods of restoring the constitutional rights of the people when they have been deprived of the constitutional means for changing a corrupt and tyrannical government . . .

A new army had however grown in Ghana, an army of men who were

348

no longer failures but part of a great country that had won freedom from British rule. An army that has come to identify itself with aspirations of the people. An army that shared their sufferings, their joys, and their hopes for the future. This army has inherited wonderful traditions from the British, traditions of integrity, fair play and above all honour. Among its ranks were men who were not only good soldiers, but men equipped with insight to appreciate every problem in this complicated world of ours. Within its ranks men had begun to ask questions about our country, about Kwame Nkrumah, about the Convention People's Party and its intentions. Men had begun to read books, to learn of the traditions of democratic institutions, and they came to know that something had gone wrong in the state of Ghana . . .

In August 1965 something else happened. Major General Otu, the then Chief of Defence Staff, and his deputy, Major-General Ankrah, were retired from active service. Ghanaians were informed that they had "retired", but most of us in the Army knew that they had been dismissed. I was only a junior officer and had no means at my disposal for finding from them the reason for their sudden "retirement". But this was not the way to treat Generals. For a long time, the Convention People's Party had made a steady assault on the Army with a determined programme to indoctrinate it with the ideology of Nkrumahism. I remember that a branch of the Convention People's Party was even opened at the Teshie Military Academy for this purpose. There was an occasion when officers were made to join the Convention People's Party by force. Forms were sent out from the Minister of Defence, Mr. Kofi Baako's office, to be completed. I refused to complete this form on the principle that the Army must be above party politics. The Army and the Police are the custodians of the nation's Constitution. If the Army was made to identify itself openly with Convention People's Party and its ideology, it was bound to lose its self-respect and independence of outlook. It was clear too, at this time, that the economic mismanagement of the country by the Convention People's Party government had affected the armed forces. Our clothes were virtually in tatters. We had no ammunition. The burden of taxation was heavy. The cost of living for the ordinary soldier was high. The Army was virtually at the mercy of the politicians who treated it with arrogance and open contempt . . .

What have we fought for? I believe that my country is a beautiful country and has everything that will make us all proud of her. It was unfortunate that we fell into unscrupulous hands, and it is again unfortunate that we had to adopt the means which we adopted. But I believe that we who were the architects of the coup owed a duty to our country. We were not unaware of the consequences in the event of failure.

We were prepared to accept the risk. We want to build a new Ghana, a country ruled by men of integrity and conscience; for when one's conscience pronounces judgment, there is no court of appeal against its verdict. It was bitter to realize that those to whom the people gave the leadership of this country had sold their souls, and thought that the use of absolute power and tyranny and the love of money were all that mattered. We will stand against anything undemocratic. I believe that all men are born free. Democracy based on the freedom of the individual is more acceptable than any form of totalitarianism. We are against fascism and communism. I cherish the hope that in our history no one man will ever be allowed to lord it over us again. I am a great admirer of the British way of life, its legal system, the Magna Carta, the Petition of Rights and the Bill of Rights. These are institutions on which the civil liberties of the people are founded. The British Constitution safeguards not only the rule of law but also the freedom of the press, of thought, of action within the law, and of the individual. It is these things that make Britain the home of democracy . . .

Let us always cherish the hope to serve God and our country above all. I can see a new society emerging in which the best and the most efficient will have a place. Our measures will be high. I have seen from the trend of events after the Revolution that the ones who amassed wealth unfairly are now the unhappiest members of our community; their wealth has become a burden. They wish they had not become rich. In public, and at press conferences, I see them denouncing their master Kwame Nkrumah. They would have us believe that they were only carrying out their master's orders. This is, however, no excuse. They all shared the collective guilt of the nightmare Kwame Nkrumah imposed on this country. I hope that they will remember that Adolph Eichmann would not have been sentenced to death if his pleas of being under Hitler's orders were acceptable to the judges. They all shared responsibility for the disgrace and the damage brought upon our country. We hope for those to come that this will be a lesson, and that history this time will not repeat itself. I belong to the younger generation; we owe a duty to our country, and this duty we shall perform to the best of our ability, in the best interest of our people, without prejudice to any cause. I have but one lamp by which my feet are guided and that is the lamp of experience. I know of no way of judging the future but by the past. The experience under Kwame Nkrumah was a bitter one, hence we must look into the future with a newer hope. I am not a lawyer to interpret the provisions of liberty, freedom, bill of rights, etc. But to me the concepts are as clear as the Ten Commandments. Among others are the freedom of worship, of speech and of the press, the right of peaceable assembly, equality before the law, just trial for crime, freedom from unreasonable search, and security from being deprived of life, liberty or property, without due process of law. Herein are the invisible sentinels which guard the door of every home from invasion, coercion, intimidation and fear. Herein is the expression of men who would be for ever free.

Under Kwame Nkrumah these principles were repudiated every day. Freedom of worship was denied, because he was held as the incarnation of God. Freedom of speech was suppressed. The press was censored and distorted with propaganda. The right of criticism was denied. Men were detained and even sent to the gallows for holding honest opinions. They could not assemble for a discussion. We spoke of public affairs only in private. We were subject to searches and seizures by spies and inquisitors who haunted this land of ours.

We must with his departure remind ourselves that liberty comes and lives only where the hard-won rights of men are held inalienable, where governments themselves may not infringe, where governments indeed are but the mechanism to protect and sustain these principles. It was for this concept that we effected the Revolution of the 24th February. We now seek for solutions to our many difficulties, and they will only come through the constructive forces which arise from the spirit of free men; we seek the purification of liberty from abuses, and the restoration of confidence in the rights of men from which come the release of the dynamic forces of initiative and enterprise. By this alone can we find our solutions and the purpose of Ghanaian life be assured.

2: I. K. Acheampong

From an interview in *Africa*, No. 19 (March 1973).
Acheampong is President of the National Redemption Council of Ghana, set up after Acheampong led a military *coup* which brought down the civilian government of K. A. Busia in January 1972.

... The protagonists of democracy harangue their people slavishly with tenets of Western democracy. In this context, I should like to say that since 1960, Africa has experienced several coups. Most of the leaders of the liberation movement were overthrown by their armed forces. Here in Ghana, we have had two successful army take-overs and two abortive attempts. Our second attempt at elective democracy ended in dismal failure after only two and a half years. The reason for this is that Africa may not have found a system of government, a pattern of democracy suitable for her peculiar circumstances.

Let me dilate here a bit on our second attempt at elective democracy. Busia was given the chance to express in practical terms his firm belief that the Westminster parliamentary model of democracy was of universal relevance to his cause. We were all witnesses to what happened. Only six months after taking power, he and his colleagues were telling us that the Constitution which they themselves had prepared was hardly operative; the checks and balances upon which his universally relevant form of democracy was based had to be upset, because effective government demanded the holding in check of the judiciary, the political control of the civil service, the transformation of the legislature into a rubber stamp, the muzzling or persecution of the press, and the subjugation of organised labour and student movements.

As I have expressed elsewhere, I abhor hypocrisy, and I could not stand the pretence at democratic rule when all the evidence pointed at the erosion of every democratic principle. Let me say with all firmness that we did not take up arms to overthrow democracy. We overthrew men who were paying lip service to democracy. However, our profession and training, and the manner in which we took power, would seem to create the suspicion that we would have no concern for democratic conditions and measures. This is wrong; I believe that no matter how power is taken, those who wield it have a primary duty to be at one with the people and with their hopes and aspirations. Being at one with them means understanding them, listening to them and taking account of their views. It is equally wrong for a military regime to behave insensitively to the reaction of the people in any given situation.

......

... Africa needs strong governments. Africa needs government with the strength of its convictions, the courage to take the most difficult decisions if they are in the interest of the people, and if I may use that word again, the strength to resist all the forces that may wish to fight against it because their interests have been harmed by the government's decisions. If strong governments are also fulfilling basic democratic functions they ought not to be castigated as undemocratic.

......

... I am reluctant to talk in terms of labels, but I do believe that the state is bound to play a forceful role, a leadership role in the development of the economy, I have said that a country with our limited resources cannot leave everything to the market forces, and I have said that we have to use state power to capture the commanding heights of the economy for Ghanaians. We can do this without curbing the entrepreneurial spirit of Ghanaians.

......

352

... My belief in Panafricanism is total and absolute. You will notice that I have built my philosophy around self-reliance. I do not see this only in terms of my country. I see it in continental terms. I mentioned this when I paid my first visit to Lomé, Togo, that the time has come for Africa as a continent to think of its development on the basis of self-reliance. I see it this way: if the development of the continent can be seen within this wider context, it will be noted that there will be many areas in which we can move faster on our own resources. We can do this only if we are all operating within a common fold, in perfect understanding that we all belong to one Continent with one destiny. You will say that others before us have said it before. It is true and what they said remains valid. What I hope to do is to join other leaders of Africa in thinking anew the methods by which we will bring to realisation the ideals of Unity.

3: J. D. Mobutu

Extracts from a Manifesto Speech for the decade 1970–80, published in *Cahiers Congolais* (October–December 1970). Translated from the French by the Editors. Mobutu is the President of Zaire, formerly Congo–Leopoldville, and obtained power by deposing President Kasavubu by military *coup* in 1965.

If we take as our point of reference a whole decade, it is to meet the programme which the United Nations sets out for the developing countries. Thus, all our action will take place within the framework of the ten-year plan.

... For our programme to be realized, there must be sustained effort and discipline on the part of every citizen, such that each one will be deeply conscious of the effort asked of him. It is most important that he should have in mind the fundamental objectives which will be assigned to State action during the next seven years.

The following exposition presents a glimpse of these objectives.

In the political and administrative field, the national Party has shown, on many occasions and above all during presidential and legislative elections, that it is solidly embedded in the Republic. However, its structure must still be strengthened if it is to become an institution that can resist ageing and sclerosis ...

Educating the young requires a maximum amount of care. Our young people are the Congo of tomorrow and must increasingly become conscious of the role they are to play. They are the leaven of the

353

bread . . . Under the banner of the Popular Revolutionary Movement, a consistent dialogue will take place between the young people and those in charge of national affairs . . .

The Popular Movement of the Revolution will not focus only on the elite of our young people but will also provide the framework, for the young people who are not part of the army, in which will take place the social service provided by the Constitution as a substitute for military service.

As for administration, public services must still increase their efficiency. To this end, civil servants and State officials, at whatever level they may be, must be aware of the importance of the mission which has been assigned to them in the city. More diligence, more discipline, more precision, more conscience, and more competence are demanded of them . . .

Our policy aiming to complete the building up of the State and to increase the public-mindedness of the Congolese citizen will be reinforced on the international level by an active diplomacy which will tend to strengthen ties with other African countries and with the States of other continents.

Faithful to the ideals of the Organization of African Unity, the Democratic Republic of the Congo will pursue a policy of help and assistance to those African territories still under foreign domination. Its objective is to contribute towards making our whole continent free, independent and prosperous.

Our Government will continue to play its part in consolidating peace, reinforcing co-operation between States and promoting world progress in all fields. Nevertheless our openness to the world does not mean that we will give foreigners a chance to damage our independence. We have neither the intention nor the means of practising an imperialist policy by meddling in the internal affairs of other States. But neither would we tolerate foreign States dividing us by sowing subversion among us. The example of rebellions with which we have been afflicted and aggressions committed by some African States incite us to take greater care.

. . . . . .

The first five years of the second Republic have been years of hard work and austerity; all energy and resources have been devoted, by priority, to rebuilding our economy ruined by years of carelessness and to establishing political, economic, financial and institutional bases favourable to a harmonious and autonomous social and economic development.

This double objective was so urgent and costly that it would have been dangerous to undertake a policy of restoration and expansion of the economic apparatus as well as an all-embracing social policy . . .

Today, thanks to the work and sacrifices offered by the Nation, our economy has been recaptured from the control of foreign monopolies. We have, as a result, restructured our economic infrastructure. The successes recorded in the economic, financial and monetary field, as well as the spiritual and moral gains which have accompanied them, have modified the conditions of national life to such an extent that we must rethink our politics in economic and social matters.

By social progress, one means progressive access to a higher standard of living by all strata of the population. In particular, the State must encourage the employers and the workers to undergo training to increase their output, and consequently their incomes ... But increasing the well-being of all is impossible without a parallel and harmonious economic development of all fields.

Could the Congolese people endure indefinitely an economic development that would systematically enrich certain areas at the expense of others? Could it accept an economic development that would favour only towns and let the rural areas suffer? Would it not condemn any policy that let some get rich dishonestly at the expense of others? Could it develop the country's economy if, within it, a war broke out between the different generations?

. . . .

The harmonious development of the Republic ... demands a balanced geographical distribution of schools of all levels. This policy is an integral part of our economic organization. Apart from this, training alone is not enough. It must be adapted to our economic programme. Outside education, other economic sectors will equally hold the attention of the Government. It is thus that a particular effort will be made to resolve the problems posed by transport and communication, agriculture, mining, industry, tourism and land development.

In the field of transport and telecommunications, our infrastructure just like our equipment is still insufficient. But the economic and social development of a country as vast as ours demands an infrastructure and equipment for transport and telecommunications adequate to ensure the rapid circulation of people, goods, ideas and techniques.

Without an appropriate network of transport and telecommunications, the integration of vast rural zones into the modern economy would be impossible; the prices of agricultural products in the Centres would constantly risk rising higher.

. . . . . .

As with transport, agriculture figures in the high priority sectors of our programme. Despite the action over the last 5 years, this sector of the economy has not yet reached a satisfactory level. We cannot overemphasize the advantages to a country of increased agricultural production. It limits the volume of imports of foodstuffs and brings the country more foreign currency. Finally, in bettering the standard of living of the peasants, who represent for our country the most important sector of the population, it expands the internal markets necessary to industrial expansion.

......

The same policy of intensification and amelioration of output will be followed in mining. We must establish a geographical balance of the production of primary products to reduce the setbacks brought about by the fluctuations in world prices of metal and we must widen the field of our mining exports.

......

The last priority sector is urbanization. In this field, we recognise that the urban population has increased considerably during the last decade. It is predictable that this rate of growth will continue. This population explosion which we have been unable to control creates, in our towns, serious problems of erosion of roads, traffic, and distribution of water and electricity.

The Government will firmly follow a rational policy of urban development. Anti-erosion works ... will be pursued. Plans of urbanization will be systematically established. Housing needs will be satisfied within the framework of State-controlled land. In the towns the necessities of hygiene and aesthetic environment will be scrupulously respected.

4: C. O. Ojukwu

Extracts from C. O. Ojukwu, *Biafra: Random Thoughts of C. O. Ojukwu* (Harper & Row, 1969). Copyright Ojukwu 1969. By permission of Harper & Row.
After the military *coup* of January 1966 in Nigeria, Ojukwu was made Military Commander of Eastern Nigeria; he then led this region into secession from the Nigerian Federation and became the Head of State of the new Republic of Biafra, until its capitulation in January 1970, when he fled to Guinea. The context of each extract is given after the extract.

In spite of all efforts since the famous Amalgamation of Northern Nigeria and Southern Nigeria in 1914, an act which all Northern Nigerian leaders to this day consistently and publicly condemn as a mistake, Nigeria as a united country was nothing but a fiction. Certain basic features mark a country out as united. Some of these features are:

1. Common or similar culture, as well as social system.
2. Common citizenship, with equal rights and privileges for all men in the country.
3. Common laws and a common judicial system.
4. A common electoral system.
5. Equal rights of all citizens before the law.
6. Rights to acquire property and make a living anywhere in the country.
7. Equal rights to employment anywhere in the country.
8. Equal rights to protection of life and property.

All these features, and more, were completely lacking in Nigeria between the peoples of the North and those of the South. While the people of the South made strenuous efforts at Nigerian unity, the people of the North did everything to stultify, indeed kill, anything that would foster it.

The constitutional arrangements of Nigeria, as imposed upon the people by the erstwhile British rulers, were nothing but an implicit acceptance of the fact that there was no basis for Nigerian unity . . . The Federal Nigerian Constitution was designed primarily to hinder all attempts by Nigerians to progress. Its aim was to create a healthy atmosphere for further imperialist exploitation after the imperial master should have withdrawn. The problems that beset Nigeria after independence were, therefore, the problems of neocolonialism – problems that have beset every country in Africa since the attainment of independent status.

The crises which rocked Nigeria from the start of independence came as a result of efforts of progressive nationalists to rid themselves and posterity of the stranglehold of neocolonialism. For this, Biafrans in Nigeria were stigmatized and singled out for extermination. In imperialist thinking, only phony independence was acceptable for the Africans. Any attempt at true independence was a nuisance which had to be abated. The sponsorship of Nigeria by the imperialists is, therefore, not surprising, nor has it been disinterested. These sponsors are concerned only with the preservation of that corrupt and rickety structure of a Nigeria in a perpetual state of powerlessness to check foreign economic exploitation.

People have sought in various ways to dismiss our struggle as a tribal conflict. People have attributed it to the greed of a fictitious power-seeking clique anxious to carve out an empire to rule, to dominate and to exploit. This is not so. Our cause is transparently just, and no amount of propaganda can detract from it. Our struggle is of far greater significance. It is a total, vehement rejection of all those evils that blighted Nigeria – evils which were bound to lead to the disintegration of that ill-fated federation. Our struggle is a positive commitment to build a healthy, dynamic, and progressive state which will be a bulwark against neocolonialism, and the pride of black men the world over.

......

Since we are not the aggressors, our war aims are quite limited. All we seek is to maintain the territorial integrity of Biafra. Ours is not to conquer Lagos or to take Kaduna or Zaria: that is not our aim. We are a peace-loving people. (Extract from Address to the people of Okigwe Province, Okigwe, December 27 1967)

There is no aspect of this war in which Britain is not involved. I do not even know where to start. The problems that bedevilled the old Nigerian Federation were implanted in that society by Britain.

It was Britain, first, that amalgated the country in 1914, unwilling as the people of the North were. It was Britain that forced a federation of Nigeria, even when the people of the North objected to it very strongly. It was Britain, while keeping Nigeria together, that made it impossible for the people to know themselves and get close to each other, by maintaining an apartheid policy in Northern Nigeria which herded all Southerners into little reserves called *Sabon-garis,* barring them from Northern Nigerian schools, and maintaining different systems of justice in a country they claimed to be one.

It was Britain, for her economic interest, that put the various nations in Nigeria side by side and called it a federation, so as to have a large market.

It was Britain, in the year 1966, when Northern Nigeria finally made an attempt to separate itself from Nigeria, that forced her into holding to the federation.

It was Britain, having thus forced Northern Nigeria into staying in the federation, that promised help to the North (the military rulers of Nigeria) the sort of help that enabled them to unleash this war of genocide . . .

It is British arms, British bombs, British technical assistance, British mercenaries, that have been sustaining Nigeria in the battlefront. A British officer boasted of having led the capture of Calabar. The same British officer boasted of having led the invasion of Bonny.

It was Britain that did, and has continued to do, Nigeria's overseas publicity, through the BBC.

I said some time ago that it might have been more realistic at the Kampala peace talks for Biafra to sit across a table, with Britain on the other side, to negotiate terms for peace.

This war will not end until Britain wants the war to end. The day Britain feels that enough is enough, Gowon cannot continue for six hours. (Extracts from International Press Conference, Owerri, 5 June 1968)

Any political arrangement must be such as to assure Biafrans absolute control of their internal and external security, including an independent international identity to prevent a repetition of the gruesome events of the recent past and to ensure that any such acts are brought to the attention of the international community without delay. Nigeria, under the plea of domestic jurisdiction, has successfully prevented the world community from taking any effective action for peace and security. (Message to the American Committee to Keep Biafra Alive, New York, 7 December 1968)

There will be a free enterprise society in Biafra. The only limitations to the freedom of the enterprise will be cash, as in all underdeveloped countries – the question of availability of capital. It is this lack of capital that in fact induces government involvement in industrial enterprise. If, on the other hand, we find other means of generating and building up capital for the enterprises, the tendency here will be to leave it free to the individual. Direction from the government will be a diminishing factor. (Interview with West German journalist, Dr. Ruth Bowert, Umuahia, 25 March 1968)

Since this is the people's war, and since it is on the people that we depend for victory, I think the revolution, which we are trying to guide, should also sweep through the army. You will find that our officers have been trained in a particular way and are tied to stereotyped military manoeuvres. They have a rather pronounced class consciousness, and a feeling of superiority to other human beings. This must be discouraged, particularly in our situation, where the only thing that matters is how well you serve the people and the state. (Extracts from Address to officers and troops, Ikot Ekpene war front, 2 August 1968)

Because of certain privileges in the Nigerian army, the British found it easy to create a reactionary group within the army that would stultify any innate desire of the people to change the various myths on which neocolonialism thrives. The British colonialists have therefore created in the army an elite corps – elite by name, but without any contributive power in socio-economic terms, nor in progress. It is a maxim of our present day circumstance that the more incompetent one is, the greater his adherence to position. This appears to be the rule in Africa today.

The army, particularly the British-trained army, has had young people transplanted very quickly from obscurity into positions of pre-eminence; they find themselves automatically in the so-called senior cadre of society, with more money than is good for them, less responsibility than is good for them. These men develop in time only a marked ability to hang on to their seats. Wherever you find people like that, people who can do so much, tied down or hampered by this form of training and experience – men so aware of their own inadequacy and so afraid of social displacement – you find the most fertile ground for neocolonialist puppetry. In a group like the army, they remain ever grateful to their neocolonist patrons. (Extract from Address at Biafra People's Seminar, Umuahia, 1 November 1967)

The working class is the backbone of any progressive state. The moribund Federation of Nigeria inherited and encouraged friction and antagonism between labor on the one hand and management and government on the other.

We had begun to witness the growing gap between the rich and the poor as well as the evils attendant upon mounting unemployment. We began to witness poor and inefficient output, wages, and salaries unrelated to production, introduction and promotion of privilege unrelated to merit, and increasing disparity between town and countryside.

Under the civilian regime our labor movement had fallen into disarray, since some of its leaders had betrayed the cause of the workers to corrupt the politicians or allowed themselves to be seduced by local or foreign vested interests. These leaders became as corrupt as the regime they pretended to attack. The result was that the role of the labor organizations in the defunct Federation of Nigeria constituted a direct negation of the real interests of the workers.

It will be the duty of this government, by eliminating all forms of oppression, exploitation, and injustice, to offer the workers their rightful place in society. The workers of this Republic will come to occupy an important position and play a healthy role in the mechanics of nation-building. We envisage that the position of our trade union movement will be one of complete cooperation with, and full participation in, government economic policies.

We consider as obsolete the separation of labor from management in industrial and, indeed, all economic activity. Such separation often creates two warring camps engaged in a power tussle which leads to strikes, retrenchments, and the frustration of economic targets. We hope to strive to achieve harmony between the two, so that the working class can itself become the driving force of our economic resurgence. To this end, the

360

government intends to take steps to set up the necessary machinery for the effective participation of Biafran workers, through their accredited bodies, in the planning and execution of our economic policy. (Extract from Address to Convocation of the University of Biafra, Nsukka, 1 July 1967)

We are involved in an indigenous revolution, not borrowed from Mao Tse-tung, or from Whitehall or the White House ... Until a society, a virile society entirely black, is established, the black man ... will never be able to take his place side by side with the white man. We have the unique opportunity today of breaking our chains.

It is not enough to fight the Nigerians or their friends. We have to fight as a starting point of the African revolution ...

If the revolution fails, we do a disservice to our race. *But, perhaps, more important, and what really frightens the white man, is the whole challenge to the direction of international economy.* The whites have created a system which is a one-way traffic – raw materials to Europe. If that is so, logic tells me that sooner or later, Africa will be sucked dry ... But Biafra, born on blood and revolution, is determined and poised to reverse the trend and challenge this economic imperialism. We are the one black country that today has the capability and capacity to buy raw materials from Europe to manufacture in Africa for selling back to Europeans. I do not say this because I believe the black man is greater. No. I believe that this is the way things should go. They should buy from us. We should buy from them. They should buy our raw materials and we should also buy their own. We should cooperate not as slaves of the European economic oligarchy but as equal partners in a world of progress and not of piracy. (Extracts from Address to passing-out parade of officer cadets, Afor-Ugiri, 2 March 1969)

5: Amin: The Coup

Extracts from a press statement by Idi Amin Dada, Head of Uganda's Military Government, issued in Kampala on 27 January 1971, two days after Amin had led the *coup* which overthrew President Obote.

What can be said without any doubt whatsoever is that Obote's regime was one of great hypocrites. Obote himself always claimed that he was a great socialist and yet there were very many things that he did that showed that he was anything but a socialist.

Obote had two palaces in Entebbe, three in Kampala, one in Jinja (fifty miles away), one on Tororo, one in Mbale (twenty eight miles from Tororo) one in Lira and elsewhere. All these palaces had to be furnished and maintained at great public expense, and yet all but one remained idle and unused almost all the time! It is no wonder that the people of Jinja, in their great joy attacked and damaged the so-called President's Palace at Jinja, total destruction of the place only being prevented by the Army.

Obote's mode of living was also anything but socialist. He heavily indulged in drink, smoking and women, and carried a big retinue (including bodyguards) wherever he went. This idle living was maintained at public expense and was also indulged in by Obote's Ministers and close advisers . . .

. . . . . .

Obote talked lofty words and wrote high-sounding pamphlets about socialism and yet his actions never matched his words. The endless taxes and high prices of basic commodities also showed that socialist Obote never cared anything about the people. As an example, the price of sugar, salt, rice, meat and many other foods doubled when Uganda changed over from the imperial to the metric systems of weights and measures, and yet Obote never enquired why this was so.

Corruption in Obote's regime was so widespread that it was almost being taken for granted. Ministers, Chairmen of parastatal bodies and top public servants owned fleets of cars, buses, scores of houses for renting, bars, petrol stations etc. and Obote never in one single instance questioned any of his men as to the way they had acquired this wealth. The Prevention from Corruption Act which was passed in 1969 was never enforced, and it remained a lot of dry ink on the paper it was written on. The worst aspect of the financial greed of Obote's men was that most of them ran the very businesses that ought to have been left to the common people, e.g. the taxi business and butcheries.

When it came to proposals for National Service it was obvious that Obote did not have the interest of the Common Man at heart. Obote proposed that 'all able bodied persons' should spend at least two years in a National Service Camp, far away from their home districts, digging and learning all about agriculture. The people were not to be paid for their work on the National Service Camps. In making his National Service proposals, 'socialist' Obote totally ignored the social problems that would inevitably arise if his proposals were put into effect, especially those relating to the split family. The people were rightly worried about the security of the family where the family head had to be away for long periods . . .

The proposals also ignored the financial problems of the self-employed man or woman who had to spend a year or two on National Service away from his trade, profession or business. Since the individual would not be paid on National Service, one rightly wondered how a self-employed individual would for that period meet his expenses . . .

Regardless of public feeling and popular opinion, Obote was determined to stay in power, together with his whole bunch of corrupt Ministers. The last elections were held in Uganda in 1962, and Parliament was given a five year mandate expiring in 1967. In 1966 Parliament extended its life for another five years, Obote having declared himself President in succession to Sir Edward Mutesa, Uganda's first President, whom he deposed.

In 1970 Obote solemnly declared that elections would be held in Uganda by April 1971, and he appointed an Electoral Commission to demarcate the electoral boundaries. He declared that candidates, all of whom would be nominated by the President's Election Commission, would have to stand in 4 widely scattered Constituencies.

This 4-Constituency idea was a trick by Obote to keep his henchmen in power since it obviously favoured the well known, and those who had funds to campaign in 4 scattered parts of the country. Obote's men obviously had funds, and moreover they all had embarked on intensive campaigns everywhere on Government expenses (under the guise of official tours) long before any official campaign period had been announced . . .

Obote deceived the public that the President would be elected by 'universal adult suffrage' – thereby giving the impression that anybody over the voting age would be free to vote for or against the President. The detailed proposals required that a candidate had to obtain the support of at least 32 of the 96 parliamentary constituencies, otherwise he could not stand as a candidate. With this safeguard Obote knew that with the necessary pressures and intimidation he would be the only presidential candidate validly nominated, thereby being elected President 'unopposed'.

Despite the fact that these confused electoral proposals were hedged around with safeguards and safety valves for Obote and his bunch of corrupt henchmen, Obote could never bring himself to announcing the date for a General Election. With most of the heavy pre-election programme not even started on by January 1971 . . . it was obvious to everybody that Obote's elections would not be held by April 1971 as he had solemnly promised. In fact he had already decided to 'postpone' the elections until October 1971, and no doubt that when that date arrived he would happily have 'postponed' the elections to some other date.

Obote (or more correctly his advisers) brought out 5 pamphlets in his so-called Move to the Left Strategy. The proposals in all these pamphlets remained a lot of hot air and they never looked like being implemented. What is more instructive is that he never dared bring out what perhaps was the most urgently needed proposal, that relating to a Code of Conduct for his Ministers and other leaders. That was a subject he never dared tackle.

Obote's actions in recent times showed that he hated and distrusted the Army which had kept him in power right from the day of Independence in 1962. He also greatly distrusted the people he ruled. For that reason Obote amassed hordes of weapons ... and they have already been shown to the local and international press.

......

6: Manifesto of The Ugandan Army

Extracts from 'Uganda : the Birth of the Second Republic' (mimeo, no date). This Manifesto contains the reasons given by the Ugandan army for their takeover of power on 25 January 1971.

1. The unwarranted detention without trial and for long periods of a large number of people, many of whom are totally innocent of any charges.
2. The continuation of a State of Emergency over the whole country for an indefinite period, which is meaningless to everybody.
3. The lack of freedom in the airing of different views on political and social matters.
4. The frequent loss of life and property arising from almost daily cases of robbery with violence ... without strong measures being taken to stop them.
5. The proposals for National Service which will take every able bodied person from his home to work in a camp for two years could only lead to more robbery and general crime when homes are abandoned.
6. Widespread corruption in high places, especially among Ministers and top civil servants has left the people with very little confidence, if any, in the Government. Most Ministers own fleets of cars or buses, many big houses and sometimes even aeroplanes.
7. The failure by the political authorities to organise any elections for the last eight years whereby the people's free will could be expressed. It should be noted that the last elections within the ruling party were dominated by big fellows with lots of money which they used to bribe their way into 'winning' the elections. The bribery, together with threats against the people, entirely falsified the results of the so-called

elections. Proposed new methods of election requiring a candidate to stand in four constituencies will only favour the rich and the well-known.

8. Economic policies have left many people unemployed and even more insecure and lacking in the basic needs of life like food, clothing, medicine and shelter.

9. High taxes have left the common man of this country poorer than ever before. Here are some of the taxes which the common man has to bear: Development Tax, Graduated Tax, Sales Tax, Social Security Fund Tax. The big men can always escape these taxes or pass them on to the common man.

10. The prices which the common man gets for his crops like cotton and coffee have not gone up and sometimes they have gone down, whereas the cost of food, education, etc., has always gone up.

11. Tendency to isolate the country from East African Unity, e.g. by sending away workers from Kenya and Tanzania, by preventing the use of Ugandan money in Kenya and Tanzania, by stopping the use in Uganda of Kenyan or Tanzanian money.

12. The creation of a wealthy class of leaders who are always talking of socialism while they grow richer and the common man poorer.

13. In addition, the Defence Council of which the President is Chairman, has not met since July, 1969, and this has made administration of the Armed Forces very difficult. As a result Armed Forces personnel lack accommodation, vehicles and equipment. Also general recruitment submitted to the Chairman of the Defence Council a long time ago has not been put into effect.

14. The Cabinet Office, by training large numbers of people (largely from the Akokoro County in Lango District where Obote and Akena Adoko, the Chief General Service Officer, come from) in armed warfare, has turned into a second army. Uganda therefore has had two armies, one in the Cabinet, the other Regular.

15. The Lango development master plan written in 1967 decided that all key positions in Uganda's political, commercial, army and industrial life have to be occupied and controlled by people from Akokoro County, Lango District. Emphasis was put on development of Akokoro County in Lango District at the expense of other areas of Uganda.

16. Obote, on the advice of Akena Adoko, has sought to divide the Uganda Armed Forces and the rest of Uganda by picking out his own tribesmen and putting them in key positions in the Army and else-where. Examples: the Chief General Service Office, the Export and Import Corporation, Uganda Meat Packers, the Public Service Com-

mission, Nyanza Textiles and a Russian textile factory to be situated in Lango.

17. From the time Obote took over power in 1962 his greatest and most loyal supporter has been the Army. The Army has always tried to be an example to the whole of Africa by not taking over the Government and we have always followed that principle. It is, therefore, now a shock to us to see that Obote wants to divide and downgrade the Army by turning the Cabinet Office into another army. In doing this, Obote and Akena Adoko have bribed and used some senior officers who have turned against their fellow soldiers.

18. We all want only unity in Uganda and we do not want bloodshed. Everybody in Uganda knows that. The matters mentioned above appear to us to lead to bloodshed only.

7: Amin: Policy Statements

Extracts from speeches and statements given by Idi Amin between 1 May 1971 and 12 August 1972. The context of each extract is given after the extract.

The question as to whether my Government will go communist, socialist or capitalist is of academic importance only. I am one of those who believe that pure capitalism like pure communism or socialism is neither desirable nor practicable. The balance of advantage clearly lies in choosing the best elements from each of these economic systems and adapting them to the private requirements of Uganda. In other words we believe that the private sector has an important and vital part to play in the economic development of Uganda. We also believe that the direction and impetus in the entire economic development of the country must be provided by the Government. This will be achieved by active participation where this is deemed necessary, by means of a well coordinated plan, and by a national strategy in which every person, every group, union or organisation will have a part to play.

My government firmly believes that economic development and improvement of social welfare are generally easier to obtain by expanding the productive base of the economy and by providing additional services. A change of ownership of existing facilities and services does not necessarily bring about the desired results. It follows, therefore, that the limited resources available to Government should be used to promote economic development and to build health centres, schools, factories and help the farmers.

Private savings and investment is of vital importance in attaining the highest possible rate of growth for the economy. But even if it were considered desirable to do away with private enterprise, the fact is that Government does not presently have the financial and manpower resources to replace private activity. (Speech, 1 May 1971)

All the people of Uganda have cause to rejoice on this day because for the first time the day is being celebrated with a difference. The difference being that unlike the past eight years the people of Uganda are not lectured to about their political indifference and differences. This used to be the forum for the politicians to pronounce their vote-catching slogans ... It is my view that all these were empty words designed to misguide the public and gain popularity in order to perpetuate the rule of those who were in power. This year I am talking to you frankly and without any political interests. I am simply discussing with you the problems that face our country and the direction which I feel we should follow. My Government believes in freedom of speech and expression and therefore, everybody is free to express their views on what should be done or what is going wrong in the country. I should add that unlike the previous regime I am not going to lock up anybody for what he has said or written about my Government. This is the game of politicians. It is those who feel insecure politically and otherwise who resort to such tactics. Mine is a Military Government whose whole purpose is to clear up the mess, put the country on a sound and secure economic foundation and guide it to greatness and prosperity ...

......

Before I finish I want to refer to a matter which has exercised the minds of many people in this country. I refer in particular to the demands especially from Baganda Elders that the monarchy should be restored ... I want to take this opportunity to state clearly and categorically that kingdoms will not be re-introduced and Uganda will not go back to the 1962 Constitutional set-up. It is my wish to see Uganda remain a strong and united country but this is impossible where you have divided loyalties. As I said before, we are today inaugurating a year which will be characterised by the promotion of human understanding. This demands, among other things, that every Ugandan must free himself from the clutches of factionalism and tribalism. Uganda must remain a strong, viable and united Republic. (Speech, 9th Independence Anniversary Celebrations, 9 October 1971)

My Government believes that one of its primary duties is to ensure the welfare of all members of the community. This means, for example, that no one section of the community can be allowed to dominate, control or monopolize the business life of the nation. No country can tolerate the economy of its nation being so much in the hands of non-citizens as is the case in Uganda today. The Asian community has frustrated attempts by Ugandan Africans to participate in the economic and business life of their country. Asians have used their economic power to ensure that the Ugandan Africans are effectively excluded from participating in the economic life of their own country. They have used their family ties, their languages which are unknown to Ugandans to exclude Ugandan Africans from the business life of their own country. They have refused to identify themselves with Uganda. For instance, at Independence, when they were offered the chance to become Uganda Citizens, the majority rejected the offer. Some of the few who became citizens of Uganda did so only half-heartedly as they had no faith in this country and also remained citizens of other countries. Asians have kept themselves apart as a closed community and have refused to integrate with Ugandan Africans. Their main interest has been to exploit the economy of Uganda and Ugandan Africans. They have been milking the economy of the country. They have exported, illegally, large sums of money from this country.

The Government has an obligation to put the economy of Uganda into the hands of its citizens. It would therefore be a futile exercise to request British Asians only to leave Uganda without, at the same time, requiring the nationals of India, Pakistan and Bangla Desh also to leave, since their presence is also not in the best interests of the economy of Uganda.

I have, therefore, today signed a Decree revoking with effect from today, the 9th August, 1972 all entry permits and certificates of residence which had been granted to the above categories of persons. They are, however, permitted to stay in Uganda for a maximum period of 90 days from today . . .

. . . . . .

We are not requesting British Citizens of Asian origin and Nationals of India, Pakistan and Bangla Desh to leave Uganda because of racialism. We are not racialists. We have no animosity against Asians or any other foreigners for that matter. The Government took this decision purely in the interests of the economy of this country. (Statement on the Asian community, 9 August 1972)

As I have repeatedly stated, whatever I do and whatever my Government does, we are always guided by God. You may have heard that even in this case, the decision was guided by God. When I had travelled to South Karamoja . . . I, on Thursday night, the 3rd August, 1972 had a dream that the Asian problem was becoming extremely explosive and that God was directing me to act immediately to save the situation. I was advised to have confidence in God through whom Uganda would win this economic war. Our war will therefore be won. (Message to the Nation, 12/13 August 1972.)

8: Amin: Foreign Policy

From 'The Foreign Policy of the Military Government of the Second Republic of Uganda'. Statement by General Amin, 15 March 1971 (Government Printer, Kampala, Uganda).

Organization of African Unity

1. The Government of the Republic of Uganda attaches the greatest importance to its membership of the Organization of African Unity.

2. The Government is committed to the principles of the Charter of the Organization of African Unity.

3. Uganda believes that no part of Africa can feel completely free and secure until the whole continent of Africa has been liberated from the yoke of colonialism and freed from insidious attempts to introduce neo-colonialism.

4. Uganda is therefore committed to supporting the elimination of colonialism and neo-colonialism from the continent of Africa and to this end the Uganda Government pledges to continue to give its moral and material support to all the liberation movements and freedom fighters recognised by the OAU.

5. Uganda will continue to participate as a member of the Liberation Committee and undertakes to pay regularly and promptly all financial contributions due to the Liberation Committee and to the general funds of the OAU.

6. The Government of the Republic of Uganda considers that its continued membership of the Organization of African Unity is automatic, in so far as the Charter of the Organization makes provision for membership of States, and not Governments. The new Government is in firm control of the whole of Uganda territory and has the support of the Uganda people, and therefore has the right to representation at meetings of the Organization.

7. The new Government takes a serious view of the support being given by

369

some few member States to the former Government. This support is considered a breach of the principle of non-intervention in the affairs of other States contained in the Charter of the Organization, and subscribed to by all member States.

South Africa, Portugal and Rhodesia

1. The Government of the Republic of Uganda condemns the inhuman and abhorrent policy of apartheid which is now practised in South Africa and believes that the evil policies of the South African Government constitute a threat to the peace and security, not only of neighbouring African States, but to the whole continent of Africa.

2. Uganda further condemns the decision of the British Government to sell arms to South Africa, which action is contrary to the embargo imposed by United Nations resolution.

3. The alarming situation in Rhodesia is also a matter which gravely concerns Uganda.

4. It is the view of the Government of the Republic of Uganda that the responsibility for resolving the Rhodesian situation lies with the British Government and that Britain should use force to establish African majority rule in that country.

5. The situation in the Portuguese colonies in Africa is also one that gives Uganda grave cause for concern, and Uganda will continue through the Organization of African Unity and the United Nations to support any policy that is based on the premise that African majority rule should be established in these countries as soon as possible.

6. It is the view of the Uganda Government that the first priority of any State is the maintenance of internal security, the promotion of internal harmony, and the resolution of internal dissensions, and that this should take precedence over any course of action.

7. Uganda also believes that any solution to the South Africa issue and those of the Portuguese territories and Rhodesia will, in the main, have to be a military one.

The United Nations

1. The Government of the Republic of Uganda attaches great importance to Uganda's membership of the United Nations and its affiliated international organizations, and will continue to work in collaboration with Uganda's brothers in the rest of Africa to ensure that the UN and other world bodies are employed for the promotion of international peace, justice and the prosperity of all nations.

2. Uganda further believes in the universality of the United Nations and

will fight for human rights the world over.

The Commonwealth

1. The Government of the Republic of Uganda believes in the principles underlying the Commonwealth of Nations and subscribes to the view that its continued existence is essential in the modern world.

2. The Commonwealth provides a unique forum, for discussion and action based on a common heritage, which usefully supplements other international agencies.

International Obligations

The Government of the Republic of Uganda will continue to respect all the international obligations and commitments undertaken by the previous Government.

Neighbouring Countries

Uganda attaches great importance to the maintenance and strengthening of friendly and brotherly relations with all her near neighbours:

1. *The East African Community*

(a) The Government of the Republic of Uganda will continue to support the East African Community of Uganda, Kenya and Tanzania.

(b) Uganda will do its utmost to see that this Community is strengthened through the improvement of relations between its members and by the inclusion of other States who have applied for membership of the Community.

2. *Other Neighbouring States*

(a) In addition to its obligations and ties to the East African Community, Uganda attaches great importance to the maintenance and strengthening of friendly relations with other neighbours: the Democratic Republic of the Congo, the Sudan and Rwanda.

(b) The Government of the Republic of Uganda will ensure at all times that no part of Uganda territory is used for subversive activities against Uganda's neighbours. Uganda, in return, expects her neighbours to reciprocate this by not allowing their countries to be used as bases against Uganda.

(c) The new Government of Uganda has pledged her good offices to mediate or otherwise participate in any attempt to effect a negotiated political settlement between the Government of the Sudan and the dissident group operating within the Southern Sudan.

The Middle East

The Government of the Republic of Uganda hopes that peace will be established in the area of conflict in the Middle East on the basis of the United Nations Security Council resolution.

To achieve this, Uganda will continue to support the mission of Ambassador Jarring, the Special Envoy of the United Nations secretary-General.

Non-Alignment

In accordance with Article III, paragraph 7 of the Charter of the Organization of African Unity, Uganda will pursue a policy of non-alignment with regard to all Power blocs.

General

Finally, the Military Government of the Second Republic of Uganda attaches the utmost importance to the principles of respect for, and the equality of all sovereign States, and to the principle of non-interference in the internal affairs of other States in accordance with Charters of the United Nations and the Organization of African Unity.

These principles are the very foundation for brotherly and friendly relations among States and are the pillars upon which all international organizations can be established and having been established, survive.

9: Kwame Nkrumah

Extract from K. Nkrumah, *Dark Days in Ghana* (Panaf, 1968). Written shortly after Nkrumah's deposition by the Ghanaian military.

It has been said, particularly by well-wishers from outside Ghana, that if I knew of the potential disloyalty in the army why did I not deal with it? The very posing of this question discloses the fundamental mis-understanding about the Ghanaian position before the coup in many friendly circles abroad.

As I then saw it, my task was two-fold. On the one hand, I had to secure a firm basis in Ghana and on the other, conduct an external policy which would lead to the liberation and unity of the whole African continent, and to the economic cooperation which was essential if any territory in Africa was to escape from neo-colonialism. In the military sense these two aims were contradictory.

I could, for example, have avoided any risk of a military revolt by maintaining the system which the British Government assumed would be maintained after independence, by which Britain would continue to supply for 10 to 15 years our key military personnel. The individual loyalties of such officers and their training, combined with political complications for Britain which would have resulted in their joining in a revolt, would have made it unlikely that a military take-over could take place. On the other hand, if I maintained a non-African officered army, Ghana could not play a significant part in the affairs of the continent.

Yet the tragedy of the Congo made one thing absolutely clear, that even small African forces on the spot at the right time could control the situation and prevent a neo-colonialist take-over. I therefore was not in a position to abolish the Ghanaian army, though this would have been an ideal course. It was a heavy charge on our limited resources for industrial development. On the other hand, looking at the problem from a continental point of view, if Ghana had no armed forces at all it must lose much of its influence with other African states. I have always said that for me the issue of African unity came before any other consideration. It was for this reason that I was prepared to run the risk of maintaining for the time being a traditional British-type army.

. . . . . .

. . . As with the army, I . . . had to accept a police force many of whose higher officers were politically hostile to the new Ghana. They, after all, had been chosen for promotion by the colonial regime and they had thus a monopoly of the specialist training required. Further, many of them were corrupt but to obtain proof of this was a difficult matter.

. . . . . .

The third element supporting the present regime is, in fact, the civil service. Again, I was faced at independence with similar problems to those that I had with the army and the police . . .

The Information Services which were the most important channel in letting the people know what was taking place and the reasons for any particular government action were all manned by civil servants originally trained by the old colonial Information Department which had been set up specifically to conduct propaganda against the C.P.P. and the idea of colonial independence.

However, I was able to pick and choose among the civil service much more than I was with the army and the police and I was able, in many cases, to reform the diplomatic and the information services. Despite this, throughout the public service as a whole, there was a tradition of serving whatever government was in power. Many of the senior officials had all originally served with the old colonial regime which had opposed trade unionism and socialism in any form and was against any real

373

representation of the people in government . . .

. . . . . .

In such circumstances it is only natural that they should have in the first place uncritically accepted the rebel government. Indeed behind the scenes the civil servants always looked back to the colonial times when their senior members were described as 'political officers' and they in practice ran the country. They welcomed the military revolt because they believed that behind the facade of military power they would be the real rulers.

. . . . . .

For some years imperialism has had its back to the wall in Africa. It has been faced with a growing liberation movement which it is powerless to stop but which, if it allows it to go unchecked, will before long end the exploitation on which imperialism's very existence depends. It has therefore resorted to a co-ordinated strategy in an attempt to preserve, and if possible to extend, its grip on the economic life of our continent.

An all-out offensive is being waged against the progressive independent states. Where the more subtle methods of economic pressure and political subversion have failed to achieve the desired result, there has been resort to violence in order to promote a change of regime and prepare the way for the establishment of a puppet government.

Fragmented into so many separate states, many of them weak and economically non-viable, coups d'état have been relatively easy to arrange in Africa. All that has been needed was a small force of disciplined men to seize the key points of the capital city and to arrest the existing political leadership. In the planning and carrying out of these coups there have always been just sufficient numbers of dissatisfied and ambitious army officers and politicians willing to co-operate to make the whole operation possible.

. . . . . .

It is necessary to realise, that, in many ways, the so-called coup d'état has not been a set-back but has been merely a symptom of how neo-colonialism is breaking down.

Almost all African countries came to independence without armed struggle. This means that it was impossible, in practice, to reconstruct these new states upon a socialist basis immediately. I was well aware of the compromises which it was necessary to make and the dangers which this entailed but Ghana's independence on any condition was the first essential in securing the freedom of Africa. . . . The circumstances under which the C.P.P. was formed resulted in it being a compromise organisation composed of some genuine revolutionaries but containing many of those who are interested in independence only so as to better

374

themselves and to take the place of the previous colonial traders and businessmen. . . .

. . . . . .

The coup d'état on its surface was a military revolt against myself and what I stood for. If it is analysed more deeply, however, it is a mark of the breakdown of the western attempt to influence and control Africa. The western countries, having failed to control democratically supported African governments, were forced into the final extremity of substituting regimes which depended upon no other mandate than the weapons which they held in their hands. Such puppet governments cannot survive for long either in Ghana or elsewhere in Africa. They are, in the first place, based on internal contradictions. Why they are tolerated is that their initial popularity is due to a sort of sympathetic magic. The prosperity of the western world at the moment depends upon exploiting less developed countries. Each year the western world pays less for its imports and each year charges more for its exports. Those who make our coups believe, however, or at least pretend to believe, that if they copy, or claim to copy, the outward image of the western world, then – in some miraculous way – they will secure the advantages which the western world enjoys. The contrary is the case. The individuals who have made the counter-revolution from Saigon to Sierra Leone are dependent for their political existence upon western support. The countries over which they temporarily obtained control are therefore exploited all the more viciously. By supporting the reactionary rebellions in Africa the western countries have dug graves for imperialism and neo-colonialism and have put before the African people the clear choice which was unclear before, either to go forward with a thorough revolution or else to continue in a situation which, year by year, impoverishes and humiliates them further.

Events in Ghana since military rebellion illustrate this admirably. Those who seized power claim they came forward to save the economy, restore prosperity, democracy, freedom of the press and the like. Instead, in order to maintain themselves in office at all they have had to impose harsher taxation, sell out state enterprises to foreign interests, murder democracy, curb the press and forcibly to suppress any type of consultation with the people. Instead, therefore, of proving that capitalism and the western way of life are the best, they demonstrate that it only brings increasing misery to all those who attempt to reproduce it in Africa. They thus, by their example, produce a genuinely revolutionary situation which did not previously exist and which was, through its absence, one of the main reasons for African disunity and for the poverty of the continent.

. . . . . .

Our success in breaking the web of economic control which Western

375

capitalism has imposed across the whole of the African continent, and our clear socialist policies, provoked the hostility of the imperialist powers. They knew that as long as I was alive and at the head of the Party in Ghana the process could not be halted and neo-colonialist exploitation could not be re-imposed. Ours was a system they could neither penetrate nor manipulate.

Significantly, one of the first acts of the 'N.L.C.' was to announce the abandonment of the Seven Year Development Plan which would have given the Ghanaian people the only worthwhile independence – real economic independence. The 'N.L.C.' replaced it with a two-year 'review period' during which the socialised industries would be dismantled and the door opened once more to unrestricted 'private enterprise' – in fact, they were establishing a neo-colonialist economic subjugation of Ghana.

The only Ghanaians to benefit from such a sell-out were the African middle-class hangers-on to neo-colonialist privilege and the neo-colonialist trading forms. For the mass of workers, peasants and farmers, the victims of the capitalist free-for-all, it meant a return to the position of 'drawers of water and hewers of wood' to Western capitalism.

BIOGRAPHIES

Colonel I. K. Acheampong

On 13 January 1972, the Ghanaian Armed Forces took over Dr Kofi Busia's government after a bloodless *coup d'état* and established the National Redemption Council (NRC). Colonel Acheampong was appointed Chairman of the NRC and Minister of Defence, Finance and Economic Planning. His first action was to dissolve parliament, withdraw the constitution and ban all political parties. Acheampong said that the *coup* occurred because Dr Busia, as Prime Minister, had mismanaged the economy and made arbitrary arrests.

A. A. Afrifa

Afrifa was educated at the Royal Military Academy, Sandhurst, and as a Colonel in the Ghanaian Army he played a major part in the *coup d'état* of 24 February 1966 in which President Nkrumah was overthrown. In the National Liberation Council, which was subsequently set up under the Chairmanship of Lt General Ankrah, Afrifa became Minister of Finance, Economic Affairs and Trade. When, in April 1969, Ankrah resigned as Chairman of the National Liberation Council after admitting to corruption, Afrifa replaced Ankrah as Chairman. Thus it was Afrifa who handed over power to Dr Busia's civilian government in September 1969, although Presidential powers were partially vested in Afrifa until a President, Mr E. Akufo-Addo, was elected in August the following year. However, after the second Ghana *coup*, in January 1972, Afrifa was arrested by the Chairman of the National Redemption Council, Colonel Acheampong, because he was alleged to have plotted to overthrow Acheampong's regime.

I. Amin

In 1966, as a Colonel of the Ugandan Army, Amin was appointed Chief of the Army and Air Force Staff. When, in May 1966, the Baganda passed a resolution to the effect that the government of Uganda should remove itself from Baganda soil, Amin led the army to crush the Baganda and attacked the Kabaka's palace. The Kabaka escaped to England and the uprising was crushed. Amin had thereby removed a considerable threat to President Obote. In 1970 Amin was accused of massive corruption in the form of misusing funds in the armed forces. For this reason, Obote planned to have Amin removed in January 1971 while he himself was attending the Commonwealth Prime Ministers' Conference in

377

Singapore. However, soldiers from the West Nile, Amin's own region, heard of Obote's plot by accident and seized the armoury at Jinja barracks to prevent pro-Obote soldiers of the Acholi and Langi tribes from getting the weapons they would need to arrest Amin and his allies. Amin then took over the government of Uganda while Obote was still in Singapore. He abolished parliament for five years, banned all parties, trade unions, and political activity of any sort and appointed himself President. He accused Obote's regime of tribalism, corruption, and of favouring Obote's tribe, the Langi. In 1972, he expelled from Uganda almost all the Asians on the grounds that they were undermining the economy.

Dr N. Azikiwe

An Ibo from Eastern Nigeria, Nnamdi Azikiwe received his university education in the United States where he obtained degrees in political science at Lincoln. In 1934 he returned to Africa and accepted the editorship of a new paper in Accra which he called *The African Morning Post*. Here he remained until 1937 when he resigned because of internal conflicts on the paper and returned to Nigeria. During the next few years he set up several newspapers in Nigeria, all of which were channels for attacks on colonialism. Soon afterwards he became directly involved in political activity when he founded the National Convention of Nigeria and the Camerouns (NCNC) which was the first national political party in Nigeria. It was largely due to NCNC pressure that Britain granted internal self-government to Nigeria in 1951, and in the elections that year the NCNC was returned to power in the Eastern Region, of which Azikiwe became Premier until 1959. At the pre-independence elections of 1959, the NCNC formed a coalition government with the Northern People's Congress in opposition to Awolowo's Action Group, and Azikiwe was appointed Governor-General of Nigeria. Then, when Nigeria became a Republic in 1963, Azikiwe was unanimously appointed President by the Federal Parliament. After the military *coup* of January 1966, Azikiwe retired from politics, although after the second *coup* in July that year he became an adviser to the military government of East Nigeria.

Dr H. K. Banda

Born in Nyasaland, Banda received his secondary education in South Africa and then went to the United States for his university education where, in addition to obtaining a Ph.D in 1931, he became a medical doctor in 1937. He studied medicine further at Edinburgh and Glasgow and then practised for years in various parts of England. In 1950, while Banda was still in England, the Nyasaland African Congress was formed to fight the proposed establishment of the Federation of Rhodesia and Nyasaland. Banda became its leader and led opposition to the idea of federation from London. In 1953 the Federation was established, but African opposition to it provoked so much unrest that Banda decided to return to Nyasaland in 1958 and lead the African Congress directly; he was elected President-General. However, in March 1959, the Congress was banned by the Federal Government and Banda was gaoled in Gwelo prison, Southern Rhodesia. Meanwhile, in September that year Banda's followers formed the Malawi Congress Party, dedicated to nationalism, socialism, Panafricanism and democracy. There was considerable agitation in Britain for Banda's release but this was opposed by Sir Roy Welensky, Prime Minister of the Federation, until 1960 when Banda was set free during a visit by the Colonial Secretary, Iain Macleod. Banda returned home to become President of the Malawi Congress Party. The Monckton Commission which, in 1960, reported to the British Cabinet that each constituent territory of the Federation should have the right to secede and that African representation should be rapidly increased, spelled the beginning of the end of the Federation. In February 1963 Nyasaland achieved internal self-government with Dr Banda as Prime Minister, and in July 1964 Nyasaland became independent as Malawi. When, in July 1966, Malawi became a Republic, Banda was the only nominee for President.

Dr K. Busia

A graduate of London and Oxford, Kofi Busia became leader of the United Party, an amalgam of opposition parties, in Ghana in 1957. He had been a member of the National Assembly since 1951 and had always opposed the policies of Kwame Nkrumah. Thus when Ghana obtained independence in 1957, Busia became leader of the Opposition. In 1959, however, he went into voluntary exile in England in order to avoid detention under the Nkrumah regime, and he did not return to Ghana until after the *coup* of February 1966 during which Nkrumah was overthrown. He was then appointed Vice-Chairman of the Political Committee, set up to advise the National Liberation Council. When the NLC decided to restore civilian rule in 1969, the ban on political parties was lifted and Busia launched his new Progress Party in May of that year. In the elections which followed, the Progress Party won a massive majority against all other parties and Busia became Prime Minister. This was the first time that an African state had been restored to civilian rule after a military *coup*. But in January 1972 a second military *coup*, led by Lt Colonel Acheampong, overthrew Busia's government while Busia himself was receiving medical treatment in London. Dr Busia is now in exile in England.

A. Cabral

Born in the Portuguese West African colony of Guinea, Amilcar Cabral went to Lisbon University to read agricultural engineering, in which he graduated in 1951.

He returned to Guinea and worked for the colonial administration for two years but came into conflict with the Governor because of his anti-colonial views. So he then went to Angola, another Portuguese colony, and helped to form the first important nationalist movement there, the MPLA (Popular Movement for the Liberation of Angola), in 1956. In the same year, he returned to Guinea and formed a nationalist movement there, the PAIGC (African Independent Party of Guinea and Cape Verde). In 1959, after violent suppression by the Portuguese administration of a strike in Bissau docks, the PAIGC decided to turn to guerilla warfare. The uprising was launched after years of preparation in 1963 and despite Portuguese retaliation it has met with considerable success. On 20 January 1973 Cabral was assassinated in Conakry, Guinea by PAIGC dissidents who had become agents of the Portuguese. His death resulted in the loss not only of one of Africa's leading guerillas, but also of one of Africa's most outstanding political theorists.

A. Césaire

Aimé Césaire was born in Martinique in the Caribbean of a poor peasant family. In 1931 he won a scholarship to the Ecole Normale in Paris. While in Paris, with some other black students, including Léopold Senghor, he started a magazine called *L'Etudiant Noir*. Although only one issue of this magazine was produced, it was important because it attempted to establish the philosophy of negritude. This philosophy had germinated with Marcus Garvey's 'back to Africa' movement in the United States, but it was Césaire who coined the term negritude and who helped to develop the concept. He became a member of the French Communist Party, from which he resigned after many years because he felt that it was not allowing the oppressed colonial subjects to think for themselves and decide their own destiny.

Dr Y. Dadoo

Yusef Dadoo is an Indian South African who trained as a medical doctor. He was, until it was banned, a member of the South African Communist Party. In 1946 he headed a movement of passive resistance, for which he was imprisoned, against General Smuts' attempts to segregate the Indians in South Africa. The following year, as President of the Transvaal Indian Congress, he signed a pact with the African National Congress to cooperate in trying to achieve economic and political equality for Africans and Indians. In the same year Dadoo spoke at the United Nations, criticising the South African Government's increasingly racialist policies. When, in 1952, the African and Indian Congresses organised a Defiance Campaign to show contempt for apartheid laws, the Government banned for life several leaders from membership of the African and Indian Congresses, Dadoo among them. He was arrested and accused under the Suppression of Communism

Act. He now lives in exile but continues to campaign against the South African Government.

Dr J. B. Danquah

Danquah was born in the Gold Coast towards the end of the nineteenth century. In 1923 he went to London University where he obtained a PhD and became a barrister. While in London he founded and became President of the Gold Coast Students' Association and the West African Students' Union of Great Britain and Ireland. He returned to the Gold Coast in 1927 and three years later he founded *The Times of West Africa*, but this only survived for five years before being put out of business by Azikiwe's *African Morning Post*. Danquah used his paper in an attempt to bring the chiefs and intelligentsia of the Gold Coast closer together on political matters. In 1946 he was one of eighteen Africans elected to the Legislative Council of the Gold Coast. The following year he founded the United Gold Coast Convention whose aim was to get rid of the colonialists by peaceful and gradual means. Nkrumah became Secretary of the UGCC but in 1949 he resigned to form the more radical Convention People's Party which, in contrast to the UGCC, demanded 'self-government now'. In the elections under the 1950 Constitution, which allowed for an all-African cabinet, the Convention People's Party won an overwhelming victory over the UGCC, from which the latter never recovered. In 1960 Danquah, as leader of the United Party, which was an amalgam of opposition parties including the UGCC, stood against Nkrumah in Ghana's first Presidential elections. Danquah was defeated but he continued to personify conservative opposition to Nkrumah's leadership until he was arrested and imprisoned without trial under the Preventive Detention Act in 1961, accused of organising industrial strikes that year in protest against the budget. Danquah died in prison in 1965.

M. Dia

Mamadou Dia worked as a teacher and journalist before being elected to the Territorial Assembly of Senegal and subsequently to the French Senate in 1948. That same year, with Léopold Senghor, he founded the Bloc Démocratique Sénégalais which claimed to stand for an African type of socialism, emphasising African values. In 1956 Dia was elected as a Deputy to the French National Assembly. He was influential in planning the Mali Federation between Senegal and Soudan of which he became Vice-President and Minister of Defence. The Mali Federation broke up in June 1960 and when, in August that year, Senegal became independent, Dia became Prime Minister. In December 1962 Dia, while still Prime Minister, attempted a *coup* against President Senghor, but the *coup* failed and Dia was sentenced to life imprisonment in 1963.

381

A. Diop

Alioune Diop is a Senegalese intellectual who started *Présence Africaine,* one of the most important periodicals produced by the French African intelligentsia. Présence Africaine also became a publishing house. In his editorial policy, Diop has always been committed to the cultural, economic and political freedom of Africa and, like his compatriot Léopold Senghor, he has contributed to the concept of negritude.

F. Fanon

Frantz Fanon was born on the Caribbean island of Martinique and trained as a medical doctor and psychiatrist. He was sent to work in an Algerian hospital during the Franco–Algerian war and his experience of the colonial conflict there made him side with the revolutionaries. But from his involvement with the Algerian situation and French imperialism, his concern broadened to the plight of the whole Third World and its struggle against colonialism. Fanon died of leukaemia in 1961 but, through his writings, he continues to be regarded as one of the most perceptive and forceful critics of colonialism as well as a leading advocate of socialism in the Third World.

R. K. A. Gardiner

Robert Gardiner is a Ghanaian who, although basically an academic economist, is equally well known for the important administrative posts he has held. At one time he was the Permanent Secretary in the Ministry of Housing and Head of the Ghanaian Civil Service. Since 1962 he has been the Executive Secretary for the Economic Commission for Africa.

J. E. C. Hayford

Joseph Casely Hayford was born in the Gold Coast in 1865. He became not only a journalist and a barrister but also one of the most influential of the early nationalists. He was a leader of the Aborigines' Rights Protection Society, founded in 1897 to protect, in particular, traditional systems of land tenure. This was one of the most important early nationalist organisations. Casely Hayford also founded the West African National Congress, the aim of which was the formation of a Panafrican movement. He was an unofficial member of the Legislative Council from 1916 to 1926 and a municipal member for Sekondi from 1927 to 1930. He always opposed the traditional chiefs, whom he regarded as barriers to an effective nationalist movement which would overthrow the colonialists. He died in 1930.

J. A. B. Horton

Africanus Horton was born in Sierra Leone in 1835. The missionaries who educated him recommended him to the War Office to train for a medical career with
the British Army in West Africa. Having studied medicine at London and
Edinburgh Universities he was posted to the Gold Coast as Staff Assistant
Surgeon in 1859. Twenty years later he was in charge of the whole Army Medical
Department of the Gold Coast. He wrote three political treatises which manifest
his mixed political attitudes. Although he was one of the elite he was devoted to
the advancement of all Africans and hoped that, eventually, independent nations
would be set up in West Africa. At the same time, however, he held a deep belief
that the British were completely devoted to the interests of the Africans.

Chief L. Jonathan

Leabua Jonathan was born in Basutoland but went to work in the South African
gold mines as a youth. He then returned to his home country to train as a Chief
and he became involved in politics. In 1959 he formed the Basutoland National
Party whose slogan was 'Bread and butter politics and a good neighbour policy
towards South Africa'. This was in stark contrast to the already powerful
Basutoland Congress Party which strongly opposed cooperation with South
Africa. Nevertheless, in the pre-independence elections of 1965, Chief Jonathan's
party won by a narrow majority and he became Prime Minister. The following
year the territory became the Kingdom of Lesotho, with Paramount Chief
Moshoeshoe II as King and Jonathan still as Prime Minister. In January 1970 the
first elections after independence were held and won by the opposition Congress
Party. The elections were immediately declared invalid by Jonathan who also
imprisoned 100 members of the Congress Party and declared a State of Emergency. By 1972 all the detainees had been released; but Congress Party refused
an invitation from Jonathan in 1973 to sit in the National Assembly.

K. D. Kaunda

Kenneth Kaunda began life as a teacher but became interested in politics, and in
1949 he opened a branch of the Northern Rhodesia African National Congress in
his home town. A couple of years later the ANC formed a Supreme Action Council, of which Kaunda was a member, to fight against the Federation of Rhodesia
and Nyasaland. In 1953 Kaunda was elected Secretary-General of the ANC, but
five years later he split with the President, Harry Nkumbula. The latter supported
a new constitution which was biased in favour of European representation. Kaunda
did not think that this was the best which could be obtained for Africans so he left
the ANC to form the Zambia African Congress, of which he was President. In
1959 Kaunda organised a boycott of the registration of African voters, in protest
against the new constitution. As a result, his new organisation was banned, the

383

leaders were arrested and he himself was imprisoned. While Kaunda was in gaol, his supporters formed the United National Independence Party (UNIP), of which Kaunda was elected President when he came out of prison, in 1960. Soon afterwards the Federation broke up, and Kaunda became Zambia's Prime Minister when it was granted internal self-government in 1964. Later that same year Zambia became independent, with Kaunda as President. In February 1972 Kaunda set up a Commission to draw up arrangements for making Zambia a one-party state. At the same time he banned the United Progressive Party, which had been set up in 1970 by Simon Kapwepwe, a former Vice-President of Zambia. Kaunda accused the UPP of being sectionalists and saboteurs of government policies and he detained all the leaders. In December 1972 the one-party state was established and the only remaining opposition party, Harry Nkumbula's ANC, was banned. A month later, the detained UPP leaders were released. In 1973 Nkumbula joined UNIP; and Kaunda was re-elected President for a further five years. Kaunda explained that it was necessary to set up a one-party state in Zambia in order to accelerate development and justice and to preserve peace and unity. Kaunda is one of Africa's leading political thinkers, best known perhaps for his philosophy of Humanism in the African context.

M. Keita

Modibo Keita helped to form the Bloc Soudanais in the French Soudan in 1945. The following year it merged with Houphouet-Boigny's RDA. In 1956 Keita was elected Deputy for the Soudan in the French National Assembly, of which he became Vice-President. Three years later he became Prime Minister of the Mali Federation (Soudan and Senegal), but the Federation split up after a few months partly because Keita wanted a strong central government, while the Senegalese favoured a loose federation. When the Federation broke up in 1960, Keita, as Secretary-General of Mali's only party, became President of Mali, the new name for the Soudan, which then became independent. In 1961, Keita joined Mali in a Union with Ghana and Guinea, which was an attempt to form the nucleus of a Union of African States with a central legislature. However, the Union was dissolved when the Organisation of African Unity was formed in 1963. In recent years Keita attempted to reduce his country's dependence on foreign aid; but in November 1968 he was overthrown by an army *coup,* and replaced by a Liberation Committee headed by Mousea Traoré.

J. Kenyatta

In 1928 Jomo Kenyatta became General Secretary of the Kikuyu Central Association which was formed to regain land taken by white settlers in Kenya. This was the first nationalist movement in Kenya. By 1955 Kenyatta was a strong force in African politics, and with Nkrumah, Padmore and others, he founded the

Panafricanism Federation whose aim was independence now for all African countries. In 1946, after spending fifteen years in Britain, Kenyatta returned to Kenya and became President of the Kenya African Union, a national movement aimed at securing the economic and political advancement of Africans. As nationalist demands for independence increased, in the face of strong opposition from the settlers, the Mau Mau revolution of the Kikuyu began in the early 1950s. Mau Mau was declared an unlawful society, and in 1953 Kenyatta was sentenced to prison for seven years for 'managing' Mau Mau. In 1960 the Kenya African National Union was formed, and Kenyatta was elected President of it while still in prison. In 1961 he was released and the following year he entered the Legislative Council as Leader of the Opposition against the Kenya African Democratic Union government. In 1963 KANU won the pre-independence elections, and Kenyatta became Prime Minister. The following year, Kenya became a republic with Kenyatta as President. In 1969 Kenyatta banned the opposition party, the Kenya People's Union, on grounds of subversion.

Sir Seretse Khama

Seretse Khama succeeded to the Chieftaincy of the Bamangwato tribe in Bechuanaland as a small boy and his uncle, Tshekedi Khama, acted as regent for him. After a year at the University of the Witwatersrand in South Africa Seretse went to Oxford, and then to the Middle Temple in London to study law. While there he married an English girl, Ruth Williams, despite strong opposition from his uncle Tshekedi who felt that the marriage was incompatible with Seretse's potential role as Chief. However, the tribe eventually accepted the marriage as they did not wish Seretse to renounce the Chieftaincy. But the British Government, purportedly under pressure from the South African Government who did not like the African Chief of a neighbouring territory to be married to a white woman, objected strongly. They offered Seretse £1,100 a year tax free if he would renounce the Chieftaincy and live in Britain. When he refused, he and his uncle were both banished from Bechuanaland, in 1950. After six years, having eventually agreed to renounce his claim to the Chieftaincy, Seretse and his wife were allowed to return to Bechuanaland. In 1962, Seretse established the Bechuanaland Democratic Party, the aim of which was to foster cooperation between Africans and Europeans and to try to gain a fair share for Africans in Government. Despite the formation of a more radical party, the Bechuanaland People's Party, Seretse continued to be an influential leader. In the elections of 1965 his party won the elections and the following year, when Bechuanaland achieved independence as Botswana, Seretse became President. His attitudes and policies are very much coloured by the fact that he is a close neighbour of, and economically dependent on, South Africa.

P. Lumumba

Patrice Lumumba was a man who, in a short lifetime, changed radically. He had only a primary education in the Belgian Congo but as a young man in his twenties he began to educate himself in an attempt to become part of the Congolese elite. He then identified with the Liberals who sought to combine Belgian and Congolese interests. By 1958, however, he was leader of the Mouvement National Congolaise which, as the first supra-tribal nationalist movement, sought independence. This fundamental change in attitude was largely fostered by his attending the first All-African People's Conference in 1958. When, in June 1960, the Congo attained independence, Lumumba became Prime Minister with Kasavubu as President. Almost immediately, Katanga Province seceded under Tshombe. Lumumba was worried because other Provinces looked as though they might emulate Katanga, which was supported by Belgian troops since the Belgian Government had large economic interests in the Province. But the United Nations and almost all other African countries rejected the use of force against Katanga and Lumumba's own troops were unreliable. Therefore, contrary to a UN Security Council resolution which banned all direct military aid to the Congo, Lumumba secretly called in Russian troops. When President Kasavubu heard of this, he dismissed Lumumba as Prime Minister and Lumumba, in turn, dismissed Kasavubu as President. The two had never been in harmony anyway, since Lumumba favoured a unitary state while Kasavubu was a federalist. General Mobutu immediately dismissed both leaders and seized power for five months. Before all this, Lumumba's troops had attacked the dissident Baluba Diamond State and killed thousands of Balubas. Now that he was dismissed as Prime Minister, Baluba soldiers went after him in revenge. Lumumba was captured and, although the United Nations tried to intervene on his behalf, he was killed. His death was announced in February 1961.

A. Luthuli

Albert Luthuli was born in the late 1890s of South African parents. He trained as a teacher and eventually became first Secretary and then President of the African Teachers' Association. In 1936 he gave up teaching when his people elected him as their Chief. He then started to organise the African sugar producers, and in 1945 he joined the African National Congress, of which he became President for Natal in 1951. The following year he was forced, by the South African Government, to resign his Chieftaincy because of his part in the Defiance Campaign. This was organised by the ANC and the Indian Congress in protest against the apartheid laws. In the same year, 1952, he became President-General of the ANC and was confined to his village for two years by the Government. No sooner had this ban ceased than Luthuli protested against the removal of Africans from Sophiatown and he was again banned for two years. In 1956, together with other leaders who opposed the Government, he was arrested and charged with high treason for allegedly organising a conspiracy to overthrow the Government, but he was released the following year. In 1959 he went on a speaking tour and addressed audiences which contained large numbers of whites. The Government, worried at his influence, immediately banned him under the Suppression of Communism Act, and confined him to his home town for a further five years. An ardent Christian, Luthuli both personified and inspired the ANC's philosphy of aiming for racial equality by non-violent means. For this he was awarded the Nobel Peace Prize in 1960. He died in 1967.

N. Mandela

Nelson Mandela, a South African lawyer, was a leader of the African National Congress. In 1952, with others such as Luthuli and Dadoo, he organised the Defiance Campaign to protest against apartheid. For this, he was tried under the Suppression of Communism Act, confined to Johannesburg for two years and banned from participating in ANC activities for life. In 1956 he was again arrested and accused of organising a communist conspiracy to overthrow the Government, despite the fact that he had always been vehemently anti-communist. The Treason Trial of the alleged conspirators began in 1958 and lasted until 1961, when all the accused were acquitted because the Court could not find them guilty of conspiring to use violence to overthrow the Government. No sooner had he been released than Mandela organised a stay-at-home campaign which resulted in strikes among seventy-five per cent of African workers in the townships. Two years later the police found documents and plans for a campaign of sabotage organised by 'Umkonto', an offshoot of the ANC. Mandela was accused of being the prime mover behind 'Umkonto'. In June 1964 he was found guilty of planning acts of sabotage against the state and he was imprisoned on Robben Island for life.

T. Mboya

Tom Mboya was born into the Luo tribe of Kenya in 1930. He began his political career in 1952 when he helped to found the Kenya Local Government Workers' Union, of which he became Secretary-General. In the same year he joined the Kenya African Union, which was banned soon afterwards during the Mau Mau Emergency. In 1953 he became General Secretary of what was to become the Kenya Federation of Labour (KFL). Since all political parties were banned during the Emergency, the KFL acted as a nationalist movement during this period. When the first African elections to the Legislative Council were held in 1957, Mboya was elected. He became closely involved in the Panafrican movement, and when Nkrumah organised the first All-African People's Conference in 1958, Mboya was elected chairman. After the Emergency, when the Kenya African

National Union was formed, Mboya became Secretary-General of KANU under Kenyatta's Presidency. From 1962, Mboya became successively Minister of Labour, Minister of Justice and Constitutional Affairs, and Minister of Economic Planning and Development. Mboya tended to become a scapegoat for all the government's mistakes. In July, 1969 he was assassinated in Nairobi. A Kikuyu was charged with and convicted for the killing.

Lt General J. Mobutu

Mobutu was born in the Belgian Congo in 1930. When the Congo became independent in 1960, Mobutu became Chief of Staff of the Army. A few months later when President Kasavubu and Prime Minister Lumumba dismissed each other (partly because Lumumba had secretly called in Russian troops to squash the rebellion in Katanga), Mobutu dismissed them both and seized power for five months. He then handed power back to a civilian government, under President Kasavubu, in 1961. History repeated itself in 1965 when Mobutu again deposed Kasavubu after a *coup,* allegedly because of a feud between Kasavubu and Prime Minister Tshombe, whom Kasavubu had just dismissed. Mobutu made himself President and the following year he dismissed his own Prime Minister, General Mulamba. Mobutu said that he took this action in order to overcome the perennial problem of having a President and a Prime Minister who could not agree. In 1970 Mobutu was elected President for a further seven years in his country, which had meanwhile been renamed Zaire.

Dr E. Mondlane

Eduardo Mondlane was born in Mozambique in 1920. He went to the University of the Witwatersrand, Lisbon University and North-Western University, Illinois, where he obtained a PhD. After doing some research at Harvard and teaching at Syracuse as Professor of Sociology, he worked as a research officer with the Trusteeship Council of the United Nations. This considerably opened his eyes to the inadequacy of the United Nations in dealing with the injustices of colonialism, so he decided to return to Mozambique and start a nationalist organisation. Three anti-colonial movements already existed there but they were either tribally or regionally based. Mondlane was convinced of the need for a national front, so the three movements were amalgamated to form the Front for the Liberation of Mozambique in 1962. The main aim of FRELIMO was to put an end to Portuguese colonialism by an armed struggle and, simultaneously, to develop those areas which came under FRELIMO's control as a result of the guerilla war they were waging. As President of FRELIMO, Mondlane provided both organisational and ideological skills. When the Second Congress of FRELIMO met in 1968, large areas of Mozambique had already been liberated from the

388

Portuguese. In February 1969 a parcel bomb killed Mondlane in Dar-es-Salaam, where the headquarters of FRELIMO is situated. It is not clear who was responsible for the murder. He was succeeded as President of FRELIMO by Machel Samora.

E. Mphahlele

Ezekiel Mphahlele was born in South Africa and became a member of the African National Congress. He was also the subeditor of *Drum*. He was banned from teaching by the South African Government because he criticised the Bantu Education Act, the declared aim of which was to produce Africans who would aspire to nothing more than certain forms of labour. Due to the increase in oppressive laws in his own country, Mphahlele exiled himself to Nigeria in 1957 where he became an extra-mural lecturer at the University College, Ibadan, and later to Paris and Nairobi and the USA. In the context of African attitudes, Mphahlele, like Frantz Fanon, is important as a critic of the concept of negritude. His best-known works are *Down Second Avenue* and *The African Image*.

Bishop A. T. Muzorewa

Muzorewa is a bishop of the United Methodist Church in Rhodesia. In December 1971 he formed the African National Council, which was not a political party but, in Muzorewa's own words, 'a spontaneous grass-roots reaction to the an-nouncement of the Anglo-Rhodesian proposals'. The ANC was formed to fight the proposals through non-violent means and Muzorewa was appointed as National Chairman. After the test of acceptability by the Pearce Commission, which found the majority of Africans against the proposals, the ANC continued in existence to try and establish a just society in Rhodesia. The ANC has asked the Smith regime to recognise it as an official representative of African opinion and to start settlement talks.

J. Ngugi

James Ngugi, a Kikuyu born in Limuru, Kenya, is a journalist and a University lecturer. He wrote the first English language novel *(Weep Not, Child)* to be published in East Africa by an African writer, but he is best known for his third novel, *A Grain of Wheat*, which deals with the Kenyan emergency and struggle for independence. A politically conscious author, Ngugi believes that 'the artist in his writings is not exempted from (the) revolutionary struggle' and 'can give moral direction and vision' to that struggle. He has also said that African writers should address themselves to the 'crisis of conflict between the emergent African bourgeoisie and the African masses'.

J. Nkomo

Joshua Nkomo is a Rhodesian who entered the political arena in 1951 when he became General Secretary of the Rhodesia Railways African Employees' Association. Just before the Federation of Rhodesia and Nyasaland was established in 1953, he became leader of the African National Congress which was strongly opposed to Federation. In December 1958, he represented the ANC at the first All-African Peoples' Conference in Accra and while he was still abroad a few months later, the ANC was banned and the leaders detained. Nkomo, in order to avoid arrest, became an exile and organised the London office of the ANC from where he continued to fight against Federation. The National Democratic Party was formed in Rhodesia in 1960 and Nkomo was elected President. He opposed the British Government's constitutional proposals of 1961 because they were undemocratic. A few months later, the Southern Rhodesian Government banned the NDP and Nkomo called on Britain to suspend the Constitution. He then immediately formed the Zimbabwe African Peoples Union of which he became President. Like the ANC and the NDP before it, ZAPU was also banned and Nkomo was restricted. However, in 1963 the new government under Winston Field lifted the ban and the restriction. Now that the Federation had broken up, Southern Rhodesia began to demand independence. The African nationalists' opposition to independence under a white regime was weakened by conflicts between the leaders of ZAPU, and eventually Ndabaningi Sithole broke away from the movement to form the Zimbabwe African National Union. In April 1964, when Field was replaced by Ian Smith, Nkomo was detained without trial and has been in prison ever since. Although ZAPU and ZANU combined in 1971 to form the United Front for the Liberation of Zimbabwe (FROLIZI) and Nkomo can no longer play an active part in politics, he is still acknowledged as one of the leading nationalists in Rhodesia. In 1972 he submitted a memorandum rejecting the Anglo-Rhodesian proposals to the Pearce Commission.

K. Nkrumah

Kwame Nkrumah was born in the Gold Coast in 1910. He worked his way through the Universities of Lincoln and Pennsylvania in the United States and, while there, he became President of the African Students' Association of the US and Canada. It was at this stage that he first began to analyse and criticise colonial policies. In 1945 he went to London to study law at Gray's Inn and he became active in African organisations in England. He attended the Fifth Panafrican Congress at Manchester in 1945 of which he was Joint Secretary, with George Padmore of the Organisation Committee. Nkrumah himself wrote the Declaration, which was adopted by the Congress, calling on all colonial subjects to organise to free themselves from colonialism. In the Gold Coast the nationalist movement had begun to organise itself in the form of the United Gold Coast

Convention, under the leadership of J. B. Danquah, who invited Nkrumah to return to the Gold Coast and become Secretary of the new party in 1947. Two years later Nkrumah resigned from the UGGC, because he found its demands were too moderate, and he set up the more radical Convention People's Party which was prepared to go to any non-violent means in order to obtain independence for the Gold Coast rapidly. However, when two policemen were killed in a riot after a CPP procession, Nkrumah was imprisoned. But the CPP was not banned and in the 1951 general election, the first to be held under a broad franchise, the CPP won a resounding victory. Nkrumah was released from prison and asked to become Leader of Government Business, the title of which was changed to Prime Minister. He led the Gold Coast to independence in 1957, when the country's name was changed to Ghana. Meanwhile Nkrumah still pursued the Panafrican ideal, and in 1958 he called the first All-African People's Conference in Accra; two years later, Ghana formed a Union with Guinea and Mali. On the domestic front, Nkrumah was steadily steering Ghana towards being a single-party state, which it became under the new Republican Constitution of 1960. In the first Presidential elections under the new Constitution, Nkrumah obtained about ninety per cent of the votes against his only rival, J. B. Danquah. From then on Nkrumah's regime became increasingly oppressive and the number of political detainees mounted. In February 1966, while Nkrumah was on his way to Peking, his regime was overthrown by a military *coup* and he was invited by his fellow-Marxist friend, President Sekou Touré, to live in exile in Guinea as Co-President. From there he continued to write and broadcast on various aspects of the African revolution until his death in April 1972.

J. K. Nyerere

Julius Nyerere was born in Tanganyika in 1922. He studied for a teacher's diploma at Makerere where he organised a branch of the nationalist Tanganyika African Association. In 1949 he went to Edinburgh University where, he says, he evolved the whole of his political philosophy. Having graduated, he returned to Tanganyika to teach and in 1953 he became President of the Tanganyika African Association. However he soon began to feel that the TAA lacked coordination and direction so he transformed it into the Tanganyika African National Union (TANU), of which he became President in 1954. TANU was now openly committed to achieving independence for the territory which, despite considerable initial opposition from the government, it did in December 1961, with Nyerere as Prime Minister. A few weeks later, however, he resigned in order to concentrate on strengthening TANU, which he believed was in danger of disintegrating now that its original *raison d'être* (i.e. the attainment of independence) had been achieved. In 1962 the National Assembly decided the Tanganyika should become a Republic with an elected executive President. Easily beating the one other contender,

Nyerere was elected. Meanwhile, Tanganyika had become a *de facto* one-party state and Nyerere appointed a commission to look into the possibility of making the situation official. The commission reported favourably and, in 1965, Tanganyika became a *de jure* one-party state. Nyerere is regarded as one of Africa's foremost political philosophers and, especially since the Arusha Declaration of 1967, as one of the leading African Socialists.

A. M. Obote

Milton Obote was born in 1925, a member of the Langi tribe in Uganda. He went to Makerere University College but left without graduating and went to work in Kenya. He remained there for several years and became an active member of the Kenya African Union before it was banned in 1953. He returned to Uganda in 1957 and was chosen to represent the Uganda National Congress for Lango district in the Legislative Council to which he was elected in 1958. The Uganda National Congress split over conflicts within the leadership and Obote left to form his own party, the Uganda People's Congress, in 1960. For the pre-independence elections in 1962, Obote persuaded the Bagandan party, Kabaka Yekka, to form an alliance with his own party in order to ensure victory over the Democratic Party. His calculations proved correct, the coalition won a majority of seats and Obote became Prime Minister with the Kabaka of Buganda as President when Uganda became independent in 1962. The alliance between the traditional Kabaka and the progressive Obote became increasingly strained and in 1966 Obote suspended the Constitution, claiming that the Kabaka was plotting to overthrow the government. The Kabaka was dismissed, and under the new constitution Obote became executive President. The following month the Baganda passed a resolution to the effect that the Uganda Government should remove itself from Buganda. Obote immediately declared a State of Emergency in Buganda and the army attacked the Kabaka's palace from which the Kabaka escaped. In 1967 Obote introduced a new constitution which abolished all the kingdoms in Uganda and created a Republic instead. In 1969 Obote began to explain plans for transforming Uganda into a socialist state. No sooner had he announced these plans than an attempt was made to assassinate him. Several politicians were arrested and all political parties except Obote's were banned. In 1971 Obote gave orders that the Commander of the Army, Amin, and other soldiers of Amin's tribe, were to be disposed of. The plan failed, however, and Obote was ousted by a *coup* led by Amin while Obote was attending the Commonwealth Prime Ministers' Conference in Singapore. Obote then took refuge in Tanzania.

O. Odinga

Oginga Odinga is a member of the Luo tribe in Kenya. He started life as a teacher but resigned from the profession in order to start a cooperative trading business because he felt that African economic independence was a *sine qua non* of political independence. Therefore, in 1947 he became full-time organiser of the Luo Thrift and Trading Corporation. At the same time he was elected to the Central Nyanza African District Council. In the early 1950s he began organising Luo support for the Kenya African Union which had been founded by Kenyatta primarily as a Kikuyu organisation. By now, however, nationalism was overriding tribalism. In 1957 Odinga was one of eight Africans elected to the Legislative Council. These eight immediately formed the African Elected Members' Organisation, with Odinga as chairman, in order to coordinate their activity in the Council with African political activity throughout the country. Odinga's contribution to the nationalist cause was given full recognition when he was elected Vice-President of the Kenya African National Union when it was formed in 1960. Odinga entered Kenyatta's cabinet just before independence in 1963 as Minister of Home Affairs, and the following year he became Vice-President of the new Republic of Kenya. In 1966, however, he resigned from this post, due to conflict with other members of the cabinet, to form and become President of the Kenya People's Union. Three years later, while Kenyatta was visiting Kisumu, of which Odinga was MP, riots broke out and eleven people were killed by the police. The KPU leaders were all arrested and Odinga and others were detained. The KPU was banned because Kenyatta said it encouraged tribalism, was involved with communism and had organised the riots in Kisumu as part of a plot to overthrow the government. In 1971, however, after eighteen months in detention, Odinga was released, but the KPU is still banned.

General C. O. Ojukwu

Odumegwu Ojukwu was born in 1933, the son of an Ibo business millionaire. He was educated at Epsom College and Lincoln College, Oxford after which he returned to Nigeria in 1955 and served as a Government Administrative Officer in Eastern Nigeria. Two years later he joined the Nigerian Army. When the military *coup* of January 1966 occurred in Nigeria, Ojukwu was appointed Military Governor of Eastern Nigeria. In May 1967, when Eastern Nigeria seceded from Nigeria, it was Ojukwu who made the Declaration of Independence and who became Head of State of the new Republic of Biafra. The Ibos of the East had been pressurising Ojukwu to pull out of the Nigerian Republic ever since thousands of Ibos had been massacred in North Nigeria in 1966. Ojukwu resisted the pressure until the Head of the Federal Military Government, General Gowon, provoked him to take action by abolishing the existing Regions of Nigeria. The ensuing war between Nigeria and Biafra lasted for two and a half years but came to an abrupt halt in January 1970 when Biafra called for a cease-fire. Just before the cease-fire, Ojukwu and his family fled from Biafra and left Lt Colonel Effiong to announce Biafra's capitulation. Ojukwu himself went to the Ivory Coast who offered him political asylum so long as he did not participate in politics.

393

G. Padmore

George Padmore was a Trinidadian journalist with strong anti-imperialist feelings. As a young man, in the 1920s, he joined the Communist Party and became Executive Secretary of the International Trades Union Committee of Negro Workers for whom he edited the *Negro Worker*. But he left the Communist Party in 1937 because he felt that communists used negroes only for their own ends. However, he remained a Marxist. In 1937 he helped to form the International African Service Bureau (IASB) which promoted Panafricanism as a political expression of Negro aspirations for freedom from white domination, whether capitalist or communist. In 1944, the IASB merged with the Panafrican Federation, which was the British wing of the Panafrican Congress Movement. In 1945 Padmore helped to organise, with Nkrumah, the Fifth Panafrican Congress at Manchester which focussed on independence from colonial domination and the establishment of socialist societies as the main aims of colonial subjects. Padmore had an enormous influence, both as a Panafricanist and as a socialist, on Kwame Nkrumah who invited him to live in Ghana after the country became independent. Padmore was Nkrumah's adviser on African affairs until he died in 1959.

L. S. Senghor

Léopold Senghor, born in Senegal in 1906, was educated mainly in France. He is both a poet and a politician. Between 1946 and 1958 he represented Senegal in the French National Assembly. In 1959 Senegal and the Soudan joined to form the Mali Federation, of which Senghor became the President. But the Federation broke up after a few months because Senegal and the Soudan could not agree on whether Mali should be a federal or a unitary state; Senghor favoured the latter. In 1960, therefore, Senegal became independent with Senghor as President and Mamadou Dia as Prime Minister. Two years later Dia attempted to overthrow Senghor, mainly because of personal differences, but the *coup* failed and Dia was sentenced to life imprisonment. Senghor then drew up a new constitution which made him executive President. In 1973 he was elected President for a further five years. With the West Indian poet, Aimé Césaire, Senghor was a major champion of the concept of negritude after the Second World War. He is also a notable exponent of African socialism.

S. Touré

Sekou Touré, born in French Guinea in 1922, began his political career in the trade union movement. He became Secretary of the Conféderation Générale du Travail's coordination committee for French West Africa in 1950. He was at that time a member of the Communist Party which he left in 1957 when he helped to form the Union Générale des Travailleurs de l'Afrique Noire (UGTAN). Meanwhile, in 1954, he became leader of the Parti Démocratique de Guinée, which was affiliated to Houphouet-Boigny's RDA. Touré was also Vice-President of the RDA. However, when the referendum was held in 1958 among all the French colonies to see which of them wished to become part of the French Community, Guinea was the only territory to vote to stay out. Since Boigny was keen to stay within the Community, Touré split with the RDA over the issue. In October 1958, therefore, Guinea became an independent republic with Touré as President. Two years later Touré took Guinea into a Union with Ghana and Mali. This Union, which was never very fruitful, came to an end in 1963 when Touré suspected Ghana of assassinating President Olympio of Togo. However, when Nkrumah was toppled from power in Ghana in 1966, Touré welcomed him to live in Guinea and made him Co-President. Sekou Touré, like Nkrumah, is basically a Marxist. In 1968, he was elected for a further seven years as executive President of Guinea.

L. Vambe

Lawrence Vambe was born near Salisbury, in Southern Rhodesia, in 1917. Having tried both the Church and teaching he finally became a journalist. He was editor of African Newspapers Ltd for several years until the company was put out of business when the Government banned the largest newspaper in its group. Then, in 1959, Vambe became Press Attaché for the Federation of Rhodesia and Nyasaland in London, but he resigned three years later because he saw that the Federation was not resulting in racial partnership. He then joined the Anglo–American Corporation of Central Africa as a public relations officer until 1970.

BIBLIOGRAPHY

The first section contains references to publications by individual Africans, or non-Africans who have influenced African thought. The second section refers to more general sources. The third section lists periodicals and publications in which major political statements by African leaders are often reproduced.

Section 1

Abraham, W. E. *The Mind of Africa* (Weidenfeld & Nicolson, 1962)

Adu, A. L. *The Civil Service in Commonwealth Africa* (Allen & Unwin, 1969)

Afrifa, A. A. *The Ghana Coup* (Frank Cass, 1966)

Ahidjo, A. *Contribution to National Reconstruction* (Présence Africaine, Paris, 1964)

Arikpo, Okoi. *The Development of Modern Nigeria* (Penguin, 1967)

Armah, Kwesi. *Africa's Golden Road* (Heinemann, 1965)

Attoh Ahuma, S. R. B. *The Gold Coast Nation and National Consciousness* (1911; Frank Cass, 1970)

Awolowo, O. *Path to Nigerian Freedom* (Faber, 1947)

   Awo: The Autobiography of Chief Obafemi Awolowo (Cambridge University Press, 1960)

   The Path to Economic Freedom in Developing Countries (Lagos, 1968)

   The Strategy and Tactics of the People's Republic of Nigeria (Macmillan, 1970)

Azikiwe, N. *Renascent Africa* (1937; Frank Cass, 1968)

   Zik: A selection from the Speeches of Dr Nnamdi Azikiwe (Cambridge University Press, 1961)

   My Odyssey (C. Hurst, 1970)

   'The Future of Panafricanism', *Présence Africaine*, Vol. 12, No. 40 (1962)

Bello, Sir Ahmadu. *My Life* (Cambridge University Press, 1962)

Blyden, E. W. *Christianity, Islam, and the Negro Race* (London, 1887)

Busia, K. A. *The Challenge of Africa* (Praeger, 1962)

Cabral, Amilcar. *Revolution in Guinea* (R. Handyside, 1971)

Césaire, Aimé. *Discourse on Colonialism* (Paris, 1955; Monthly Review Press, 1972)

'Culture et Colonisation', *Présence Africaine*, Nos. 8, 9, 10 (1956)

'The Political Thought of Sekou Touré', *Présence Africaine*, No. 29 (1960)

Danquah, J. B. *Journey to Independence and After: Dr. J. B. Danquah's Letters*. Compiled by H. K. Akyeampong (Waterville Publishing House, 1971)

Historic Speeches and Writings on Ghana. Compiled by H. K. Akyeampong (Accra, no date)

Dia, Mamadou. *Reflexions sur l'économie de l'Afrique noire* (Présence Africaine, 1953)

Contribution a l'étude du mouvement coopératif en Afrique noire (Présence Africaine, 1958)

The African Nations and World Solidarity (Praeger, 1961)

Diop, Cheik Anta. *Nations négres et culture* (Présence Africaine, 1954)

L'Unité culturelle et l'Afrique noire (Présence Africaine, 1959)

Les Fondements culturels, techniques, et industriels d'un Futur Etat fédéral d'Afrique noire (Présence Africaine, 1960)

Diop, Mahjemout. *Contribution a l'étude des problèmes politiques en Afrique noire* (Présence Africaine, 1958)

DuBois, W. E. B. *Color and Democracy* (New York, 1945)

The World and Africa (New York, 1947)

Fanon, Frantz. *Black Skin, White Masks* (Paris, 1952; Paladin, 1970)

A Dying Colonialism (Paris, 1959; Pelican, 1970)

The Wretched of the Earth (Paris, 1963; Penguin, 1967)

Toward the African Revolution (Paris, 1961; Pelican, 1970)

Graft Johnson, J. W. de. *Towards Nationhood in West Africa* (1928; Frank Cass, 1971)

Gardiner, R. *A World of Peoples* (BBC, London, 1965)

Hayford, J. E. Casely. *Gold Coast Native Institutions* (London, 1903)

Ethiopia Unbound (London, 1911)

West African Leadership: Public Speeches and Letters of J. E. Casely Hayford, ed. Magnus J. Sampson (Frank Cass, 1969)

Horton, J. Africanus B. *Letters on the Political Condition of the Gold Coast* (1870; Frank Cass, 1970)

Itote, Waruhiu. *Mau Mau General* (East African Publishing House, 1967))

Kariuki, J. M. *Mau Mau Detainee* (Penguin, 1963)

Kaunda, Kenneth. *Zambia Shall be Free* (Heinemann Educational Books, 1962).

A Humanist in Africa (Longman, 1966)

Humanism: A Guide to the Nation (Government Printer, Lusaka, 1967)

Zambia's Economic Revolution: The Mulungushi Declaration (Lusaka, 1968)

Towards Complete Independence: After Mulungushi (Lusaka, 1969)

A Nation of Equals (Lusaka, 1972)

Keita, Modibo. 'The Foreign Policy of Mali', *International Affairs,* Vol. 37, No. 4 (October 1961)

Kenyatta, Jomo. *Facing Mount Kenya* (Secker & Warburg, 1938)

Suffering Without Bitterness (East Africa Publishing House, 1968); 'African Socialism and African Unity', *African Forum,* Vol. 1, No. 1 (1965)

Lumumba, Patrice. *Congo, My Country* (Pall Mall, 1962)

Luthuli, Albert. *Let My People Go* (Fontana, 1962)

Ly, Abdoulaye, *Les Masses africaines et l'actuelle condition humaine* (Présence Africaine, 1956)

Mandela, Nelson. *I Am Prepared to Die* (Christian Action pamphlet, no date) *No Easy Walk to Freedom* (Heinemann, 1965)

Mbeki, Govan. *South Africa: The Peasants Revolt* (Penguin, Baltimore, 1964)

Mboya, Tom J. *Freedom and After* (André Deutsch, 1963)

The Challenge of Nationhood (André Deutsch, 1970)

Mlambo, E. *No Future Without Us* (E. Mlambo, London representative of the Zimbabwe African National Council; no date)

Mobutu, J. D. 'Manifesto for the Decade 1970–80', *Cahiers Congolais* (October–December 1970)

Mondlane, Edouardo. *The Struggle for Mozambique* (Penguin, 1969)

Mphahlele, Ezekiel. *The African Image* (Faber, 1962)

Ngugi, James. *Homecoming* (Heinemann Educational Books, 1972)

Nkrumah, Kwame. *Towards Colonial Freedom* (1947; Heinemann Educational Books, 1962)

The Autobiography of Kwame Nkrumah (Nelson, 1957)

I Speak of Freedom (Heinemann Educational Books, 1961)

Africa Must Unite (Heinemann Educational Books, 1963)

Consciencism (Heinemann Educational Books, 1964)

Dark Days in Ghana (Panaf, London, 1968)

Handbook of Revolutionary Warfare (Panaf, 1968)

'African Socialism Revisited', *African Forum,* Vol. 1, No. 3 (1966)

Obote, A. Milton. *The Common Man's Charter* (Kampala, 1969)

Odinga, Oginga. *Not Yet Uhuru* (Heinemann Educational Books, 1967)

Ojukwu, C. O. *Biafra: Random Thoughts of C. O. Ojukwu* (Harper & Row, 1969)

Okello, John. *Revolution in Zanzibar* (East Africa Publishing House, 1967)

Padmore, George. *Panafricanism or Communism?* (Dennis Dobson, 1956)

Quaison–Sackey, Alex. *Africa Unbound* (Praeger, 1963)

Rabemananjara, J. *Nationalisme et les problèmes Malgaches* (Présence Africaine, 1958)

Samkange, Stanlake. *On Trial for My Country* (Heinemann, 1967)

Senghor, Léopold Sédar. *Nationhood and the African Road to Socialism* (Présence Africaine, 1962)

On African Socialism, ed. Mercer Cook (Praeger, 1964)

Liberté I: Négritude et Humanisme (Présence Africaine, 1964)

Selected Poems (Oxford University Press, 1964)

'Negritude and African Socialism' in K. Kirkwood (ed.), *St. Anthony's Papers, No. 15* Chatto & Windus, 1963)

Sithole, Ndabaningi. *African Nationalism* (Oxford University Press, 1968)

Thiam, Doudou. *The Foreign Policy of African States* (Praeger, 1963)

Thuku, Harry. *An Autobiography* (Oxford University Press, 1970)

Touré, Sékou. *Guinée; Prélude à l'Indépendence* (Présence Africaine, 1958)

Toward Full Reafricanisation (Présence Africaine, 1959)

L'Expérience Guinéenne et l'Unité Africaine (Présence Africaine, 1959)

La Revolution Guinéenne et le Progrès Social (Conakry, 1962)

L'Afrique en Marche (Conakry, 1967)

'Africa's Future and the World', *Foreign Affairs,* Vol. 41, No. 1 (October 1962)

Vambe, L. *An Ill-fated People: Zimbabwe before and after Rhodes* (Heinemann, 1972)

Section 2

Organisation for African Unity. *Basic Documents and Resolutions* (Addis Ababa, no date)

C. Legum (ed.). *Panafricanism* (Praeger, 1965). The appendices are valuable basic sources on the Panafricanism movement.

American Society for African Culture (ed.). *Panafricanism Reconsidered* (University of California Press, 1962). Record of a conference of black American and African intellectuals.

Africa Report. 'The Dakar Colloquium on African Socialism', *Africa Report,* Vol. VIII (1963).

Kenya Government. *African Socialism and its application to Planning in Kenya* (Nairobi, 1965)

The Ndegwa Report on the Public Service (Nairobi, 1971)

Tanganyika African National Union. 'Mwongozo Wa Tanu (Tanu Guidelines)', *The African Review,* Vol. 1, No. 4 (April 1972)

British Government. *The Report of the Pearce Commission on Rhodesia,* Cmd. 4964 (HMSO, May 1972)

D. Duerden and C. Peterse (ed.). *African Writers Talking* (Heinemann Educational Books, 1972). Interviews with leading African writers.

C. Gertzel (ed.). *Government and Politics in Kenya* (East Africa Publishing House, 1970). Selections from a variety of documents to illustrate all aspects of political, social and economic development in Kenya.

D. Rothchild (ed.). *The Politics of Integration* (East Africa Publishing House, 1969). Selections from a variety of documents to illustrate the problems and progress of recent cooperation in East and Central Africa.

Section 3

Africa (London)

Africa Report (Washington)

African Affairs (London)

African Review (Dar-es-Salaam)

Foreign Affairs (Washington)

International Affairs (London)

Journal of Modern African Studies (Cambridge)

Présence Africaine (Paris)

West Africa (London)

An annual collection of African sources is C. Legum and J. Drysdale (ed.), *Africa Contemporary Record* (Rex Hollings). They cover to date the years 1968–9, 1969–70, 1970–1, 1971–2, 1972–3.